A
Different
Woman

Books by Jane Howard

Please Touch:
A Guided Tour of the Human Potential Movement

A Different Woman

Jane Howard

A
Different
Woman

E. P. Dutton & Co., Inc. | New York | 1973

Library of Congress Cataloging in Publication Data

Howard, Jane.
A different woman.

1. Women in the United States.   2. United States—Social conditions—
1945–   I. Title.   HQ1426.H69   1973   301.41'2'0973   73-79557   ISBN
0-525-09310-9

10 9 8 7 6 5 4 3 2 1

Published simultaneously in Canada
by Clarke, Irwin & Company Limited, Toronto and Vancouver

Four of these chapters first appeared, in different and much shorter form, as
magazine articles. "No Chocolate Eggs This Easter" is based on a *Mademoiselle*
article entitled "Growing Up Midwestern." "What's So Great About Sofas?" and
"A Tunnel's No Place for a Woman" are elaborations of *Life* articles. "Didn't
You Almost Drown While Interviewing Saul Bellow?" originated with an article
for [*MORE*].

To my father

to the memory of my mother

and to Ann

Jane Howard

I could not have lived through the time described in this book without the buoying support of a good many people to whom privacy is precious. Largely for that reason, several names have been changed, a few characters appear as composites, and some who have mattered are not here at all. To everyone who helped, my thanks.

Contents

1. Put Your Feet Under My Table   17
2. No Chocolate Eggs This Easter   33
3. Mark Van Doren, the Dalai Lama, and Jimmy Stewart 49
4. The Osborne Agreement   61
5. What's So Great About Sofas?   63
6. When Shall I Wash My Hair?   83
7. Pierced Ears   101
8. Pomp and Circumstance in Groundhog Hollow   104
9. I'm in Love with a Handsome Mommy   116
10. When I Grow Up   130
11. Somebody's Got to Get a Loser, Right?   144
12. I Didn't Bring Enough Burnt Sienna   155
13. The Only Man in the Polo Lounge with a Learner's
    Permit   167
14. Area Code 415   184
15. None, They Say, Have I   204
16. I Wanted Just What I Got   212
17. A Citizen of the Realm   220
18. Achieve, Achieve   234

11

Contents

19. The Cat Lady   240
20. Honor Your Corner Partner   253
21. Tears of Joy   269
22. Potentially Frivolous   275
23. A Tunnel's No Place for a Woman   281
24. Cream Can Curdle   293
25. Tooth and Nail   305
26. Didn't You Almost Drown While Interviewing
    Saul Bellow?   308
27. Fragments of Comfort and Joy   317
28. Oh Taut Stretched Beam   331
29. You've Got to Be Buried by Oliver   348
30. Carrot Juice   360
31. Rapid Pips and Bongo Drums   365
32. Chicanos Don't Say *Olé*   375
33. Vodka Gimlet to Go   388
34. Is That Miss or Mrs.?   402

One's grand flights, one's Sunday baths,
One's tootings at the weddings of the soul
Occur as they occur . . .

Wallace Stevens
"The Sense of the Sleight-of-Hand Man"

Jane Howard

A Different Woman

A
Different
Woman

1

Put Your Feet Under My Table

My mother and I had a sure instinct for riling each other, like stalking beasts in a forest. Once, in my adolescence, I can't remember why, I made her so mad she threw a hairbrush at me. Often, in those days, I would sigh heavily and say things in an annoyingly well-modulated voice like, "That's precisely what I *intended* to do, Mother," and although I was nearly thirty-six when she suddenly died of a stroke in 1971, there was still something of that tone between us.

There were other things about her, though. Once, endearingly I thought, she had a laughing fit in a Quaker meeting. She was an inspired maker of turkey stuffing, steamer-off of old wallpaper, refinisher of furniture, dressmaker for her granddaughter's toy bunnies, and arranger of dried weeds and pussy willows. She cared about the trees my father planted, and noticed owl's nests and the songs of bobwhites. When I had to go on bird walks very early in the morning for high school biology class, she went with me.

"It's a most gorgeous day," she wrote in the last letter I ever got from her. "You'd go out of your mind. The redbud and dogwood should be in bloom when you come here. If I hurry I can burn some leaves (pollute) before the church circle meeting at Corinne's." The sociable aspects of church meant more to her than the theological. She felt most herself, I think, in a roomful of approving others. She could always be counted on to volunteer to have foreign students to Thanksgiving dinner, and she liked big, convivial sit-down breakfasts at which she would declare, "I feel sorry for everybody who doesn't have the other half of my grapefruit."

She had a litany she would repeat every night when my younger sister, Ann, and I were small: "I love you up to the sky and down again and around the world and back again." As unloveable as we sometimes were, I think she always did. When I would arrive home for a visit, there would always be a multicolored Crayola sign she had made, taped to the kitchen door. It said WELCOME HOME! YEA, JANIE!, as if I were a basketball team. And when my visit was over, she would stand there at the airport gate waving until not only I but my airplane had vanished entirely from sight. Not everybody is a waver, but my mother definitely was. And before I left the house she would always repack my suitcase, a gesture I found at once thoughtful and inquisitive. Into it she would tuck a dishcloth she had just crocheted, or a box of Auntie Pearl's ranger cookies, or both.

Often, as we drove around the prairie, she would observe that pin oaks were her favorite trees, because they didn't know which way they wanted to go. Neither, a lot of the time, did we. Indecision seemed to be in our genes, like big feet and high foreheads. Options bedazzled us. Okay, we had decided we would definitely go out for dinner, but where? The candle-lit Sangamo Club, where we would be observed and greeted by other residents of Springfield, Illinois, and asked, "Would you like some *au jus* with your roast beef?" Or, perhaps, smoky, funky Gabtoni's, where there were these knockout sandwiches and where we might see some of Dad's cronies from the State House press room? Or the Dew #2 Chilli Parlor, whose proprietor Joe Bockelmann always made such a heartwarming fuss over us? A lot of what we decided would depend on how our hair looked that day, and how many comps we were likely to get. Comps—compliments—were at all times welcome.

"That's a pretty sunset," I might say as my mother and I drove along.

"Thank you," she would reply. The Blithe Spirit, she said her kinfolk used to call her, not only for such flashes of zaniness but because as a teen-ager and young woman she had gallantly, without much complaint, endured a long series of maladies. She had diphtheria, a tracheotomy, recurrent sinus trouble, and surgery which robbed her of her sense of smell. Nor did she later call much attention to her severe phlebitis, which obliged her to wear elastic stockings, and other medical misfortunes. Toward the end, abrupt though her end was, she might have been more sick than she let us know, because she once asked Mabel, the cleaning woman, if she knew how to get hold of Mr. Howard at his office, in case anything should happen.

With Ann and me, our mother was not often blithe, nor were we with her. It's odd. We were thought in our circles to be amusing, and so was she in hers, but regrettably seldom did we laugh together. We never developed enough rapport. Sometimes mothers and daughters do have strong rapport; I have seen it. But in those cases, the daughters seem less close to each other or to their brothers. Can this be some new maxim of human nature, or is it somewhere written that you can have real, ready access to your parents or else to your siblings, but not to both?

Although my mother was vain about her Davidow suit and her elegant engraved informals from Black, Starr & Gorham, and hardly ever could bring herself to throw out invitations to parties, she had a snakeboot side, too. "Snakeboot" has become family slang meaning unpretentious and practical, because snakeboots, with anklets under them, are often worn by my unpretentious, practical Aunt Millie in the Catoctin Mountains. It was snakeboot of my mother, for example, to enter her cookies in the state fair and to stuff wadded-up toilet paper into the locks of the booths of ladies' rooms, so the next customer could get in free. And she was a connoisseur of snakeboot vernacular.

"It'll do you good," she would say, "as well as helping you."
Much of this talk was related to food. (Food was a handy idiom
for a lot of other things.) If Ann had just finished a painting,
or I a troublesome magazine article, our mother would ask us,
"Did you get a good scald on it?"

"Scald?" we would ask her. "What's that?"

"Oh, I don't know," she would say. "It's from some old cookbook somewhere. Corinne told me about it. She doesn't know
exactly what it means, either. It has to do with having things
turn out right."

She wanted exceedingly for things to turn out right, including birthdays. What a champion rememberer of birthdays she
was. When she was eleven, in 1916, her grandmother gave her a
birthday book with an Emerson quotation for each day of the
year. In this book all her life she noted not only the births,
weddings, and deaths of the human beings in her vast ken but
such entries as this one, on March 3, 1956: "Copper Jones—
nine Golden Retriever puppies." In the flyleaf of the birthday
book she wrote, "MIZPAH—Engraving in Mother's Wedding
Ring—May the Lord watch between thee and me while we are
absent from one another." She also inscribed a poem by her
cousin Edna Tratt: "They come, they go, we meet, we part/
And there the pleasure ends/ Save for the few who really care/
Our joys increase, our sorrows share/ And these we call our
friends."

Friendship was her vocation. "Your mother," one of her
neighbors once told me, "always thinks everybody is just darling." She wanted to think so, anyway. She had, undeniably, a
heart rather easily made glad. Another little litany she liked to
recite went: "There's so much good in the worst of us/ And so
much bad in the best of us/ That it hardly behooves a one of
us/To talk about the rest of us." She kept confidences; she did
not gossip. Instead, she was always doing people, who in turn
did her, preferably when her feet were under their tables, or
theirs under hers.

Let me explain. "Do," in this context, is a transitive verb. It
takes an object. It can, in fact, overwhelm its object. "Do" thus
means to take under one's wing, to shelter, succor, nurture,

concentrate on, listen to, cause to feel central. It is not easy to do people in absentia, which was what my cousin Mary Louise was implying when she said to my mother over the phone, "Oh, Eleanor, I just wish you'd come over to Oak Park and put your feet under my table."

The practice of doing continues. "Hey, go do Dr. Covington, she's standing all alone over there," Ann or I might whisper to each other at a party. We all do and in turn are done by our friends, who are all, from time to time, our caseloads, just as we are theirs. Everyone, according to an as yet unpublished monograph on the Caseload Theory of Interpersonal Relationships, is entitled now and then to be a caseload. We become caseloads when we are Worse. Worse is one of the three possible human conditions, applicable alike to men and nations. The others, as you might expect, are Better and The Same. This method of explaining things may lack refinement, but it offers a convenient shorthand.

"How's Julian?" I might ask Peggy.

"He's The Same," she might reply. "We're not going to have to do him just yet. But Liz is Better." (Julian's wife Liz, annoyingly enough, is always Better.)

"Max," we once said to another friend, "we have something to tell you: you used to be Worse, but now you're Better."

"Better than what?" asked Max, but that was before he caught on.

These people constitute part of what if I were Jewish, which I sometimes wish I were, I would call my *mishpocha*. If I were a social scientist, which I almost never wish I were, I would call it my extended, as opposed to nuclear, family. By this is meant not just a string of unconnected wellwishers but a network of persons who have some kinship, by blood or spirit, not only with me but with each other as well.

New links must be forged as old ones rust. Only children should be brought up close to other only children, so they will not someday have to reminisce alone. We who are unmarried, only children of another sort, must deepen and cultivate our friendships until water acquires the consistency of blood, until we develop new networks as sustaining as orthodox families.

It may be hard, but the need for some such arrangement, whatever one may call it, has I think been established almost beyond doubt. I, for example, have or have had an answering service and a biweekly cleaning woman and a superintendent and an agent and a certified public accountant and a psychoanalyst and an orthopedist and more peripheral friends than I can have occasional lunches with. I usually get quite a lot of Christmas cards. A book I wrote is being translated into Japanese, Greek, and Spanish. I am resourceful. I know the second and third verses to a lot of songs. Like a proper Miss Subways, I enjoy funny little out-of-the-way foreign restaurants, not to say foreign movies. I forgive myself for falling asleep in movies and am resigned to waking up in the morning before whoever else is around, almost always. When I want to be soothed I listen to WNCN; for energy I turn to WLIB. I prefer tubs to showers, bridges to tunnels, and I like to, and sometimes do, wake up in country rooms with U.S. Geological Survey maps tacked onto unfinished wooden walls. It really isn't bad, my life, except that once in a while, when I am in need of someone's shoulder, the right one isn't nearby. At such times my thoughts turn first to the possible benefits of living on a commune—only I'm too bourgeois and too private for that—and next to the idea of a nuclear family.

I am not at present part of any nuclear family, nor can it be said with certainty that I ever will be. One doesn't know. I have spent weekends and sometimes entire weeks with nuclear families, but I rely more on the *mishpocha*. It supplies me with the feeling of connectedness my mother got through her sixty-six years from her seven aunts, the Hoard sisters, four of whom still live together in the Pomona, California, house their parents bought before 1920.* Although Auntie Grace, the senior member of that household, is at this writing a regal ninety-seven, she still chainsmokes happily, does paintings, and joins her sisters in frequent games of Canasta.

* The similarity between my own surname ("a wonderful English name," my mother used to tell us) and "Hoard," the maiden name of her mother, is a coincidence.

One thing that sustains those women, I think, is their fierce sense of clan. Since the clan in question is a fertile and mobile one, keeping track of it can be a full-time job. On my father's side, too, there is a strong tradition of family reunions. Some sheep have strayed far from the fold, but everyone knows where they are and how to reach them. My sister and I reach each other quite often, mostly by phone, on which our voices sound uncannily alike. Now that the scars of our combative childhood are well healed, we sometimes talk for more than an hour at a time. Her husband, who knows a lot about real estate, has suggested that we use this money instead to buy a high-rise in Phoenix.

"You girls," our mother would sometimes marvel, "have a precious thing going." It gratified her to see us laugh even when our humor was, shame on us, at her own expense. I guess I like to laugh about as much as I like anything, and I wish that my sister and certain others who can readily make me do so lived closer at hand, but mine is not, alas, a geographically feasible *mishpocha*. It is damnably inconvenient, in fact, to have its members scattered so widely. I'm not talking about people who say, "Lunch, *soon!*" Plenty of them are well within reach, as are a few whom I really do love. I'm talking about the remote others whose proximity would be such a delight that we tease each other by asking long distance questions like, "What are you wearing?" and "We'll be having the lamb tonight; why don't you come over?" as if "over" didn't mean a couple of thousand miles.

On Sunday, April 25, 1971, Suzanne Szasz and I were too busy running around Milwaukee in our rented yellow Mercury to think of calling the Ramada Inn for messages. Suzanne was taking pictures and I was getting quotes for the story *Life* had assigned us to do on feminism in the heartland. It was an unwieldy story, hard to pin down, but we were beginning to feel encouraged. A couple more days ought to wrap it up, we agreed over a leisurely German dinner. Then we drove to a 7 P.M. meeting at the Non-Violent Feminist Center, a green-painted frame

23

building at the corner of North and Buffum. That was where I heard the news.

My thoughts and heart pounded as I raced south in the yellow Mercury, driving the 250 miles toward Springfield, asking myself: Is? Was? What's a stroke, anyway? Struck? Stricken? Did people recover from massive cerebral hemorrhages? Dying? Dead? Me, a motherless child? How had I lived this long without losing anyone close? If it has to happen, isn't this a good way? Is there ever a good way? Why hadn't I looked more attentively at the old magazines she had brought up from the basement, just to show me, the last time I saw her?

On the car radio, which I dared not turn off, was an inane talk show on the nature of humor. I arrived at the hospital, the same one where Ann and I were born, at about 2 A.M., clutching a stone I had picked up the day before at a beach in Milwaukee. I thought maybe I could give her the stone to hold.

"Her toe just twitched," said the nurse in the intensive care room. "That might be a good sign." But Ann and I could tell that there wouldn't be any good signs. We just knew. Dad and David had gone home, as I did after a couple of hours, but Ann refused to. When I did arrive home, just a while before dawn, my father came downstairs in his pajamas and said, "Well, she sure raised a couple of fancy daughters, anyway."

In the other bed in that intensive care room lay a very young woman who had nearly bled to death in the course of a Caesarean birth and still was bleeding. The infant had died, but the mother was going to be all right. Her husband, who appeared to be about fifteen, wore elevator shoes and had a slicked pompadour. He looked like someone in a Diane Arbus photograph, as I'm sure we did, too. He brought his wife a cellophane-wrapped rose from a wreath on their stillborn baby's coffin. He kept telling us we would be surprised how much it helped to pray. Thanks, we told him, but we did not pray, not the way he meant. We waited.

We waited until nine the next night. At that hour we sat in the lounge, talking with the interim Presbyterian minister. A Scotsman whose son liked snakes, he was telling us about haggis and herpetology. My goodness, we said. Imagine. How strange. Then the doctor appeared, with news. He had been going to unplug the mockery of a breathing machine, but it turned out he didn't need to. It was over. We started making phone calls. Neighbors arrived with casseroles and pies. "We thought a lot of your mom," they assured us. Relatives came. We made decisions. King James, not Revised. Bach, don't you think? Okay, "A Mighty Fortress." Just the white dogwood, forget the pink. The undertaker asked who her hairdresser had been. What difference does that make, we asked in turn, since she is to be cremated?

"If we'd had a little advance *notice*," said the voice at the lumberyard, "then maybe we could have had a plain wooden coffin ready."

That Friday I had meant to attend a free-for-all sort of rally on feminism at Town Hall in New York. Norman Mailer and Germaine Greer and Jill Johnston would be there. The multi-vehicle collision sure to occur would offer a vivid contrast, I figured, to what I had found in Milwaukee. It would have, too, but I was not in New York that Friday. Instead I was witnessing the burial of my mother's ashes in the Bangor, Iowa, cemetery, which is a secluded and pretty place, if you like cemeteries.

Dying was one of the few controversial things my mother ever did. Her generation recoiled from unpleasantness. "Don't bring the black doll," she told my sister, "when your Southern cousins are here." In life and on stage her generation yearned to be soothed and reassured, I suppose because they had known enough real fear about money and health. She did not thank me, not at all, for taking her to see Edward Albee's *American Dream;* she liked a musical from which she could emerge humming, because life was tough enough. But for us it had not been, not yet. Brought up after the Depression with polio shots and gold inlays, which my dentists invariably marvel at, we could take sterner stuff. Privation, as we knew it, meant having to buy raincoats on sale at Marshall Field's and not going to fancy summer camps in the Rockies with our classmates.

The generation before ours meant well; I don't doubt that. They did what by their lights they had to, which meant presenting to us a spectrum we were to find sheltered and narrow. It took us a while to figure that out, though, and within that spectrum, meanwhile, we found nuance enough to feed a habit of self-scrutiny which startled our mothers. "You sure didn't inherit that," they seemed to be saying, "from *us*."

The death of my own mother made me feel like a deck of cards being shuffled by giant, unseen hands. Parents, however old they and we may grow to be, serve among other things to shield us from a sense of our doom. As long as they are around, we can avoid the fact of our mortality; we can still be innocent children. When a parent goes, half of that innocence goes, too. It gets ripped away. Something, someday will replace that innocence, maybe something more useful, but we cannot know what, or how soon, and while we wait, it hurts.

Since this was the spring of 1971, I saw my own hurt, or something akin to it, multiplied wherever I looked, not by private grief but by a public and resolute assault on a whole matrix of attitudes about the female sex. Everybody else seemed to feel unmoored, too. It was not only personally, I began to realize, that I would have to do some overdue growing up. I was a thirty-six-year-old motherless child and that was too bad, that was something I would have to get used to, but I was also going to have to try to figure out what it meant to be a woman.

One afternoon I sat in a bar in Greenwich Village, talking of such matters with the wife of a colleague. Feminism, we agreed, had become a proselytizing religion, with a lot of evangelists around, and woe to the unconverted. "I used to think I was happy," she told me, "but suddenly I started wondering: was I really? Before, I never used to question the woman I was; but now I *am* questioning, and I'm dissatisfied.

"All of a sudden we're being put down. Maybe they're right,

the people who say we're jerks. Maybe I really *am* stupid. After all, all I went to was high school. I used to think college women were idiots who only had book sense, no common sense, but then I started wondering. This past year I decided that's it, no more, I'm going to be me; it always worked before, it better work now. Then I thought, 'Oh, Christ, I really *am* becoming neurotic.' This is ridiculous, this Women's Lib. It's really screwing me up."

Needless to say there are those who find it anything but ridiculous. Another woman I chanced to talk to, whose job is to travel around the country recruiting nurses, could not say enough for the new exhilaration she found wherever she went. "In middle America," she said (using the term sociologically), "women are a lot more ready than they used to be to try new things. They're listening more and seeing more and feeling a lot more impatient with what they used to think were their limits. They'll never be the same."

She was right, I think. Women won't ever be the same. I have hardly found a one of late, of any age or station, who has not to some degree been affected by the new wave, an inescapable tidal wave, of feminism. Even those who loathe it, and they are many, can hardly deny it. Nor can men. One of this movement's male champions, a forty-four-year-old musician I know, delivered some impromptu thoughts on this subject with such feeling that although I had not meant to I ran to get my notebook.

"Women's Liberation," he said, "is much bigger than the black revolution or the proletarian revolution or, so far as I'm concerned, anything in my time. It's changed my whole life, my whole way of looking at people and at myself. I wish it had come along fifteen or twenty years earlier. I wish I had learned sooner that I didn't have to measure up to the image of Don Juan or Gary Cooper, that it wasn't sissified or girlish of me to love and need someone. But there are still a lot of men of my age who have to bluster along."

Aren't there just. "Oh, kiddo, look," I heard a junior high school principal say, "Women have it easy. There's a lot less pressure on women. They don't know how to take orders, follow a chain of command, be obedient. I've got a wife and I bought her a car—now *that's* what I call liberation. She can go wherever she wants. I'm the one who has to worry about gas and insurance. A man's got to get out of the sack every morning whether he feels like it or not, but a wife can just lay there and dawdle with magazines for an hour or two. Women can just sit and chew the rag, while a man's got to *produce.* Women of today have lost what the older generation had: love and respect for their husbands. Irregardless, in the old days, the man was boss, the father had the final word."

My own thoughts on this omnipresent subject keep shifting back and forth between the general and the personal. They often involve my mother. Quite often I wish that we had talked to her, and she to us, less guardedly. Now and then I see some woman on the street or in a store who from a distance, for a split second, looks like her. If it were, I would go talk with her, with fewer evasions and nervous silences than we had when she was around. What, I wonder, were we all afraid of? Why was there so much pretense on both sides?

Maybe it is to atone for my own pretense, my own evasions, that I have been preoccupied since my mother's death with what I hope has been honest talk with surviving women. Maybe that is why I have been traveling around this country with a dogeared *Rand McNally Road Atlas* and an uncommonly thick address book. I go around calling up people whose names are in that book, visiting with them, listening.

Sometimes I wonder if there is any place I truly belong. Springfield, where I was born, to which my parents returned only after I left home? Chicago, where I sold Kool-Aid and bought war stamps? Winnetka, where I went to dancing school and baby-sat? Ann Arbor, where I was talked out of depledging the sorority after all, but spent most of my time at *The Daily?* New York, the only city in which I have ever voted? Surely not those distant other places which I passed through just long enough to say phrasebook things like *"Dove il gabinetto?,"* *"Haben sie ein zimmer fur eine nacht, bitte?,"* *"Petit à petit l'oiseau fait son nid,"* *"Porqué no hay camarones?"* and "Where is the pectopah?"—all, you will notice, in the present tense.

But given a choice, and I guess I have been given a choice, I have so far preferred brief bivouacs to being trapped. It is hard for me to resist going anywhere, but the places I like best to visit, which seem to me the most exotic, are those with the thinnest phone books. Perhaps because I am not very rooted myself, I am most charmed where roots are deep, and the smaller the town, it seems, the deeper they grow. I mourn, incidentally, the loss of postmarks. On two occasions I have driven miles out of my way just so I could send postcards from a hamlet called Bumble Bee, Arizona. The last time I was in Bumble Bee I visited for a bit with the postmistress.

"Many people stop by here?" I asked.

"Not too many," she admitted. "Day like this, I wouldn't be surprised if you'd be the only customer I had."

"Don't you get lonesome?"

"Oh no, I bring my ironing."

I wish I had talked more with that lady (I am sure she would wish to be thought of as a lady), but one of the lessons I am slowly coming to accept is that it is in fact not possible to go everywhere, meet everyone, and do everything. One must choose from the options, however painful the act of choice may be. So I didn't really talk to the Bumble Bee lady, not at the length I might have liked, or to the woman on the Michigan Avenue bus in Chicago whom I overheard say, "It's bad enough that my father is passive-aggressive, but now it turns out my *step*father is passive-aggressive, too."

I wish I had talked more with my Aunt Martha the last time I saw her, too. Aunt Martha takes a folding chair with her to the 40-yard line of high school football games in Cambridge, Minnesota. Once she went to an open installation of the Eastern Star Lodge, "the twinklers" as she calls them, and decided not to join. Uncle Henry, her husband, used to be Justice of the Peace, which meant that weddings were held at their house, and Martha always made it a point to serve coffee and have candles. I think she could tell me a lot I would like to hear.

So could the cook with plucked eyebrows in a Colorado café where a homemade sign said NOTICE! IF YOU PUT YOUR

CIGARETTE IN YOUR PLATE, PLEASE NOTIFY THE WAITRESS AND SHE WILL GLADLY SERVE YOUR FOOD IN AN ASHTRAY. I love signs like that.

So could the very young woman who was leaning, crying, against a frail new tree for a long time at my street's block association fair last spring. She just stood there crying for a long time while other people bought brownies and plants and rode the Ferris wheel.

My quest, if I had talked at any length with these women, would have been to try to find out more about the texture of their lives, whom and what they loved, what was on their minds, and in what ways they were like and unlike each other and the rest of us: what it is, if anything that is unifyingly "American" about us. I wonder whether it is true, as a British-born photographer friend of mine once said, that "there's more antagonism between the sexes in America than anywhere else —something happened with American women back in the frontier times. It has to do with pedestals. They really screwed up their men; they haven't learned the language." Or are there seemlier traits we share?

How many of us would meet the approval of President Lyndon Johnson, whose daughter Luci Nugent told reporters at his post-funeral collation that "He wanted his women to have their hair combed, their lipstick on, and to be strong and brave"? Does good grooming imply valor? Does lipstick, for that matter, imply good grooming? Is it significant that more and more women address each other in manless groups as "you guys," and individually as "man"? What, if anything, does it mean that only in the South is "girl" used in conversation as "boy" and "man" are elsewhere, as in the phrase "oh, girl, you just can't imagine"?

These are among the things I have had on my mind in the course of talks I have had in the past two years, with women and ladies and girls and gals and broads and chicks and matrons in zip codes all over the country. Thinking to try to sing the unsung, I avoided celebrities. Few whom I talked to were especially famous or especially militant or especially anything.

Certainly none of them was on any list of Most Admired Women, except maybe now, in some cases, my own.

This book is, by design or deliberate lack thereof, more a patchwork quilt than a balanced, definitive survey. Look elsewhere if you want to read about senators or newly ordained ministers or Radical Lesbians in Cleveland, Ohio. But you will read rather a lot here about the first American woman I ever met. She and my sister and some of the other members of the network I have mentioned will keep recurring through these pages, and so will I. In a sense this book is a journal of two years. They were two years in which Nixon got reelected, George Wallace got shot, China got opened. Two years of Saigon, Munich, Khartoum, Managua, Belfast, warmer winters, Watergate. Twenty-four full moons (of which I noticed probably five), in the course of which I have tried, at long last, to come of age.

A word about the pattern by which I proceeded: there wasn't one. My experiments along these lines never led to any foolproof formula, so what I did was play it by ear. Sometimes I would just walk up to a strange woman in a public place, gulp, and ask if I might visit with her for a while. Other times elaborate advance arrangements had been made. Some talks lasted less than an hour, and other times I would hang around for a week. Often chance conversations with my dearest friends became "interviews", too. Usually I had a crumpled list of questions somewhere in my purse, questions like, "What's the most you've ever spent on a dress?" But as time went on I referred to these less and less.

Question-and-answer interviews seem to me a stultifying approach to colloquy. If you want to find out what is on someone's mind, you don't sit there staring at her and asking what she thinks are the central issues facing her community today. Take a drive around the mountain together, or have her teach you how to make popovers, or at least go with her while she picks up the dry-cleaning. Try, if you can, to see for yourself where she lives and with whom and to get some sense of how she and they seem to feel about each other. And never dare to suppose, however much rapport may develop, that you are getting anywhere near to the core of her soul. Doris Van Velkinburgh was right when she told me, in the bar of the Ocean Grove Lodge in Trinidad, California, that "women like to blab a lot; you won't have any trouble getting them to talk."

No, not much trouble at all, in most cases. But the more a woman talks, however candidly and trustingly, the more mysterious and complex she proves to be. "What would happen," Muriel Rukeyser asks in a book of poems called *Speed of Darkness,* "if one woman told the truth about herself? The world would split open." Perhaps it would at that.

2

No Chocolate Eggs This Easter

"But you're not from here *originally*," fellow New Yorkers sometimes say, almost accusingly, when they learn that I have been in their city since the fall of 1956. They are quite right. It's a good thing I have no yen or cause to conceal my midwestern origins, because to do so would be exhausting, involving at the very least a lot of elocution lessons, and maybe impossible. If I should live to be ninety-six without ever again beholding a cornfield or eating a sweet roll (as opposed to a Danish) over a copy of the *Chicago Tribune,* I would still look and sound midwestern. I do not, it is true, say things like "real fancy" and "prit-near" and "extry," or use "deal" as an all-purpose noun, or address my friends as "kid." I have never given or even been to a party called an "ice-water sit-around," nor do I drink coffee *with* dinner or order "Scotch and seltzer." But I am marked for life with the amply nourished, lantern-jawed look, the telltale broad "a" and the resonant "r" of the prairies. And if you ask me if I'd like some more turkey stuffing, I'll answer "shirr."

Anyone given to crossing state lines these days knows how deplorably similar American cities are getting to look. Over all their superhighways crane white-lettered green signs that say "¼ MI. TO EXIT 47N." Their downtowns are reached by streets clotted with franchised tacos, donut and phrostee-phreez shops, karate parlors, and intersections with plastic-pennanted gasoline stations on all four corners. The more I see of this sort of thing, the luckier I feel that in my own past there figured a town so tiny and proud that a sign on its outskirts could boast "CLEMONS, IOWA. POP 200. SIZE OF A DIME, HEART OF A DOLLAR."

Now I did not technically grow up in Clemons, but I put in a lot of impressionable weeks on a farm near there. The farm, called Homelands, consists of the same 640 acres my father's grandfather homesteaded and is presided over to this day by my Aunt Janet. My mother's childhood was more nomadic. Since her father worked for the Milwaukee Railroad, her memories were of Miles City, Aberdeen, Ottumwa, and Spokane as well as Montevideo, where she was born, and Wausau, where she went to high school. Still, she was indisputably midwestern too, and with such a heritage I ought to be much abler than I feel to define what distinguishes us from people who came of age in other regions. It pretty well goes without saying that we are not as charming, and need not be as defensive, as those from the South, that we are not as breezy and effusive as westerners, nor as reticent as eastern Yankees. Maybe the essential thing we share, apart from the look and sound of us, is more subtly paradoxical: an attitude compounded of naiveté and mobility. Landlocked, we were raised to wariness of things and people and ideas from afar. But we were also brought up equidistant from two oceans in as nomadic an age as the world has seen, and nothing really seems inaccessible to us, either.

Nor is the Mother Midwest inaccessible to us, her exiled children, at least not to those of us in whom was stamped early an instinctive family loyalty. One way or another, you go home a lot if you are such a midwesterner. If you fly, you can tell the minute you step off your plane at O'Hare in Chicago that you aren't in the East anymore. Trousers are baggier, neckties are narrower, men's hair is cut shorter, waitresses and cabdrivers are friendlier. Everyone is friendlier. Strangers, quick to offer thumbnail autobiographical sketches, expect the same of you. Later, if you are a visitor, you discover that midwesterners are not only more trusting and more affable than people in the East—nearly as much so as Californians, in fact—but also more readily appalled. Their shock threshold, one might say, is low. Gentility reigns. A midwestern woman I know once daringly lowered her voice a bit to say, "He didn't have the G-U-T-S, if you know what I mean," which from her was racy language indeed.

Genealogy is an honored calling in my Midwest. In close-knit clans it is tacitly assumed that one in each generation will serve to tend the family tree. Ann and our cousins and I would be drilled as if for a surprise quiz with the names of our antecedents. James begat Henry begat James begat Henry who begat James who has since, rather startlingly, begotten a Timothy. William D. governed a state, Patrick H. superintended a railroad, James R. was once seriously considered for Secretary of Agriculture. We learned of these and of any number of humbler men who threshed grain, milked cows, kept books, preached, taught school, and once in a while were wards not, God forbid, of the state but of each other. And we would learn the names of their stalwart womenfolk, who kept (and still do keep) track of family pregnancies, graduations, weddings, illnesses, and plans for the summer and who saw to it that nothing interrupted the steady flow of thank-you notes. I was alarmed recently to find this thank-you note vigilance emerging in myself. "Tell them you had a nice *time!*," I found myself virtually hissing to my nephew and niece, as we all departed the house of some friends.

It is generally assumed that everyone is gainfully and, if possible, charmingly employed. "Why didn't you write a *charming* book?" an aunt asked me a bit sorrowfully, when one I did write contained words she was not used to seeing in print. One aspect of charm is hospitality among kinfolk. Even now I feel a twinge of guilt if I plan a vacation that does not include homage to, and free board and room from, some relatives along the way. Nor is such largesse restricted to blood kin.

"You don't know me," I said to a strange man on the phone

35

once, "but I'm Bob Howard's daughter, and he said to call you to say hello." He and my father had last seen each other when they were college roommates, something like forty years earlier. Regardless of that gap in time, he and his wife insisted I come right over and spend the night.

We of the Midwest deserve at least some of the credit other people get for regional traits. We are as hospitable as southerners, the mothers among us are fully as *kvetchig* as our New York Jewish counterparts ("If I, a mother, won't tell you," my own once said to me, "who will?"), and our upper lips are at least as stiff as those of stoic New Englanders. Nobody ever told us in so many words to brush our troubles under the rug because if we did they would disappear, but that was the general idea.

It was often implied that if we couldn't think of anything nice to say we had better keep still, that it didn't do to argue all the time, and that controversy was somehow in poor taste. Why, my mother would ask us, did we always have to *analyze* everything? Why were we so critical? What did we mean, asking whether she liked Mrs. X more than Mrs. Y—why, of course she liked them both exactly the same. During my high school years the parents of a couple of my friends were divorced, but those friends never, ever talked about it, and nobody else did, either. The worst thing the Winnetka *Talk*'s movie critic could say to damn a film, and did say often, was that it "reflects the acceptability of divorce." Monogamy, in our sheltered world, was the overwhelming norm. Not until years later did I hear the rumor that Mr. Baldwin, down the street, might not have died in his office, as we had been told, but in the arms of his paramour. Adultery, as far as we knew, only happened to people in books.

Books were held in high esteem. I developed a precocious taste for them, perhaps in part to vex my mother, who often said "Shirr, shirr, shirr, I'd like to read more, too, if I had time." Maybe she was more literary by nature, or once had been, than she seemed to be to me. The caption next to her graduation picture in her high school yearbook said, "There was a young woman and what do you think? She lived upon nothing but paper and ink." Before she married my journalist father, when they both were twenty-eight, she had worked for a while as a newspaper reporter herself. But for one reason or another, by the time she and I got at all acquainted, she was more preoccupied with things like cleaning up the house really well because tomorrow Julia, the cleaning woman, was coming.

I was not destined to be such a *balabosta*. No place I have ever lived has had that immaculate Bauhaus look about it. I don't even like to think how close I came to living a whole life without contour sheets and dishwashers. Having little taste or talent for housework, I was always sneaking off to read. Janie, Janie, I was often warned, you'll ruin your eyes, and it may be that I do owe my early myopia to the first three grownup books I can recall devouring: Louis Adamic's *What's In a Name?*, Betty Smith's *A Tree Grows In Brooklyn,* and Dr. Morris Fishbein's *Modern Home Medical Adviser.* Dr. Fishbein and the much-publicized Seven Danger Signals of Cancer held my rapt attention. I was sure at any given time that I harbored at least two of the Danger Signals, and never really thought I would make it to my next birthday. After visits to the family cemetery, not far from the farm near Clemons, I would sit in my grandfather's study lugubriously designing my own tombstone. It was a modest thing not more than four or five feet high, to be carved, if it wasn't too much trouble, of rose-colored marble.

When my father could take time off from covering the state legislature and other political matters, the whole family would take trips south or east or west by car. When he couldn't go, the rest of us went without him. He could not go to California in 1940, when our mother took us on the train to present us to our great-grandmother, but every night, as we strolled down the streets of Pomona, she would point upward and say, "See, girls? That's Daddy's star." After a few weeks we had a rendezvous at last with Daddy in Iowa. "All roads," my mother used to observe, "lead to the farm," a place where, as Ann has since recalled, our male relatives were miraculously able to give us ceremonial hugs, upon arrival and farewell, with their hands still in their pockets. If they were a demonstrative lot by nature, they hid it well. It is said of one of my great-grandmothers that when her younger daughter died she broke the news to the dead child's sister this way: "Mamie is gone. The Lord hath given, the Lord hath taken away. Blessed be the name of the Lord." With that the mother turned on her heel without a word or gesture of affection to her surviving daughter, and left the room.

"Hello-grandmother-and-granddaddy," we were trained like seals to chant on arrival at the farm, "it's wonderful to be here." It was also quite restful. On many hot, shimmering afternoons it was an event of some note when a car drove past. "Well," someone would comment, "I wonder who *that* could have been? It looked like Delbert's car, but he just went to town this morning to get the separator. Why would he be going again?"

Once, my mother wrote in her diary, "Bob's father walked in on me while I was smoking. I was a little relieved, because I always felt so sneaky, but he was terribly disappointed in me— just walked out and didn't say anything. I'm simply sunk about it. It just makes me heartsick." Unaware of such contretemps, we would wait for Christian Endeavor hay rides or trips beyond Clemons to Marshalltown where there were movies and a restaurant that served world-famous lemon chiffon pie. We would take forbidden, unsanitary dips in the horse trough and try the patience of hired hands by asking them what were the pet names of all the sheep and hogs and cattle.

Aunt Janet, who had been a Tri Delt, would drive us sometimes over the roller-coaster, Grant Wood landscape to county fairs. Once or twice we went to the huge state fair in Des Moines, where there was always a life-sized cow carved out of butter. Often enough there were family reunions, at which Whiteys and Bobs and Jacks and Pauls and Jims would assemble over midday dinner for reminiscences about the old days at Homelands Farm (ours) and Friendly Acres (Aunt Nora's, fifteen miles away) and impromptu debates as to whether second cousin once-removed meant the same thing as third cousin. Aunt Martha would tell of her days as a Theta at Iowa State, and she and my mother might join in a chorus of "Casey Would Waltz with the Strawberry Blonde."

38

Ann and Judy and I would make up songs. Jimmy and Johnny, destined to be high school basketball stars and SAE's at Ames, would chase us. Uncle Andy, once a Beta, would sneak us dollar bills and bubble gum. Aunt Bessie, a sweet librarian from Oskaloosa, would invent stories to tell us, and Uncle Jack, our soldier of fortune and raconteur (who had not yet discovered Aunt Millie), would reminisce about his army days in India.

World War II seemed less important than, say, thank-you notes. "No chocolate eggs this Easter," my mother wrote in her diary in 1942. "The country is just going crazy," she had written on Pearl Harbor Day. "Nothing counts now except our families. Wonder what is in store for us and our little girls and what kind of world they will live in. God bless them. All I hope is that all my dearest ones will be well and safe in this crazy world of ours, and that we can always keep our little group safe and intact." Five weeks later: "Bob wished my ring on again. Anniversaries are the only time it is removed. Took a long walk in the most delightful snowfall. Green moiré taffeta curtains."

We sang lines like, "Hi-hi-hee for the field artiller-ee," and drew caricatures of Hitler, Mussolini, and Tojo, and seemed to be sick a lot. "Drove to Glencoe," my mother noted one day. "Ann *didn't* get carsick. Found Jeanette had permitted children to play with my cards. Seven decks are ruined. I am furious." "Ridiculous weather for June. Janie greeted me when I came home saying, 'Ann is awfully naughty. She put all the company towels in the toilet, pulled the leaves off of your new plant, and wrote all over her blanket!' Bob's new boss may take us to the Pump Room Saturday. Hope it will work, I'm crazy to go."

"Today we had the ghastliest, funniest time. Jane W. and I took our kids to Dr. Hardy's. They never acted worse but it was so funny. Stopped at Tratt's [an interior decorating showroom] and Mike and Janie got in the show window, knocked over pictures, and stepped on samples. Then on the way to the car Janie fell and tripped Mike. They both landed in puddles, Mike said Janie pushed him on purpose. Ann was coughing very hard and wound up vomiting all over her snowsuit. Then we got Wacky the cat from the animal hospital and she was scared of all of us. I whooped constantly from my own cold. We just howled. What a day."

Much later, in Winnetka, we got a holiday from school so that we could cheer General MacArthur as he faded away, before our very eyes, en route to Wisconsin, but we were really more interested in movie magazines (why do I remember even now that Alan Ladd liked lamb chops?) and in the Hit Parade. By the time I cared about the Hit Parade enough to sigh impatiently waiting for the Lucky Strike Extras to be over, the Number One song bade the legendary ballerina to "do your pirouettes in rhythm with my aching heart" and "just ignore the chair that's empty in the second row." Ah, they really aren't writing songs like that any more, or lines like " . . . their faces gaunt, their eyes were blurred, their shirts all soaked with sweat," from "Ghost Riders in the Skies."

Tratty, as we called our distant cousin Edna Tratt, would drive out to Winnetka from Chicago on Sunday afternoons to keep my mother company. Tratty, fifteen years my mother's senior, was long divorced and had twin sons who were both interior decorators, one of whom had died. Tratty had fine auburn hair and a wry, droll manner. She went to a lot of movies and played bridge with socialites and colonels. To Ann and me she seemed the very height of urbane sophistication, living as she did in a sunless apartment on the Near North Side all done in dusky French rose and smoked mirrors.

Tratty would sit there at our piano, on those long Sunday afternoons, and play "I'll See You Again" and "Alice Blue Gown," with considerable feeling. Ann and I would do our homework and consort with our friends, most of them girls who had sisters and female pets. Later we might go for a drive in Tratty's car past the houses of the Old Money ("Gol," our cousin Judy once marveled, "they look like *fraternity* houses!"), and eat out at the Indian Trail, waiting until ten or so for our father to come back from work at the *Chicago Tribune*.

If anyone ever said anything unkind about the *Tribune,* our mother told Ann and me, "just tell them it's your bread and butter," which, since for most of his career our father worked there, it was. Mother was not much given to philosophical discourse as to why elephants were so much better than donkeys; they just were. In 1970, when my father retired, his associates planned an enormous testimonial dinner. They gave him a good selection of plaques and a check which he turned over to a college scholarship fund. So much did this occasion make Ann and me feel like Tricia and Julie that we referred to it as "The Coronation." "I've never made a speech in my life and I'm not going to break that record now," Mother said, "but I think you're all just divine!" When the speeches were over someone came up to me and said, "Well! I saw you sitting with a *Democrat!*," hardly less startled than if I had taken up with a Maoist pygmy.

Then, as often, one of our mother's chief concerns was how our hair would look. She even worried about the coiffure of four-year-old Sarah, who was not even going to the Coronation at all but staying behind with her brother and a baby sitter— "a registered nurse with a lifesaving degree," Ann said—at the Lampliter Motel. (The house was filled with other relatives from farther away.) Ann spun a fantasy about the motel's other guests, tipsily busy yelling things like "Bring your bottle on up to Room 235!" How dreadful if they should disapprove of Sarah's hairdo! She imagined demonstrating different styles, as if working from a trade magazine at a beauticians' convention, on the child's little head. "Just sneak a bobby in here for Style K12 and here, for J14—would you believe such a difference, folks, with just a flip of the barrette?"

Another time, when we were fooling around with a tape recorder, Ann did a spontaneous account, as if for a television special commentary, on "The First Indoor Brain Surgery." That inspired us to make several other such tapes, all in the manner of mindless radio interviews. Our subjects included medical ankle bracelets, child-oriented households, bake-offs, Astronauts' wives, an animal hospital offering the ultimate in privacy for "male masters and their female dogettes," and a lengthy debate between two clubwomen as to whether Quito or Glasgow should be their town's sister city. We had the tape re-

41

corder with us one day whan a contractor arrived to begin
work on a tennis court on the property of some friends. "Could
you tell us, please," Ann asked the startled man as she held the
microphone up to his mouth, *"What was your real emotion*
when you came up this driveway?"

Ann's own life had its surreal moments. David, her husband,
once owned a motel which nearly burned down. "Have you
ever seen a melted phone?" she wrote after the fire. "Have you
ever washed ninety-six sheets and forty-eight pillowcases at a
laundromat and been told 'you really *should* bring your laundry in more than once a year?' "

Before a party which neither Ann nor I much wanted to go
to but which was not optional, I said, "Well, I guess we'll just
have to grit our teeth and be nice and think of compliments."

"Right," she said, "like 'How'd you ever get these ice cubes
so perfect?' "

In 1952 our dilemma was whether the Republican nomina-
tion ought to go to General Eisenhower or, as more of us
tended to think, to his opponent, Mr. Integrity. My friends
and I wrote quite a snappy little campaign song, which began,
"Off the graft raft with Taft," and my father supplied us with
free passes to the convention, which meant we could march
right past the Andy Frain ushers, second in vigilance only to
Secret Service agents. Our debutante friends envied Ann and
me such worldliness. I guess the feeling we gave them was akin
to what would later be called Radical Chic. Such were the limits of some of our classmates that we, those crazy Howard girls,
were the most unorthodox mavericks they knew.

My mother came to like Ike a lot, especially when some wire
service photographer caught her husband walking right behind
the grinning president and his grandchildren. "SAVE," she
wrote on an envelope, "VALUABLE NEGATIVE OF BOB
WITH IKE!" Up that picture instantly went, framed of course,
to join the series of Bob with Adlai and Bob with Governor
Horner and Bob with all the other politicians. On other walls
there were just as many pictures of Ann and me, at all stages of

our development, including the desperate smiles I hope we reserved for graduation photographers. Eleanor never talked of finding work outside the home, but if she had wanted to, she might have had a promising future as an archivist. As it was, her intense sense of history was focused inward, upon us.

Midwesterners who come to New York have as much in common, are as much *landsmen,* as people who have come from County Mayo or the Ukraine. When we get together, we talk of old folkways. With my friend Russell Oberlin, who comes from Ohio, I have often discussed midwestern attitudes toward matters of taste. Russell remembers how, when he was a boy in Akron, certain of his neighbors thought that aluminum storm doors with an initial on the front were "just a little nicer" than plain ones. "We didn't fall for that *ourselves,*" Russell says in quick defense of his own family. "After all, we were Episcopalians. But the phrase 'just a little nicer' is one I can remember having heard all my life." I can too. My own first such memories concern snapshots; I remember being told that those with a dull finish were just a little nicer than glossy ones. My mother probably told me this as she sat pasting the products of her cherished Brownie box camera, which really *was* brown and which later was replaced by an Instamatic, into Ann's and my separate but equal Kodak books.

Those books grew chubby, as did we, with the passage of time. There we still are, The Girls, barely past the stage when we fought over whose side of the back seat was whose, gazing up in a snapshot at the Rockefeller Center fountain, in stunning homemade twin denim costumes known as Our Lavenders. The Girls: at the seashore or the skating rink with friends, on the farm with cousins, secured forever in albums with those black Nu-Ace corners. And if ever anyone in any group snapshot did not look his or, much more likely, her best, do you know what Eleanor Howard would do? Why, she would go get her manicure scissors and deftly trim off a fat hip here or a double chin there and paste the picture in with Elmer's glue instead of Nu-Ace corners. She would write who it was in white ink. She was quite fond of monograms, name tapes, and all forms of identification. She even put our initials on all our toothbrushes, with nail polish, as though we were a family of eighteen instead of four.

Once, when someone asked what she would save if the house were burning down—what possession, in other words, she cherished most—she said she would run for her husband. No, whomever she was talking to said, what *thing?* Easy: Ann's and my baby books, as opposed to Kodak books, mine with a blue cover and Ann's with a white, full of tiny footprints and first Valentines and cute sayings. Could any two children of our station and period have had a more extensively documented childhood? Maybe we would have grown up sooner had less attention been paid to our early feats and antics; maybe not.

It was one of the sorrows of my mother's life, I think, that she herself did not appear in a single one of the many pictures taken at Ann's and David's twilight garden wedding. The photographer simply forgot. He caught all other possible combinations of ushers and bridesmaids and in-laws and Ann coyly feeding David a piece of cake but not a one of the mother of the bride. When the honeymoon was over, accordingly, the newlyweds were asked to put their costumes on all over again, so that someone could take flashbulb pictures of them, this time with both the bride's parents. Only those flashbulb snapshots never turn out awfully well. The pupils of everybody's eyes always seem to look red.

Mother didn't think it was nice for us to say mean things about Spiro Agnew when he made a speech in Springfield once, and she most certainly was not amused when Ann wore a dress to a Fourth of July party that looked quite a bit like a flag. Going through her drawers we found a DAR Manual of Citizenship, and once she alluded in the presence of some of my bleeding heart New York kneejerk liberal friends to "that *darling* Nixon." The aunties in Pomona, when I advised them in 1968 that I thought I would vote for Humphrey, were worried. "Have you told your *father* that?" they asked.

Winnetka was and is a handsome town. Noble trees arch along its lake shore and over roads and lanes well tended by people most of whom moved there specifically to give their children the proverbial advantages. But in some ways, in my time anyway, it was about as open to change as a walled medieval city. There were a few scattered Catholics and Christian Scientists and Jews, but almost everybody belonged either to the Episcopal church or, as we did, to the ever so slightly less fashionable Congregational. Our choir was impressive. I was never good enough even to try out for it, but exposure to it gave me an abiding fondness for hymns of all kinds, from Gregorian chants to fundamentalist stuff. I don't even switch the radio dial away from church services on Sunday mornings.

Rites of passage in Winnetka would have made anthropologists yawn. Upon reaching the eighth grade, children were funneled off to one of two dancing schools, Mrs. Wilson's or Mrs. Woolson's, or, as the vernacular had it, "Wil or Wool." Other decisions of like magnitude arose. Should we swim at Maple Street Beach or Tower Road? See a movie at the Teatro or the Community House? Return from Chicago (where we had our braces tightened, or saw the Cezannes at the Art Institute, or ordered furtive cocktails at the Tip Top Tap of the Allerton) by the North Shore electric railroad or the Northwestern? Get our ice cream at Conney's Drugstore or Hammond's on Green Bay Road or Florence Beach's? In the undemonstrative Midwest, where "not so bad" can mean "marvelous and wonderful," ice cream is a common metaphor for love. Maybe that is why a lot of us do not look as lean and rangy as we might like to.

Autumn Saturdays we would sit on the bleachers outside New Trier High School, which we were endlessly reminded was one of the nation's top ten or top two or something, and sing, ". . . three thousand strong we march, march along, for the school by the lake see-rene. . . ." Earlier, in Memorial Day parades, we had literally marched in Scout troops to the Village Green. At Christmas there would be mother-daughter teas and maybe tasteful little dances. Our vices, those of which I was aware anyway, were laughable. Some of us experimented on the sly with nail polish, but it was considered "cheap" to smoke, much less drink even beer, before college.

45

We had crushes on unattainably older boys—"But of course it's hopeless, he's a *senior.*"—and passed more evenings than it is comfortable to recall either baby sitting or else having giggly slumber parties. At these we would shriek when boys tapped playfully on the windows, talk soulfully about Keats and Edna St. Vincent Millay, listen to Aaron Copland, and bewail the frizziness of our godawful home permanents. It was little comfort that these permanents, as their name did not imply, lasted about a semester. We'd always have another. We would sit there feeling doomed, passing curlers shaped like chicken thighbones to our beautician mother, as the sharp smell of neutralizer fluid filled the house.

The bolder ones among us would run sometimes for class or girls' club offices, being careful, of course, never to vote for ourselves. Among the all-school girls' club committees, secretariats really, were two called Friendly and Social. It was surpassingly important to be friendly and social. We would smile, and hope desperately to be popular, and apologize a lot. One of my most cringing memories is of making my self-conscious way, imprisoned in braces and glasses and more girth than manicure scissors could trim away, from locker to classroom. On the way I would hail people by saying "Excuse me: hi."

I cannot say how different it would have been if I had been raised in the sphere of Coney Island instead of Riverview, or of Lord & Taylor instead of Marshall Field's. I only know that to me at least Winnetka seemed fawningly reverent about things eastern. We would positively lionize anyone's house guest from Massachusetts who came through saying things like "Heavens, Mummy, it wasn't all that *hideously* obnoxious ennaway." We had Moms, not Mummies, and we said "anyway," and we seldom spoke in italics. Two kinds of American women talk in italics. *One* is the kind you *simply* can't have missed if you *ever* read *Cosmpolitan* magazine, which has all these *marvelous* hints for girls who are *trying* to make a *go* of it in the city, which for *all* its dangers is the *only* place I can *imagine* actually *living.* The others who talk in italics are a little more *subtle* about it. They come from houses filled with porcelain and crystal and photographs in silver frames and fading, expensive rugs, and the monograms on their stationery are always palpable. They say "ennaway" and "ennathing" and if you tell them something faintly improbable they interject "Stop!" I used to think, when such things mattered to me, that these people had secret signals they sent back and forth, as impossible for the rest of us to hear as silent dog whistles.

Summers, while our classmates sent us postcards from Banff and Wianno, Dad got jobs for Ann and me in offices in Chicago, so we could help pay for tuition. The offices were not air-conditioned, and we felt like grim martyrs, and it was probably good for us. One summer, loath to use my father's pull in job hunting, I decided to find something myself in "publishing" and was hired to write form letters to people who had not paid their installments for F.E. Compton's Pictured Encyclopedia. A month or so later I was fired for making up my own form letters. Ann was quite embarrassed, maybe that same summer, when some of her colleagues at the C.T.A. Charter Services (which you would call if your club or fraternal order wanted to hire a bus for a day) noticed a picture of her at some debutante picnic in the *Daily News* society page.

Some of my friends had been dispatched in glory to Mount Holyoke and Smith. I, with lower grades and leaner funds, made it as far east as Ann Arbor, which even in the apathetic fifties was a vast and rich cafeteria of a place, where midwesternism was diluted. I met not only rural Michigan Elementary Ed majors who made light of lesson plans but New York Jews who seemed far more exotic than turbaned foreigners, with their talk of *yentas* and *tsuris* and hocking me a *chainik*. Ah, Jews, with their liquid eyes and tragic sense of life. Clearly mine was to be a schizophrenic future, torn between prompt thank-you notes to patrician summer houses on the one hand and huggy Seders on the other.

Before I left Ann Arbor I learned among other things that by no means everybody thanked Senator Joseph McCarthy (R., Wis.) for "rooting out the Commies" and that there were some perfectly darling people who didn't even want to be DGs or Phi Gams. I got a bachelor of arts degree in a singularly anticlimactic rainy day ritual and not long afterward took an all-night, sit-up train to New York City to seek, as they say, my fortune. Dad was out of town the evening I left, covering the convention in San Francisco, but Mom determined that I should have a proper send-off. Before I got on the sit-up train she took Ann and me to dinner at the Pump Room.

3

Mark Van Doren, The Dalai Lama, and Jimmy Stewart

Lord Baden-Powell, founder of the International Scouting movement, is said to have decided whom to marry on the basis of her tracks. His heart stood still, apparently, the moment he first beheld the future Lady Baden-Powell's footprints in the dirt.* On behalf of the unattached women in late twentieth-century America, I both salute him and envy him his moment of epiphany. I wish our search were anywhere nearly as simple. But in these complex times, with so many of our streets being paved, it is not easy to locate the partners of our dreams. Our dreams themselves, to make matters worse, are mystifying and confused. I once heard a woman, more sure of herself than many, declare that she personally was on the lookout for "a good dresser who knows how to order." But most of us ask more. Once some friends and I made a list of the Forty Most Important Qualities in the Opposite Sex. The Quality that sticks most in my mind, after quite a few years, is Affinity for Wood.

* Conscience compels me to add that Lord Baden-Powell's biography says it was the future Lady's gait, not her tracks, which caught his notice on the promenade deck of a ship. I still prefer the apocryphal version of the story.

Two or three times a year, at about four-thirty in the morning, my phone rings and I groggily pick it up to hear the voice
of my sentimental old roommate Bonnie. Having had several
drinks in Redondo Beach, California, where it is three hours
earlier, Bonnie wants to know whether I have met Mr. Right
yet and to reflect with nostalgia on the good old days when we
first came to New York and lived together, first at Katharine
House, then on Ninth Street, and later on Perry. In those years
she and I and most of our friends were programmed to prosper
in our chosen professions (or hurry up and choose them if we
had not done so) and to find men, not necessarily in that order.

Our programming had been subtle and happenstance, for
the most part, but every now and then my mother, who was by
default the source of most of my instructions along these lines,
would let slip some specific hint. My sister and I were not only
to empty-the-garbage-and-sweep-the-floor, leave the kitchen
spotless, try if possible to be dainty and have tiny waists like
Tiny Babs across the street, but, should it please God, "settle
down someday with a big, handsome, wonderful hunk of an Ivy
Leaguer." More she could not wish us.

In the early part of my quest I therefore looked with concu-
piscent awe upon that species, not yet aware that Ivy Leaguers
could have clenched fists and clenched minds just like the boys
back home. To this day, although that particular set of scales
has long since been ripped from my eyes, I swear I have a soft
spot even for guys who went to Princeton. I certainly rejoice
for my late mother's sake that, totally though I failed to make
this dream of hers come true, Ann at least bestirred herself to
locate a handsome hunk of, if not an Ivy Leaguer, a Big Ten
man.

My mother more fundamentally hoped, she said, that we
would find men who loved us as much as our father did her,
and vice versa. Apparently they really did love each other. At
least after she died, when Ann and I went through all her stuff
(a more painful ritual, by the way, than any of the formal ceremonies), we kept finding these Valentines they had sent each
other and notes he had left her saying things like, "Good morning, it's a real nice day and I love you and hope you sleep late."

Had the occasion arisen, Mother would have given me three further lessons she vouchsafed to Ann: always have placemats on the table when he comes home, never go to bed mad, and always be home when the kids come home from school. Well, fine, although the latter point may be arguable, but where were we supposed to look for the senders of such Valentines? How would we know if we met one? Would the earth move? Did it really matter, as my mother once hinted it might, "if your gent's parents would get to be friends of Bob's and mine"? Was it true, as she and probably most other mothers observed, that "it's just as easy to fall in love with a rich man as with a poor one"? I didn't and don't think so. Once, when she quizzed me about some man whose name I had mentioned a couple of times, she asked me what his background was.

"Well," I began, "he went to Yale Law School . . . ."

"He sounds *wonderful,*" declared my mother. Her curiosity was sated. When she learned that my friend Carol was going to marry my Harvard alumnus friend Tom, and that they had met each other at a party I gave, she could only keen, "Oh, Janie, and you introduced them!"

"But Mother," I should have explained, "I'd never have had a chance against Carol. She comes of such impressive stock."

"As you can see," Carol used to announce, "I am the great-granddaughter of the furrier to the Czar." She really is, too. I often did, and still do, find myself scribbling notes from phone conversations with Carol. Once, when she had been putting up preserves, we talked of the menace of botulism.

"You might think I'm a little too how you say rigid about it," Carol said, "but I always feel that one marmalade fatality is one too many."

My guarded letters home did not go into great detail about my efforts to find any sort of big, wonderful hunk, but I did once allude in my mother's presence to having spent a weekend off somewhere with a man. Correctly intuiting that there had been no chaperone at hand, she winced helplessly and said, "Well, that sure wasn't the way we did it in *my* day."

"How *did* you do it in your day?" I somehow never asked. "Please," I never could quite bring myself to implore, "tell me

51

how you're supposed to do it. Not how to be an English major, not how to work up a good case of guilt, not how to be career-oriented, but how to live! What are the rules?"

I suppose if she had known she would have told me, or the word would have got around somehow. I guess none of my friends at Katharine House on West Thirteenth Street knew either. Katharine House was a residence for genteel, allegedly young persons, run by something called the Ladies' Christian Union. In the fall of 1956, when I moved in, one could get a room and two meals a day for $18.75 weekly, which wasn't bad. That was where Bonnie and I and two other recent college graduates gravitated together and plotted our escape. Not only was the place oppressively genteel, but some of our fellow residents seemed neither all that young nor all that mentally sound. Quite a few of them talked quite a lot about their pet parakeets, and there was one who used to hum "Home on the Range" all during the whole leisurely elevator ride from the basement laundry room up to the fifth floor.

The West Ninth Street apartment we moved into was like a stage set for some comedy about ingenues in the big city, a drama which we proceeded to enact. The place had two tiny bedrooms and an air of claustrophobia when we were all home at once, so we tried not to be. With easily acquired new friends we went to Rienzi's coffee shop and other places on MacDougal Street and to bars like the White Horse and Romero's and Julius's and, on special occasions, to Marie's Crisis and the Five Spot. For even more special occasions we would go hear Mabel Mercer. Doggedly eclectic, we also kept up on lectures at the New School and woodwind quintet concerts around town. We made a point of discovering the Bronx Zoo, the Aquarium, the Pierpont Morgan Library, and Ripley's Believe It Or Not Odditorium on Times Square where, after considerable debate, we decided we did believe that a cow had licked a block of salt into the shape of a swastika.

Weekends we would ask each other, "Where are the parties?" There always were some. On occasion we would give them ourselves, rarely if ever providing the liquor; nobody expected us to. Once there was a New Year's Eve party given by two roommates named Shag and Shirley, who always made you sign their guest book. It must have been my twenty-second birthday when a friend named Larry, whom I had met at a production of Sartre's *No Exit,* took me to El Morocco, dutch treat. That Easter we were given a tiny chick we named Fink, in honor of a landlord across the street. We taught Fink to Charleston and soon thereafter he died in his dish with his beak up.

We had a playreading group and argued over who would get to be Blanche DuBois. Once we sang *Guys and Dolls.* There was such a thing as the *My Fair Lady* look in those days, and we still wore girdles or garter belts under our Lanzes. Marimekkos, panty hose, and slacks in midtown were no more discernible on our horizon than peace demonstrations or grass. A number of our gentleman callers were uncontroversially in the military, and when they dropped by on furloughs there would be talk of M-1 rifles and where they had taken their basic training. Nancy moved off to marry Mickey when the army transferred him out of clerk-typist school, and she was replaced for a while by Sonja, who was replaced by Ingrid, who in turn was replaced by Sue. Sonja and I, having decided we were made of finer clay than Gail and Phyllis, once announced that we were going to have what we chose to call a Renaissance Kick. It didn't last long, nor, with that name or in that spirit, did it deserve to.

Somewhere along there I craved, and finally could afford, more space. I moved into a third-floor floor-through on Perry Street, with two other roommates instead of three, and a room of my own. My room had an enchanting view of other people's back gardens and its own fireplace, which was astonishing luck, but there was a catch: there was no other way for anyone to get to the bathroom. Nobody minded much, though.

"Dear Miss Howard," begins a letter which came in the Perry Street days. "On several occasions Mrs. Vanoff has brought to my attention that your visitors persist in stomping up and down the stairs, and recently she spoke to your guests asking them could they please walk up and down like normal people. The answer was somewhat terse to the effect they can't." We could, however, stage elaborate Thanksgiving dinners and other rituals, including a surprise twenty-sixth birthday party for me which lasted, as I recall, three days. It really was a surprise, and it has caused me on every subsequent May 4 to wait in vain for a horde of well-organized loved ones to leap from behind some door. Maybe such things are only supposed to happen once. The cake said *"Ça va sans dire."*

One morning I woke up and decided I was sick of having any roommates at all. I went out with the *Times* real estate section and signed a lease for the first apartment I looked at, a fifth-floor walkup at Fourteenth Street and Seventh Avenue, above a Nedick's and across from the Federation for the Handicapped. Once a truckful of mooing cows passed by that always noisy intersection. Ever since I have longed to see, somewhere in Manhattan, a sign reading "MOOSE CROSSING."

Moving into Fourteenth Street meant I had to acquire furniture of my own, among other things a bed.

"Double, huh?" Bonnie observed when she saw it.

"Same price as single at Gimbel's," I said defensively.

"Yeah, right, sure." Only very privately, say among ex-roommates, was it conceded that a hale unmarried woman in the second half of her twenties might succumb to an occasional craving, of an evening, not to sleep alone.

In those years I was starting to write bylined articles for *Life,* because it was clear that I was supposed to, and a number of Dear John letters, because it was not at all clear that I was ready at that point to marry. The very idea of going steady seemed alarming enough. I announced an odd triumvirate of heroes: Mark Van Doren, the Dalai Lama, and Jimmy Stewart. These, I said, were my ideal men. It figured. Homage to the cinematic idol of my youth, along with wistfulness at having been born too late for the grand old days at Columbia's English Department, and too soon for Hare Krishna. Totally unrealistic expectations, and therefore totally safe. There was not a chance in the world that I would encounter anyone who could begin to match these, these . . . dare I call them standards?

I felt scared whenever things got complicated with the actual men—boys as I believe they were often still called—who did enter my life. Hence the Dear John letters. Dear Lloyd, You deserve someone better, and besides our metabolisms are different. Dear Louis, You're too old. Dear Warren, You're too young. Dear Jerry, You're too married. No, Al, I said NO. "Wise?" that same Al once asked rhetorically, "this girl knows *all* the answers." In fact I knew damned few. I did not, as they say, know even the questions.

"Pardon my male tendencies," an Ivy Leaguer named Tim once memorably said at the end of an evening, as he began a tentative assault on my person. "Why, Tim," another friend reported having once said to him under similar circumstances, "What are you *doing?*" In God's name what did she think he was doing? What did any of us think we were doing? Why were we not born in time of coeducational dormitories and reality?

I wasn't the only one who could write letters of rejection. Once in the surf at Nantucket I met a man who had beautiful teeth. We literally did meet in the surf, and it was all very sun-drenched and salty and exhilarating. He used phrases like "let's just sort of prowl around" and "to be quite candid with you," which should have been a tip-off, but I didn't realize what he was like until later, when we were waiting for a light to change in Providence, Rhode Island. As we watched the crowds cross the street he said, with something frightening in his voice, "Don't you think some people are so ugly they'd be better off dead?" Still, I had been so smitten I tried to overlook his being a Nazi, and I wrote to him faithfully when he went off to teach in the West. In late November, eager for his promised return over the Christmas holidays, I ordered a monogrammed tobacco pouch for him at Mark Cross. He did not, of course, come back for Christmas. "Social life here," he wrote, "really has become rather amusing."

Some chord in me responded when my friend Grace once said she always felt she was supposed to be Daddy's boy. Now her nice midwestern daddy and mine probably would recoil in equal horror at the very suggestion that they ever made us feel this way. It certainly wasn't deliberate on their parts, but as the older daughters we were both given the idea that our mission in life was to achieve, even as our younger sisters were exhorted, just as unconsciously, to go forth and be popular and pretty.

"Big deal, so you were programmed," a man once said to me. "It's better to be programmed, even badly, than not. Whatever you're told to be—a cheerleader, a surgeon, a roengenologist— it's better than nothing."

"I guess so," I told him, "but it seemed so *arbitrary*." Our sisters didn't have to get good report cards, and Grace and I didn't have to have a flair for romance.

As a result, we certainly hadn't. But slowly, a decade before consciousness-raising came along, we began to realize that even we, in our late-blooming way, could at times secrete a certain emanation we referred to as Musk. Musk was an ephemeral fragrance which could and, sometimes even did, drive men mad with desire.

"If only," my friend Grace once mused, "I could turn my Musk on at will!" She had been enduring a long dry spell.

"The trouble with you," our other friend Andrea told Grace, "is that you don't get around enough."

"Andrea's right, Grace," I said. "You ought to get out of the rut you've been in."

"Why don't you let *us* plan some weekends for you?" Andrea said. "If you do what we tell you to, you'll find happiness."

"Happiness," I promised, "and romance. You won't feel like Daddy's boy any more, either." Andrea and I shared a strong managerial streak, a confidence that in small ways, if not large ones, we could make order from chaos. We set to work changing Grace's life. We told her to loiter around men's accessory boutiques off Madison Avenue in the Fifties, fingering the merchandise as if in search of the perfect gift for a certain absent someone—monogrammed tobacco pouches, perhaps. Now and then she was to ask the advice of fellow customers, one of whom might ask her out for coffee. If this didn't happen she was to go to the Palm Court of the Plaza Hotel and look mysterious as she read a slim volume of Randall Jarrell.

The Modern Art Museum, we ruled, was a cliché. We dispatched Grace instead to the Museum of the American Indian, preposterously far uptown, where she might be found by some footloose ethnologist. Concerts at the Cloisters and the Frick were recommended, and on Sunday mornings she could have her choice of the hearty Unitarians, the pensive Quakers, or other houses of worship where services were conducted entirely in French, Greek, or sign language. You never knew. Our programs for Grace were not rigid; we gave her a lot of latitude. On Saturday we suggested she go on an Appalachian Mountain Club hike over some trail in the Berkshires. She did, and met a cardiologist whose effect on her own heart, at least for a while, was salutary.

Gleeful over our modest success at matchmaking, Andrea and I later turned to the personals column of the *New York Review*. By this time she was married and I was happily involved, so the ad we placed was on behalf of our friend Barbara. It said:

> ADVENTUROUS WOMAN seeks to share energy, warmth, humor, intellect with outdoors-minded potential husband.

Replies, to our amazement, poured in. Those who sent them didn't sound bad. The one man we went so far as to screen, a diplomat, seemed worthy. Without telling Barbara how we happened to have met him, we arranged for him to call her. He took her to dinner and a concert, but sparks did not fly.

"Maybe there's something just a tiny bit manipulative about messing around this way with other people's lives," Andrea suggested.

"You could be right," I said. "Somehow I don't even have the heart to screen those other guys, have you?"

She hadn't either, so we did not, but we became addicted to the euphemistic prose of personals ads. How, we and other friends often wondered, could such hip, supple, sensitive people be at such loose ends? Were they really finding one another? Would anybody even answer an ad for someone who sounded humanly flawed and real? One evening, after a dinner party, eight of us set to work composing such an ad. It was notable, we thought, for its economy:

FAT, uptight wallflower, approaching
her prime, seeks Heathcliff.

The wallflower was a figment of our collective imagination,
but plenty of Heathcliffs wrote in to declare their eager interest. Of course for all we knew they were fictitious too, the products of other similar dinner parties, but on the chance that we
might hurt somebody's feelings we decided not to answer the
letters.

"Had you thought of reading the *reviews* in the *New York
Review?*" a friend inquired, and we decided he had a point
there.

On a slip of paper stuck into an old journal I recently found
this note, in my own hand: "Guilt about Ron. Guilt guilt guilt
guilt guilt. Oh shit." I could not recall whether this particular
attack of guilt pertained to restraint or to excess, but I did suddenly feel that those of us who were born in the middle 1930s
would have grown up faster and clearer-headed had we been
given a less distorted, less idealistic picture of the opposite sex.
We didn't think they were our enemies, we just assumed that
they were beyond reach. At some rally in my third year of high
school I can remember being given hectographed new words to
"Onward Christian Soldiers," which we were supposed to, and
did, sing *en classe:*

> Onward junior gi-i-irls,
> Marching after men,
> Til they leave the freshmen,
> We'll be hags til then . . .

Hags. *Oi.* The very idea. Hag parties. Slumber parties. Pro-
longed and unsought separatism. It turned out that not all the
boys in our class were enchanted with this state of affairs either. At least Peter Yorkus had not been. Peter Yorkus was my
classmate in high school, and I had not seen him in nearly
twenty years when we suddenly were both asked to the same

dinner party. He still had a sweet face and I confessed to him, freed by the passage of time, that I had always secretly thought he was rather nice. He told me he had secretly thought I was too.

"Then why," I asked in exasperation, "didn't you invite me to the prom or anything? Do you know I never went to one of those damned proms?"

"Me neither," he said. "Come to think of it, I wish I had asked you. But I guess I was afraid."

I am much pleased to report that the general feeling these days is considerably less hectic and desperate. The shackles of inhibition are being shaken off, and high time. I have even spent interludes with several different good dressers who had marked affinities for wood and were absolute wizards at knowing how to order. Since I do not think, upon reflection, that any of these alliances was destined to last, I cannot regret their temporary nature. Anyway, it isn't pathetic anymore to be single. As a friend of mine had the wit to reply when someone asked if she were married, "Good God, no, are *you?*" As much as anything, an unmarried person nowadays is the object of envy. I have not felt for some time that I had to apologize for my state, to myself or to anyone else, nor that I must fill my unplanned hours with nonsensical encounters designed to prove (to whom?) that even I, though a firstborn, can be popular. Who needs all that "servitude and flutter," as Marianne Moore characterized courtship, unless there is some point to it?

Not to say that I rule out the prospect of matrimony. That state is becoming so unfashionable, and I have all my life been so consistently out of step, that my time may well be drawing nigh. The subjunctive mood grows wearisome; commitment sometimes beckons. It's not that I want someone to watch over me; I want continuity. It is sobering, of course, to note how disillusioning how many other people have found such things, but I still might have to try it, someday, for myself. I may be able to summon a spirit other than resignation in which to do it.

If I do, it will probably happen, as most things do, when least expected. That's the way it was with Bonnie out there in Redondo Beach, when she became a wife, though not for long, and a mother. I'll wager, come to think of it, that even Lord Baden-Powell may have had something else on his mind the day he spied that fateful set of tracks. And so, I say to my several selves, let us declare the old criteria obsolete and get on with it—get on, that is, with not looking for it. Let us rule out the idea of placing any more personal classified ads, certainly any that read:

> IVY HUNK with donnish dignity,
> solid karma, and boyish charm sought
> by chronic seeker. No phonies, please.
> Photo a must.

That's not the way we're going to be doing things, in my day.

4

The Osborne Agreement

For six years or so I lived in an august and imposing large brownstone apartment building, at the corner of Seventh Avenue and Fifty-seventh Street, called the Osborne. It was as splendidly ugly as it was conveniently located. It had a great deal of what is called character, and I liked my three rooms in it, even though they were not situated so as to admit much in the way of sunlight. Certain people were unduly impressed when I told them where I lived; the Osborne was an address with cachet.

Once, the first man who ever truly mattered to me, whose name is Lloyd, passed through town as he sometimes does. This was years after we had parted, which in turn was years after we had first interlocked and "made a mess", as Mabel Mercer used to sing, "of both of our bright young lives." The afternoon he dropped by, Lloyd and I agreed over not a little Irish Coffee that in view of the fact that we were both such superior human beings, it was a damn shame that things hadn't worked out between us. Lloyd is tall and unassuming, with a cellist's hairline and profound reserves of erudition and gentle irony. I still keep all his letters.

"Do you remember," I asked him, "the afternoon we got on an elevator somewhere on West End Avenue in the nineties and a black woman got on with us and looked at us and said, 'Nice man, nice woman, you be having nice childrens.'?"

"Of course I remember," said Lloyd. Lloyd, it was said, had a mind like a steel trap. "It's probably just as well that we didn't have childrens, though, because we might have driven them and each other crazy."

"We drove each other a little crazy anyway," I said.

"Maybe if we'd got married and divorced," said Lloyd, "we'd at least have something to show for it. It was all so ambiguous."

"What's ambiguity? The last refuge of the scoundrel?"

"Hobgoblin of small minds, I think."

"Anyway, it was all so unresolved and *vague*."

"You know what we need? We need some sort of quasi-legal document to show for it all."

"Why not? Everyone else has marriage licenses and divorce papers. We ought to at least have something."

Suddenly, as persuaded of the therapeutic value of paperwork as if we were a couple of minor airlines officials in Bengal, we set to work. We drew up a pact, Lloyd and I did, with several whereases and six or seven different clauses. The gist of the pact was that we both sure did have a lot of esteem for one another and wished each other Godspeed in the years to come.

I typed the pact, making two carbons and being finicky about centering and interior margins. Because of the effect all that Irish Coffee had had on my motor skills it wasn't so easy to achieve a flawless copy, but finally it was done.

We called the pact the Osborne Agreement and went downstairs to walk two blocks south to the Park-Sheraton Hotel. In the downstairs lobby we paid a woman sitting at a desk fifty cents to have our pact notarized. She was blasé, as I suppose most notary publics must get to be with the passage of time, and she did not treat us any differently than if we had brought her an application for a driver's license renewal.

Returning to the Osborne, we celebrated.

5

What's So Great About Sofas?

If I had an acre for every hour I have spent in rap sessions, I would own the equivalent of, at least, Connecticut. Rapping, by the spring of 1971, had come to rival baseball as our national sport. No issue was so complex that someone somewhere did not propose to unravel it in the course of a simple five- or six-hour rap session, in which it did not go without saying (nothing went without saying) that everyone would let everything all hang out.

Margaret Mead and James Baldwin had recently published their *Rap on Race*. The Jesus people were rapping about the imminent Second Coming, Hare Krishna devotees were rapping, when they were not chanting, about the Godhead, La Leche League women were rapping about breastfeeding, and members of Mensa were rapping about how nice it was for them to have IQs in the 140s. Unofficial groups like the Radical Moms of Decatur, Illinois were rapping far into many nights about the problems and promises of alternative schools. In my head still echoed the earnest rapping of encounter workshops and the weekly sessions of a New York consciousness-raising group. Wherever one turned, it seemed, one heard the sound of voices confessing, responding, explaining, reemphasizing, paraphrasing—rapping. At first all this was refreshing, but one's appetite had its limits. The following autumn I wrote an article on silence; my first suggestion for a title was *Oh, Shut Up.*

But meanwhile my lot was at all times to heed, and when possible to take part in and even initiate rap sessions, structured or otherwise. At the very hour my mother lost consciousness, Suzanne Szasz and I were rapping about feminism in a small house in South Milwaukee. We had been invited by Pat Baranek, a new recruit to a group called the Non-Violent Feminist Co-operative, who lived there with her parents and her grandmother, an immigrant from Yugoslavia. Pat was a twenty-three-year-old student whose other interests included Young Americans for Freedom. Suzanne and I reasoned that if the women's movement in Milwaukee had reached such converts as Pat, it was a force to be reckoned with indeed.

When news of Pat's involvement in the movement spread through her own family, her parents received calls of condolence from other relatives.

"Oh, no, Mary!" an aunt had phoned to say. "Not *Patty!* In Women's Liberation? How awful!"

"What's your new name?" her brother-in-law asked Pat when he heard the news, "Butch?"

Before the movement touched her, Pat told us, she had thought of herself as "twenty-three and over the hill." A heavy woman with extremely blond hair, she had once aspired to be a beautician and had only recently enrolled as an Italian major —"Can you *imagine* anything so impractical?"—at the local branch of the state university. Her grandmother, wearing a babushka that Sunday morning, sat and watched and plainly wondered what I was doing there with my notebook and to what end Suzanne, festooned with cameras, was setting up strobe lights all over the living room. Pat's mother had to explain to the older woman, translating to and from the Serbo-Croatian.

"She wonders," Mrs. Baranek told us, "why I don't buy Patty some clothes. She doesn't understand that all the girls wear pants these days. She thinks it was better in her time, when the man was the boss in the home. She says God took the rib from Adam and made woman, which is why the woman should serve the man."

"That's okay, if women want to," said Pat, "but that's not the kind of life I want for myself."

"But why not?" her mother asked. "I *like* doing womanly things."

"Oh, Mom," Pat said. "You know that's not all you do. You've worked for fourteen years as a bookkeeper, too."

"Even so," Mrs. Baranek said, "I like cooking for my husband. I like being on a pedestal. I love being pampered. I like nothing more than having the door opened for me. And as far as men staying home and being mother, I don't think men are *equipped* to stay home and take care of itty-bitty babies."

"They don't have to," said Pat, "but women shouldn't have to, either, if they'd rather spend their lives doing something else."

The women's movement had come to Milwaukee in 1968, when the small and self-described "hard core bunch of nuts" who founded the original chapter of the National Organization of Women decided to stage a sit-in at an all-male restaurant. The restaurant manager obligingly called them something like "Communist, Fascist trash," so silly a claim as to catch the eye of numerous housewives who had been reading Betty Friedan and wondering. "That was the time," one housewife said, "when I'd think, 'Oh, goodie, the Di-Dee Wash man comes this afternoon! I'll have someone to talk to besides the kids!'"

Before long she had plenty of others to talk to. Women's consciousnesses were stirring in every neighborhood of Milwaukee. NOW was quickly gaining strength and numbers, and other new groups and acronyms emerged fast. Members of the guerrilla chapter of WITCH, the Women's International Terrorist Conspiracy from Hell, got mad at the newspapers and sprang a surprise skit, on women's rights, for the edification of what they called the Oppress Club. Over on Wells Street, across from a pornographic movie house, the West Side Women's Center painted giant flowers on its pink walls and threw open its doors. Everybody was invited in for coffee, to read magazines, to rap, and for lessons in driving, macramé, and nutrition. In one corner was a free clothing and toy exchange, with a sign that said TAKE WHAT YOU NEED, BRING WHAT YOU'RE THROUGH WITH.

What the West Side women were through with themselves was the coeducational Left. Most of them had come from the civil rights and peace movements, in which they had felt demeaned by their male colleagues. Their political aims had not changed, but they weren't going to be subordinate to men any more. They held no special brief for the nuclear family— "Ultimately," one said, "our goal is to smash it."—or for such established conventions as heterosexuality.

In patriarchal Milwaukee such notions made a lot of people edgy, including even some ardent feminists. Another schism engendered the Non-Violent Feminist Co-operative, whose members did not spell their country's name Amerika, or long in public for the doom of capitalism, or discuss their orgasms. "I'd bop my husband one on the head," one NVFC member said, "if he talked about our sexual experiences with any group of men." Except for three or four young unmarried women, the NVFC consisted of middle-class housewives who had, or had had, or expected to have, tricycles cluttering their not very spacious front hallways. On their kitchen bulletin boards hung signs that read SHALOM and ANOTHER MOTHER FOR PEACE.

I first met Bede Yaffe over lunch and told her that I had been hearing so much talk about feminism that it was time for me to take a break and go someplace like the Milwaukee Zoo. At once she gave me the keys to her car and urged me to be off. Such an act of charity and trust was, by New York standards, amazing. I had a good time wandering around the zoo. On returning I reported to Bede the lyrics of a song I had heard on the car radio: "Hey, little woman, please make up your mind/ Come on into my world and leave your world behind."

"So," she said to me, "it's getting to you, too, is it?"

"Sort of," I said, "but I have an aversion to groups and movements."

"Then how come you write about them so much?"

"Fair question," I said.

People never believed Bede at first when she told them that her oldest son was twenty-eight. She looked more like a Cub Scout den mother. When I first met her she had a part-time job at an art gallery, where the following fall there would be a one-woman show of her paintings. Painting was coming to matter to her more and more.

"When people say, 'Oh, painting, that's a nice hobby,' I'm just now starting to be able to reply, 'It's not a hobby, it's my *guts!* '" Bede, a sort of freelance evangelist for the women's movement, was not precisely a member of the NVFC, but she hung around with them a lot and went to their rap sessions and was designing for them a felt collage to be hung in their headquarters, captioned FEMINISM LIVES. There were those in the NVFC who thought she might be a spy from some other group.

That night Bede and I went to an NVFC rap. One woman there was a former beauty queen who had only lately let her hair grow back to its natural color, because she was tired of having men on the street say, "Hey, Blondie, you walk kind of fast, don't you?" Another was a fifth grade teacher who had just persuaded her not very religious husband that it was hypocritical of them, and inconvenient for her, to keep a kosher household. Few of the NVFC members had known each other socially—"Who has *time* for social life, anyhow?" one asked—and few were joiners by nature.

"I always had a horror of women's groups before," one of the unmarried members said, "but this is different. Once I got into this, I knew I wouldn't be comfortable leaving it."

Not long ago I talked to an old friend, a friend I have had since sixth grade, who was working in the national headquarters of what used to be a formidable Greek-letter sorority while she waited for her divorce. It pleased me to hear her say that "working there is like trying to keep an elderly patient alive in a hospital." I worry when I hear trend-spotters claim, as they do now and then, that we can expect a revival of the customs and styles of the fifties. I still have dreams, disturbing ones, about my four years in a college sorority, starting in the fall of 1952.

At our Rushing Parties we, the Actives, were divided into three categories: Floaters, Stabilizers, and Watchdogs. The purpose of these Parties was to assess, and be assessed by, the horde of generally terrified Rushees, of whom twenty or thirty would become our Pledges. They would come to cohabit with us and learn our sacred secrets. They would not, God forbid, reflect discredit upon the House.

At Hash Sessions following the Parties, dressed in bath-robes and with our hair rolled up in pin curls, we would vote on whom to bid and whom to blackball, on grounds perhaps that *"she* would be a detriment to a *dogfight."* Once we wanted to bid a girl who was half Japanese, but were urged not to "because she wouldn't be comfortable with the way she might get treated by the alum chapters in California." (It was assumed by alumnae that all our fu-ture friendships for the rest of our lives would stem from such Alum Chapters: wherever we might move, our first act would be to get in touch with this Sisterhood.) We were obliged to extend bids to our Legacies, whose moth-ers or sisters were Alums, but beyond that our quest was for girls who would prove to be Dolls, Queens, or Workers and Thinkers. (This structure was rather like that of an apiary, now that I think of it.)

My own sister, which is to say my parents' other daugh-ter, belonged to such an organization too. In her sorority, when Rushees or other guests arrived, someone had to go "take them off the door," which meant greet them, over-whelm them with cordiality. We took them off the door too. And on Final Dessert night, at the end of Rushing, we would all stand on the stairway, wearing white robes and holding candles, our eyes misting a bit as we sang a certain song about a certain species of rose. Some of us might wink at our favorites among the departing Rushees, hoping they would not decide to pledge another House.

Before every dinner we would sing a special grace, and at compulsory Monday evening Chapter Meetings we would memorize the names of our organization's Founders, which I still could recite on demand at any time. **Friendships** developed in spite of all this mystique, not because of it. The system's only defensible function I can think of was to certify to the world that somebody had found us acceptable at a time in our lives when a lot of us were not sure we were.

I would give a great deal to have had the wit to spend all these Monday evenings in any number of other ways—learning German, say, or trying to do cartwheels. Whenever I have reservations about feminism, I think of my sorority, and raise a clenched fist.

For different reasons, latter-day sisterhood in Milwaukee seemed puzzling to friends of Bede Yaffe. They could not see why she had taken up what struck them as so unseemly a crusade. "You have everything you want," they told her. "Why this?"

She did "have" a lot. She dressed impressively, went to encounter groups, and talked of Jung and Krishnamurti. By her first husband she had three grown sons. Her second was a kind and prosperous businessman, with whom she lived in a comfortable house where there was a studio in which she could paint, sculpture, and make rugs.

"Of all *people*," her friends went on, shaking their heads. "You're so *feminine!* Why *you?*"

"I felt like a misfit and a freak at first," Bede said, "because it seemed very radical and strange for me, who used to be afraid of my own shadow, to go around wearing buttons with equality signs and clenched fists. But I've always been a late bloomer. It's taken me a long time to realize a lot of things. Let me tell you how stupid I was when I was divorced after twenty-three years of marriage—which is one of the ghastliest experiences anyone can go through.

69

"I was so crushed and broken that when I went to the attorney all I could do was bawl and say, 'I don't want a penny of *his* money; I just want out.' It took that poor lawyer three or four months to make me see that I was *entitled* to some of that money—that I had put in twenty-three years of my life and raised three sons and been a good wife—and that he, as a lawyer, could not in good conscience let me go out without any money. Was I stupid! What if I'd been paid by the week for twenty-three years?

"Now people ask me, 'Does Frank give you *permission* to go to all those meetings?' Well, he isn't exactly jumping for joy, but he's come to realize that if he can go away all the time on business trips, which he does, and play poker with the boys one night a month, and spend the whole weekend in the fall watching football on TV, then I should be able to get away and do things that are important to me, too. It can be such a spiritual awakening. When you open yourself up, a whole world opens up to you. But maybe you have to suffer before you can know this. There's great suffering and loneliness in the upper middle class.

"I keep trying to tell people it's as important for men to be liberated as for women. I'm sure a lot of women of my age and station in life agree with our principles, but the connotations and the image scare them off."

By "connotations," Bede of course meant homosexuality, a word about as popular in Milwaukee as carcinoma. The subject was rarely discussed, but it did come up in the course of an impromptu rap session held in, of all places, my room at the Pfister Hotel. Bede had helped me organize this session, which was open to Milwaukee feminists of all sects and persuasions.

"'Lebsian' is a potent, damaging label that scares a lot of women away," observed one of the women who came to this *salon.* "It cuts down deep into the gut, in a very irrational way."

"But it's one of the most important steps toward liberation," argued another of my guests. "For most women at least a try at a partially sexual relation is a step toward liberation. It's silly

70

to talk about trust if you don't go all the way. Just being able to touch, hold hands, hug a woman is a huge step."

"But," broke in an NVFC woman who sounded a little nervous, "you have to be able to go that far without going farther."

"Nonsense," said a West Side woman who was holding a friend's hand. "The only answer when someone asks if there are a lot of Lesbians in the movement is 'Yes, and right on.' "

"But since this is the *key* taboo," said her friend, "we'd better quit emphasizing it, or we'll never get power."

"I can't imagine loving, in any sense, anyone who wasn't a feminist," another woman said.

"Not in *any* sense?" asked Virginia Ray, an immense twenty-five-year-old in Granny-glasses and a long skirt made out of a curtain. "That's heavy. We could at least try to love them the way Jesus loved the sinners."

"You don't really think *all* men are oppressors, do you?" I asked one of the women from the West Side.

"Some of them may be coming out of it," she answered, "but how long is it going to take? What would have happened to the black race if they'd waited for the whites to come around?"

"But if you're involved with a man," said an NVFC member, "you can recondition him."

"Or else leave him."

"It's like the difference between reupholstering an old sofa and buying a new one."

"Or maybe having none at all. What's so great about sofas?"

"Come on, how can a straight woman get along without a man?"

"I have, for over a year."

"Aren't you—well, horny?"

"No. I'd rather have no sex at all than sex without love. Sometimes I think celibacy may be an even bigger taboo than lesbianism."

"But a whole *year?*"

"It takes practice. You have to learn to love yourself."

I called room service and asked them to send more Seven-Up.

"I don't just hate men," Virginia Ray said later. "I hate some women, too. I don't feel any sisterhood toward women who oppose abortion legislation."

"That doesn't mean you hate *them,*" someone assumed. "You hate what they *do.*"

"That's not so," said Virginia. "I hate them personally. If I had had the kids I aborted myself, the possibility of me being free would have been between zil and voich. One thing the movement's done for me is make me no longer afraid of anything except my own strength, my own anger. I was raped once, but I knew instinctively there was no point in my calling the police, because they'd just tell me I'd been asking for it. But if it happened now, I'd knock the rapist down."

I could see why Bede Yaffe liked Virginia, who had helped establish, but later quit, the NVFC, "because she was such an absolute purist. She was happy at first to try to live and work with middle-class people, but it didn't work." Still, Virginia was cordial to Bede and me. One night the three of us went to look in on a Jesus rally and stopped for ice cream with Virginia's niece and nephew before returning to her two-room basement apartment. She had mattresses on the floor and psychedelic lighting. She was of Italian descent, on welfare, uncommonly bright, and uncommonly sensitive, too.

"Every time I try to be myself," said Virginia, "I get called a bull dyke. I know we should learn to live with that, but when I finished a sculpture at the Y and stood there in goggles and levis looking at it, feeling really happy, somebody said, 'Hey, look at that bull dyke.' It really crushed me. All the joy of creation was gone.

"I used to be a masochist," she said. "I'd want men to hit me and beat the shit out of me, because only when they did could I feel submissive. My shrink says Women's Liberation means we're all looking for the little girl in us. He looks like a grandfather, and I want to tell him things that will make him happy, and they *do* make him happy. He says that psychologically I hate myself.

"I do get angry sometimes when I think of the NVFC. Sometimes I think I ought to go back there and just be their dictator, because a dictator is what they need."

Joanie Sloane and Barbie Hartsman, blood sisters as well as fellow members of the NVFC, were going to entertain at the forthcoming grand opening of the NVFC headquarters. Joanie would play her guitar and Barbie would sing, the way they had been doing for years. One bright Saturday afternoon in April they met in Joanie's living room, to practice their songs. For quite a while, though, they forgot about the rehearsal. In Washington, as we could all see on Joanie's color television screen, one of those giant, convivial peace demonstrations was going on. I felt nostalgic. I had done a bit of marching myself in the years before—an Aldermaston march once in London, the Jeanette Rankin Brigade, the big Moratorium. I knew that the main benefit of these events was to make the marchers feel a righteous camaraderie, but still, I wouldn't have minded being in Washington right then.

Finally the sisters got out their music. "Our repertoire has changed a lot," said Barbie. "We used to do 'Queen of the House' and 'As Long As He Needs Me' and 'Chin Up, Ladies' at bridal luncheons and temple affairs, but I can't do that fake, sweet stuff any more. Now we only want to do feminist songs. In fact I've dropped out of organized religion altogether: I happen to feel that it's manmade and sexist. We offered to do a program on Women's Liberation for our B'nai Brith chapter, but they said it was 'irrelevant'.

"We've both been dropped by a lot of acquaintances. I was kicked out of the temple choir because I don't like to wear a head covering. The acting cantor came up to me and said the rabbi didn't like to see me there with my head uncovered. I said okay, you've just lost your best singer."

"Barbie never even used to open her mouth during our raps," Bede had said, "but now she's one of the angriest, most outspoken ones among us."

"When we were married seven years ago," said Barbie, "I was *everything* to my husband. I didn't even realize I was doing a change until I came all the way over. Joanie was interested in civil rights first, and in this too, and I'd never have dreamed I'd get into either one. But now Bob's changed too. I guess he didn't have much choice. He had it rough when I first got into this, because he came from a family where women worked but also did all the housework and cooking. Now, if he leaves his pajamas on the floor, they stay there until he picks them up. Now sometimes I think he's a better feminist than I am. Or at least let's say he knows the story pretty good."

Joanie tuned her guitar, and the two sisters began to rehearse a song that began "There was a young woman who swallowed a ring/ Looked like a princess but felt like a thing . . ." Then they sang one whose chorus was:

> Look at that mirror upon the wall
> Is that a toy, girl, or is it a doll?
> Is there anybody there, behind the mask?
> What is the answer? Are you too scared to ask?

"We've had a sister act since we were kids," said Joanie, "called—are you ready?—Barbie and Joanie." An able guitarist, thirty-two years old when we met, Joanie was the wife of a furniture store owner. She taught Sunday school, had a lot of bowling trophies on her piano, and was a chronic battler against overweight. To her three daughters, then four, nine, and twelve, she seemed a devoted mother.

"When I heard that my last baby was a girl," Joanie remembered, "the first thing I thought was, 'How shall I break the news to my father?' But he took it all right." Liberation, for her, had begun at home a couple of years earlier, "at a time when everybody else seemed to be walking around with protest signs, so I decided I'd have a strike too. I decided I was sick and tired of washing all the dishes by hand. So I got a shirt cardboard and made a sign. The sign said I WILL NOT WASH ANY MORE DISHES UNTIL WE GET A DISH-WASHER.

"I paraded back and forth in the living room and everybody laughed, but the dishes piled up in the sink and sat there. We bought paper plates. Dick got very angry, but every few days he would wash the dishes. This went on for a year. He wouldn't give in, and neither would I. Finally my mother-in-law, who has a thing about cleanliness, gave us a dishwasher as an anniversary present."

The preceding August, Joanie had taken her feminist consciousness outside the home. She decided to join the Women's
Equality Day parade downtown, where Milwaukee feminists
would march dressed as suffragettes, pregnant brides, Playboy
bunnies, and in other costumes. Joanie had her hair done and
put on her best red dress. Before she left the house she also put
on chains. To the chains, borrowed from her sister's dog, she
attached a whiskbroom, a toilet bowl brush, and the dust jacket
of a book by Dr. Benjamin Spock.

"Now just a minute," said her husband when he saw her
array. "Women's Lib is fine up to a point, but you've reached
that point."

"Oh, no I haven't," said Joanie.

"When people ask me what I want," she said at an NVFC
rap, "I tell them that all I want to do is change and restructure
the whole society fast enough for my three daughters, because I
figure it's already probably too late for us."

"But not just daughters," said Bede. "Sons, too. Men have
been just as injured by this society as women have. And it's
our fault, partly. When my middle son had appendicitis and
was in terrible pain, his girlfriend had to teach him how to cry,
because I never had. When I realized that, I had to cry too.

"I was the one who molded his character, who had always
told him and his brothers to hold back their tears and be brave
little men. I made them go through baseball and Cub Scouts
and all the rest of it, whether they liked it or not, so they
would be All-American he-men. Now I see I should have tried
to make them feel the humane side of things too."

Barbie Hartsman and her husband planned to adopt a baby
but had been afraid to tell the social worker of Barbie's involvement with the movement. Linda Majchszak, one of the
single members of the NVFC, said she would not have children
even if she did marry. "I personally don't feel like going
through all the hassle and pain of pregnancy. Besides, the
world is too much of a mess to bring any more kids into it. If I
ever feel the need to have children around, maybe I'll adopt
ten, but I won't have them myself."

By her own admission, Linda used to be "a bitch and a tease

75

and a flirt." One of her feminist friends said that "walking down the street with Linda was like walking through the hall of mirrors. Men kept turning around all the time to say things like, "Hey, Baby, where ya goin'? Wanna come with us?" Linda advised them quite pungently that she didn't want to do that at all, but to little avail.

Until quite recently, Linda had no use for the movement. "I was totally against Women's Liberation," she said, "because I felt I already *was* liberated and all the organizations were a waste of time. But then I went through some terrible changes, and I'd wake up crying and thinking, 'My God, it's true, I really *am* oppressed.'

"Oh, I could tell you so many times I've been angry, since I've been into Women's Lib. This one male I knew wouldn't bring back the facial sauna I lent him. 'I thought I'd be doing you a favor,' he said, 'taking away one of your supposedly feminine articles, now that you're liberated.' Now isn't that ridiculous? And when I bought a bike recently, one guy asked me how come I hadn't got a boy's model."

The movement, Linda said, had helped her realize the error of her previous assumption "that all other women were giddy, stupid, fluttering butterflies, or competitors, or both." She also realized that a lot of men she had thought were her friends really only wanted to seduce her. Lately she had been trying some experiments. "I notice that men don't like it when I turn the tables and put *my* arm around *them,* or give *them* a pat on the rear end, or suggest to *them* that we go out for dinner." At her own expense, because "my father wants me to *marry* an attorney, not be one," she was putting herself through pre-law courses.

Other changes the NVFC had brought were spectacular only cumulatively, not in themselves. Carolyn Mueller wasn't sorting her husband's and children's socks any more—"They can just all find their own or go barefoot." Patti Novak had quit plucking her eyebrows. Sue Williams, who looked, and for most of her life had acted, like a madonna, had told a man at a party to go fuck himself when he made disparaging remarks about his wife who "had it easy," staying home with their three children while he went off to conventions in the Caribbean. Joanie Sloane put a new sign on the mailbox outside her house. The old one had borne only her husband's name, but the new one read RICHARD AND JOANIE SLOANE. "We drew lots," she said, "to see whose name would come first—fair is fair. And I finally worked up enough nerve to ask Dick to take care of the kids when I went off for a weekend bowling tournament. He did it."

Steve Kutner lost four buttons off his sport jacket, and his NVFC wife Jan had said, "Look, I hardly know any more about buttons than you do, and what I do know I am now about to teach you. I'll sew on three and then you do the fourth, okay?" It was okay, except with Jan's cousin, "the one I gave *Sisterhood is Powerful* to for Hanukkah. You know what she said? She said 'How emasculating! How castrating!' "

"Oh, that word 'castrating,' " said another feminist. "I used to play Ping-Pong with some guys in an office where I worked, and if I won, they'd talk about castration. If their balls are that fragile, who needs them? Who wants to spend a whole life with someone like that?"

"Marriage brings sex and social approval: a lot of women only get married to have the stigma of old-maidiness removed. But who needs it, if it means playing games and stopping your growth and whining?"

"Who even needs dates? Dates are just one miserable big play-act. If you could really be comfortable and yourself, okay, but that game-playing business I can't stand. When you act like yourself men are threatened."

"Husbands just croak anyway; who says they give you all that emotional support and financial comfort?"

"Hey, *girls!*" said a regressing NVFC member.

"Not girls, women."

"Well, hey, *women,* do you know how we're *sounding?*"

"How? Like manhaters?"

"Manhating is a stage," said a seasoned feminist. "You get over it. Anyway, when men get used to the idea of liberation, they're relieved. It takes a load off everybody's shoulders. Sometimes I wish I were meeting my husband now for the first time, instead of thirteen years ago, when I did."

"Would you still marry him?"

"I think I would, but I'd like to have grown up first."

I went to the Watts Tea Room for ginger toast, as had become my custom when Milwaukee perplexed me, and visited a bit with a kindly waitress named Mabel Suemnich. "My generation," she said, "has raised a bunch of crybabies. I had to work like a man from the age of thirteen on, because my father was one of those unfortunate farmers who had no sons. I took care of the cow barn, and my sister was in charge of the horses. I'm sixty-five, and I've been working here for twenty years. I first came in to 'help out' for a while, and it's been a long while. Before then, my husband, he was a linotype operator, wouldn't hear of my working, but after that I loved to hit him over the head with a signed paycheck.

"I may be a little old-fashioned," Mabel said, "but I like to see the father honored as the head of the family. Fathers can't have children, after all, so the least they ought to get is not to be degraded."

That afternoon I talked to a woman editor who said, "*My* constant fear is that I'll show my husband up. It's a real effort not to, because by the time he's up and dressed I've cleaned the house and made ten phone calls and put everything in order and gone off to work."

"Isn't there anything he can do better?" I asked.

"Well," said the editor after a long pause, "he's better at golf."

"Swell," I said.

Late that night in the bar of my motel I sat alone with a stein of beer, reading the notes from another consciousness-raising rap I had been to the week before, in Minnesota. At the table next to mine sat four men. "Excuse me," one said, "but would you like to join us, dear?"

"No thanks," I said. Might as well be civil. "I've got something I have to read."

"You must be a schoolteacher," the man said. I kept on reading. "*Are* you a schoolteacher?" he asked. I stared at him and did not answer. He shrugged to his companions and turned away.

The Minnesota rap had been held in the living room of my old roommate Leslie, now a college professor's wife, the mother of two boys, and a fervent feminist.

"I might have known you'd be ripe for this movement," I told her. "I remember a letter you wrote me right after you were married. You quoted Barney asking, 'How do you expect me to keep a clean house when you throw your clothes around like that?' "

"As you can see," Leslie laughed, "things haven't changed. Our group thought of having a Messy Homes Tour, as opposed to Stately Homes. We also thought about having a work crew go around to people's houses to get the work done, since everyone hates housework."

"How did your group get started?" I asked her.

"Some women from Chicago came up to give a talk during the student strikes. Then a girl here rode a bicycle around town asking people she thought might be interested if they'd like to form a group. A small group met all through the summer, and got bigger in October, and has been getting bigger and bigger—past the point of intimacy—ever since. We had a lot of new members who came because they were turned on by Kate Millett's book."

"Has the movement affected you a lot?"

"Oh yes, in all kinds of ways. For one, I'm through with all that stuff about flirting with men, making a hit with them. I've come to see that it's just as important to make a hit with women and kids."

"Me too," said a black woman in Leslie's group. "Did I tell you about the stockbroker who took me out? He did it, he admitted, to find out what blacks were all about. That gets to be a bore, you know? I think I'll charge a fee for my services as a racial consultant. But get this: before the evening was over he said, 'Boy, I'd like to get hold of one of those radical feminists to see what makes *them* tick too.' I said 'Well, buddy, here I am, try me.' He said—if you can believe it—'What is it you women want?' After asking him if he couldn't think of anything more original than that, I told him, 'We want what *you* want.'"

"But as a woman, you're *told* what you want," said another group member. "As a woman, you never feel you have to make a decision or that you're expected to know what you want. The way to free yourself from all that is to take risks, but I grew up afraid of taking risks."

"I think we were all brought up afraid," said a woman who taught in a Roman Catholic school. "It's in the church too. When a priest comes into a schoolroom the kids have to stand up and say, in unison, 'Good morning, Fa-ther,' and open doors for him. Do you think nuns get that treatment? I assure you they don't."

"Once you do start to open doors," someone observed, "people help you push. But we couldn't even *be* here, do you realize, if our husbands wouldn't let us come."

"What can we do? I guess I'll try to infiltrate my mother's Ladies' Aid."

"And we can keep trying to open a women's center, a place where women can just drop by to rap and get counseling on abortions and birth control."

"Did I tell you I called about that one ad for a vacant apartment, the one we thought we might use for a center?' The landlady asked 'for how many?' I said, 'Well, one, actually.' And she said, 'What do you mean, *actually?*'"

When I was nine or so, my mother and Lois Buesch, a neighbor of hers who had four children, used once in a while to hire a babysitter for all of their six progeny so they could simply walk together three blocks to the Village Green in Winnetka

and talk without distraction. Would they have gone to a wom-
en's center, had there been one? Would they have supported a
women's movement, had there been one then? If there had
been, would their lives have been richer and freer? Would they
have said things like "Oh wow" and "Right on," and fancied
the term "Herstory"?

I thought about all this at the grand opening of the headquarters of the Non-Violent Feminist Co-operative which was,
I am sorry to say, anticlimactic in spite of the excellent homemade chocolate chip cookies and spirited singing by Barbie
and Joanie. One of the NVFC members read "a poem by a seven-year-old women." Not too many of the neighborhood
women, at whom the center had been aimed, dropped by.

"We're going to have to be careful, or we won't reach the
women who really need help," one NVFC member observed.
"We can't tell them how to look—if they want to wear a lot of
makeup and spray their hair, then that's their business. And we
can't just pull the rug out from under them when they start
going on about how old their babies were when they learned to
walk. If that's what they want to talk about, fine. It's just that
there should be options."

"I've just discovered a new option," said another member.
"I've made a new arrangement with my husband, just like the
one he's had with me all along: maybe I'll be home for dinner,
and then again maybe I won't."

"That's what stops me when I think of getting married," said
a single woman. "The idea of not being able to come and go as
I please. In Biblical times, you know, when they said 'til death
us do part', it meant until they were thirty-five, because that's
what the life span was then. But the idea of living with someone forever today? It scares me, to tell you the truth."

"I have to admit that *not* being married would scare me," replied another.

"We're into that old game again, aren't we? You show me
your scars; I'll show you mine. Ha-ha, my scar's bigger than
yours."

The next afternoon, I arranged to meet an old friend who
had moved to Milwaukee. Her feminist consciousness had not

as yet been raised, but her human decency level was right up there where anybody's ought to be. She came to fetch me at the Pfister and said she would wait outside the NVFC center while I went in for a last-minute errand. On an impulse, she drove to a nearby florist shop and came in the center with a geranium plant.

"I heard it was your Grand Opening," she said to the Non-Violent Feminist in charge, "so I got you a flower to wish you luck."

"Oh," said the Non-Violent Feminist.

Once when Suzanne and I arrived in Milwaukee, some feminists met our plane. The one who drove apologized for their lateness, "But Mike," she said, "is the one who usually drives to the airport, so I never noticed what the routes were before."

"Women get lost, right?" chided her companion. "Women can't read maps, women can't balance checkbooks, women can't open bottles of wine, women all compete with each other, *right?*"

"All *right,*" said her friend, "I get the point."

My own moment of raised consciousness had occurred a bit earlier, when a male attendant, probably in his forties, helped Suzanne and me sort out our baggage. "Here you are, girls," he had said.

"Thanks, boy," I replied.

I thought of something Linda Majchszak had said: "I'm sort of fluctuating between what I used to be and what I am."

6

When Shall I Wash My Hair?

"Why, that darling girl," my mother once said of someone we knew, "why should *she* have to go to a psychiatrist?" Because the darling girl was having trouble putting one foot in front of the other, that was why, but such unsettling ambiguities were not something my mother wished to confront. Neither, for a long time, did I. I brought with me to New York the firm midwestern prejudice that only gibbering looneys went to shrinks: that if you were reasonably bright, and had friends who would listen to you, you ought to be able to figure out your troubles for yourself. It was itself an admission of lunacy, I thought at first, to pay huge sums for such dubious commodities as "therapy" and "analysis," whatever those words might mean.

But time chipped away at this notion. The tussles and minuets and fencing matches of which my life seemed to consist became awfully repetitive. I kept having the feeling: haven't I been here before? Maybe there were patterns I wasn't seeing, or was afraid to recognize. Maybe I, even I, could use some help. Not, mind you, that I was on the brink of madness. "You're not nearly as neurotic as you'd like to think," a shrewd boyfriend told me once. I don't think I've ever had what could be called even a marginal nervous breakdown. But I did burst into sentimental tears once over the lyrics of "My Grandfather's Clock Was Too Large for the Shelf"—surely a danger signal, I thought—and I did keep having these two recurring dreams. In one, upon discovering a whole room in my house (sometimes it was an apartment) which I had never noticed before, I would wonder with urgent panic how that room should be furnished. In the other dream, I had just boarded some train or plane or ship bound for a remote destination I suddenly realized I had no wish whatever to visit, but it was too late to turn back and go home.

I figured it might not be a bad idea to hire some wise navigator to point out the shoals where my craft was prone to get stuck. Walter G. Dyer M.D. proved a providential choice, if hardly a showy one. In a crowd of the mod swamis and groovy, flowing-sleeved gurus with whom I had been consorting in the course of my work as a journalist, Dr. Dyer would have gone unnoticed. He could pass for a periodontist. His thinning gray hair is not combed forward to give an illusion of youth: it is obviously tended by a neighborhood barber, not a stylist. His eyes, blue and kind, are what one notices about him. So is his perspective, which soon came to seem as exalted as his office, eighteen floors above the park.

I liked at once the forthright way he stated his misgivings about encounter groups, to twenty-five or so of which I had been in the previous year, and "peak experiences" and oversimplified shortcuts of all kinds. I liked his flashes of irreverent humor and his calm decency. Intolerant of nonsense, he proved to have an elegant, graceful mind. Besides, he didn't pretend I wasn't there if we happened to ride down together on the same elevator. There are analysts, I understand, who do.

One day I wore a wig I had just bought to his office. Even Dr. Dyer, not ordinarily one for *ad feminam* small talk, observed that I seemed to have changed my hair style. My friends were more direct about that wig. They hated it. If I continued to wear it, they made clear, they would not be seen with me.

"But," I told them, "it cost forty dollars at Bergdorf Goodman."

"Tough," they said, as one. "Deduct it and throw it out, or hide it away and wait for Halloween."

"But I'm not going to have time to be getting my hair done," I explained, or tried to, "I have to make all these *appearances.*"

That was my most surreal summer. Because my first book, on the topical subject of encounter groups, had just come out, it was my lot to rush around the country to publicize it. I made speeches and went on a good many television programs, discovering a hammy streak I had not known was in me. On a talk show in San Francisco I ad-libbed for a while about, of all subjects, original sin. On the quiz program "To Tell The Truth," when the wives of two members of the New York Mets pretended to be me, there came the moment when the emcee said, "Will the real Jane Howard stand up?" Although it occurred to me to just keep sitting, on grounds that I wasn't sure who the real Jane Howard was, I stood.

Dr. Dyer helped keep me sane that summer, and so did a house whose rent I shared on Springy Banks Road in East Hampton, Long Island, a tiresome drive from the city at best. Few sensations I know of can match the abandoned, whelming surrender of leaping into the surf out there on a hot day. The afterglow of that feeling, if it is let be, can sometimes linger for hours or even days, but that summer it never did. That summer I always had to be thinking about promoting the book in Washington tomorrow or Chicago next week, and when, I always wondered, can I wash my hair?

Loath to face the clotted traffic of the Long Island Expressway on Sunday evenings, my friends and I would tarry late on Springy Banks Road to eat leftovers and watch the sun go down behind the trees. Not until midnight or so, when we were sure the roads would be clear, would we head back west, keeping the radio on loud so as not to be lulled to sleep by the sameness of the exit turnoff signs. We played guessing games ("If you were a felony what would you be?") and tried to keep alert by watching the changes on the odometer and noticing how the traffic lamps changed shapes when we got to Douglaston. When you get to Douglaston, on the edge of the borough of Queens, you are technically in New York City.

"Well, at least driving by night means postponing the visual shock of returning to ugliness," we would yawn and tell each other. (We were all quite sensitive.)

"Have you noticed that more and more people you see on the streets are getting to look like some police artist's composite drawing of a rapist or a mass murderer?"

"Yes, but if we didn't live here who would we talk to? We could live without movies and delis and bookstores, but if we lived in Baton Rouge or Sioux Falls who would comprehend us on a sullen Thursday evening?"

"Maybe we'd be surprised; maybe we'd find people who would. Maybe we're too provincial. Maybe if we lived somewhere else—*anywhere* else—we'd have more of a sense of community."

"We'd also probably get more sleep." But sleep is not the only thing one sacrifices if one returns from the Hamptons at three in the morning and has to get up early the next day. One also loses the margins, the white space in one's life, and this is a loss that comes to seem more grave with the passage of time.

Before and during my television summer I saw a lot, socially, of a man who did know the value of white space. He had a way of just sitting in a room or park or anywhere, not reading or talking or even listening to a record. He'd just sit there, and I'd get strangely jittery.

"What are you *doing?*" I would ask him, even though I knew.

"Reflecting," he would answer. Rationally I knew that this was an admirable and even modish pastime, being cultivated by new devotees of transcendental meditation as well as by my friend, but even so it made me nervous. Even though I had come close to being initiated into the mysteries of TM by the Maharishi Mahesh Yogi himself, my own bent was for action, not stillness.*

---

* This happened in the course of a magazine assignment. I thought it would be an honor indeed to have the Maharishi tell me, in a secret, private ceremony, what only he could discern to be my own personal *mantra*—a sound for me to meditate by—but I backed down when I learned what the initiation fee was. You had to give six fresh flowers, a clean white hanky, four pieces of fruit ("Pears," it was suggested, "would be nice"), and a week's pay.

It strikes me what a paradigm of an American I am, with my domestic glut, confused foreign relations and implicit credo that if something is possible, or somewhere accessible, I'd better get busy and do it or go there, and make it snappy. I talk such matters over with Dr. Dyer, who agrees that mobility is a useful thing, "but why, with you, does it have to be such a *principle?*" He suggests that for me a saner course might be to try slowing down and staying in one place, just to see how "dailiness," as he puts it, might feel. He does not say so in so many words, but he hints that the marginless, seemingly adventurous surface of my life may represent a clever trick to evade the fact that real risk scares the hell out of me. From him I get no praise or M & Ms for having done seventeen things in one day or seen six different people in six evenings. He succeeds, or begins to, where well-meaning, like-minded friends have failed: he makes selectivity seem alluring.

But Dr. Dyer notwithstanding, I still make mistakes. An advertising man who saw me on the Johnny Carson show phones to invite me for a drink. Like a fool, I go. He compliments me on my "knockout smile. *Just keep that smile.* If you keep on smiling like that," he advises me, "you can get anything you want in this world." Maybe, if life were a rush party and the world were the Theta house.

A husky-voiced woman who thought she had read a personal message between the lines of my book keeps phoning me so persistently that finally, out of curiosity and to shut her up, I agree to meet her for lunch. She arrives at the Time & Life Building in a chauffeured limousine and asks where in all the city I might like to go for lunch: Voisin? Lutece? The sky's the limit. Name it. Gee, no thanks, I say, let's eat right here at Ho Ho's; it's my favorite.

"You're shy, aren't you?" she asks over the lichee nuts. Why should I seem otherwise? Trust is a prerequisite to the sharing of confidences; I always am silent with people like her. Still, the fact that I met her at all encourages her to make several more follow-up phone calls, until I am obliged to tell her in so many words to leave me alone.

"But we could be *friends*," she says.

"I already have more friends than I can keep up with."

"You just *think* you do," says the woman, with what I believe could be called a hollow laugh. "In your whole life you won't have as many friends as you have fingers on one hand."

An engaging, literate letter arrives from a man who, having read my book, wants to take me to dinner. I accept. He helps me into my side of his fancy, low-slung sports car. I reach over to unlock his door, to save him the trouble. "I always know," he says as he slides into the driver's seat, "that when a girl does that, I'm going to score."

"One of the hardest things in a person's life," another kinder letter-writer tells me when I finally meet her, "is to learn to shut certain doors. You don't just shut them; you barricade them." I guess you do have to, like Emily Dickinson: on her divine majority obtrude no more. Once, when a perfectly nice friend says he is going to Antarctica so why don't I contrive to get sent too, which I could probably manage to do, I elect instead to stay home and alphabetize my herbs. Most unlike me. But I invest three hundred dollars in an Off-Broadway show I can tell in my bones won't really work, because I feel sorry for the producers: go back six places. I pay for a four-day junket to Paris, France, a *Life* assignment, with a week of incapacitating flu. Besides, *Life* decides not to run the story.

I have just left *Life*'s masthead, a volunteer refugee in what comes to be called the Great Purge. The staff must be shrunk by many salaries, so I decide after fifteen years to go off the payroll and take a contract. I am to do four stories in the coming year for only a little less money than I had been earning. How nice and free it will be, with all the new time to myself, right? Wrong. The bond to that place and its people proves as absorbing as ever it was. I won't really leave *Life,* as it turns out, until *Life* leaves me and everyone else.

But the profit-sharing money I get, combined with some royalties, enables me to buy an apartment overlooking the Hudson, and the cherry trees of Riverside Park, and the sunsets. At last, a room of one's own to work in, and daylight enough to sustain spider plants and *draecena marginata*. The aging couple who sell me the place, a brother and sister, are a little hurt that I don't want their chandelier. I buy the apartment from them with the help of a petite and persistent broker still in her twenties. Earlier she must have shown me at least a dozen other places on the Upper West Side, a neighborhood I guess I have chosen for the same reason some of my contemporaries want to leave it: because it's so Jewish. I love seeing all those Mr. Sammlers on Broadway.

A year later my friend the broker tells me she has switched to commercial leasing and is on the verge of making a killing, "but you know me," she says, "I'm keeping a low profile." So am I, I guess. The vistas from my square footage slow me down. Dailiness doesn't seem so dull any more. My father comes, soon after I move in, to wallpaper the bathroom. He is skilled at things like that. His visit touches me. We have a good time. We eat in Japanese restaurants and go to the Natural History museum. He discovers Zabar's Delicatessen, and goes there every morning. Someone calls to ask if we want a pair of last-minute seats for an oboe concert at Philharmonic Hall. Sure we do.

Shower curtains, and like matters, obsess me for months. A superb procrastinatory device for a writer: how can I possibly work until I have the ideal environment?

My friends make me throw out a lot of stuff. Without such encouragement, I never would.

"You *know* you'll never wear that dress again," they say. "*Out* with it!"

"But not these Christmas cards," I say. "There're some interesting samples of handwriting . . ."

"Oh, for Christ's sake . . ."

"That's Him, that's whose birthday . . ."

"Don't be funny. Out with them too."

One afternoon I take several boxes of things to Mary, my cleaning woman in Bedford-Stuyvesant, in return for which she gives me two gilt-edged plates showing Jesus knocking at the door.

"It's not right," she says, "to get without giving." One Sunday I go to her place for an early breakfast and then spend all day at her church. Once a year she runs for Queen of the Church. The Queen is whoever brings in the most money.

That church is surpassingly important to its members, most of whom are female domestics. I am moved by a procession of Mary and a couple dozen of her friends, marching with a stately hesitation step down the aisle, all dressed in white. Since Mary always calls me Miss Howard, I start to address her as Sister Collins, by which name she is known to her churchmates, but she doesn't seem to want me to. Not one for the twenty-four part handshake, Sister Collins.

I see Dr. Dyer less frequently, busy as I am with shelf paper and all, but I don't quit. Something has happened between us: I suppose it is that phenomenon known to some in his trade as transference. His approval can make me feel in a state of grace. Not that he always approves; far from it. Once, when I recount to him how I have stalked back and forth in front of the brownstone of a man I crave to talk to, instead of calling up that man on the phone, Dr. Dyer looks at me and says, "You know what, Jane? You're crazy."

"I guess that's why I'm here," I say. We both laugh. We often do. If we didn't, I'd have drifted off long ago. But at times, with Dr. Dyer, I also stammer, and swear, and weep. Sometimes, I am sure, I must bore him: why not, if I bore myself? There are days when I wonder to what end I am buzzing that doorbell up there on the eighteenth floor only to announce, "Well, nothing too much has happened since Tuesday; I really don't have anything special to tell you," with the meter ticking away at a dollar a minute. But life is often commonplace, and I can't expect my every summary of new events and thoughts to inspire a fortune cookie insight. I guess it's okay for us to digress about our tastes in music, movies, and food. Once he gives me a handwritten recipe for clam chowder. His handwriting is lucid and simple.

On two occasions I stay up there in that room for much longer than the allotted fifty minutes. He does not look at his watch and say, "Well, we'll stop here." Instead he offers me instant coffee, which seems almost a sacrament. One of these extended visits comes just after I return from the burial of my mother's ashes. The other is on an autumn Saturday afternoon when the cause of my gloom is a good deal less specific. It is so vexingly untraceable, in fact, that I spend the morning trying to figure it out, typing a list of twenty-two reasons why I am depressed. Dr. Dyer listens, as he always does, with his whole being. He convinces me, in the course of a long and gentle talk, that the fundamental reason is a twenty-third which had not crossed my mind. So much for lists.

Another time, to my delight, he answers a letter in which I explain why I am too busy to see him for a while. In it he tells how his own summer has gone: "Had meant to steep myself in Proust's excruciating ruminations, but try reading Proust with a noisy baseball game going on outside the cabin. Come to think of it, can't really imagine what the right setting would be for reading Proust. Prison, maybe."

Among doctrinaire feminists the party line is that women should see women analysts: keep it all in the family, don't you know, because They, the enemy men, will only scheme to get us married off. I did see a woman once for a while, some years back, and she was a decent and worthy person, but no special rapport arose between us. Several years later, socially, I met a female Jungian analyst in California. I liked her. She had a fascinating office. In it there was this sandbox with a whole bunch of tiny different toys. She said she sometimes could tell a lot more about her patients by which little toys and figures they picked up to fool around with than by what they actually said.

"Some of the stuff in that sandbox is junky," she said. "Most of it is pretty. There's one terrible pink plastic woman whose posture suggests, 'I'm waiting for it to happen to me,' and I myself hate it, but I keep it there because it's plastic, terrible, nonfeeling, which is the way a lot of people are. There are hundreds of figurines, a mermaid with great bazooms and terrible little hands. She's a terrible sex object, romping around mindlessly."

Gee, I think, it would be fun if Dr. Dyer had a sandbox full of toys, but he would no more do that than take up with the Primal Scream crowd, or give his practice over to consciousness-raising sessions. The female Jungian had her doubts about consciousness-raising groups too.

"Sometimes they raise false bravado," she said. "They can lead some women to go home and make confrontations they can't back up with their own strength, because the strength is vicariously borrowed from the group. The poor guys they confront at home are slumped over and confused."

The Jungian and I had a quick Mexican supper together. It had to be quick, or else she would be late for her cello lesson. Funny, Dr. Dyer plays the cello too. After a full day of fifty-minute hours of words, these doctors must crave a wholly other vocabulary. "I couldn't manage if I didn't have my fiddle and my tennis," the woman analyst says. "You're on the line all the time, thirty-five hours or so a week, and if you're really *there* all those hours, trying to figure out the larger ideas behind every specific conflict people tell you about, you really need distraction. One of the frustrations is that you can't talk about your work, not to anybody, because it's all private.

"Very different things happen with a male analyst than with a female," she said. "I can't prove it, but I strongly suspect that totally different stuff comes out of the unconscious. A woman analyst activates the psyche in different ways. Outer reality is where the female analyst might have a little more to offer. A female has her whole psyche there when a patient chatters on, whereas a man may go to sleep on it and think, 'Well, we'll get to the real stuff later.'

"At first I heard many times over, 'Oh, I'd *never* see a woman analyst.' Probably from the same women who used to say, 'I can't *stand* women; give me a man any day.' This might really mean fear of women, because they had got out of the habit of identifying with women.

"I have several patients who are afraid that if they ever saw a man analyst, they would be too flirtatious, because they'd always had success charming men. But sometimes there are very successful analyses when a doctor uses the female, nurturing side of his nature."

Food for thought, all this. Had I been unconsciously flirting with Dr. Dyer, trying to con him? Hope not. Does he come on like a motherly male nurse? Maybe, some. (Come to think of it I did once dream he was a woman.) Is there anything I've held back from telling him? Probably. But would I have been any more open with a female paid confessor? I doubt it. One thing I have never lacked for is confidantes of my own sex.

My sister phones from Illinois to ask whether I think she should keep or cancel an appointment with her psychiatrist, a Dr. Hahn. Her town is intimate enough so that school lunch menus are announced on the radio but complex enough to support five or so analysts too. She has not seen hers on anything like a regular basis, just four or five sporadic visits since our mother died.

It touches me that Ann should seek my help; it used to seem that I was the only vulnerable one. But I don't know how to solve her present problem which, so far as she can pin it down, is that she has just turned thirty-five.

"For one thing," she begins, "three and five are eight, and eight's always been a bad one for Mom's gal. Oh, I almost wish I could wake up and be thirty-six."

"Soon enough you will," I told her, "and that you'll like, because three and six are nine which is, as it happens, the most auspicious of numbers, being as it is the sum of the digits of the totals of my address, Social Security number, and birthday."

"You're trying to distract me with all that numerology nonsense," she said.

"Look at it this way," I suggested. "Two years ago I was thirty-five myself. David used to be thirty-five. Dad and Beth used to be thirty-five. Dr. Hahn and Dr. Dyer and Tratty and Tukie and Mrs. Van Der Vries are all former thirty-five-year-olds. If I had time I might even be able to think of some others."

"But thirty-five is half my life, if I'm lucky," said Ann, "and what have I got to show for it? I'm getting to the point where I can predict how my obituary will read, and it bores me. What can anyone say of me other than, 'Oh look, she got her car started all by herself.' And, 'Isn't she wonderful? She's so together she remembered to put on both her shoes.' I have the feeling that I'm on hold, that nothing promising is happening."

"What about your painting class?" An art major when she quit college to get married after her junior year, Ann had only lately resumed painting.

"Oh, it gives me a real high once in a while, but those highs are ephemeral, like taking a really neat bath . . ."

"Name me something that isn't ephemeral."

". . . and the others in the class are all nineteen-year-old kids; nice, but their company doesn't stimulate me. To them I'm the honey-darling, finger-snapping, thirty-five-year-old mom who always has enough alizarin crimson to share around."

"Could you study art somewhere else?"

"I'd like to work toward my degree at Champaign, where there's a much bigger department. I'd really like to take an apartment there and spend three days a week by myself. Not leave David and the kids, just be gone three days at a refuge of my own."

"You can always come here, you know."

"I know, thanks; David urges me to go see you, but I don't need New York now. I need solitude. I'd like to go alone to a north woods cabin."

"How *is* David?"

"Resilient. He always is. He's not like me. He doesn't brood, pout, sulk, mope. If he's mad he blows up and gets it out of his system. Right now he's just terribly busy, and he doesn't need all this flack from me just because he forgot to remind the kids that it was my birthday. How were they supposed to know? They don't have little date-bookettes at their age—what would they be if they had? And what's such a big deal if he and they *don't* remember?"

"I know, though. I always carry on about birthdays too. I always secretly think alternate-side-of-the-street parking regulations should be suspended on mine."

"All David really needs," Ann said, "is another month or two to get his new project ready. He needs a Barbie Doll wife to have the table all darlingly set every evening and act concerned when he comes home and say, 'Would you rather go to a movie tonight, or have me organize your socks?' He's excited about what he's doing right now, and he actually told me, in so many words, that he could not at this point invest the time to communicate with me. I resented the financial metaphor, but I guess I should have just ignored it. He ignores enough of my faults."

Once in a while Ann and I write letters. "My begonias are blooming," she said in one, "and I don't even *like* them." Only between ourselves and a very few others dare we expose such examples of ugly ingratitude. When we meet, twice a year or so, we discover odd similarities. We both smile at ourselves in the mirror and say "Hi!" even if nobody is looking. When we wake under the same roof and meet in the kitchen for breakfast, we stride manfully toward each other, parodying *macho* salesmen at a conference, with hearty jock handshakes and deep-voiced self-introductions:

"Ann Condon."

"Jane Howard."

Sometimes we relapse to bratty sibling rivalry. One summer we all rented a tiny house on a cove in Maine, and when I complained of the early morning noise made by lobstermen's motorboats, she looked at me witheringly and said, "That's *ethnic,* you jerk." Ethnicity means things regional, special, and therefore sacred. Wherever we meet, I tell Ann where I have been, geographically and otherwise, and she is likely to reminisce about Chile and Puerto Rico and Greece and Philadelphia and Chambersburg, in all of which she and David lived before the children were born. Chronically they wonder whether it is time for them to get on the move again.

In Fort Lauderdale, where our paths once crossed for a day or so, she and I had a binge with Reese's Peanut Butter Cups and saw our first exhibitionist, in a parking lot. We talked of cartwheels, which we both wish in vain we could do. Endlessly, everywhere, we discuss the domestic heroes of our shared youth, trying to puzzle them out, feeling sorry for only children who must solve such matters for themselves. We agree that in most of the households to which we have been privy, the moms, as Ann puts it, seem to exert more influence than

95

the dads. The women shield and protect and manipulate the men, and secretly, if not openly, run the show. We further agree that this is not necessarily a laudable state of affairs but that we can't think of any solutions.

To the bafflement of her and David's insurance agent, Ann took it upon herself to "do a whole unit on the merits of life as opposed to term insurance. He'd never seen a woman bother with that stuff before. And this summer I made it my life study to understand all the codicils of our wills. It *is* interesting, isn't it, that everything in my will is in reference to his?

"Sure, I'm getting to be something of a feminist," she says on the phone, "but in most ways the movement seems redundant, as far as I'm concerned, because I felt liberated before it came along. I've never felt I was an appendage of David socially. If anything, it's the reverse: I'm the one who controls who we play with, not him.

"Last night we were over at Sheila and Luke's, and we were all talking about the wheat surplus. I asked why we can't just *give* our wheat to the Russians, if they're starving, and the others all said, in effect, 'Oh, dummy, we can't do that, we need our money to subsidize the toaster factories, so we can keep on making newer, better toasters that do five slices at a time, varying in color from dark mulatto to light beige.'

"Tonight we're supposed to go to a twelve-dollar fund-raising thing to see *Fiddler On The Roof.* I'd rather pay the money and stay home and read, but most of our Jewish friends here are such Zionists, and our constellation of friends is so small, that if we didn't go they'd say, 'What's wrong? Don't you like Yids this week?'

"I'd like to intensify my relationships with everybody and everything. The way it is now, it's all too comfortable, knowing who the kids' bridesmaids and our pallbearers will be. If we're going to be staying here forever, which for all I know we will, then I'd better get used to it."

"You haven't found anyplace else you'd like to live?"

"We keep looking, we'd like to find a safe place—safe not so much from your typical axe murderer as from boring Jell-O—but other parts of the country don't seem that different in the ways that matter to me. So, if this is my mother decade, I figure I might as well do it Akela."

"Akela?"

"It's a Cub Scout word that means, you know, good, perfect, excellent, the right way. If I have to live the kind of life I've been living, in this town, I know damn well what the remedy is. The remedy is get in there and FOLD."

"Fold what?"

"Bandages, Red Cross stuff, laundry, beaten egg whites. Lead a troop of Cubs or Brownies. Make a quadruple batch of brownies today, and eat half at one sitting, and go to Weight Watchers next week. Progress from Hostess Cream-Filled Twinkies to Adelle Davis. Keep busy, onto the treadmill, into the gerbil cage. Appease everyone. Make Xerox copies of the chicken casserole recipes. God forbid you should just groove on the whiteness of the walls. Talk about central casting. Here I am at the actual core of it all, the quintessential thirty-five-year-old mom.

"I find it esthetically offensive to have such a banal malady. If it were ice cream it would be brick bulk Neapolitan from the supermarket. Some shrinks ought to hire me and put me in a cage at a convention. I'm such a case study they'd be fools not to.

"Carole came over the other day and noticed the silver cigarette box the FMBC gave me for a wedding present, and asked what those letters meant. [The Friday Morning Breakfast Club consisted of some of the female elite of New Trier High School's class of 1955.] When I told her, she said, 'Aha, that's really not so different from what we're into *now,* is it? Even though our symbols are different—we deal with recycling bottles and starting new schools—we still aren't so very different from that sort of thing.' "

"Or from our card-playing mothers," I said. "I hate to tell you this, but I have a new hangup: when I come to an impasse in my work, I play solitaire. Do you think it could be hereditary?"

"Solitaire may be the secret underground vice of American womanhood," said Ann. "I have more friends than you might

97

think who say, 'Well, I think I'll just flip through this deck one more time.' Oh, we're all festering masses of one sort or another. We all just *seem* not to be, sometimes."

"You're not lonely, though, are you?"

"I could use more sophisticated communication than I get, but I do have people to talk to, people I like, sure. I've only felt really lonely in places like Chile, where my only women friends were very formal, and just did me to be polite instead of to communicate. That sort of thing won't do. It's a cruel parody. I need somebody I can hash it all out with."

"David?"

"He's not bad at it, but I don't think very many men are good at it. They aren't bred to be."

"The quality of talk does usually change, doesn't it, when a man walks into a room where two women are deep in conversation? Certain nuances are lost. There are a lot more signals and subtleties between women and women than there are between women and men."

"Which is sort of a cop-out," Ann said. "I guess you have to be a pro to really talk to coherent members of the opposite sex, because it's harder and therefore more worthwhile. But a lot of the things I think about might not endear me to either sex around here. For instance, the ponies Yorkie Madigan rented for her little boy's birthday party. I think I'm turning into more of a Commie pinko than anyone might realize, because it seems to me those ponies should have been attached, figuratively speaking, to a plow to raise wheat germ. Why should Yorkie's kid have two ponies when some don't have birthday parties at all? Maybe you wonder who I am to talk this way, sitting poolside as I sometimes have at the Sun & Fun Club, reading Mary McCarthy."

"Look at it this way," I said. "You don't read Ayn Rand. Or do you?"

"If I did I wouldn't tell *you*," said Ann.

"Even so," I said, "you've come a long way since the days when you made posters for Barry Goldwater."

"A million thanks for reminding me. Well, at least I've got

past the point of thinking that all there is for me to do, now that I've mastered Canasta, is go on to learn Samba. You know, I used to criticize Her [our mother] because all she seemed to specialize in was circulating her recipes . . ."

"Remember all the things we found in the freezer after she died? Those frozen casseroles she'd made, and pies with perfect-ly-fluted crusts?"

"Sure I remember. That's part of what I'm talking about. That's what I don't put down any more, and I'm ashamed I ever did. Now that I'm older, and realize I probably won't be coming across a Salk vaccine in my own basement, I think what she did—keeping everybody fed and together—was a lot."

"You know what I ran across this morning?" I asked. "That speech I made right after she died, at the Springfield Mental Health Association. Remember?"

"I'd rather *not* remember," she said. "It's still painful for me to think of you standing there in front of that banner that said FIGHT MENTAL ILLNESS, nearly breaking down in front of—how many was it?—two hundred people. I'd never have made that speech. I'd have cancelled it, if I were you, on grounds of death in the family."

"You would not," I said. "You'd have had the same Kenne-dyish show-must-go-on feeling. Anything to get over the stage of being hooked on reading all the fine-printed obituaries in all the papers, even of people we'd never heard of."

"Oh yes, all their viewing arrangements. I guess anything would be more therapeutic than that. Even talking about grief."

"But the way I managed not to break down was I *didn't* talk about it. I left that part of the speech out."

"Have you got that speech handy?"

"It's right here."

"Read me the part you left out, the sympathy note you got from that guy in California."

"Okay," I said. " 'Theirs was a generation'—he's talking about his father's and our mother's—'sadly perhaps the last, with a definite sense of place, a definite idea of who they were,

99

and that survives in us, no matter what the buffeting. It's not a bad legacy, and I hope that in some deracinated way we can pass it on.' "

"I guess that's what I hope, too," said Ann. "You know what I've decided?"

"What?"

"I think I *will* cancel the appointment with Dr. Hahn. There must be somebody who needs him more. I think maybe I can make it on my own."

7

Pierced Ears

"There's no heat or hot water in my apartment," John Kolodny calls me up to say one cold Sunday noon in the middle of
November.

"Want to come over here?"

"No."

"Want to come over later and have lamb chops?"

"No. No thanks."

"Don't you like lamb chops?"

"I *do* like lamb chops, but I want to get started with that
speech." John devotes his energies to excellent causes.

"You're going to write it in the cold?"

"Yes."

Is it possible? Me, a clinging vine? Me, to whom, if I do say
so, a few other vines here and there have tried in vain to cling?
John is actually shorter than I am, so this botanical metaphor
is not ideal, but as I have been learning for the past several
months there is something imposing and resolute about John,
with his thick dark hair and broken-looking nose. I had not
previously found low foreheads attractive, nor had I known
anyone so evasive.

A week later he tells me about the romantic adventures of his friend Henry, whose girlfriend Francesca until recently had been content to see him 1.6 times per week. This arrangement had suited both Henry and Francesca just fine. Then Francesca got to thinking about it, and changed her mind. She decided that 1.6 times per week was not enough, after all. A scene of sorts ensued. Henry won.

"You mean Francesca still sees him?" I ask John. "You mean she didn't kick him out, or give up?"

"I'd have said *he* didn't kick *her* out or give up," said John.

"Yes," I say, "I suppose you would have."

Thanksgiving approaches. John says our friends the Sandlers have invited him to dinner and that I would also be welcome there. I had thought of going to my family's, but on the other hand it would be nice to be with John that day.

"Look," I say, "do you *want* me to stay here for Thanksgiving?"

"Well, you *do* have a four-day weekend. I don't, you know. There's a conference I have to go to on Friday."

"I'd like to ask you an embarrassing question," I say.

"Oh?"

"Yes, I'd like to ask you this: how committed am I supposed to feel to you?"

"I don't like answering questions like that," says John.

"I suppose you think I adore asking them?"

He still does not answer. He is accomplished at not answering. As he leaves, I announce that I guess I'll take a bath.

"Remember," he says, "it's just a bath. It's not the all-time metaphor. You are not going through a spiritual ablution ceremony. You are getting physically clean."

"You mean I shouldn't think of it in terms of Growth vs. Decline, Concentration vs. Dissipation, Consecration vs. Vulgarity, Commitment vs. Indecision, Passion vs. Indifference?"

"Just so," says John as he heads for the door. "You're grasping the idea. It is just a bath."

Later that day I buy and eat two different thirty-cent slices of pizza.

A vine not given sun and water will cease to cling and climb.

A few months later I am struck with the realization that I don't even care whether John Kolodny has a starring role in my life. Somewhat to his amazement, I tell him so. We stop seeing one another. I learn a few months afterward that he has been seen around with a spirited young woman in his office, whom I have met once or twice, named Caroline.

Once, in Milwaukee, an Italian woman was telling me how her former loves never became her friends.

"Really? Mine nearly always do," I said.

"Maybe that's because you're not Italian," she told me. Maybe so. In any case, it did not surprise me when, after a year had passed, John called to ask me to have lunch with him. The year had given me a boldness I lacked before.

"How did it work out," I dared to ask, "with Caroline?"

"You didn't hear?"

"Hear what?"

"She's gone."

"You mean she got fed up with all that hard-to-get business of yours?"

"The funny thing is," John said, "I didn't *play* hard-to-get, not with her. I guess she was the only one I ever didn't play it with."

"What did you play?"

"No games. I fell for her."

"You did? Well, I'll be damned. What happened?"

"I told you about the conference I had to go to in Budapest. Well, when I came back, Caroline had found someone else."

"Some other guy at the foundation?"

"Not a guy at all."

"*Caroline?*"

"Caroline," said John, "has moved upstate, with her new friend. They're living in a gay collective. It's what I believe is called an alternate life-style."

That afternoon I figured I might as well go ahead and have my ears pierced.

8

Pomp and Circumstance in Groundhog Hollow

Every morning Matilda Titus Hastings fixes her husband, Wayne, a panful of biscuits and gravy to go with his specially fried eggs. Perhaps as a subtle consequence of this repeated alchemy, in the same way that dogs come to resemble their masters, Matilda looks something like a biscuit herself, wholesomely puffy. "Only one woman in Atkins, West Virginia," she likes to say, "is bigger than I am—the lady who runs the tavern."

But Tildy, as she is usually known except to the twelve who call her Mama and the three dozen or so to whom she is Granny, is not really all that fat. What she is is comfortable looking. Her hair, which never in her life has been cut, is pinned up in braids. "Before it got so thin," she says, "the braids were about as wide as my wrist."

She wears glasses for sewing, the only work for which she has ever been paid, and for reading, which is her furtive pleasure. (She reads on the sly, the way some people gamble.) Outside, on bright days, she puts on a homemade sunbonnet. Most of her dresses she makes herself, for about a dollar each, but once she spent sixteen dollars on a three-piece lace outfit. She owns two costume-jewelry pins. One, crown-shaped, is composed of the birthstones of her ten daughters and two sons. The other, made of coal, is shaped like West Virginia.

I met Tildy through my friend Sally Wells. Sally, for nearly three years, was the director of a West Virginia cooperative named Mountain Artisans. All over the state groups of rural women like Tildy were organized to work from Mountain Artisans designs. They filled orders for patchwork quilts, pillows, and quite a lot of such improbable high-fashion items as evening skirts. Painstakingly marketed by Sally and her staff, these products were sold in stores like Nieman Marcus and Bergdorf Goodman, for prices which allowed seamstresses to earn more money than they ever had. Some of these women never left their own counties, and the fact that what they made was sometimes billed as Resort & Cruise Wear transfixed me. So did the patchwork itself, especially the quilts, which were showier than those my grandmother made for the beds of her farmhouse, but in the same spirit.

Sally would come north regularly to do business in the vernacular of Seventh Avenue, in which she had become fluent. She also learned the argot of Appalachia, a more appealing one to a New York ear. The more she told us all about her new friends the seamstresses, the more I wanted to meet some of them myself. I resolved to visit West Virginia. Finally, one week, I went.

The Hastingses' two-story house is modest by many standards, but in West Virginia it is thought to be imposing. To get to that house you have to take a rough ride up Groundhog Hollow Road. The car bounces and jounces and rattles and shakes and so, if you are a passenger, do you. "I tell people that's how come I had so many girl babies," Tildy jokes during one such ride. "Going up and down this road all the time, I shook the balls off them."

Groundhog Hollow Road leads down a steep hill to Atkins, where the Hastingses shop. Turn right there and drive four miles and you will come to Rollo, where they get their mail. All around that region you will see cars with Kentucky and

Virginia license plates, because both state borders are nearby. Medical facilities, however, are not. If something is wrong with the Hastingses' teeth, for example, they have to drive thirty-five miles to Welch. "There's supposed to be a dentist in War, sixteen miles over," says Tildy, "but seems like you never can find him in."

McDowell County, in which the Hastingses live, has been called the Coal Bin of America. Slag heaps in the wake of strip mines desecrate the lyrically lovely hillsides. Abandoned car hulks rot, with all deliberate speed, in stream beds. The best of the roads are poor. All change comes slowly. Incest is not unheard of—"They try to hush it up, but word gets around."—nor is illiteracy. "A lot of people," says Tildy, "have to have the postmistress read them their Black Lung checks." Ninety percent of the men in McDowell County who work or have worked in mines, including Wayne Hastings, suffer from silicosis.

Movie theatres and libraries are scarce, but churches abound. Just down the road from Groundhog Hollow, in Atkins, is a church whose members believe that the command given in Mark 16:18, "They shall take up serpents," must be followed literally. On Saturday evenings they really do handle real snakes. I wanted to visit this church the weekend I spent with the Hastingses; to me it sounded as exotic as a mosque. Wayne said we could, but first we would go to the Church of Christ, where he sometimes preaches. The service there lasted so long that by the time we got out the snake-handlers had gone home.

Tildy does not share her husband's enthusiasm for the Church of Christ, by which he is in fact ordained and to which he converted dramatically in 1953. Nothing can lure her away from the Jacob's Ladder Branch Church of the Old Hosanna Regular Primitive Baptist Association. She and Wayne can argue for hours about theology.

"It like to kill her daddy when Grace Ellen joined the Primitive Baptists," Tildy said of one of her daughters. "He said he'd rather see them dead than join my church. Several of the others joined his. On the surface you might think they cared more for their daddy than for me, because they make over him more. But they feared him, while I was more their friend. I'd stop them if they ever said anything disrespectful. I'd say, 'That's your father, so don't you *say* that.'

"Wayne is interested in death and the hereafter," she says. "He believes in hell and damnation, everlasting fires. I'm interested in Christ and salvation. I believe we get our punishments and our blessings right here on earth. I can't believe I need to be water-baptized in total immersion to avoid eternal damnation. You should come here sometime the first Sunday in August, when we have, in my church, our old-time foot-washing.

"We wash each other's feet with two towels sewed together. Ladies wait on female members, men on men, and it doesn't matter whose feet we wash, because we all just love each other so much we want to be at each other's feet in humility. As we wash each other's feet, we keep on singing."

If you were setting Tildy's life to a musical score, you would draw from three sources: "Earnestly, Tenderly, Jesus Is Calling," "Turkey in the Straw," and "Pomp and Circumstance." Nothing in all the Hastings house is more arresting than the array in the living room of twelve high-school graduation pictures. Six graduates on top, six below, born between 1928 and 1947, each one dressed in cap and gown, some with diplomas clutched close to their cheeks.

The youngest of these children did not technically get a diploma but a certificate of attendance. "She had to fight to finish high school; she wanted so bad to have that picture up there with the others. Her I.Q. is 85, and she doesn't retain information. Wayne thought it was the teachers' fault; he thought they didn't try hard enough to pound the learning into her. In his own childhood, you see, people weren't retarded. They were crazy.

"But Wayne is as proud of those pictures as I am. He drives around even now, with all our children grown and gone, to visit the schoolrooms, or he tries to, anyway." In one schoolroom, a couple of years ago, a teacher told Wayne he could not pay an impromptu visit without special permission from the Board of Education. This hurt him. "If that ain't communism," he asked rhetorically, "could you tell me what is?"

Tildy herself, the second of nine children, only went as far as the eighth grade, because her father didn't believe in sending girls to high school. Sometimes, even when ice covered the ground, she would walk to school barefoot and contemplate stealing something from the country store so that she might be sent to reform school, "because at least it was a school.

"I was born in nineteen and eleven and raised up at the top of this same mountain," she says, "and I like to say my father moved just about every time the moon changed. We had a lot of superstitions in those days. If your nose itched, it meant somebody coming. If a rooster crowed on your porch before breakfast, you'd have company. If you stepped on a rusty nail, the thing to do was pull it out, rub it with bacon rind, and hang it on a hook. If you got a snake bite, you'd wrap the bite in black tape and try to kill the snake before it got to water— then the bite would heal."

From the moment she first saw Wayne Hastings, "I thought he was about the handsomest guy in the world. I was at a spring, dipping water, and he passed by and said, 'How do you do?' There was never another man in my life before and there hasn't been one since. Once I said I knew of two women around here who were decent, and someone said, 'Oh? Which two?' I said, 'Well, I know *I* am, and I'm pretty sure Mama is.' Mama was there, and she said ' 'Pon my word, daughter, I am.'

"One night Wayne walked me home from a tent meeting and we started keeping company. He never proposed and I didn't, either. One day he said, 'I'm not going to walk this ridge so much.' I said, 'Oh? Why not?' He said, 'I'm going to make *them* come to see *us*.' He was twenty-two and I was seventeen when we got married on September nineteenth, nineteen and twenty-eight. It was a Wednesday, a popular day to be married in those times, and we never knew what a honeymoon was, except that somebody caught us a catfish so long it wouldn't lay flat in a three-dollar washtub.

"My mama warned me that Wayne was from a family that drank right much, and for a long time he did. He could be mean: he'd fuss at the children and once when he was cleaning onions with a butcher knife he looked at me and said, 'I ought to cut your throat.' I said, 'Go ahead, if you can,' and took off my glasses and stood right there, but he didn't. I left him once, over drinking, but I couldn't abandon the babies, so I came back. He never missed a day's work over it, and he was always a good provider. In October of nineteen and fifty-three he joined the church and never had a drop since, not even after the accident."

A rock "as big as a mattress on a bed" fell onto Wayne's spine inside the Island Creek Coal Company mine in 1959. "He was hunkered on his heels—they were blasting to get the coal out and he was shot fireman. Compared to what could have happened he was lucky. The hole he was caught in, they said, didn't look big enough for an eight-year-old child to survive in. And they weren't sure he would be able to walk at all, or have any use whatsoever of his sexual organs." A two-year period of rehabilitation at a United Mine Workers hospital in New Jersey restored partial use of the lower half of Wayne's body, but life has been difficult ever since then both for him and his wife.

"His morale was right bad after the accident. Once he said he felt so worthless we'd be better off without him, and he told me to get a divorce. I said, 'You can't drive me away—I don't want a divorce and you can't get one. When we were married I said it would be for life, and I've always held to that.' My one prayer is that I'll outlive him, so I can care for him as long as he lives. I don't think the children could cope with him. When I'm gone he subsists, but he never eats the right food, and he won't go visit his sisters. They offer to do for him, but he won't have it."

Tildy still likes to read visitors a letter she once received from her eighth child, Louella: "I think about when I was younger," Louella wrote, "maybe twenty or twenty-five years ago. I think about good things. I see the beauty of the mountains we lived in. All the fields cleared, with all the dandelions growing everywhere and the milkweeds and polk berries, the log house and the spring in the holler. Beautiful, beautiful sunshine everywhere. The cows, chickens, cats, and dogs. I don't believe the sun could shine any brighter than in the spring and fall as it did then. In spring everything seemed greener than green and in fall, everything red, yellow, and colors that can't be named. Hickory nuts and walnuts and squirrels. Watching the house being built was one long, beautiful movie."

Before they moved into their present house, in 1949, the Hastingses lived in a four-room log cabin half a mile or so down Groundhog Hollow. Before Wayne's illness there was no telephone; only since 1962 have they had indoor plumbing. Tildy can remember the first car she ever saw: "In nineteen and eighteen it sounded like a helicopter sounds now. When I heard it coming up the hill, I ran and hid." Not so long ago she herself washed on a board, cooked on a wood stove, and hand-ground entire 250-pound hogs, storing the meat in Mason jars.

Her babies were delivered in the old log cabin, with the help of a midwife. "When it was time, we'd send a neighbor boy over the mountain on a mule to fetch her, and she'd walk down with a bag that had in it a scale, a scissors, and a cord. Her fee was five dollars, and if she had to she'd stay around for a week at a time. She wasn't in any hurry to go. She was a wonderful woman, and I was blessed to sit by her bed and hold her hand when she left this world.

"If I had it to do over I'd have fewer children, because there isn't room enough in the world for everyone to have as many as I did, but I sure can't tell you which of them I'd give up. Without anesthetics it wasn't easy having them, but you just grit your teeth and bear it. Once I had six under the age of five, and when my youngest daughter was three months old my system wasn't too strong, and I almost had a nervous breakdown. If the company doctor hadn't got my tubes tied, I might have had more still. Wayne would divorce me if he heard me say so, but I feel more strongly about sterilization than abortions, though I think there are times when abortions should be permitted too."

Tildy tells of a doctor's visit to an equally fecund friend of hers. The doctor, calling on the woman in another old log cabin, suggested that properly timed cold baths might help to reduce chances of pregnancy. "Doctor," the woman asked him, "do you see that creek down there?" He saw it, a good 150 yards away. "Doctor, do you think I'm going to go down there four or five times a night to take a cold bath? Because, Doctor, if you do, you'd better think again."

Wayne and Tildy, like many American couples, have their failures in communication. "A lot of times I find out from other people what's going on with him," says Tildy. They have chronic disagreements, too. Wayne, for example, is still not persuaded that reading anything other than the Holy Scripture is a worthwhile activity. "Wayne says that reading costs money and that time spent reading could be better spent doing something different. But I've always read, all my life, and I'm not about to stop. I used to read to the kids, one on either knee, whether they wanted me to or not. Once, when I was missing my copies of *Life* magazine, I went to ask the postmistress how come they hadn't been coming, and she hinted that Wayne had them sent back. I said to him that if my magazine didn't come that next week, I'd go to the drugstore and buy a copy, so that was the end of that.

"But when the children were in school and he was working on the night shift, I'd read all the school books I missed as a child, and a novel a night. I've read *Franklin and Eleanor* and *My Life with Jackie* (I liked it but thought that author lady was very disloyal) and several of Taylor Caldwell's books and *Jane Eyre* and *I Know Why the Caged Bird Sings* and *Tap Roots,* a Civil War story that dealt with the Negro race, and a lot of Reader's Digest Condensed Books and *A Lion in the Streets* and *For Whom the Bell Tolls* and *Forever Amber* and another one I can't remember.

"I watch television some, but not as much as a lot of people do. Television's changed things a lot. Before television people used to be more friendlier, pay more attention, be more relaxed and settle-minded. Used to be whole families would come for a visit and stay overnight. Now sometimes weeks pass and nobody stops by here."

Not one of the Hastings children has settled in West Virginia: "They all went other places to find work, and they all found it too." It saddens the parents that none of the children wants to inherit the house they struggled so hard to build. "It's a dream," says Tildy, "but we'd like to make the house, after we pass on, into a home for wayward girls or old people or maybe disabled miners."

Most of the children live close enough, in neighboring states, to make occasional visits. Once in a while, in a masterful triumph of choreography, the whole family is reunited. On one such occasion somebody had made a sign which still hangs: OC-CUPANCY BY MORE THAN 25 PERSONS IN THIS BATHROOM IS BOTH ILLEGAL AND UNLAWFUL. And one July, when many of the dozen came home, they chipped in to buy their parents a new dinette set. "A couple of them took us down to the store in their car," Tildy remembers, "and when we drove back, they'd keep saying, 'Wonder if Santy Claus has been here?' When we got home, we saw the old chairs we'd been using out on the porch and the new set inside. Both our reclining chairs were gifts from the children too. Oh, we couldn't be more proud of them all."

Had she not had so many children, Tildy thinks she might have been a nurse or a writer. "I love to take care of people and I love to tell about people. You don't raise twelve children and help with a lot of grandchildren without doing a lot of nursing. I've helped in hospitals and had patients to ask me how long I've been in nursing. I delivered a baby one time in an emergency and helped with a lot of other deliveries. I put the first diaper on Clifford's wife's baby and the first diaper on Clifford's wife herself too.

"Once, out on Atkins mountain, a favorite uncle of mine had a stroke. I was out there caring for him when another daughter in Indiana was about to have surgery, and another one's babies were ill, and Wayne's mother had taken a turn for the worse. I debated which to go to: Grace Ellen or Velma Jean, and decided Velma Jean needed me worse. I stayed at the hospital a couple of nights and helped in the house, too. Wayne called and said Grace Ellen had to have brain surgery.

"Wilma, the one whose husband was in jail for being an alcoholic, she was about to go to the hospital for a baby. So I called her the next morning in Dayton, and the nurse said she was coming along fine. Wayne and I went to see Grace Ellen and found her mother-in-law already there. She said Grace Ellen was getting along all right, but Lord, how she looked. I got home Saturday evening, went to church Sunday morning, and on Monday morning went to Tennessee to get Wilma's boys. Tuesday morning I went to the hospital myself, from what I guess you might call an overdose of motherhood. I've had a heart condition, and spells off and on, ever since. I have to take it pretty easy these days.

"But there's lots of things I want to do. For one, I'd like right much to look into genealogy. They tell me my people go back to 1066, and that we're descended from a queen of England. I'd like to travel too, right much more than Wayne ever wanted to. It's hard for the kids to entertain their daddy when he and I come to visit. One thing he did like, when we went to Washington to see Louella, he liked the Wax Museum."

In West Virginia, as in other stops during my journey, I was struck by evidence that American women seem to be more venturesome than their husbands. I thought of the Hammills, a couple my parents' age who lived in Indiana. All her life Laura Hammill had wanted to go to Europe, but her husband, Arthur, had always found a reason why they shouldn't. Not money; they had plenty. Not sickness; both were robust. Not time; they weren't all that busy. Finally, after a year in which her friends and relatives had joined her in a campaign to persuade Arthur, he relented. They ordered plane tickets, round-trip to Paris, and flew first to New York. After two days at the McAlpin Hotel, they had gone back to Indianapolis. What, everyone wondered, had happened? The answer was simple: "Arthur got scared." Poor Arthur. No, poor Laura: doomed, as long as she was his wife, not to see the other side of the Atlantic.

Blanche Griffith had been luckier. Blanche is another Mountain Artisans seamstress, who lives in a village called Sod. Sally sent me to Sod one afternoon to talk to Blanche, but in the several hours of my visit I said very little. What impressed me most about her near-monologue was what she had to say about seeing the top of the clouds.

"I always declared that nothing would ever possess me to get on an airplane unless him"—Blanche indicated her husband —"or one of the children was someplace dying. But honey, I tell you, there's never nothing in this world more wonderful than getting above the clouds. How could you get any closer to heaven than that? We flew to Dayton once, to talk about Mountain Artisans on a television show, and another time we flew to Washington and landed at night. It sure was beautiful to see all them lights. All four times I was on a plane I seen something different.

"My husband, he don't want to fly on a plane, but when I'm back up there on that hill seeing them clouds floating along, I just wish there was some way in the world for me to describe them clouds, the way they look from the other side, so that anyone would understand. It's just absolutely wonderful.

"Mountain Artisans," Blanche said, "has made people find out that all the women in West Virginia wasn't stupid, that we could make beautiful things. The wonderful people I met through Mountain Artisans I wouldn't trade for all the money on earth."

"Lord only knows what might have happened to women like Tildy and Blanche if they'd had more options," Sally reflected as we had dinner that night. "Their lives have been so limited it's a wonder they've even met each other."

"And they only live—what?—sixty miles apart, as the crow flies," I figured.

"I don't think I can stay on the Mountain Artisans board," Tildy had said, "because of my health. But being *paid* to do the kind of work I've always done anyway since I was seven has given me a self-confidence I never had before. Somebody said the quilts we make aren't art, because we make them to a design and art's something there's only one of, but I said, 'What could be more artistic than something our grandmothers taught us how to do?'

"Besides, one year I earned $841, and some have made plenty more than that. For some, including me, it's the first money we ever made in our lives, and for others it's the only source of income at all. Not that I expect to be paid for all I do. I like working in the community too, trying to get school buses to go up into the hollers to get to the children, organizing a buyers' club, helping with Head Start, and helping with the old people too. Seems to me whatever more pleasure they can get, they sure do deserve it.

"Old women seem to me more lonely than old men, because old men can get together more, on street corners and in barber shops. Women are more sure of themselves than men, in this area anyway, but to me women'll always be women, and they shouldn't try not to." Tildy put on a checkered sunbonnet and walked out her back door to look up over the hill. "But I don't think any person, male or female, should be a doormat," she went on. "I've heard married couples to say they've never had an argument in their lives. All I can say to that is they must be mighty meek and mild. I'm sure glad *I'm* not married to a man like that, and I'll bet the men wouldn't like it much either. I guess it works out about equal most of the time, but you could put it this way, if you understand what I mean: we make men *think* they run the show."

9

I'm in Love with a Handsome Mommy

"*What?*" Marcus was saying. "I can't *hear* you."

"I guess I should have called you from someplace else," I yelled into the phone. Almost any phone booth in the city would have been quieter than this one, just east of the Empire State Building on Thirty-fourth Street. Toward me, that April Saturday afternoon, were marching a couple of thousand women, my sisters, all chanting "WOMEN UNITE! ABORTION IS OUR RIGHT!" They were coming closer, and getting louder, every second.

"Listen," I said to Marcus, "I'll meet you and the Regans at around four by the playground." The Regans and their daughter Hannah had weekly picnics in the park, and Marcus liked to join them. I liked to too, but I'd have to be late this week, because I wanted to see more of the abortion parade. Having just returned from West Virginia, where Matilda had had her sixteen pregnancies, I was much concerned with the business of the unborn and the born. Wombs, and what use we women might or might not make of them, were on my own and, it seemed, everybody else's mind. We are the first generation to see the clouds from above and to choose whether or not to reproduce ourselves. I had been brought up as well-bred as could be managed; the question now was whether I wished to, or could, breed myself.

Abby Heyman and I had come to the parade together from her apartment in the Village. I had gone there earlier for coffee and to look at the prints from two rolls of film she had shot, a couple of months before, of her own abortion. The pictures were good; Abby is a gifted and energetic photographer. I had lost her a few blocks back, where she had become engrossed with a fierce band of people from the Right to Life League. The Right to Lifers were holding up posters of fetuses in jars and chanting their own message: "NOT YOUR BODY, NOT THE STATE, LET YOUR CHILD DECIDE HIS FATE."

"I've come to feel very involved with the whole women's movement," Abby had said over coffee. She was a short, earnest, red-haired twenty-nine-year-old, and I admired the photographs she had been taking of other women as well as those of her abortion. "The movement has affected me just the opposite of a lot of women. It's given a lot of women the courage not to get pregnant."

"You mean they feel they can be defined other than as mothers?"

"Right, but what it's made *me* feel is that *I* can be defined other than by my work. I used to be afraid that if I had a child, I would stop working—that I had to make a clear choice between children and work. The movement made me see I might do *both* things."

"Then why . . ."

"Why did I have the abortion? Because I feel the need to be established in terms of work before I become a mother. When I say 'established' I don't mean in terms of public reputation, I mean in terms of my own self-image."

"I didn't think you meant publicly."

"Anyway, I haven't been serious about my work for that long, so it became a question of energy. During the two months I was pregnant, there were days when I was too tired to get up and do what I was supposed to do, and that scared me.

"The operation was kind of weird," she said as she showed

me her pictures. "I went in the hospital at one and came out at five. The operation was over at 2:40, when the nurse showed me the bottle with the fetus in it and all the blood. She said there was nothing to see, really, and it was too early to tell what sex. The whole thing took ten minutes.

"I can actually say that it was fun in a way. The doctor clued me in to each new procedure. It put the nurses in a very good humor, to see me wheeled in there with a camera and two rolls of film under the sheets. The doctor got special permission for me to take the pictures, because he wanted them published."

"I want people to see how simple, available and safe abortions can be," Dr. Richard Hausknecht told me when I went to see him later in his office. He had been part of the abortion reform movement, he said, since 1964. "It was sensible and calm of Abby," he said, "to use her own unwanted pregnancy to try to help other women. She's a bright, sensitive woman who understands her own body better than most women do."

"But isn't there some problem of—what would you call it— post-abortal *tristesse?* Isn't she, or won't she be, depressed?"

"Unwanted pregnancy," he said, "is the only psychiatric disease curable by a surgical procedure. Most women who've had abortions experience a colossal sense of relief. The whole abortion thing has helped women to learn about their bodies. Women are just now feeling free to talk in detail about their sex lives, which is a healthy side feature of all this."

"Hey, did anyone see three index cards with the Groovy Orgasm speech notes on them?" Somebody called this out in the break between workshops at an all-day sex clinic at the Andrew Warde High School in Fairfield, Connecticut. Scores of women were milling around looking at their programs trying to decide which workshops to go to next. I had asked Peggy and Snowflake to drive up with me from New York. When we stopped to ask directions of two Texaco station attendants, they guffawed. Pretty funny, they seemed to think, the idea of a bunch of women in Fairfield County spending a whole day talking about sex in some high school.

From past trips with them both, I knew Peggy and Snowflake to be amiable companions. Peggy and I had once gone impulsively to Montana, where she had sat on mountaintops with her recorder and played such diverse airs as "Jesu, Joy of Man's Desiring" and "Hitler Has Only Got One Ball." Snowflake and I had spent a week together in adjoining tents at a campground in Jamaica, scraping fresh nutmeg into our coffee and hiking off to beaches.

All three of us had been around the world a good bit, but none of us had beheld a more startling sight than that of twenty-two-year-old Jeanne Hirsch. Jeanne was lying on two pushed-together desks in a high school classroom with her panties down and her skirt up. Thirty or so of us crowded around to see. Jeanne had inserted a plastic speculum into her own vagina. With the help of a mirror and a flashlight, she and all of us could see her healthy pink cervix—a vista such as hitherto had been visible only to gynecologists.

Had her cervix not been healthy, Jeanne would have recognized the danger signs and decided for herself whether or not to go see a possibly insensitive, probably male gynecologist. She could have recognized the signs because she and her mother, Lolly, had become a team of missionaries, part of a nationwide movement for "women to know and rightfully reclaim our own bodies" and to control the quality and price of health care.

"In spite of the most expensive gynecological care that money could buy," Lolly Hirsch wrote in a letter to the *Village Voice*, "I came out of my first child delivery March 16, 1944, with my arms, legs and face black and blue. I had fought the straps and anesthesia like an animal for no one had informed me that I would be shaved, enemaed, strapped, and gagged to deliver a child. . . . We are convinced that brutality toward women is unnecessary. I will devote the rest of my life to the determination that women will be treated humanely and kindly by the field of gynecology."

A speculum for every woman was one of the goals of the movement the Hirsch women represent. Another was access, for every woman, to self-help gynecological clinics,* where in-

---

* Described at length in Ellen Frankfort's *Vaginal Politics* (Quadrangle, 1972) and in *Our Bodies Our Selves: A Book By and For Women* by the Boston Women's Health Book Collective (Simon and Schuster, 1973).

formation would be available about contraception, abortions, and the insides of women. I thought of Tildy. If there had been some such clinic near Groundhog Hollow, might she have had fewer pregnancies?

These missionaries' most ambitious hope is that it may soon be possible and safe for women to team up each month and extract all their menstrual blood at once. We would use suction devices on one another, in a sort of Mutual Aspiration Society, and thus accomplish nothing less revolutionary than a death blow to the tampon industry. Myself, I don't mind bleeding; in fact it is a ritual whose color and rhythm I rather enjoy. What I wish some pioneers would research, so as to end it forever, is premenstrual tension. Not that these moods of ours, I rush to add, are more incapacitating than those of any man. They're annoying, though: more annoying than blood.

This possibility of menstrual extraction, another missionary told me later, "is the biggest outcome of the whole movement. It's really making an impact on women's lives, changing attitudes and changing the politics of health care for women."

My own gynecologist, a kind, efficient woman who looks like Mary Worth, has doubts about self-help clinics, and graver doubts about menstrual extraction. She is opinionated and always has something to tell me. "We've lost thirty-three beds in the maternity ward here," Dr. Newton said the last time I went to see her. "How's *that* for proof of the declining birth rate?"

"It doesn't seem to have made *you* any less busy," I said. Like most doctors, she ordinarily books appointments three or four months in advance.

"I've been spending more time in the clinic," she said. "You ought to see what goes on there. It's ridiculous. There's one law on the books that we can't examine girls under the age of eighteen except for suspected VD. We had one girl coming in who was in *labor,* and we couldn't legally examine her. What we're forced to do, sometimes, is look them in the eye and say, 'You *are* eighteen, *aren't* you?' It's rare to find a *fifteen*-year-old virgin anymore.

"Another thing that's been bothering me," she said as I put my clothes back on, "is discrimination against women in medi-

cine. It's subtle in this country, but far worse here than anywhere else. Nobody regards women doctors as freaks in Europe,
Russia, the Middle East, or the Far East, but in this country it's
a feat for a woman to get into medical school in the first place.
And once you get in you have to be extra clever and sweet and
delicate. You have to work harder and try harder, so as not to
antagonize the boys, because if you don't be nice they won't
refer their patients to you.

"If it hadn't been during World War II, when all the men
were off, I probably wouldn't even have had a chance to do
OB/GYN surgery. That's what burns *me* up. I can't get too
excited about women marching and antagonizing people and
saying we don't need men. That's where they're wrong; we *do*
need men. We can't overcome anatomical differences; they've
got something we don't have and we've got something they
don't have."

I'm in your camp, Dr. Newton, if it is a camp, even if I don't
like your annual answer to my question: how risky is it for me
to keep putting off having a baby? Chances of fertility go
down, she always tells me, after the peak age of twenty-five, and
chances of having a Mongoloid baby rise to ten percent after
age forty.

"But remember," as Snowflake tells me, "Margaret Mead had
her first at thirty-eight."

"Remember Svetlana Stalin," said Peggy. "She was forty-five,
and the baby was okay."

"But that baby wasn't her first," said Snowflake.

"It just seems so unfair," I said, "that Segovia can sire a son
when he's nearly eighty, and my own bearing years should be
coming to an end."

"But you can't even play the ukelele."

"Very funny."

Not that a baby, were I to have one, wouldn't radically alter
the tempo of my life, a tempo I have spent years working on to
get where I want it. How do I know I would not suffer a
three-year postpartum depression, which is the self-diagnosis of
one of my friends? How do I know I would have nearly as
much patience as my friend Alice, with whom it has been so
difficult of late to carry on a simple phone conversation?

"Could you hold on for a second?" Alice is always asking. "GABRIEL! Take your hands off that sewing machine. *Oi.*"

"You never used to say *oi* all that much."

"I'm reverting to ethnic type. You would too. It *is* trying, you know, and he's not even hyperactive. May God have pity on the parents of the hyperactive. Let's not waste paper towels, Gabe, they have to cut down trees to make paper towels."

"I see you're not being overly permissive."

"Sometimes I think I'm too permissive. One does want to swing with the pendulum, not to say roll with the punch. God, bringing up a human being is such a *responsibility,* and when you think that almost everyone you know is some sort of emotional cripple, and that it all stems from around the very age Gabe is now . . ."

"Sobering, all right."

"But next week—did I tell you?—I'm going away for three days, the only three days in our entire three years together, and the very prospect feels like two weeks in the Caribbean. He has been at home all this week, as you know, with an ear infection."

Like the children of many of my friends, Gabriel is adopted. Finding him, which took just about a full nine months, was scarcely less demanding than the process of gestation. It was, said Alice, "a *rull* learning experience." Alice and her husband used to think they would try to adopt another, but now they aren't so sure. An official at one agency told them that "the only *reasonable* approach" would be to take a year off and conduct a worldwide search—a prospect which suited neither their finances nor their schedule.

Alice defends the women's movement at dinner parties, but in private she has her reservations. "What makes me mad," she says, "is the way it makes kids seem a burden, an impediment, something to be stashed away in some day-care center and forgotten about. They don't seem to realize the fact that if you have a young child, heavy demands are made on you which are hardly of an intellectual nature, and that's that. For all the madness of it, I can't think of anything I'd rather be doing just now."

"It was strange when I heard I was pregnant," Abby Heyman told me. "In spite of everything, even though I wasn't sure I wanted to have the baby, I was actually happy, because at least I knew that it was possible for me to conceive."

"I'd be reassured if I knew that for a fact too," I told her.

"A lot of people ask how an educated person like me could have been careless about contraception," she said, "but I guess in a way I doubted whether I really could get pregnant, so I figured it wouldn't matter."

"Sort of testing fate?"

"In a way. Of course some of my friends had the old moralistic idea that it's bad for a single girl to be pregnant: what was I doing having intercourse in the first place? Wasn't that a sin? Wasn't it immoral? A lot of people still think in those terms. But what's so moral about divorced parents bringing up children? What's so sacred and ideal about nuclear families? I can see 'moral' ways of bringing up kids that seem to me a lot more dangerous."

"What about the baby's father?" I asked. "How did he feel about the whole business?"

"Guilty, a little," she said. "He and I had been involved for a long time. I wish I could have shared more of the whole experience, though. There's no such thing as sharing an abortion. My lover volunteered to go to the hospital with me, but I said, 'Oh no, I can go by myself.' Maybe I shouldn't have; I felt the aloneness very acutely."

"Would he have helped you bring up the baby?"

"No, we agreed that if I'd had the baby he wouldn't have been a father to it, financially or in any other way. That was okay with us both. I could have supported the child. The first doctor I went to, when I told him I wasn't married, said I should get an abortion because he didn't see how I could support the child myself."

"Pretty presumptuous."

"I thought so. I was annoyed at his automatic assumption that a woman would have no economic ability. I said I was pretty sure I *could* finance the child—that money wasn't the reason for my misgivings. He said, sort of jokingly, 'Well, I guess a husband isn't needed, then.'

" 'Not for that,' I told him, and I wasn't joking."

"What name would the baby have had?" I asked.

"My own of course," said Abby. "Why not? I guess I'd have had to make a lot of changes in whom I associated with, though. I guess a lot of people would have dropped me and not let their children play with mine. I guess I'd have had to look for some communal arrangement with other single parents."

"You don't quite feel like doing all that?"

"Not yet. For now it's important for me to keep on the way I am," said Abby. "Now my whole life is geared to being flexible and free—not just free to travel, though that's part of it, but free to *grow,* whenever and in whatever ways may seem necessary."

That's how my life has been, too, and the price I have paid for freedom is childlessness. On bad days I brood over children I might have had. On good days I think about her or him or them whom I might someday still bear. On all days I reflect with gratitude on the existence of a certain few, borne by others, whose company matters as much to me as anything in the world. I need kids in my life as much as I need men. To hold a snuggling, trusting child on one's lap is to feel a deep and peaceful intimacy as necessary, to me at least, as any feeling I know.

No more any old kid than any old man. Some children, like some men and for that matter some women, leave me neutral or downright hostile. Janie McPherson, who calls herself Jane One and me Jane A so that neither of us will have to be second on the list, is not among these. She and I have had some good talks.

"What do you worry about," I asked her once, "before you go to sleep at night?"

"Whether we're going to have a substitute at school tomorrow," she says, "and whether people misunderstand something I say. Sometimes the message gets changed from going through so many ears, and people might get real mad. Do you know how that feels?" I assure her I do.

My nephew John, at age ten, purports to be a misogynist. Assigned in school to compose a five-line poem in which each of the interior lines was to have two syllables more than the preceding, he wrote:

> Stupids.
> You know that's girls!
> All girls are so stupid.
> Boys are great but girls are stupid.
> That's all.

Feeling that someone should raise his consciousness, I sent him a letter in the same mode:

> Dear John,
> I think you're wrong
> To say all girls are dumb.
> Some girls are smart; some boys are not.
> Love, Jane.

No answer came. On the phone I asked my sister if John had liked my poem. It turned out he had not, not at all. I didn't worry. Nor do I mind when John addresses me as "How-weird," which he has discovered was my nickname when I was his present age. Then, on the sixth-grade playground, I minded it hugely, but from him, at this point in both our lives, it's fine. If he called me Aunt Jane I would somehow be offended.

Tom Jacobs, of his own seven-year-old volition, bought me a souvenir china cup and saucer, decorated with a saguaro cactus, at the Arizona-Sonora Desert Museum. When he brought it home it broke. So, momentarily, did his heart and mine. But he gave me a carved wooden squirrel instead, which I treasure. His brother Henry, nearly nine, suggested on the fourth day of my visit that he and I have "a chat." I felt singularly honored. "Well," he began, "how's New York these days? Are the subways as smelly as they were last summer?" We covered that and many other subjects, including his hair, for whose somewhat unconventional length he is persecuted.

Jane Howard Jacobs, at three, was known to her intimates at times as Monkey Cow and was praised for the way she and I helped her father to gather the seeds of African daisies. She amuses herself by making up songs when her parents go driving in the Land Rover. Once, when her mother was at the wheel, Jane, in the back seat, was heard to sing, "I'm in love with a handsome mommy."

"What'd you do?" I asked Kathy, her mother.

"I probably stopped the car," said Kathy, "and got out to give her a great big hug."

Kathy and Ann and their husbands are all inspired parents, with a genius for sanctifying the mundane and making a special occasion of the most lacklustre day. One summer Ann and David and their children were to pay a week's visit to the house I helped rent on Springy Banks Road in East Hampton. It would be our first reunion in a good while. The thought of leaping with the children into huge waves we called "Maytags" (because they made us feel like laundry being washed) and of pretending to steal bites of their ice cream on grounds that "it looks as if it's about to turn" filled me with impatience. Driving eastward from the city, I couldn't get there soon enough. When I arrived in my Volkswagen, their station wagon, with the Illinois plates, was already there. Sarah heard me pulling in and rushed out to the balcony of that house to shriek, "SHE'S HERE!" I don't think I have ever felt more purely welcome in my life.

In another workshop at the all-day sex clinic in Fairfield, a woman was talking about when she Came Out, and she did not mean at a debutante cotillion. "When you're Out," she said, "you put yourself in the reject bin, but before you're Out, it's worse. It's like you're constantly waiting for a shoe to drop. 'If they *knew*,' you think, 'I couldn't be here. If my boss knew, he'd fire me. If my friends knew, they'd reject me, and I'd reject me too.'

"If my parents knew, they'd hate me. I haven't written to my parents for five months, because I don't know how to tell them. But on another level they *do* know, and I know they know, and they know I know they know. Can you see how ridiculous this all is?

"My lover," this woman continued, "is in the New York City school system, and she had to wait five years before she could Come Out, because she had to get tenure first. The day she got tenure officially, all hell broke loose. Now that she's Out officially, everything is beautiful."

One of the women in that chemistry classroom, during the Lesbian workshop, was a black minister of the gospel. "It's going to be very fashionable to be gay in another year," the minister predicted. "It'll be a fad. It'll be, 'If you're not gay, you're not with it.' What I mean is not necessarily in terms of sex, but an alternate life-style."

"Not sex?" asked a woman who looked as if she could model for Peck & Peck.

"What a lot of you straights don't understand," the reverend told her, "is that gay women aren't looking to other women for what men do. Women look to each other for something more, something far removed from face and figure and all that. Gay people can have long-term relationships without having to go through all the hassle of divorce, the whole heavy bit of role-playing."

I suppose people must wonder whether I am gay. Why should I be exempt from such universal speculation about all single people and in fact some married ones too? My voice, after all, falls in the alto register: those high notes about the rockets' red glare confound me every time. I hail cabs and catch waiters' eyes better than many men do. I am more likely, when doodling, to draw men's heads than women's. (For whatever it may be worth I am unable to draw anything below the head with any skill whatever.) But nobody ever said I ran like a boy or threw a ball like one. As a matter of fact I don't feel like one. I wish women in the gay liberation movement God-speed, although I take issue with their premise that all men, without exception, are intruding vandals bent only on the oppression of womankind. I submit that some of them can be welcome guests.

At a cocktail party in Cambridge I met a woman of forty-eight or so who told me that her marriage had broken up a couple of years before. Oh, I said, that must have been painful. Not too, she said. It took a while to sort things out, but it worked out okay. Her husband had remarried and the kids were all off on their own. Aren't you lonely, though? I asked. No, she answered, I don't live alone. Oh, I got it: she lived with that buoyant, smartly tailored woman across the room, passing the cheese around. They seemed to be the happiest couple in the room.

"How is Emily?" I asked a woman over lunch in Seattle. Emily was her daughter, a freshman at Reed.

"I think she may have had a sexual escapade over the summer," the mother confided.

"Considering she's—what?—seventeen, I guess that's not so surprising these days," I replied.

"But I don't think it was with a boy," said the mother.

"Oh."

"Well, *que sera sera*. Waiter? Check, please."

"It would have been just horrendous to have had an abortion without a camera," Abby Heyman said. "Otherwise I'd have been agonizing over nothing, because it's completely painless. The one moment when I was completely terrified was when the nurse was strapping my legs, so that my most vulnerable parts were exposed, and there was a scary feeling of 'no way out.' No matter how much it hurt (and I didn't know then that it wasn't *going* to hurt) there was no way I could get away.

"In the middle of the operation, as I was taking pictures, the doctor said, 'Well, you're not pregnant any more.' I smiled, but I realized I was happy for *him,* not for myself. I was thankful to him, for letting me photograph it and all, but I wasn't so completely happy.

"I went back to my hospital room to rest. I tried to read— I'd brought along *The Female Eunuch*—but I couldn't get into reading. There was a phone by my bed so I called friends, because I didn't want to think. I could hear other women phoning too. It struck me that nobody was talking about their men. I didn't see or hear any men there all day—and there

128

seemed to be a whole floor full of abortions—except for one who tried to force his way in to be with his girlfriend. They wouldn't let him in. I found that offensive.

"When the idea of having given up the child really hit me, I started to cry. A nurse came in, the same nurse I had heard telling another girl in another room not to cry. That annoyed me tremendously: why shouldn't she cry if she wanted to? Why shouldn't I? I told her I was upset about the *child,* not the operation. She said, 'Well, you have to take the sour with the sweet.'

"I feel wistful now when I see people with children, especially if they're the age mine might be, but the other side of being wistful is knowing I have a choice. I think my choice was rational. I think and hope that when I'm ready to conceive, I'll be able to."

At the all-day sex clinic in Fairfield I had bought a speculum, for two dollars.

"Don't you want to get one too?" I asked Peggy.

"Not much," she said. "I'm not all that curious. I've never seen the inside of my ear, either, and I don't hold that against the otologist."

One afternoon in the privacy of my own bedroom I decided I would try to use my speculum, a strange translucent gadget which somehow reminded me of a duck. I had trouble figuring out how to see my cervix. As I was trying to do so, fussing with the speculum and a flashlight and my mother's old monogrammed silver hand mirror, the telephone rang in the other room. As I hastened in to answer it, the speculum fell to the floor. It broke.

10

When I Grow Up

"Well, sure, an omelet *would* be nice," I told Alison Busch, "but I don't want to put you to any trouble."

"No trouble at all," she said as she began to slice the scallions, "but I'll have to leave for class in an hour, so we won't have much time to talk."

She had moved only recently to this apartment in Austin, Texas, but the place had a settled, snug air about it. Monogrammed towels. Japanese woodcuts. An antique globe. Framed pictures of her four children and two grandchildren. A portrait of her venerable late father, a navy captain. Hand-caned chairs. The Old Testament in Greek. An English-German dictionary. Complete Sherlock Holmes. Complete Gilbert and Sullivan. *The Better Homes Handyman's Book.* A. A. Milne. Roger Tory Peterson. Pretty silverware. Nice china.

Alison had the look of a gentle, alert rabbit. Her brown eyes missed nothing, and her cashmere cardigan matched her tweed skirt exactly. At fifty-two, she wore size eights and looked as if she got a lot of exercise. There was one thing missing: a husband. A couple of years before, after nearly three decades of marriage, "a man from the court came up to me and handed me divorce papers. I wouldn't file, because I had no grounds whatsoever. Bob said, 'I'm not good for you,' but I wondered, if that were true, why he hadn't told me so years before.

"I had to find out from the children, not from him, that the real reason was he wanted to remarry. His doing it that way didn't sit well with anybody. He finally said to me, 'We have nothing in common.'

" 'No, nothing at all,' I said to him, 'just four kids, twenty-seven years, and a lot of shared interests—can you call that nothing?' " He could. Alison became the first woman in her social circle, "and Lord only *knows* the first in my family, ever, to have a divorce. I guess I'm socially and sexually obsolete."

"Armagnac!" Ted shouted when he opened my house present. "Ah, Jane Howard, what a memory you've got."

"Who could forget those evenings?" I said. "And it's pretty lucky for me that you just happen to be home, the first time I call you in eight years for a bit of free hospitality."

"Where else would we be?" asked Kate. Nice floppy old red-haired Kate, she'd always reminded me of a Raggedy Ann doll. She had always been relaxed at times and in places when the rest of us were nervous. She had an air about her of contagious poise, and the passage of years had hurt her none at all. A lot of my old friends seem defensive or shattered when I see them after a long separation, but Kate and Ted did not. They appeared to have grown parallel and close, the way we all used to think was our birthright.

"Where else would you *want* to be?" I asked. "This is an outrageous old gingerbread house, but great. It suits you both exactly."

"It's an hour's commute to the campus for Ted," said Kate, "but it's worth it to be out here in the country. It's worth it for him to go there, too, because he really likes what he's doing."

"I never thought we'd actually like Detroit," said Ted. "We came here on sort of a trial basis. But it grows on us. It has its points."

There had been a period, in our early New York days, when Kate and Ted and a dozen or so other people and I had got together at least two evenings a week. That was when Ted was a graduate student at Columbia, and Kate a teacher of high school French. When they got married, in the big house where Kate grew up outside St. Louis, I was invited. The wedding was lavish, and Kate's gregarious parents asked me to stop by sometime on my way to visit my own family. Two or three times I had. I had sent baby gifts to all Ted and Kate's three sons, but of late we had barely exchanged Christmas cards. On a last-minute impulse, as part of a trip to the West, I had phoned to ask if they would like to have me stop in Detroit and drop by. Their response was heartening.

"Now tell us, just what *is* it you're working on now?" Ted asked me as he poured us each a snifter of armagnac.

"Oh, traveling around, trying to collect impressions about women."

"Where women's—how you say—heads are at?"

"More or less."

"Feel like talking about it?"

"Not all that much, right now. You know what I really would love to do?"

"What?"

"I really feel like going ice-skating."

"Who can blame you? The pond's frozen up on the hill there; why don't you girls go try it?"

"*Women,* darling," said Kate.

"*Je vous en prie,*" said Ted, giving her a fast little backrub.

"There's one problem," I said. "Difficult as it is for me to travel light, it didn't occur to me to pack ice skates. I mean I didn't even know I was going to stop here at all."

"Such a madcap," said Ted. "But don't worry, you can use mine. Have you forgotten the evening you and I traded shoes?"

"Of course, how prescient we were, foreseeing the entire concept of unisex," I said. "I'm not even embarrassed any more to wear Size 10 shoes, that's how raised *my* consciousness is. But if I wear your skates, what'll *you* do?"

"I'll stay home," said Ted. "For a while I will anyway. Later I've got to go to campus; I've got a conference."

"Oh, Ted," said Kate, "on *Saturday?*"

"It couldn't be helped," he said. "But I'll be back in time for the veal—the what kind of veal?"

"Marengo," said Kate. "It's out of the new James Beard. The new James Beard, I think, is terrific," she said as we walked toward the hill, "and there's this other new cookbook I'm quite smitten with called *Home Made:* it gives all these atavistic, nineteenth century recipes."

"I guess atavism is having its day," I said. The afternoon was brilliant, and for a wonder nobody else was there on the smooth ice of the pond. We had it to ourselves and glided around with matronly sedateness.

"Can you skate backwards?" Kate asked.

"No more than I can speak Swahili," I said. "Can you?"

"No, though I've tried incessantly to learn. I guess we all have to have one tragic flaw—that might as well be mine."

"I remember your father once showed us slides of you and Liam skating."

"Ah, yes, Daddy and his slides."

"Come to think of it, doctors are always showing slides. They've always just come back from the Yucatán or Switzerland or somewhere, always first-class, and they always want you to see where they've been."

"I guess they have to prove they have other interests besides medicine," said Kate.

"Where've he and your mother been lately?" I asked.

"No place," said Kate. "I guess I didn't tell you. Are you ready? My father, Dr. Martin Gorman, has left my mother for another woman."

"He's done *what?*"

Lois Ross mixed good margaritas. She gave me a second one as we sat on the patio outside the house she shares with her younger son in a Boston suburb. His older brother, to Lois' pleasure, won a scholarship to Brandeis, and she hoped her younger son might get one too.

"It was too much of an uphill struggle for me to get my own education," she said. "I realize it's very chic to be disdainful of college, for my boys' generation, but it would kill me if they didn't go."

"You just got your doctorate in psychology yourself, didn't you?"

"Yes, which is partly why the company decided I was over-qualified. That's why they're going to lay me off, and that in turn is why I'm filing the class action suit." Lois was one of the women I met in the course of a search *Life* asked me to make, for a victim of corporate sex discrimination. She was a short, feisty woman of forty-five or so, with thick black hair, and a good laugh.

"The thought of being laid off makes me absolutely livid," she said, "but one thing I've been learning in therapy is how to deal with anger. Do you know I didn't use to even *know* when I was mad? Can you imagine such a thing?"

"Sure," I said. "I'm that way myself."

"But now I *enjoy* being angry. Funny thing about anger: it's the only emotion men can show, and the only one we can't. I so much prefer it to weepy, plaintive petulance."

"You? Petulant?"

"You should have seen the way I carried on for the first two years after my husband left."

"He left? Why?"

"For someone else."

"In my sane moments," Alison said as we ate our omelets, "I wonder how I could have put up with Bob for as long as I did. When I can be objective, I realize that I'm well rid of a lot of things about him. Boats, for one thing. We were forever making payments on boats we couldn't afford. Here, have some endive."

"Thanks. Was he smart?"

"I think mine was the higher I.Q., but he was smart enough. He was five days younger than I am and two inches shorter."

"Why'd you marry him?"

"Oh, there was a war on, brave boys were going off to the front, everybody else was getting married, why shouldn't I? It looked like security, and it would get me out from under my parents' thumbs, which were some thumbs, let me tell you."

"Did you have a big wedding?"

"It was all I could do to round up one bridesmaid. I wanted the wedding to be at Beloit, where Bob and I met and where all our friends were, but my father said, 'Come home to Pensacola and let your mother participate,' so I had to say, 'Aye, aye, sir.' I stepped, as it were, from his bed and board to my husband's. Bob was an orphan, and do you know who put him through law school? My father did."

"Was Bob attractive?"

"I guess so. He's always been terribly concerned about his appearance. He has quite a thing about not getting old. Once when he was in a plane wreck accident, which proved to be quite a forceful reminder of his mortality, he remarked, 'My Peter Pan suit is getting tight.' His birthday, as I say, is five days after mine, and we always used to have parties together. On our fiftieth birthday, he hired a caterer and invited friends to *his* party, without telling people it was my birthday, too. I guess that should have been a clue that I didn't matter to him any more."

"What's his new wife like?"

"She's a lot younger, with four kids and a richer father than I had. A friend of mine, who knows her, says they deserve each other. She likes sailing and parties and I hear she's just as demanding as Bob is. One reason she got rid of her first husband, I hear, was his financial irresponsibility. Wait until she finds out what she's in for now! If she's also the type that has to get all the time without giving, they can't last long."

"Have you met your father's friend?" I asked Kate as we unlaced our skates.

"Yes, once, and she seemed a nice enough woman, ten or so years younger. It was a nervous occasion all around, but I sort of liked her. Later he asked what I thought, and I told him, 'How you live is your own business, but I think it was cruel of you to leave Mother so abruptly, never really explaining to her what had happened.' You know what he said?"

"What?"

"He said, 'The only *kind* way I could have done it would have been to shoot her.'"

"I guess that's true," I said. "I've always been undone by even trivial partings, and I've never even been married."

"But you should see their apartment—they moved out of the big house—did I tell you?—and into an apartment after Molly and I left home. The stuff my father left behind is untouched. It's like Lenin's Tomb. There should be ropes across the doorways. My mother just sits there, waiting and hoping he'll change his mind and come back."

"She must be wretched."

"You can't imagine. At least if she were a widow, it would be respectable. The *ambiguity* of it is what she can't stand. What's she supposed to say to their friends? Now she has nobody to take her out on Saturday nights. I'm afraid their whole lives have been lived on a kind of high school level: just one Saturday night date after another, getting all dressed up and going to the country club dance as though it were a prom, planning where to be seen and in what and by whom, and what cruises and trips to take."

"Can you talk to her about all this?"

"You want to know something sad? I don't think I've ever talked to my mother in my whole life about anything important. She never did anything to encourage it. She'd probably be devastated to hear me say so, because she thinks she's led this perfect, exemplary life. The way she sees it it's simple: another woman stole her husband."

"Are they divorced?"

"I'm not sure they ever will be, because she'll have to agree to it, and if she divorced him she'd be acknowledging that all this really happened. She'd rather pretend it hadn't. She used to boast, 'Look at us, forty years of marriage and we've never had a cross word, never an argument,' as though that were something to be proud of. Even as a kid I could figure out that if you never disagreed, you never talked."

"When my husband left I was a basket case," Lois Ross told me. "It was the shock of my life. He had apparently been

trying to get me to divorce him, had behaved in such an irrational, unusual way. He got a psychologist friend to tell me
that he was very seriously mentally ill, but it turned out the illness was nothing more serious than another woman.

"I was a housewife for all the years of our marriage. I'd had a
master's degree in psychology and did personnel work for a few
years with all sorts of fancy titles, but what all the titles really
meant was that I was the one who turned on the lights."

"Did he want you to quit working?"

"Well, we had the two boys, and I thought I should spend
time with them. At least I had sense enough to do short-term
deals for the League of Women Voters and Democratic politics.
I was always involved in something, because I'm convinced that
a woman regresses in a home role. If she has no interaction
with adults, she gets to talk and speak and think as children
do."

"Even though I'm a grandmother," said Alison, "I still feel
like a kid. I still wonder what I'm going to do when I grow
up."

I had met her only once before, and briefly, following a
panel at the Conference on World Affairs in Boulder, Colorado, the previous spring. That was the spring I was in constant orbit. No invitation seemed irrelevant to my quest to find
out what was on the minds of American women, so I went
wherever I was asked. At the same time, I was trying to finish a
story for *Life* on brain waves and serenity. In search of serenity
I was racing around like a frenzied madwoman. The day before
my flight to Colorado, I had been sitting in the San Fernando
Valley in an approximation of the lotus position, plugged into
a biofeedback machine with sawn-in-half Ping-Pong balls over
my eyes, trying to experience something called a "total cosmic
whiteout."

Year after year students and townspeople keep showing up
for the panel discussions of which the World Affairs Conference
consists. Panel discussions are of course a preposterous format
for the exchange of ideas, but some of the panelists return annually, because there is something addictively merry about the

frenzy of that week. It is all so intense and sleepless and convivial that a camaraderie develops of a sort rarely found outside
foxholes. Nor need the panelists make any decisions. All they
have to do is show up to be lionized at nightly dinner parties
and to discourse from platforms two or three times a day on
such absurdly juxtaposed topics as "God," "Cable TV," "The
Military Mind," and "Terrorism."

Alison had been in Boulder visiting her sister, and she had
come to a panel I was on, entitled something like "Whither
Womankind?" She waited by the door of the classroom with
tears in her eyes, maybe because something I had said struck
some chord in her. Or maybe she just wanted to tell someone,
anyone, how wretched it was to be an abandoned fifty-one-year-
old woman whose so-called friends not only didn't introduce
her to any new men, but wouldn't even have her over for coffee
in the morning.

"I haven't met anybody new at all," she said, "and I don't
even know where to look. Singles parties? What a sad bunch.
All I met at the one I went to was a man who works at a dairy
—good-hearted, but hardly the answer to my search for com-
panionship. My husband never liked *my* friends, so our friends
were his. Even those I assumed were our mutual friends, the
couples we knew together, they dropped me. I had the feeling
nobody would care if I were dead or alive. That feeling, like
going the wrong way down a one-way street, can really drag
you down."

I had to hurry elsewhere, as I always seemed to have to that
spring, but I took down Alison's address and phone number
and said I would look her up if I ever got to Houston. Seven
months later, I did. Her phone number, the operator said, had
been disconnected, and when I rang what had been her doorbell the new tenant said she had moved to Austin. Having
done that much detective work, I stayed on an extra day when
my other business was finished, and drove the 150 miles to see
Alison.

While hardly a stand-up comic, she seemed a good deal more
cheerful than she had in Boulder. Moving to Austin from
Houston had been the right step. All her four children were

grown and gone, and she had decided to work toward a master's degree in education.

"How are your classes?"

"Demanding, but I don't see why I shouldn't get A's—I don't have that many distractions. I have to fight feeling lonely, and I have to fight anger. A couple of times this past fall, just thinking back on all that happened, I've got so mad I haven't been able to study. There's a Women's Center here, mostly for young girls having abortions, and sometimes I've thought of going there, just to ventilate."

"My mother has turned into a ranting banshee," Kate said as we walked back toward her house when our weak ankles had had enough of skating. "She was enraged when she found out that my kids knew what had happened to her, but I said, 'How could they *not* know, the way you scream so loud about it into the phone?' "

"Has she thought of doing anything else?"

"What's so sad is that she's always just defined herself as Mrs. Martin Gorman: as the doctor's wife and Angela's and my mother. All she's ever done has been to make a home for him. In their social set it's always the man who makes the money and the woman who spends it. They always say '*she* decorated *her* house,' as if it weren't the man's house too. It's always '*my* child,' '*my* house,' '*my* curtains,' never 'ours.' "

"Didn't your father ever care what furniture she got?"

"Once he tried to. Once he happened to be at Stix, Baer & Fuller, buying some pajamas, and on an impulse he went to order a new chair they needed for their den. I don't think he'd ever ordered anything like that in his life before, so it must have been a kind of adventure for him. I remember the way my mother sort of sneered when he told her what he'd done. She laughed, not in a nice way, and said, 'Well, I can *imagine* what *that'll* look like. Back it will have to go.' "

"What pathetic division of labor," I said. At least my own parents had done wallpapering and gardening together.

"I'm afraid I really do feel," Kate said, "that my mother has

wasted her life with cards, golf, window-shopping and luncheons. She had the time and energy and wherewithal to do a lot
of other things, but I guess she never wanted to."

"Did she ever think of getting a job?"

"If she had ever even suggested it, my father would have
been horrified. It suited her better to seem dumb, act helpless
and dependent like a little girl who needed her daddy. Besides,
the way she sees things women only work for two reasons: if
they're brilliant, as in 'Oh, she's such a brain, such a whiz, she
goes to business, you know,' or if they're destitute and need the
money. God knows my mother never needed money, and although she has plenty of native intelligence, she's never
thought of herself as being smart."

Lois never had doubted her own wits. "My parents were
Russian immigrants on welfare, with absolutely no education,
but my father had a fantastic mind. Even though he could
hardly write, he always encouraged me to use my head; and I
always have, or tried to anyway. Some women say getting married was the only thing they ever did that made their parents
feel they were worthwhile, but my parents weren't like that.

"One of my problems," she said, "is I'm afraid I threaten
people. I feel like a Mrs. Milquetoast, but my vocabulary is too
big; I guess I use words that intimidate men."

"You mean four-letter words?"

"No, that's *not* what I mean, but I have used them in self-defense. Our company has big conferences, a lot of men at these
meetings have felt threatened by my presence, and said, 'Well,
we'll have to watch our language while *you're* here.' Fellows at
the lower levels feel especially uptight; they can only deal with
me by saying, 'Look, sister, you don't really belong here.' Once
I said, 'Wait until after the meeting, and I'll tell you my
motherfucker story,' and they were stunned.

"At one meeting one of the men begged me to help him field
questions he couldn't handle. Finally I did, but he didn't introduce me to his group, which would have been simple courtesy.
After I'd bailed him out, one of the other men in the group
looked at me and said, 'My, you have a lot to say, girlie.'

"I felt like telling him, 'Why shouldn't I have a lot to say? I have a doctor's degree!' but I don't like to pull that rank unless I want someone to take my call, in which case I'll say to someone's secretary, 'It's Dr. Ross,' and the darned secretaries say, 'Put him on,' and only giggle when I say, 'But *I'm* the doctor.'"

"Can you make friends with the women in your office?"

"The only other women are secretaries, and I can't be too friendly with them, because then I'd be identified with them. Men never ask me out to lunch, but I can't have lunch with the secretaries either, because if I did I'd lose status."

"That," I said, "is appalling."

"You know what's *more* appalling?"

"What?"

"I almost forgot to tell you this: when a woman applies to work at my company, one of the questions on the application blank is, 'Date of last menstrual period.'"

"Good God."

"Good God is right. But I'm not going to let all this get me down. If I survived my divorce, I can survive this, and win the lawsuit. It's no joke for a woman to get out in the real world of competition without any seniority. It's more difficult than you might think. I did everything I could to transform myself, including plastic surgery: a face-lift and the whole works. And I got my degree, by the way, with distinction, with all kinds of honors.

"I'm an absolutely different person now, because success breeds success. Russians, of whom I am one, are supposed to have a capacity for misery, but I was determined I'd show the goddamn world it wasn't going to get *me* down. That's why I took the trip to Europe too."

To judge by what Lois and Alison told me, the solo postmarital trip to Europe is an effective *rite de passage* for newly abandoned women of a certain age and certain income level. Here's what you do when your husband suddenly leaves you for someone else: you cross the ocean and go someplace where nobody ever heard of you and buy a phrasebook and change your traveler's checks into an odd currency you study at night in your hotel room so you won't have to read the coins, looking conspicuously foreign, when you pay for a coffee and pastry (your order for which, to your amazed delight, the waiter just now actually understood).

You feel euphoric just looking at the doors of the houses, more portals than doors really, so much nobler than what we walk through at home. You notice the second and third stories and rooftops of buildings, you think about architecture, you take delight in the curved pats of butter, the patterns of cement on the sidewalks. Your exhilaration mounts as you discover you can get on the right train at the right time all by yourself and that you can go whenever you want wherever you want, without having to argue with anyone. With luck you might meet congenial soulmates to eat dinner with or maybe do more than that with, but even if you don't, you feel buoyed as you write your postcards home.

For Alison, whose previous vacations had mostly been afloat in the Gulf of Mexico, Europe had been intoxicatingly different. "I was warned that it would be hopeless to go anyplace without a reservation and that I'd end up sleeping in parks with flower children, but I always managed to find myself a place to stay, even when it was most crowded. Did I tell you what happened in Bayreuth? I went there impulsively during the festival, at the last minute, and I ended up sharing a room with a man! He was a homosexual, I could tell, an art historian on a sabbatical, but still—can you imagine, little Alison from Houston taking a chance like that? We met in a cafe, and when I told him I hadn't found a place to sleep, he said he didn't see why I shouldn't use the other bed in his room.

"And I made a side trip to Scotland, from London, with another divorcee, from Miami. We just rented a car, just like that, and went on up. Her husband pulled the same trick on her as mine did. I'll tell you something: the women men pick out to marry and have their children with are superior by far to those they choose to have fun with later."

"Tell me something, Alison," I said. "Have you ever given any thought to polygamy?"

"I have, in fact," she said. "Maybe if a man had *four* women to mother him, it might almost be enough. But the ideal thing would be polyandry."

"You mean us having four men to father us?"

"Does it sound so bad?"

"It could be quite a nice stopgap solution, if hardly a final one," I said. "More privacy, less possessiveness, less jealousy. I've heard worse formulas. It would mean a lot of logistics, though. I wouldn't like all that furtiveness."

"Are you ready for it on a non-furtive basis?"

"I suppose not. I guess the real adventure, for me, would be old-fashioned, hard-core monogamy."

"That's because you didn't jump into it automatically when you were twenty-two," Alison said. "In a way, I envy you. You already know how to live alone: you must know how to, because you've always done it. I'm having to learn now what you already know, because before Bob left me, the bastard, I'd never lived alone in my whole life! What a thought! But it's true.

"My daughter came over on my fifty-second birthday. She brought me four cupcakes, figuring I wouldn't eat a whole cake by myself, and a dozen yellow roses. Before she left, she said, 'Well, Mother, you're just going to have to learn to run the dishwasher before it gets full.' "

A month or so later I had a call from Mrs. Gorman, the mother of my friend Kate. She had come to New York to visit her son, and I was astonished to hear her voice.

"What a nice surprise," I said, not quite sure whether I was supposed to know all that had happened to her. "Maybe you heard that Kate and Ted and I had a good visit a few months ago. It was great seeing them again after so long. How are they now, by the way?"

"You haven't heard?" asked Mrs. Gorman.

"Heard what?"

"They've split up," she said. "Ted has left Kate. He's living now with one of his graduate students."

11

Somebody's Got to Get a Loser, Right?

"Listen," Arlene Zermiak asked me as we drove in my Volkswagen down a parkway in Brooklyn toward the tavern where her husband tends bar, "would you mind if I introduced you as my girlfriend Sharon from New Jersey? See, I've never lied to Dom in my life before, but I don't think he'd like it—in fact I know he wouldn't like it—if he knew I let some strange lady writer come into our house. If you don't mind, I think it would be better not to say who you really are."

"Well, okay, I guess," I said, "but what if he asks me something about what I do or how things are in New Jersey? *Where* in New Jersey?"

"Never mind," she said. "He won't ask. He don't know my girlfriends and I don't know many of his man friends. Oh, we have people over sometimes, but not too often. Home to him is a very special place."

Home to them is the second floor of a house with an asbestos-siding facade and a backyard vegetable garden, across from a playground in the Bensonhurst section of Brooklyn. All the rooms are spacious. The bedroom, facing the street, has a collage of snapshots of both their families. In the living room is a phonograph. (Arlene likes music, "especially ballads I can relate to.") The kitchen has the television, flower decals on the refrigerator door, plastic flowers here and there, and three pairs of plaques on the wall:. a pot pouring into a cup, a couple of masks, and a couple of cats. A couple of real cats, Tiny and Jinx, referred to as "the kids," slink around and, Arlene said, provide good company.

I had a hard time finding her place; I probably shouldn't have taken the Williamsburg Bridge. Although we live only about twelve miles apart, I knew as little of her borough as she did of mine. Manhattan, to her, is a place the catering service sometimes sends her on jobs. Brooklyn, to me, is a place I pass through sometimes on the way to the airport. The odds against our ever meeting, we agreed over rye whiskey mixed with Seven-Up and crackers covered with Kraft cheese spread, were great, but we are both uncommonly curious.

"I don't have too many friends," she said. "Friends need a lot of time, and if you don't have the time, why bother? I can't see picking one person out of a crowd and saying, 'You! You're going to be my friend!' I'd rather have fifty thousand acquaintances, because they don't ask much, and I don't feel like committing myself. Besides, I can't see letting friends interfere with my own life."

There wasn't much she didn't tell me about her own life in the three hours we sat in her kitchen. No topic, from contraception to death, was overlooked, and I began to suffer from wrist cramp.

"I love subway trains," she was saying. "I like to ride them back and forth. When I was in my teens I'd get up at three, four, five in the morning, get on the train, get off at Coney Island, look at the water for a while. It really worried my mother but I loved to do it. I'd stay twenty minutes or so, walk along the water, then get back on the train and come home."

"I've got this idea," I interrupted. "My car's outside. Why don't we drive and go look at the water now?" So we took rather a long drive, to see the boats lined up at Cross Bay Boulevard, near where Arlene lived as a child. "The change in this neighborhood is really something," she said. "Like when I was little there was nothing here but the Bow Wow and the pizza palace, and look at it now. Hey, want to get a hamburger?"

Sure. She insisted we go dutch at a neon-lit Wetson's, where she said "Thanks, hon," to the waiter who passed over my cheeseburger and her Big W Special. And then, since Dom wouldn't be home until very late, how would I like to drop by his bar? Why ever not? Inebriation, it was clear, was a strong motif of our acquaintance, whose beginning she recalled more clearly than I did.

"I wanted to get a glass off you," she said, "and you didn't want to let go of it. It was toward the end of that wedding— no, it wasn't a wedding, was it? We usually work weddings, but this was some other affair." It had in fact been the annual extravaganza of the American Academy of Arts and Letters, up on the mall at 155th Street and Broadway, at which painters and writers get awards and feel silly and are engulfed by hangers-on like me, who feign jaded cynicism, deplore the lack of eye contact but keep assenting to maybe just one more daiquiri. If I'd had one less I probably would not have confided in a waitress what book I was trying to write. It's a good thing I did, though, because Arlene had said, "You ought to talk to *me:* I'm only twenty-five and I've had three marriages and a nervous breakdown and *I* know a thing or two about how it is to be an American woman."

Arlene took pains with her appearance. No dark showed at the roots of her pale blond hair, tied back with a coral-colored scarf which just matched her bell-bottom slacks. She had plucked and arched her eyebrows carefully, and gone to the trouble of putting on green eye shadow and mascara. Her blouse was black nylon, her cardigan embroidered with flowers, her shoes white wedgie sandals, and on her face was a look of nervous native wit.

For a twenty-five-year-old she had indeed known her share of anguish. Her present husband, the bartender, had terminal cancer. "We were married last September and found out in October." Arlene made me feel that for all my travels out of and back to JFK and LaGuardia, and for all my twelve years' seniority, of the two of us she was by far the more experienced.

"Before I married Dom," she said, "I was always in such a hurry to get no place. My first husband, I knew him since I was thirteen, I married when I was seventeen, earlier than the other girls in my crowd. They waited until they were nineteen or so. (As a kid I was always wild, a leader, I'd take chances, and I'd think of my girlfriends, even the ones who were older than me, as little children.) I was two months pregnant when we got married; we eloped down to Virginia.

"He was a very smart, intelligent man, more educated than me, but we never discussed anything, never went out. I always figured he'd loosen up when we were together more, but that didn't happen. He worked for a beer company and we had a pretty house with a yard out in New Jersey. I didn't know I was missing anything. I had a part-time job as a floor girl in a dress factory, and I'd come home to watch Jack LaLanne and do housework.

"Well, one day I came home too early and found him with a man. When that happened I just turned away, seeing I wasn't needed, and tripped down the stairs. When I came back he was gone, and he never did come home that night; we never did discuss it. He knew I knew, so that was it. He went to Mexico and got a divorce. I can't even read the divorce papers; they're in Spanish, but a lawyer told me it was okay. I had a miscarriage. I was six months along; that marriage lasted four months.

"A year and a half later I married again, this time a big deal with the white dress bit and 250 guests, because my second husband's idea was he didn't want anyone to know I was divorced, because you don't take in someone else's laundry. The whole image of divorced women is garbage, it should go down the drain, but that's how he felt.

"He was a bookbinder, and we'd go to this yacht club. His father belonged, so we got to go. Listen, if you ever want to meet a bunch of phonies, just go to a yacht club someday. All they do is lounge around and feel like hotshots because they're there. My husband liked it, and he liked photography and fishing, and he got a second job as a painter. He was also fooling around. See, we had sex problems.

"He was a supersexy man, and I couldn't reach a climax. I

didn't know how to fake it. Now I'm better at faking it. You learn. Hell, I like the emotion part of it, but it's not the end of the world if I don't click. I didn't worry about it for a while, but then I'd read those books and think Jesus, everyone else is having them but me.

"But even if I would have clicked with him, he still would have gone after others. He started on narcotics after we were married too. He said pot made him see visions clearer. I've never wanted to try drugs myself, my own worst vice is drinking.

"So that marriage didn't work either, and then I had another boyfriend, and that didn't work, and that's when I had my breakdown, when I needed some assistance psychological-wise. I just retreated, I didn't even eat or wash, I'd sit on my bed or else I'd sleep. I tried to kill myself by taking a bottle of rye and a bottle of aspirin, and I got deathly ill, all right, but not the way I wanted to. They brought a stomach pump and all that.

"The psychiatrist I had at the hospital was a woman, and she did me good. She'd never answer anything, she'd bounce my questions back at me. She'd say, 'Your own brain has all the answers, so if you have a problem you take a sheet of paper and write down all the pros and cons.' So that's what I do now, that's how I keep sane. I haven't seen her in three and a half or four years, but I'd go back again, sure, because I'd rather get a little help than flip out and hurt somebody.

"My health's okay otherwise, except I have a bad heart. There's some valve supposed to open and close that when I get nervous it stays open. That's why I flunked the physical to get on the police force. I'd like to have been a detective, but they'd probably just have made me a meter maid even if I got in. Or some kind of social worker, maybe, but that would have been bad because I'm the kind, I take my problems home with me. My husband laughs at the way I do that, but somebody's got to, right? I figure there's less problems in the world if people listen to each other, so I take it upon myself to be one of the ones that listen.

"I've traveled some to different places and I always expect people to be different, but they never are when you actually talk to them. Basically they're the same as you, they just want to survive. I've been to Virginia and North Carolina and Florida and Canada, mainly around Niagara Falls. I don't like traveling alone, if I don't have somebody to say, 'Hey, look at that mountain.'

"I'd like to go back to the South; I liked the people and the climate there. I like New York, but I'd get away if I could, it's too fast here, and down there it's so much more relaxed, you have more of a chance to unwind, and maybe it's easier to talk to people.

"Who do I talk to here? My mother, and one married woman lives near her. I save all my mending for my mother when she comes over, because it makes her feel like I need her. She pretends to complain, but you can see right through it, she really loves it. She's a pretty religious person, she goes where I used to go as a kid, the Lutheran Church. I only went because I had no choice, I sang in the choir and in school choruses, but I blew my career when I took up smoking. I can't hold the high notes no more. I'm not too keen on Jesus Christ, but I do believe in God; I think there must be somebody or something in charge. I'd go to church now if I didn't have to get up so early. With Dom not coming home sometimes until four in the morning, we like to sleep late.

"My parents are Austrian descent. My mother plays bingo about every night, but she just uses two cards. She goes to a bingo parlor where you can win twenty dollars a game. I'll go sometimes, or I'll visit, or go to the movies once every two weeks, but it has to be when I want to go. If Dom and I go out we usually end up in a bar.

"My mother and dad were separated for ten years and they just got back together again. She cried her heart out while he was gone, but now they're getting along good. He's an alcoholic, but he's cured. He works as a quality-control tester for a real benevolent paint company, they give you your birthday off along with all the usual holidays.

"My father is a handyman too; he taught me how to do electricity and plumbing and all that stuff. I'm as good at that stuff as Dom is. He'll wash my floors and he'll vacuum; he feels he

149

wouldn't ask me to do anything he wouldn't do himself, and vice versa.

"I've got two older brothers. I miss the one who's in the navy, who lives in Florida, because we used to be very close. The other one's in the police force. Even though his precinct is right across the street, he never stops or waves or anything. He went into the police full of the milk of human kindness—he was going to help people and all that—but now there's so much red tape he just looks the other way a lot of times. He ain't even going to give a ticket, with all that red tape. It could all be so much easier, so much of it's ridiculous with the post-poning and court calendars and all that.

"The idea of stronger gun laws makes me laugh. To be truth-ful, I have a gun in there in the bedroom. It's not registered; it's illegal. And I can tell you, if you want a gun for an illegal reason, nothing can stop you. I wouldn't know how to shoot it; I'd probably shoot myself, but I keep it just in case. My father used to have a philosophy: if you're gonna shoot anybody, do it in your own house; drag them in your house first. Sometimes I think the old West, like in the movies, was better: shoot first, ask questions later. They didn't kill innocent bystanders in those days.

"I think if I wanted to vote—I don't, because I don't follow it that closely—I'd join the Conservative party. Dom doesn't vote either. We both figure whoever you get in there can't be any better than the one before, or any worse. I guess we shouldn't have got into the Vietnam war, but once we did it was too bad they never sent enough men over there to do a job.

"Dom was in the army for about eight years, in the time of Cuba and all that. He went to a couple grades in high school but he didn't finish. I quit after the third year, not so much be-cause of finances (my mother's a financial wizard, in fact) but because I wanted to. If I'm smart it's from talking to people, not writing or reading or math. I can add up a column of fig-ures, but I need all my fingers and toes. I've read books like *Oliver Twist* and *A Tale of Two Cities*, though. I don't read the newspapers, it's all the same stuff all the time. I'll watch TV. In fact my programs are on tonight, Adam 12 and Perry

Mason and Cannon. I like mysteries and musicals and anything to do with the police. I have a great respect for law. Even though I jaywalk and stuff like that I'm basically a very law-abiding person.

"My first job was as an operator in the telephone company, and it bored me to death, not being able to see the people I was talking to. I've done other stuff in between but nothing I cared about a lot. Now I work for this catering service that gives me waitress jobs at weddings and big parties. I serve food and drinks. I don't bartend, because barmaids have to be like truckdrivers and know how to handle six-foot drunks.

"If there's a fight in Dom's bar, though, I'm right in the middle, trying to calm it down, instead of in the corner where he wishes I'd be. He's protective, and he thinks I'm very gullible because I have a lot of faith in people. He's Italian and Polish, he's still got relatives in Poland. He was brought up in Ozone Park, and he has an adopted brother married to a Jew and a sister married to a Filipino who has multiple sclerosis. His parents burned to death in a fire.

"The guy Dom works with is a hypochondriac, and Dom's always covering for him. He worries more about that bar than the boss does. He don't like cursing there, either—that's one thing he can't stand—and he doesn't like me to be around when that happens. He's there at that bar until two-thirty, three-thirty, sometimes four in the morning. He drinks a lot himself, but he holds it well.

"You know what he looks like? He looks like a kewpie doll, you'll see. He's a supergreat man; you should hear how he listens to the troubles of everyone in that bar. He's a bank, he's a carry-home taxi service, he's a shrink, he's an everything. He's thirty-two, which is late for a man to marry, but I'm his first wife. He used to be a machinist for twelve years, but his temper got the better of him one day and he slugged his foreman, so that was the end of that job.

"When he gets mad he has a muscle that twitches in his cheek. Somebody else might not notice it, but I always do. I think knowing a person that well is really a part of loving. I never knew anyone so well before, and I only knew him six months when I married him. If nothing else it proves that there is such a thing as a good marriage and that if you be patient you *can* find someone who cares, no matter what happens.

"I have a great need to be needed, it's been a fault of mine all my life. I truthfully don't think I could make it on my own, without a man. I don't mean financially, I could make it all right financially, but emotionally.

"As far as Women's Liberation, I think it's dumb. Those women seem not to need men. What those women say they want and what they really want is two different things. A man's ego is really super, it's something you shouldn't play around with. These dumdums who want every single right a man has, to tell you the truth they look to me like dykes. They're weird; they're not feminine. They seem to be striving for a world without men, and if they get it, they're going to be sorry. What's so great about China and Russia, where everybody wears the same thing?

"I think a woman has much more chance of individuality than a man. You take twenty men, they all work at the same job and do the same thing all day, but twenty women—why, you can go into all their homes and every one of them will be differently decorated. Women can wear whatever they want and look different every day. I never felt I was missing any freedoms; lack of education hasn't stopped me from getting any jobs, and I don't think the men I worked with were paid any more, either, but maybe they *should* be, like in the catering men have to set up tables and do more work than we do.

"After all, a man don't ask much. He wants his dinner, he wants clean socks, what's wrong with that? And Dom, he likes me to look nice. I like nothing better than running around in dungarees and pajamas, but if we go out, I'll wear a dress.

"He wears dark glasses all the time, because he has ulcerated eyes. Nothing aggravates me more than when someone says to him, 'take off your glasses, I can't see your eyes.' People put too much emphasis on stuff like that. What's important about Dom is the way he treats me, and other people too. Generous? You ought to see: I ask him for potatoes and he brings me a fifty-pound sack. Ask him for a slice of watermelon, you get the whole thing.

"He's a very good-natured man most of the time. He's one for helping people, and he's very protective of me. When we're in public, he's in charge completely. He'll listen to my logic, if I make logic. If I think he's wrong, I'll wait until we get home before I tell him, because I don't want to embarrass him. If we're out and I do a booboo, I get a *look* from him that if looks could kill, forget it.

"Yeah, Dom's got cancer in the lungs and stomach. Oh, yeah, it's terminal; he's got about a year yet, but I figure you can store up a lot of memories in a year. He's not much for painkillers; he likes to keep active. He eats a good meal, even though he's not supposed to. He figures if he follows all the doctor's orders he may live another six months, but it would be very boring, so who needs it? He's a very heavy drinker; he can kill a bottle of Scotch in a day, easy. Not me, I get looped on less than a bottle.

"I'd like to have his child, because I've never found a man who deserves one more, but even though it would be nice not to be alone when he's gone, I don't want to stand by a grave with a baby in my arms. And he'd worry thinking how he wouldn't be here to see it raised. There's lots of things a father can do that a mother can't, like give the child strength and extra affection when the mother has to do the discipline. Besides, with a child where am I going to find another husband? And even if I had one I wouldn't want to go back to work and leave the child with a baby sitter and have him wonder who's Mom. 'I've got to face facts: each week Dom gets sicker—and if I had a miscarriage, I think that would cut my heart out.

"Abortion? I believe in it, but not at six months, maybe because I lost one of mine at six months. (I had two other miscarriages, too, at four months.) I'll give a woman three months not to notice—maybe she's busy—and one month to make the arrangements, but no more. I think if a woman's gone six months she should go the other three and give the baby up for adoption, because after six months it's not just something like a clot or cyst growing in you, it's more like a person.

"But first of all you shouldn't get pregnant in the first place, there's no excuse with fifty thousand contraceptives on the market. If you use two at a time like I do—I use pills and foam—

you have no excuse. I've been told to get off pills, but I won't, because when your husband gets romantic there's nothing worse than ruining the whole mood by running for a diaphragm.

"Our honeymoon was our only vacation. All we did was watch my brother's house while he took his vacation. Don't come here the second and third week in July, though, because we'll be together here then, and I'm hoping it'll be romantic. We like to stay home. We play cards, chess, checkers, and right now I'm working on a hooked rug, too, to put at the bottom of our bed. You like it? Well, it keeps me off the streets, anyway.

"How do I feel about what's happening to Dom? Well, I figure somebody's got to get a loser, right? If I get a loser, somebody else won't. I try like heck to reason things out, and I think I'd rather have him going this way than all of a sudden someday a knock on the door and some stranger saying, 'Sorry about that, lady.' I really don't know how I'll react when the time comes, but I'm getting used to picking up my marbles and going home."

On the way to the bar we noticed a spider on the inside windshield of my car. Arlene asked if we could please stop and get it out. "I wouldn't want you to kill it, but if there's one thing I really don't like, it's bugs. Dom says I have a special voice I use to scream for him to come and kill bugs or get them out."

The spider wasn't hard to get rid of, and then we went into the bar. It was dimly lit and convivial. I guess like most neighborhood bars are anywhere. Dom really did wear dark glasses and he really did look sort of like a kewpie doll; I could see what Arlene meant. When she told him I was Sharon from New Jersey, all he said was, "Oh, yeah, hi."

"I'm not coming home tonight," he said to Arlene.

"You're not?"

"Not until two-thirty."

"Good," she smiled. "I'm making you steak with wine sauce."

12

I Didn't Bring Enough Burnt Sienna

You wanted to fly in the daytime to Tucson, fifteen hundred miles farther west than you ever had been before, so that you could see the terrain from above. You have a special aversion, you said, to arriving in a new place after dark: you like to see what you're getting into. Fair enough. Since you are an artist or, as you sometimes put it, an *artiste,* we arrange to arrive in midafternoon. As our plane descends, you look down onto the desert and sigh.

"I didn't bring enough burnt sienna," you say.

Our trip is fraught with possibility. We have come this far to find out whether we can stand each other. We are here because, okay, you're right, it's true, in all these off-and-on years of our entanglement, I never have given you my whole attention. Always there has been somebody else around the corner, or waiting in the wings, maybe because I was afraid for there not to be. Maybe we've both been afraid it might work. At heart, perhaps, we don't want to trade our familiar, comfortable sighs of resignation for the strange new oxygen of hope.

But of late I have been having what some call fantasies, starring you. Having no idea whether you were still available, I counted to ten and took deep breaths and called you. You answered. After some nervous parrying about the *New Yorker*'s two movie critics—reading Penelope Gilliatt after Pauline Kael, you said, was like drinking a cool glass of champagne after slivovitz—it turned out you still were interested. We reunited. We talked anew of a possible joint future. We brushed this prospect off as if it were something from the attic, blowing the dust away, examining it. Might it work? A lot has happened; maybe we have changed for the better since the last time we gave up on each other. Our temperaments are flagrantly different, sure, but maybe that's good. Maybe with the new me around, you would be inspired to do more of your magnificent, tender landscapes. Maybe with the new you around I would uncoil and stop being so flippant and hectic. Might we after all forsake all others, cleave together, merge? On the chance that we might, we have made what, for two such wary people, is a serious emotional commitment. We have agreed that as soon as the semester is over and you stop teaching, we shall journey together to the West, where in all your five decades you never have been. A native New Yorker, a street kid grown up, your travels have been to Sussex and Tuscany and the valley of the Rhone, except for that one time in Iowa City. Now, since you have the whole summer off, you will accompany me to the West, where I have to go anyway in the course of my work.

We stay up late poring over the *Rand McNally Road Atlas*, humming songs from Woody Guthrie and imagining how it will be. We shall go out to where (as the postcard verse has it) the handclasp's a little stronger, out where the smile dwells a little longer—out where in public places you automatically get home fries and a twist of orange with your breakfast, where the gas station attendants are not sullen all day, where the vistas ought to make a painter's heart, such as your own, leap. And while your heart is leaping, while you perhaps are making sketches (you do such exquisite sketches, truly), I shall be gathering material for the book I am doing on our countrywomen. We've both got to do what we do, right? You, a reflective artist, will contemplate the scenery. I, a hyperactive journalist, will talk to women. Whatever happens between us will somehow be more valid than what has happened at home. For the constricting impasses of New York we shall trade the fresh new realities of the road, thereby discovering our true selves and, with luck, each other.

Oh, and you'll finish learning to drive. Since from Tucson onward we shall travel by rent-a-car, and since you say it isn't fair for me to have to drive all that way, you have actually hired Tony and Al, at the AAA Academy, to teach you enough to get a learner's permit. In so doing you have begun to overcome a lifetime phobia, to a standing ovation from all our friends, who join me in urging you to go the distance and get a license.

The fact that you don't drive obsesses me unprettily. I am not mollified to know that Vladimir Nabokov and Jules Feiffer don't drive either, or that Edmund Wilson couldn't. I forgive them, but I have too mean a spirit to forgive you. I am a willful, limited, grownup brat from Sangamon County, Illinois, and any man who aspires to be a man of mine had better be able to do a mean U-turn. Oh, I make a real metaphor of it. Driving means going where you want when you want—get it? —not having to rely on bus schedules or friends. What driving really mostly means, in the matter of you and me, is that I have an outsized fear of being, or even seeming to be, the one who is in charge.

"Come to think of it," you say at one point, "I can't recall ever seeing *you* with a needle in your hand."

"I can't sew."

"Why not? Sewing is womanly."

"Sure it is. That's what my mother used to say. She *was* good at it, and she was always trying to teach me, giving me little sewing kits and things. But somehow, for me, sewing is like playing tennis: I just can't do it." Accordingly, we are both disgraces to our genders. In an ideal picture of us as the perfect all-American duo, you would be sitting in the driver's seat, maybe whistling as you wove expertly into the far lane of a freeway at rush hour while I, beaming at your side, would be busy with my crewel embroidery. But although we fall far short of this idyllic vision, we claim to be willing to change, or try to. We agree that when we get to Tucson, which will be a sort of orientation week for our month together in the West, I will finish teaching you to drive.

My cousin Kathy, our hostess, thought this plan was really funny. She thought it was hilarious. "The Jane T. Howard Driving School? It would be as if I were to open up the Kathleen M. Jacobs School of Art Appreciation [she never had been much of a one for museums] or my father the Paul M. Mitchell Last-Minute Travel Agency."

"Or mine the Robert P. Howard Dance Studio."

"You could also, of course, consider the Jane T. Howard Remedial Tennis Clinic."

"Just as you could sponsor a series of Kathleen M. Jacobs Silent Retreats."

"What about the Marcus D. Hillel Academy of Optimism?"

"All *right,* girls," said Marcus, "I get the idea." On a drive the day before to the border town of Nogales, Marcus had fretted over what would happen if our car should break down on the giant, four-lane federal highway. He was pretty sure that it would and that nobody, well-traveled though that road was, would come to our rescue. Behind every silver lining, for him, there was always a cloud.

Tucson proper is not especially beguiling. It has a lot of orthopedic supply stores and a goodly number of people who are old and gray and full of sleep and nodding in the sun. But two things keep drawing me to its outskirts, time and again, on the slightest excuse. One is the sense of fresh welcome Kathy generates. "At last!" she always in effect says to me and all her other repeat visitors, "You've come! How have we ever survived since the last time you guys were here?" The other reason I go back is the look and feel of the place. The clarity of the air, the changing shadows on the Catalina Mountains, and the abundance and variety of cactuses have an instant tonic effect on me. I am no botanist, but the very names of the desert flora entrance me: cholla, ocatillo, brittlebush, saguaro. Joseph Wood Krutch and Edward Abbey and, most of all, my own senses persuade me that the desert here is anything but hostile. Besides, there are places where you can turn your head for 360 degrees and not see anything in the way of the works of the hand of man. From Kathy's house, until quite recently, you could only see one other.

It is Steve's house too, of course. It was he, after all, who was lured out here to work in the state university's Optical Sciences Center, who fathered, and who nightly bathes and sings to, Henry and Tom and Jane who reads to them: "Put on the pan, said Grrreeeedy Nan," who figured where to put the tennis court and the swimming pool and the greenhouse and who has caused so many flowers to thrive. It is he who plays the banjo of an evening, if he feels like it. If he doesn't, no matter how many guests are present, he is likely without a word of farewell to disappear to bed. Steve and I have come to know each other well enough to fight over what is left of a quart of Baskin-Robbins English Toffee, which is pretty well, but until you do know Steve you tend to think of the place more as Kathy's, because hers is the more forceful persona.

Kathy and I are not much alike. She was a champion figure skater in high school, who in her time has been paid to manage personnel for department stores and to teach infants to swim. Her sewing is legendary. When Angelita, who worked for the Jacobses, decided to get married, Kathy made her a silk-organza-over-double-taffeta wedding dress, appliqued with white Chantilly lace. I could no more do that than I could do open heart surgery. But she and I are not only second cousins and contemporaries, we also both grew up in what the *Tribune* used to call Chicagoland. For a year or so in New York, where she worked at Stern's and I clipped newspapers for *Life,* we were roommates on Perry Street. We saw each other through some ill-fated romances and some which, at least temporarily, seemed promising. She has never let me forget the time I invited a number of guests to dinner who got there before I did, "which gave *me*," says Kathy, "the opportunity to greet them and starting mixing the refreshments you had chosen which were, as I recall, mint juleps—and I had a *serious* hangover."

I am no less in her debt now, but she doesn't want to acknowledge such things. "Relationships with people," she says, "are my religion. That guest room in there saves my life. I sometimes think we ought to separate the boys, so that each of them could have his own room. Adjacent boys, somebody told me, are the most trying combination there is. But that would mean putting one of them in the guest room, and then we couldn't have Steve's friends from the department, or the grandmas, or you guys staying here. Having guests is what keeps me sane."

The Jacobs household rises early. Somewhere a rooster crows, and woodpeckers and flickers report to the feeding station right outside the window above the kitchen sink. Before Marcus and I are about, Kathy has begun a sour cream coffee cake, made a batch of cucumber soup, put the wash in, started the coffee, and packed a lunch bag for Steve, who meanwhile is saying "I'll *pork* you!" to one of his children. Ernst von Schlibberschlobber, the long-haired dachshund, cavorts about and overturns the garbage can, so that the forty or so sparerib bones we stripped clean last night litter and gum up the kitchen linoleum. No matter; Kathy has it fixed in a moment, and meanwhile, noticing that Marcus has lost a button from his shirt, she proceeds to sew it back on, before she addresses herself to a pile of a dozen or so pairs of kids' levis, in varying sizes, all in need of patching. When Steve has watered his garden, before he drives off to the campus, he and she go to the tennis court to volley for a while.

Kathy's mother and Steve's both worked when their children were young for, respectively, Planned Parenthood and the Children's Book Committee of the Child Study Association. Both estimable women, they were away from home a lot, in reaction to which, probably, Kathy seldom is. Maybe Jane will work when her children are small, if she has them. At the moment, aged not quite four, she is sitting on my lap and singing, "Oh Mrs. Grady, she was a lady, she had a daughter I adore . . ." as we drive up Mount Lemmon. We are driving up so that Marcus can observe the miraculous changes in botanical zones. Why is he not *kvelling?* Why does it matter to me in the least?

He has dared to suggest that to see one saguaro—*sir-wa-wa,* he persists in pronouncing it—is to have seen them all. He approves of the Arizona-Sonora Desert Museum, to which we go in the course of one of our driving lessons, but he is disappointed in Nogales, on the Mexican border.

"Kitschy," he calls it.

"You should see Tijuana," says Kathy. "Tijuana makes Nogales seem like Pocantico Hills."

Evenings there are banjos, guitars, and sangria. Kathy and I, at nobody's request, sing "In the Garden" and "That Great Speckled Bird." Marcus and Steve disappear. She tells me, during a walk we take by moonlight, that Steve had influenced her, programmed her, more than anyone or anything else ever. She lives to please him. No other man ever made her feel that way. She learned how much he mattered when he quit seeing her for a while, back in New York.

"I decided it would be therapeutic to go skiing alone in New Hampshire. Nobody else was in the place where I stayed except four or five carloads of Episcopalian young people. I couldn't stand being there, or anywhere, without him. Maybe I was destined to be a housewife." For myself, I wonder if I am destined not to be. I wonder if I could ever find the capacity for that much devotion. Maybe it's a gift, like being able to skate or sew.

Marcus says he likes the Jacobses, but that Kathy talks a lot and Steve is enigmatic and haven't I been gaining a bit of weight? Do we have to go to that Mexican place tonight? Will there be anything unspicy on the menu? What time are we going to eat? Not late, please God, like last night. He spends a morning writing postcards. It has been said of his postcards that they make the Lord's Prayer on the head of a pin look like skywriting. We have a long argument about probable postage rates to Europe. I am ashamed at my pettiness. He has brought imaginative presents for the children, whom he had never seen before we came here. He does not complain when, in the bathroom he and I share with them, the toilet goes unflushed and there is Crest on the towels and bathwater left in the tub. Can anyone say he is not a model guest? No, no one can. Is there any logical reason why he and I should feel quite so irked with one another? Probably not, but we slip dangerously back into our habit of diminishing each other.

"How many fights did you guys have between here and the post office?" Kathy says when we return from one of our driving lessons.

"Just two," says Marcus. "You ought to see Jane's knuckles. I'm not sure the blood will ever return to them."

That afternoon, starting to feel guilty about my unwritten book, I go into town alone to have some interviews. Marcus sunbathes, and Kathy sews. At dinner that night we all tell how we wish we could change ourselves. Steve says he wishes he could care more than he does about other people, or show it when he does. Kathy wishes she were smarter. Ginny, another guest, wishes she were more organized. I wish I had more direction. Marcus wishes he could understand profounder things.

For some reason he likens himself and me to Abe and Mary Lincoln. Having a strict constructionist view of that First Lady, I of course take offense. I am generally advised to be less petulant. To change the subject, I ask Ginny how she cut out the letters so evenly on the felt banner she has made for Kathy, which hangs in the kitchen. The banner says: IT IS THE TIME YOU HAVE WASTED ON YOUR ROSE THAT MAKES YOUR ROSE SO IMPORTANT.

"The letters aren't even at *all*," says Marcus. "What makes you think they're *even?* They're *crooked!*"

"Well, they're a lot evener than *I* could make them," I say.

"Actually," says Ginny, "they aren't *supposed* to be perfectly even." She is sure we both have a point. She is from the South, and tactful.

The road between Tucson and Phoenix is straight, uncomplicated, and not very interesting. Marcus drives, and ably, too. I switch the car radio on, hoping to hear a bit of Country Western, maybe a chorus of "Water Can't Quench The Fire Of

Love," or some superb line like ". . . you may be too much for Memphis, honey, but you're not enough for L.A." Marcus writhes and winces for a while and reaches down to switch the dial off, giving a discourse on the cultural poverty of the American interior. A while later, since it is high noon and we are in the desert, I switch on the air-conditioner. He writhes again.

"Would you mind not turning that thing on?" he asks. "It seems unnatural."

"Fine," I say. "We'll just sweat. It's probably not quite in the hundreds yet." Miss Technology, Miss Detroit, that's me. Oh dear. Some of the best conversations of my life have been in cars, on long trips like this one. There is something freeing about being encapsulated and uninterrupted, something conducive to the heights of humor and depths of gravity that separate good talk from blather about logistics. I guess I had hoped that Marcus and I would have such conversations on the open roads of America. I guess we aren't going to.

I am at the wheel at dusk, when we get to the Grand Canyon. I drive past several Outlook Points, trying to find one which will give the most spectacular view of the setting sun. Marcus seethes: he is afraid it will be dark before I stop. I finally do. We get out and stare down the south rim. I know exactly what he is going to say, and he does not disappoint me.

"That," he announces, "is a *big* mother." He cannot see enough of it. The next day we are both happy. He makes sketches of the canyon. I ask why he didn't do sketches in Tucson, knowing I sound like some parody of a production-oriented member of the Nixon administration but unable to help myself. He says he didn't feel like it. It pleases me immoderately to see him engaged in a pursuit of his own. I ask if he would like to stay here a couple of extra days while I go on ahead to Los Angeles, where I shall be busy with a lot of appointments. I have a foreboding he isn't going to like Los Angeles. Oh no, he says, he'll come along with me. He doesn't want to stay here alone, or take the bus.

Something about Prescott, Arizona, through which we pass on our way to Los Angeles, enchants me at first sight. I am smitten with the courthouse square and its big old trees and the men sitting around on park benches. I love the lady who waits on us in the coffee shop and am tempted when a man in cowboy boots whom we talk to there suggests we stay on that night for a street dance. Marcus says he will if I really want to, but that we ought to get going. Prescott seems just another town to him.

Since I am expected in Los Angeles Monday morning, and this is Saturday night, I agree that we should proceed. We look for a motel reputed to have old-world Spanish charm in the border town of Blythe. Nobody is there to let us in, so we stay instead in a franchised place right on the highway, hearing the traffic all night. Our waitress at the adjacent Denny's, which never closes, is named Donna. She has moved here from San Diego, she tells us, because the job market isn't so good down there. A quartet of Mexican bridesmaids and their dates sit down next to us.

As we head relentlessly westward on U.S. 60, I grow more fidgety about the juxtaposition of Marcus and Los Angeles. That place can unsettle me enough when I go there alone; how am I going to handle it with the most discerning companion in the Western world at my side? Eager for distraction from this train of thought, I feign more excitement than I feel at the sight of signs pointing to the Joshua Tree National Monument, within which, I recall hearing somewhere, were amazing botanical wonders.

"Okay, why not?" agrees Marcus. "We might as well have a look." But the place is very much bigger than we had expected it to be, and harder to figure out. We stop to ask some questions of a U.S. Ranger, "a very proper Randolph Scott goy guide," Marcus later calls him, who shows us a chart and tells us that the actual Joshua trees are quite a distance away. Marcus is at the wheel. After he drives a short way he stops. Soon we are deep in another argument, our best to date, or our worst. My position is—Resolved: that there probably *is* enough gas in this rent-a-car (whose fuel gauge is out of order) for us to get all the way through this interesting and important horticultural shrine.

Marcus took the negative. Certain that the gas tank could

hold but a few drops more, he instead evoked an image like the last scene in "Greed," of the two of us stranded in the cruel, parching desert with no sustenance other than half a pack of Wint-O-Green Life Savers. They wouldn't last long. We would perish of thirst, unnoticed by Rangers or fellow tourists. Only vultures would find us. Cremation would be unnecessary.

"Oh, come on, look," I said, "there's a car right over there. *It* would stop for us if we broke down."

"But why should we break down?" he asked. "I'm not sure we have time to go through here, anyway."

"I thought that as long as you were out there you'd want to see things you couldn't see in the East or anyplace else."

"Of course I want to, but what if . . ."

"Oh, all right," I sighed dramatically. "I don't care. Turn the car around and let's get back on the superhighway."

"I'm not going to," he said. "I'm going to prove that I've got as much balls as you have."

"Excuse me?" I said. "Did you say balls?"

"You heard me," he replied. With that I took my folded cotton sun hat and hit him on the arm. "Don't you ever *dare* to strike me again," he said with something new and terrible in his voice.

"Well you struck *me* with your words," I said, and began to cry.

What if he was right? What if I was coming across as one of those coarse, tough bitches of whom someone had said, "Boys will be boys these days and so, apparently, will girls"? Maybe it was true, as I once had heard someone else observe, that "men and women snipe at each other because they no longer need each other, which is why it's so appalling for the word 'ballsy' to be applied to women. All that word really means is that a woman's got presence."

Some presence I had, sobbing there in the desert. Marcus got out of the car and stalked off into a cholla grove for a bit. Then he came back to tell me it was nice there and that I should have a look too. I did, and caught a cactus spine in the canvas part of my tennis shoe. He hugged me and said he was sorry. I said I was too. Our fight, I suggested, probably had nothing to do with Joshua trees. Probably not, he agreed, and made a joke about Jews in the desert and Exodus. We never did see the rare and fabled upstretched arms of the forty-foot tall trees, a branch of the lily family according to our *Mobil Travel Guide*. To be safe we turned off at the next sign pointing toward a town which happened to be Twenty-nine Palms. A newly discharged female Marine, tending the pump at the first gas station we came to, confirmed Marcus' suspicion that our tank was all but empty. She was saving money to get her own car out of hock, she told us as she wiped the windshield, so that she could drive on home to Maine. Meanwhile, if we liked that sort of thing, there were some really mellow dog races around these parts. Thanks, we told her, but we had to head on West. Briefly whistling "The Halls of Montezuma," we proceeded, detouring at Palm Springs, where the fabulous homes of the superstars somehow depressed us. We had pastrami sandwiches at a place called Sherman's, where the waitresses were all bored and rude. We stopped next at a flamboyant place off the highway where dates and figs were sold to load up on Macadamia nuts. And then, since it was getting late and there weren't any more excuses, we continued toward Los Angeles.

13

The Only Man in the Polo Lounge with a Learner's Permit

The Beverly Hills Hotel is a sumptuous pink monument set off Sunset Boulevard by an imposing horseshoe drive. You don't park your own car there, attendants do it for you. Inside the corridors have jungle foliage wallpaper, and if records show you to have been a guest there before, you will find a basket of fruit when you first reach your room with a "Welcome Back!" card from the manager. The desk is good about messages and whenever you pick up the phone in your room the switchboard operator greets you by name. The orange juice is expensive but obscenely delicious. All over the premises you see lithe, bronzed, gilded people with unlikely teeth, standing around oozing importance, paging each other at poolside and having phones plugged in at their tables in the Polo Lounge so they can call New York. Once I did that myself. When I would go to Los Angeles for *Life,* to do stories on people like Jacqueline Susann, a room would always be booked for me at the Beverly Hills.

I had not planned on staying there with Marcus. Intuition told me that with him I should stay in some modest place right on the ocean, so that he could swim or sunbathe, if he wanted to, while I was off working. This was the week in which I would pay for my part of our trip, and I would have plenty to do. Besides two magazine assignments, I hoped to gather some material for my book on women. While I was doing all this, Marcus and I had agreed, he would discover the city for himself. Since I would need our rent-a-car he would get around by public transportation. It was more or less true that nobody we knew had ever known anyone, socially, who ever had taken a bus in Los Angeles, but so much the better: his forays would be the stuff of anecdotes. He was and is, among other things, a skilled raconteur. Anyway, had he not thus explored Vienna and Rome and Edinburgh and any number of other cities? Was he not the compleat tourist?

Maybe, if he gave Los Angeles a chance, he would even like it. A lifetime movie addict, he could steep himself in the mystique of Hollywood. A painter, he could assess the museums and galleries. A committed *nosher,* he could compare the Farmer's Market with Zabar's and Balducci's. Meanwhile, we had to hurry up and find a place to stay. The Santa Monica motel where we had made reservations, out of the *Mobil Travel Guide,* turned out to be seedy, which was why I was telling Marcus about the Beverly Hills.

"It *is* a legendary place," I told him. "Staying there is sort of a sociological experience, even if it isn't on the Pacific. Since I'll be on expense account, maybe we ought to stay there after all."

"You know I'm a bed and breakfast man at heart," he said. "But if you say so, okay, let's go there."

Before we could sign in at the Beverly Hills, I had to pull the car over on a side street and slip a dress on over my shorts.

"Jesus," said Marcus, "you'll be arrested for indecent exposure."

"I'm not taking anything *off*," I told him, "I'm *adding* a layer. I don't think I've ever seen anybody checking in there wearing shorts." Nor could I recall ever, there or anywhere, being the one of a couple to register for a hotel room. I was feeling, you might say, skittish.

"The gentleman?" asked the hotel clerk as I signed in. Marcus, standing off to one side, was obviously with me.

"He's my, uh, friend," I said, with all the savoir faire of a 4-H Club member on her first trip to the state capitol.

"It might have been a little more clever, dear, to say I was your *husband,* give them my name too, and say you used your maiden name professionally," Marcus said as we inspected our ominously posh corner room on the second floor.

"I guess you're right," I admitted as I stepped out onto our own private balcony. "Do you like palm trees?"

"Those out there are quite handsome, in a certain way."

"I don't like them. They've never seemed real to me. They remind me of overbred poodles. They look fake."

"Real trees are supposed to lose their leaves and shiver naked in the rain, huh?"

"Yes, all that Joyce Kilmer stuff."

"And you say *I'm* the negative, critical one?" asked Marcus. "Come on, let's have a drink." In addition to the balcony and a fireplace we had a little kitchenette, in whose cute icebox we could keep our Boissiere. One of the few things we never disputed was that all other brands of dry vermouth were swill compared with Boissiere. We sat down and had a drink, and I pretended to forget the advice I had got back in New York from my friend Snowflake.

"Let me get this straight," Snowflake had said. She is famous for her intuitions. "You're going out West with a man who has never been there before? You're interested in him, and you expect to get some work done at the same time?" I nodded. "Doesn't sound too promising," Snowflake said. "I'd say either do your work and meet the man later, or concentrate on him, but don't try to do both at once." Ah Snowflake, I should have listened to you.

"Hey," I said when I returned to our hotel room a couple of nights later, after an interview in Pasadena, "have you been watching the election returns? McGovern won the primary, and he hasn't even been assassinated."

"Rlmph," said Marcus, who had fallen asleep with the light on. "Good for him."

"Sorry to wake you up."

"That's all right."

"I tried to call you this afternoon. What'd you do today? Swim?"

"It was too cold. Wasn't it cold where you were?"

"No, in Compton it was hot, hot and smoggy. The smog never seems to lift there. Where did you go, then?"

"The County Art Museum. Not a bad collection. You've seen it, haven't you?"

"I've always meant to go there, but . . ."

"In all the trips you've made to this city you've never once been to the County Art Museum?" Now Marcus was fully awake.

"As I say," I called from the bathroom, "I've meant to."

"But these sociological trends you write your stories about keep you pretty busy, huh?"

"You put it so graciously."

"Sorry," he said. "How was the woman you talked to this evening?"

"She was a sixteen."

"A what?"

"That's how the Bank of America categorizes its employes, by numbers. It's so personal and nice. The president of the bank is a thirty, and file clerks are ones, and my new friend Betty is a sixteen."

"I assume she doesn't *like* being a sixteen?"

"She's got a law degree and a *summa cum laude* in math, and she's forty-four years old with a lot of experience, and in the five years she's been there, they haven't given her one promotion."

"How come she doesn't split and find some other job?"

"Because she has this uncanny loyalty to the bank. She wants to help change it from within."

"Will she fit into the article you're doing?"

"I hope so," I said.

"I don't see how you'll ever get it done," he said.

"Thanks."

June, everyone said, is considered the worst month of the year in Southern California. The weather was wretched, and so were my spirits. I filled several notebooks with the minor key plaints of women whom society had neglected and abused. In turn I neglected and abused the man I came home to, if you could call the Beverly Hills our home. True enough, Marcus had his share and more of shortcomings, but I in my insecurity chose to focus glaring light on these, instead of being charitable. One of the things that had drawn us together at first, several years back, had been our congenial humor, but these days we rarely laughed. We were either elaborately polite with one another, or openly mean, perhaps because proximity scared us.

Mornings we would lie there on the rug of our extravagant hotel room, each doing exercises, somehow not companionably. I did a series meant to fight off fat and sloth, to the dulcet, tape-recorded voice of a Viennese physiotherapist: "Right arm and left leg *together* . . . and enough." Marcus went through a series for a bad back. He had a bad back and a bad knee. Indigestion troubled him. I summoned compassion. He also had a sore on the roof of his mouth, which probably was a sign of the most dreaded of maladies. And what could it mean, he asked, that he felt so tired all the time? I tried to banish it, but it kept coming back, that vision of myself as an unlicensed practical nurse to an elderly grouch—a role for which I felt about as suited as I would have been to conduct the Chicago Symphony doing Mahler's Fourth. I was mean-spirited. We both knew women of about my age who were devoted, happily, to men older than Marcus ("*even* older," he would say), but somehow their example seemed not to apply. He talked a lot about his infirmities. He also talked a lot about mine, which were mostly psychic and spiritual.

"Maybe we were wrong," he said at one point, "to take this show on the road. It's not a realistic experiment."

"I'm afraid it is, though," I said. "What's being revealed, what hurts so much, is the difference in our temperaments. My temperament comes from the compulsive Protestant work ethic. Yours is to . . ."

"To be a *schlemiel?* A parasite?"

"Your blazer looks nice," I said, trying to change the subject.

He had bought it just for the trip. It was navy blue, with brass buttons. He hadn't wanted to get the brass buttons, because he thought they looked too military, but a lot of us told him it looked better that way.

Betty, the sixteen, was suing the bank she worked for. This was as alarming as it would have been for her dogs Phaida and Burgermeister, the only other occupants of her spacious house, to bite her hand. Many of her colleagues at the bank had ostracized her; clearly her bosses would have rejoiced if she just gave up and quit. When she told her midwestern father that she had joined in a lawsuit against her employers he was as worried as he had once been years earlier, when she broke an engagement.

"The way I was raised, you always remembered to be thankful for what you had, no matter what you didn't have," Betty said the evening she and I talked. "That's why I haven't been militant in the women's movement up until now. But now I go to work every morning with a sense of dread. Somebody at the office advised me, 'Look, for the sake of your friends here, don't be too friendly, because friendship with you could be a handicap.'" Such a remark was like throwing acid in the face of Betty, who delights in having annual house parties every Rose Bowl weekend and who goes out of her way to make a cake if she finds out it's somebody's birthday.

"All my working life," she sighed, "I've been told, 'You're doing great, but we can't give that promotion to a woman.' What am I supposed to do, go to Sweden and get a sex change operation?"

Every day while we were in Los Angeles I was to drive for nearly two hours, over a complex labyrinth of freeways, to get to a certain home-economics classroom in a certain high school in the forlorn town of Compton. The girls in this class, mostly from welfare families, were being exposed to a program on vocational guidance, organized by a team of vivacious social workers from the YWCA. The program, its director said, was "geared to go against the American mania for testing and self-fulfilling prophecies. Tell a young kid she's too dumb to achieve anything, and she'll believe you." The social workers had a lot of tricks and paraphernalia: a wheel of fortune, games, skits, improvisational dramas.

They had presented this same program in other similar high schools all over Area Code 213, they told me, with stunning results. They had changed the courses of a number of young lives. This week, however, their magic wasn't working. Perhaps because it was the last week of the school year, the home ec students were much more interested in other things. Fewer and fewer of them came to class each day, and on Thursday the class was cancelled altogether. I called the magazine editor in New York who had assigned me this story to say things looked bad. She asked if I'd like to do another piece, instead, on the battered child syndrome.

What I remember about the abortive YWCA program was the passion in the voice of Jeanne Scott, its director. It was clear that she really cared what happened to the girls in that home ec class, and other girls like them. "The Greeks," she said, "were a lot kinder about it: they threw girls in the river when they were born and that was it. What boils me is that as much as we claim to love children in this country, those in power put every possible obstacle in front of children who happen to be female.

"I tried to get a job for one darling twenty-three-year-old I work with, under the Manpower Development Training Act, but it turned out she wasn't eligible. For one thing, she's over twenty-two. For another, she makes just a bit too much money to be classified as 'disadvantaged'. They asked me, 'Is she an ethnic minority? Is she a criminal? Is she handicapped?'

"'No,' I told them, 'but maybe I could push her down the stairs, if that would help.'"

Once, over egg-salad sandwiches in a Compton luncheonette, Jeanne told me how she used to be a nun. "I was aghast, when

173

I first got into the convent, to hear the other girls' stories about how they got the call. Call? I didn't know what they were talking about. I'd never had any sort of emotional call at all."

"Then why did you join?" I asked her.

"The only other option I had was marriage," she said, "and I didn't like what I'd seen of marriage in my own family. The way I was brought up, an unmarried career girl was the work of the devil."

"I think, for myself, that I'd rather be called almost anything than a career girl," I said.

"How about career *gal?*"

"You're right," I said. "That *is* worse." The difference between a career and a job, I read somewhere, is that a career means unguaranteed risks and long-term decisions. Well, so does living.

"Anyway," said Jeanne, "I was a basket case when I changed from Mrs. God to Miss Scott. I guess that's why I'm so concerned about these girls. The establishment's attitude about welfare is, 'She must be dumb or she wouldn't be poor, so why should we send *her* to college? Why give *her* any training that would require any intelligence?' "

"Maybe," I suggested, trying to save my story, "I could go to the homes of one of these welfare girls in the class? Maybe I could sort of try to absorb the texture of the life in Compton?"

"That wouldn't work," said Jeanne. "They'd assume you were a Women's Libber. Women's Lib isn't big in places like this. To the matriarchs of Compton, it seems derisive and threatening."

Matriarchs, it appeared, were everywhere. Consider those great-aunts of mine out in Pomona. They all have outlived their husbands or menfolk, and they all still have brown hair, even though the youngest of them was born in 1896. They live in the house they inherited from their parents, among massive pieces of carved walnut furniture, a Rogers sculpture called "The Scholar," and a piano with an open hymnal.

It strikes me, of course, that I ought to go call on these

women at that shrine in Pomona, but just now I don't think they and I would ask each other the right questions. I feel too distracted. Not, God knows, that they don't mean well; a better-intentioned household would be hard to find, anywhere. I thought of the time when I came out here to do the piece on Jackie Susann, whose husband had mused, on the way toward Malibu one afternoon, that, "I like to live life from the left-hand side of the menu, and Jackie does, either."

The day after that, Jackie was due for an autographing party at the Pickwick Bookstore on Hollywood Boulevard. Now nobody seriously doubted that a crowd of adulators would materialize spontaneously, for the sake of the *Life* photographer, but it might not hurt to be sure. When I suggested that I might produce a few relatives for this purpose, everyone in the Susann entourage was pleased. All it took was one phone call, to Aunt May in Manhattan Beach. (Pomona is by no means the only stronghold of my Southern California kin.) May rounded up three sporting great-aunts an uncle and a cousin, none of whom otherwise probably would have read *Valley Of The Dolls*.

"Gadding" is an activity esteemed by these aunts of mine. They are a peripatetic lot. Marguerite, known as Peg, is the champion gadder of them all, having ventured on her own across the Atlantic and never once missed a field trip of the Bs & Ps—the Business and Professional Women—when she lived in New York. From her quarters in "a kind of a club" up near Columbia University, she daily rode the IRT to and from her job at the Brooklyn Navy Yard. I suppose you think I went to see her as often as I might have.

Aunt Frances sleeps out on the screened porch in Pomona, and will not hear of having curtains there, because curtains would obstruct her view of the trees. "Wave on the pine trees," she once wrote me in a letter. "They always wave back." When Les, her husband, died, she wanted to stay on alone up where they had lived together, in Placerville, but it was decreed that she should return instead to the ancestral home. It was not good to live alone; had she not read about the woman across the street who was found dead after four days?

"But I *like* being alone," Aunt Frances said a bit wistfully. At present she is the household's official correspondent. "Lois and Peg don't get along," she once said, "because they're both Capricorns. We try to move Gracie, to change her position every hour or so, but she stays in there and does her paintings. At ninety-seven she looks not a day over eighty. She has a new kind of medium, crayon and oil, that doesn't need a fixative. She's as keen as ever at cards—'I cheated,' she said after a solitaire game, 'and I'm *still* losing.' "

"Far out," said our friend Luther. "Think of it, Marcus, the only man in the Polo Lounge with a learner's permit." We were having dinner with Luther and his wife Gwen in an Italian place on Sunset, and Marcus was telling of his adventures with public transportation. He had transferred with bravura from one bus to another that morning, making his way to Farmer's Market, which he pronounced excellent. Never, he said, had he met more courteous bus drivers. His only regret, he told us as we ordered zabaglione, was having allowed a Zionist, pro-Nixon barber on Fairfax Avenue to cut off rather too much of his hair.

"You should have seen the way Marcus's hair was starting to look," I said to Luther and Gwen. "It was thick and luscious."

"A bit too Ben-Gurion, though," said Marcus. "But it'll grow back. It'll be *perfect,* you know what I mean?" He was making a determined effort, it was clear, not to be negative. "Hey, guess what else I did? I paid homage to the footprints at Grauman's Chinese Theatre! Quite a thrill, for a kid from Eighty-ninth and First."

"If you'd like to have a tour of one of the studios," said Luther, who was writing a screen treatment, "we could lay that on for you."

"Thanks," Marcus said, "but the only thing of that nature I'd really like would be to meet Jimmy Cagney."

"So would I," said Gwen, "but who knows how to do that?"

"These zinnias are magnificent," I said to Gwen and Luther. "It was great of you to bring them to us."

176

"It *was* thoughtful of them," Marcus said later as we drove homeward along Sunset Strip, "but how come they didn't invite us to see their house itself?"

"Maybe their house was a mess," I said. "After all, they just got back from Mexico. Maybe they just didn't want to. There are times when I don't feel like having people over, either."

"Still," he said, "it gave me an odd feeling."

"Look over there," I told him. "See those sort of gable roofs? That's the Chateau Marmont, where I once lived for three months."

"Maybe we should have stayed there instead of the Beverly Hills."

"Maybe so, but I didn't think you'd like being right here on the Strip."

"It's a weird phenomenon, all right," said Marcus. "To tell you the truth, I don't know what you see in it."

"I don't recall ever saying it was pretty," I told him. "But as American thoroughfares go, it's about as vital and revealing a one as any I can think of. Look at the energy of it."

"I suppose so," he said, "if what you're interested in is history, or sociology, or the future."

"And you're *not* interested in those things?" I asked. "I guess you're really not, are you? Wow: you're ruling out a lot." I couldn't help myself: since we weren't far from home, I reached down to turn on the car radio. After half a minute he switched it off. The ensuing spat did honor to neither of us.

"Silence is intolerable to you, isn't it?" asked Marcus.

"Yeah, right," I said. "That's why I once spent two months doing a piece on it. I like an occasional cantata and madrigal too, you know," I reminded him pompously, "but it also nourishes my soul to keep abreast of the Top Forty once in a while."

"Your soul," he said, "is so wonderfully protean."

The song we heard a bit of, before he turned the radio off, was my personal Number One favorite that summer, for its high *schmaltz* content. It was the wail of a rejected suitor, whose loved one would not even deign to talk to him on the telephone. It went, in part: ". . . Sylvia's mother says Sylvia's tryin' to start a new life all her own. . . ."

Sylvia, I thought, and everybody else. At least everybody else in Greater Los Angeles.

"I can't wait until Brandace gets old enough to give me some really good advice," Karol Hope was telling me over Eggs Benedict in the hotel restaurant, the next morning, as Marcus slept late in our room. "At eight and a half she's doing pretty well already. She's amazingly grown-up. She wishes a man would come along that we both liked at the same time, and I guess that's what I wish, too."

But Karol, who is six feet tall, has a number of other wishes. "The new culture we're trying to create," she said, "seems drastic to those who guard the traditions we're trying to get away from. Even the women's movement is only slowly becoming aware of single mothers. What we're essentially trying to do is to make our lives more than just a foggy limbo between one heavy relationship with a man and another."

When Karol Hope says "we," she is talking about 250,000 other single mothers—one doesn't say "unwed mothers because some of them have been wed,"—in Los Angeles, and more than seven million others in the rest of the country. *Momma,* a magazine Karol conceived and edits, was founded to meet the needs of these mothers, most of whom are divorced and a few of whom are widowed. These needs concern welfare, jobs, housing, child care, and a lot more sociability than is readily to be found in cities like Los Angeles.

"In other cultures," Karol said, "single moms aren't isolated, but in ours they are. I think fewer and fewer people are going to have kids, as they find out all that being a parent involves. It's really hard to be a single mom in a city like this. There's so little sense of community. The ideal way would be to go to a bar or coffee house on Monday night where you could meet somebody you could be sure you'd see there again on Wednesday."

"If there were a place like that in my own neighborhood," I said, "I'd go there all the time. If only we had pubs like the Irish, or cafés like the French, where you could just sit for as long as you wanted to, alone or with other people, and read, or talk, or sing, or whatever."

"Bars here are especially unsatisfying," Karol said, "because the social expectation is that if you're a divorced woman you're on the make, and you have to spend all your time and energy letting people know you don't want to be approached. It's really hard, in a transient place like this, to build up the kind of slow, solid friendship you might have a lot more easily in other places."

"How come you live here, then?"

"Because of the innovations, the imagination, the openness. It's such a change from the authoritarian way I was raised. Sometimes I wonder if I'll end up in a mental institution, for having stepped so far from the mainstream."

"Were you ever really *in* the mainstream?"

"I had a church wedding," said Karol, "and I wore all the things my mother wanted me to wear. I was afraid that if I didn't marry this man, he would split or pull away. I really married him because I was into getting out of the house, and I was afraid to hurt his feelings." There was a time, I remembered, when I almost had done that myself.

"What attracted you to him?" I asked her.

"He represented adventure, excitement, do-it-a-different-way-ness. He'd been married before, he was ten years older, six inches taller—for the first time in my life I could wear heels—and he was very powerful in my life. I listened to him a great deal, and I guess he liked me because I was young and enthusiastic. At that point—I was nineteen—I was incredible, tragically unaware of relationships, love, and how marriage really could be. What scared me was confronting him with how I really felt. We were married for four years, and like so many of us, I walked into that life-style without knowing what I was doing."

"What do you think the answer is?" I asked Karol. "Communes?"

"Not exactly. I studied communes in anthropology, and there are two things that make or break them: enough space so that everyone can be alone, and honesty, so that people really can say where they're at and how they really do feel, as opposed to how they ought to.

"Single mothers," she said, "are forever being told how they *ought* to feel about things. We always live under the burden of someone else's expertise. Scientists, churches, psychologists, parents, teachers, whoever's around, everyone tells us what to do. Still, we feel total responsibility for the care and well-being of kids. It's amazing what effect it can have on your energy to know you can't possibly say to someone else, 'Here, *you* take over for ten minutes.'

"It's scary, but single mothers have an overwhelming necessity to survive. There's a lot of consciousness-raising going on, and a lot of single mothers are starting to reject the pressure they've always had, especially in ethnic communities and in suburbs, to be linked up with a man—any old man will do— just for the sake of the landlord."

"What'd you talk about at breakfast?" Marcus asked when I went back to our room.

"Oh," I said, "the problems of mothers who don't have husbands."

"What about men whose women are never on the scene?"

I looked at him and said nothing. A short while later I was due at another high school, to talk with a seventeen-year-old girl named Darnella. The appointment had been arranged by Jeanne Scott of the YWCA, and I didn't feel I could cancel it. Darnella, who had a husband and a two-year-old son, was one of the girls whose horizons had been expanded by the vocational guidance program.

"My mother, she used to make me go to catechism," Darnella said, "and I'd ask the nuns questions like why we born, and who is God, and how come I'm going to die, and stuff like that, and the nuns would say: you too young to want to know about stuff like that, wait until you're older. Well, now I'm older."

Darnella's husband was a cashier in a linoleum company, who worked evenings as a custodian in a school. Their son stayed with her father while Darnella was in school. "I get to the door after school, my father's there waiting with him; he say, 'Here he is, he's your baby, now *you* take him.' My sister used to be the one who took care of him, but she got into one of those new gangs, so now she not around so much."

"Gangs a big thing around here?"

"Yeah, they starting up. There's this gang of girls called the Cripettes. They be doing bad stuff, like they pull your hair out, set you on fire, take your purse. They go with the Crips. The Crips are the ones killed a boy at the Hollywood Palladium. They're at Washington, Horace Mann, Henry Clay, John Muir, Bethune. The Crips do the killing, the girls be doing the stabbing. There's the Hoover Groovers, too, at Fifty-fourth and Hoover, but that's a lot of big talk and no do. And there's the Blackstone Rangers."

"I'm in a gang," said another girl in Darnella's class. "I'm in the Thorsen gang. We stab my mother, with words."

"She just jiving," said Darnella.

Marcus loves all bodies of water. He was happy that we were invited to dinner with some friends who lived right on the ocean in Malibu. He was not happy, however, when he met one of our fellow guests. Her name was Hedy, and she was what was coming to be known as a Movement Heavy.

"It's disheartening to be an activist," Hedy said over the artichokes, "because right now there *is* no movement."

"Can you be serious?" asked Marcus, who was the only man at the table of eight with a jacket and tie. "The movement is all I ever hear about."

"What you're hearing about," Hedy told him, "are the *results* of the movement." She wore a black and white striped caftan and held her cigarette between thumb and forefinger. "By now the movement is in every woman's heart, and there's more cultural change all around us than any of us ever anticipated."

"I suppose you've been involved with that speculum business?" asked Marcus. "Girls sticking plastic things up themselves?"

"I was for a while," said Hedy, regarding him coolly, "but I didn't like the way the self-help groups were going, politically. I'm more into sociology. The *timing* was way off with the self-help clinics. Two years ago, they would have been fantastic."

"What did you do *before* you got into the movement?" I asked Hedy.

"Oh, I was a typical faculty wife. I did all the usual entertaining, but I never had anything *like* the fun and hard work I'm having now. I wouldn't *dream* of getting out of the movement."

"Where's the movement going next?" our host asked later, as he was pouring brandy.

"Women now have got to push into a really political dimension," Hedy said. "And we've got to do it in a positive way. The next thrust will be a sort of organizational period."

"Thrusting," muttered Marcus, "used to be thought of as a man's work."

She just looked at him. "Now that we've described the problems," she said, "now that we understand what we want, we've got to go out into the community and get it, because it'll never be given to us."

"*What'll* never be given to you?"

"Basically," said Hedy, "I always come from the concept that women should control and stabilize the birth rate. On this issue I'm almost matriarchal. The movement is fragmenting now, and the new organization will be in terms of more politically assertive groups, organized around the issues."

Marcus, who is not especially fond of dogs, led our hosts' Schnauzer out onto the patio. Undaunted, Hedy continued.

"In the past year," she said, "there's been a fantastic change in the consciousness of professional women. They're starting to organize now. The ones who used to say, 'I made it; why can't you?' are showing a new kindness to each other. They're identifying, and that's a *lot* of progress."

For a long time, as we drove southward toward the hotel, Marcus said nothing.

"She did go on some, didn't she, that Hedy?" I said.

"Some of what she said even made sense," he replied, "but in the whole evening I can't recall a single *instant* of humor or levity from that woman."

"How'd you like the food?" I asked.

"In general I'd give it an eight," he said, which was almost immoderate praise.

"Did you notice the artichokes?"

"What about them?"

"You *didn't* notice them. Well, that says something. Liza cut the tops of her artichokes off squarely, just the way I did that night when we had the Alfreds to dinner. When *I* cut them off, you publicly denounced them at the table in front of four other people, saying it was an outrage to ruin their beautiful shape that way. You'd have thought I was tearing down the Frick Museum to build a swinging singles' high-rise."

"Oh, baby, baby," he said, as he reached to stroke my hair, "You can hold a grudge, can't you? That was a month ago."

"Yes," I said. "I know it was."

The next afternoon we checked out of the Beverly Hills and stayed in Redondo Beach with my friend Bonnie, the one who sometimes phones me late at night. She urged us to join her and her date in a tour of their favorite bars, but we declined, and baby-sat instead for her six-year-old son, Terry. Terry climbed all over Marcus and begged him to play catch and any other game he could think of. Bonnie's door was closed the next morning, so I made some coffee and wrote her a note while Marcus and Terry played a last quick game of catch. When we drove away, Terry looked downcast.

We drove off to see the Watts Tower, that splendid mosaic masterwork of broken china and old Seven-Up bottles which it took the obsessed immigrant artist Simon Rodia thirty-three years to complete.

Oh Simon Rodia, I thought, may your spirit be reborn. We could all use somebody who knows what to do with shards and fragments.

14

Area Code 415

"Now *this*," said Marcus as we drove north on U.S. 1, "is my idea of California."

"Yes, this is the kind of day people write songs about."

"And the kind of landscape, and seascape. No wonder Big Bill Hearst put his monstrosity up on that hill."

"You know what else we ought to stop and have a look at?"

"Esalen? I wouldn't mind seeing that place, after reading and hearing so much about it. But will they let us in? Don't they have a problem with curious tourists sneaking around?"

"We're not tourists. I'm an old grad—I've been there, after all, five or six times. If we just act casual, it'll be okay. I don't think you'll want to wear your cord jacket on the grounds there, though."

"You mean there isn't a whole lot of emphasis on clothes?"

"Well, *some* people there wear them. Oh, listen, I know what we have to do when we get there! Have massages!"

"Pretty terrific, huh?"

"My dear, an Esalen massage is to your standard well-meant backrub as—"

"As Bach's B Minor Mass is to a chorus of 'Happy Birthday To You'?"

"I knew you'd come up with the right analogy."

"It sounds X-rated."

"But it's not sexual, it's spiritual."

"They massage your *spirit?*"

"In a sense, yes."

"Oh, my mystical little flower child. Well, I guess we can both use a little dissolving of tensions."

Sometimes Esalen's masseuses and masseurs were booked solid for days in advance, but we were lucky. Bridget could take Marcus at three, and Gary could fit me in at three-thirty. As we waited, we sat sunbathing on the lawn, much landscaped since I had been there last, and listened to flute music as we looked out at the sea. After a time we walked down the path to the cinder-block bathhouse, where the massages were given, and soaked in the hot sulphur tubs. Things didn't seem so tense and terrible after all. Maybe swords could be beaten into plowshares. Then we lay on parallel wood tables, in the sun, and waited for Bridget and Gary to do away with all our anxieties. I had begun to doze by the time Gary touched me on the shoulder to say he was ready.

He spread a white cloth on the table and anointed his hands with oil, and I closed my eyes and silently purred as the knots of the past week disappeared. It was all quite innocent and exquisite, just the way I remembered it from the old days, Class of '68, and I was happy for Marcus that he too must be feeling healed and soothed in the warm, strong sun. But when it was time for me to turn over so Gary could tend to my flip side, I looked over at the table where I had last seen Marcus and found it vacant. He was standing over by the clothes hooks, getting dressed, and looking enraged.

"What's wrong?" I asked.

"Do you know what *time* it is?"

"No." Who cared?

"It's 4:15, and that masseuse girl or whatever she is hasn't even shown up." People doing their Hatha Yoga *asanas* on other tables, unused to such tones of ire, looked gently perturbed.

"Why didn't you *say* something to someone?" I asked.

185

"I kept thinking she'd get here. Well, now I'm sunburnt to a crisp. I'll go wait in the car for you."

"Oh, dear, if I'd known I'd have given you *my* appointment. What could have happened to Bridget?" I asked Gary.

"Some hassle or other," he guessed. "But maybe someone else can take care of your friend."

"*I* can," volunteered a young woman named Nicki, who must have been moved by the depth of his gut-level feeling. To Marcus's delight, she spoke in the accents of the country he loved more than any on earth. Not only did she come from Liverpool, but she gave as fine a massage as any anglophile could wish. When it was done, Marcus was quite mollified, if also quite sunburnt. We spent a sacred hour watching the sun disappear behind the rocks at Pfeiffer State Park, and had a noncombatant supper at Nepenthe, up the road a bit.

The next morning our abdomens resembled extremely rare roast beef. Yesterday's nice snuggly warm sun, beaming for hours on our pallid nether regions, had led to agony.

"So the Fun over Fifty tour was a disappointment?" Jim Hutchins asked his mother-in-law.

"I tell you, Jimmy, I'm never going to go on one of those things again. Ridiculous bunch of geriatric people, can't even make a decision for themselves. Now you take the seventy-third birthday party you and Joan planned for me; *that's* more my idea of fun."

"What'd you do for her birthday?" I asked Joan. She and I were in the kitchen making more Bloody Marys.

"We took her down to Big Sur for a weekend of jade-hunting with a bunch of twenty-year-old hippies," said Joan, "and she had the best time of anybody. I think she's enjoying herself now more than she ever has in her life." Joan and Jim seemed to be doing pretty well, too. Maybe deciding definitely not to have children—"At least we don't feel *guilty* about it any more," Joan said—had relaxed them. A well-matched couple, Joan and Jim: both psychiatric social workers, employed by dif-

ferent agencies, both musicians, both rockhounds, and both
naturally hospitable. As soon as they heard that Marcus and I
were in the vicinity, they insisted that we come to their house
in San Bruno for brunch. Paul and Amy Feldman came too,
along with Joan's mother. Paul was a freelance writer with no
assignments, but apart from that he seemed euphoric. He had
grown a beard since I'd seen him last, and he and Amy kept
holding hands.

"Hey, darling," Amy said to Paul, "Marcus has never been
out here at all before. Wouldn't it be nice to take him and
Jane with us to the Napa vineyards tomorrow?"

"Oh dear," I said. "I've got to go to Berkeley tomorrow, to
see a couple of people. For me this is partly a work trip."

"Partly?" said Marcus. "This girl is the true embodiment of
the Puritan Wasp ethic."

"But why don't the three of you go anyway? Maybe we can
all have dinner together later."

"That sounds like a good, emancipated suggestion," said
Jim.

"How do you stand on all this emancipation business?" Marcus asked Jim.

"I'm learning," said Jim, "but it takes some doing."

"Tell them about your office Christmas party," Joan
prompted.

"You tell them," said Jim.

"Jim's office Christmas party was scheduled for a Friday
night," Joan said, "so he volunteered to bring a ham, which
meant I'd cook one at home. Fair enough, until it turned out
that *my* office party was going to be the same night, and I
thought it was important for me to go so I could get some re-
ferrals. I got a canned ham and gave it to Jim with an electric
frying pan and some sauce in a jar and told him he could just
fix it that afternoon in his office. You know what he did? He
had a woman social worker make it instead."

"Men always take advantage of women when they get a
chance," said Joan's mother.

"My stepfather sure took advantage of you," said Joan. "He

187

didn't help at all around the house, even though he was unemployed most of the time. I don't recall your complaining about that."

"What I *did* complain about," said the older woman, "was getting paid a lower salary than the male bookkeepers in my office. They were paid more," she said, "on the grounds that men support families. When I pointed out to my bosses that I supported a family too, they said 'You can't buck city hall.' "

"These days," said Marcus, "it seems you can."

"Can and should," said Joan. "What worries me is that what we're having now will turn out to be temporary liberation, like they had in Elizabethan England. Women could own property then—and Mesopotamia and ancient Egypt, too, I think—but it didn't last. They lost their rights."

"We won't lose ours," said Amy Feldman, still holding her husband's hand.

Once, several years back, I thought perhaps I had left my heart in San Francisco, somewhere in the vicinity of Telegraph Hill. It turned out I was mistaken, as I often have been in such matters, which is perhaps why I always return to that city with somewhat ambivalent emotions. I can sympathize alike with the contempt heaped on San Francisco by chauvinists from the South and the genuflections of pilgrims from the East, but it is not a place that stirs the depths of my own soul.

But Marcus, that savorer of cities, adored it on sight, even with his Esalen sunburn. When he rode up in the same Huntington Hotel elevator with Karl Malden one morning, his cup all but overflowed, having been less metaphorically filled, earlier, in the coffee shop of the Mark Hopkins, where to his intense pleasure copies of the *Times Literary Supplement* were kept on racks for guests to peruse. "Peruse," that's a word Marcus uses a lot. It's a thing he does a lot.

"We decided you were an adverb," some friends and I once told him, in the course of one of those conversations that tend to develop in the course of long car rides.

"Oh?"

Shattuck and Alcatraz. Now's there's an intersection with some meat to it. The sound of it, I mean. Like Miracle and Oracle in Tucson. I said the words over and over to myself. The only trouble was, I wasn't supposed to be there at Shattuck and Alcatraz. Shattuck and Alcatraz meet in Oakland, and I was supposed to be in Berkeley, at the Women's History Research Center. How had I got so lost? Daydreaming, I guess. The Bay Area does that to me. But I had better find my way to my destination, which I had heard was one of the vital ganglia of the whole feminist movement. Since I seemed to be making pilgrimages to such ganglia, I had phoned there to ask directions. The feminist who answered sounded so formidable I asked her name, and she told me.

"Is that spelled E-C-K?" I asked.

"No, X. The letter X. Just plain X."

Laura X proved to be a blonde native of St. Louis, born in 1940, who had gone to Vassar and moved to Berkeley in 1963 to work with the archives of the Free Speech Movement. Her conversion to feminism, although gradual, sounded as intense as some of the accounts in James's *Varieties of Religious Experience*. She lives on a small income from the estate of her late grandfather, a shoe company executive. She has invested the principal and sacrificed all of her house to her part of the cause, which she describes as "the world's only complete archive of the present women's movement."

To reach this archive, in a residential neighborhood of Berkeley, you climb up an outside flight of stairs and announce your name, speakeasy style, before you are admitted. The atmosphere within is very busy and, as Laura puts it, "very nonprofit," more so since the federal government has withdrawn support of libraries and work-study programs to help hire college students. Although it is a library, a repository of information, the tempo is like that of a 1920s movie. Laura and her assistants rush from room to room as if to make up for lost time, which in fact is what they are doing.

Even the shower of that house is somebody's office. Only half of Laura's bed is used to sleep in; the other half is in effect a desk, piled high with printed matter. All over what was once a living room are the elements of a topical research library of two thousand miles, along with two thousand books, twelve hundred pamphlets, five hundred and fifty periodicals, folders, photographs, four hundred "herstory" tapes and clippings. Laura has faithful operatives around the world who supply her with clippings on feminism from their local papers.

"We also have manifestos," she told me, "and syllabi, theses, term papers . . ."

"This place probably proves more visibly than anywhere I've been how far the movement has come in four years' time," I said. "It's odd, though, that nobody else has assembled such a library."

"Nobody has," she assured me. "At least not on a scale like this. Ours was the first network that held everybody in the movement together. When we first started this center we put out a newsletter that just tremendously, algebraically facilitated communication. Now our index is all organized by topics, and it goes out to libraries. It's available on microfilm through Bell & Howell. Why don't you sit down, if you'd like to, and browse through some of the files? I've got a couple of people waiting for me on the phone."

The diversity of Laura's files dumfounded me. My own task of finding out what was on women's minds these days seemed more amorphous and audacious than ever. Everything, it seemed, was on women's minds. What could I possibly rule out? What, so long as I was here, would I like to enlighten myself about: women bartenders? Women cops? Women steeplejacks? Women leaping over the walls of convents, or out of marriages, or into bed with each other? Women blazing trails literally and otherwise, or writing herstory books? In the introduction to a women's songbook, by "a wandering menstrual! for hire," I read that in Laura's archive "the song file is getting bigger rapidly; so is the tape library. The whole library serves women doing things from setting up women's courses to looking for decent gynecologists, from doing articles on rape to researching the lives of women, including the woman who invented the cotton gin and got ripped off by Eli Whitney.

"Laura X," I read on, "especially treasures photos besides

the pre-McLuhan things she's harassed for collecting, graffiti, autobiographies, biographies, old books on tokology (midwifery) *, poems, love and hate letters, diaries, graduation books, and children's books."

Once Laura's surname had been Murra—Rumanian, she told me, for blackberry. She changed it to X, she said, on November 19, 1969, when an arrogant male professor, with whom she was working to plan a women's studies seminar at Berkeley, asked, "Is there enough about women to fill a quarter course?"

"I was so angry that the women were made to suffer, by obnoxious men like that, that I thought of Malcolm X, and figured, 'I don't want to have *my* owner's name, either.' I sure as hell didn't change it to be cute."

"What owner do you mean?"

"My father."

"How did *he* feel when you dropped his name?"

"Distressed, at first, but now that I'm internationally famous and respectable, his daughter the foundation president, the librarian, the writer—now he doesn't mind so much."

"How international are you?"

"Well, we just got a bibliography the other day from Uganda, which I did *not* solicit, and all the women's periodicals everywhere mention us."

"What part of this work do you like most?" I asked her.

"Oral herstory. The tape archive is very important to me. What I'd really like most to do would be to go around getting women to speak for themselves—suffragettes, union women, all kinds of women. It's been very demoralizing for me to have to spend all my time fund-raising—it costs $100,000 a year to run this place—especially since it's turned out to be such a mistake."

"Mistake?"

"Well, two and a half years of beseeching fifty foundations, and no results—what else would you call it? They all say we're either too new an area for them to give funds to, or else that

---

* "Did you know," Laura later asked me, "that in the nineteenth century doctors would identify any disease they couldn't diagnose as menopause? Wasn't that convenient for them?"

we're not new enough; they'd been looking for an action-oriented pilot project. It makes me furious. We've been pioneers, but they treat us like old mothers put out to pasture. You know who we get most of our contributions from? Women who have so little money they don't even have to pay taxes."

"How long have you had this house?" I asked Laura.

"Since my marriage. It wasn't a technical marriage, but we considered ourselves man and wife. At that time I was the compleat housewife. I'm such a Scorpio, such an all-or-nothing. When I was with the Free Speech Movement I devoted every second to that. It's probably a good thing I don't have a child. Not only are there too many children in the world as it is, but if I had one I'd be an overly attentive mother." Photographs Laura had taken herself, of children in Puerto Rico, hung on many of the walls, as did a giant relief map of Puerto Rico. "I taught there—there and in Harlem," she said, "and working there was a very special learning experience for me. Those children taught me everything I know about being human. Oh, there's the phone again."

I had to go meet Marcus, who had been strolling around the Berkeley campus, but Laura said I could come back later. When I returned, she offered me buttermilk, of which there were numerous cartons in her refrigerator. Buttermilk, she said, was part of a special diet to control her diabetes. "The diet isn't so bad," she said. "Honey's what I miss the most; I used to put it in my tea. The doctor said if I didn't work so intensely I wouldn't have got diabetes till I was fifty-five. I also have twenty-two gray hairs."

"I have a couple myself," I told her. "But we're both lucky: with fair coloring like ours, it won't show."

"Mine will," she said, "they're right around the forehead. If you *have* to smoke, would you mind going outside?" She put on a fur coat and told me more as we sat on a balcony where there were a hammock and a water bed.

"The basic thing I'm trying to do here," she said, "is to save libraries money. I'm not a maniac; it's not an obsession. It's just that I feel responsible for all this material, and if I have to work 120 hours a week—which I always seem to—then I will."

"What would you do if you didn't work here?"

"Sleep, first. Sleep and *read* some of these books. My idea of utter nirvana would be to use this library myself. I used to have a sense of humor; I used to have something to say other than moaning about the federal government and its priorities. Well, if they shut us and other libraries down, I guess I'll have time to read then. No, that's not true, I'll have to get a job— and who wants to hire a used librarian?"

"Maybe it won't be shut down."

"If we were men it wouldn't be. If we were men, people would assume we were doing serious, dignified work, and be more likely to pay us for it. As it is, we have to spend nearly all our time fund-raising. Since we're women, we're eccentric, right?"

"That's your word," I said, "not mine."

"I don't care if they do call us that, because it's really nice to meet fellow fanatics. I've been like this all my life. I've always been a bookworm; even as a child I always read biographies of women. Now I sort of feel that all of us who used to think we were freaks—by which I mean lonely bookworms who cared about improving human nature—have managed to find each other."

"When did you think you were a freak? At Vassar?"

"Long before. Before Vassar I went to an upper-middle-class girls' school. As a matter of fact I started going to girls' schools when I was three years old. In schools like that you get a double message. They tell you that women can and should think independently, but only for one reason: so as not to bore their husbands."

"I know some victims of that mentality too," I said.

Laura's two younger sisters are married and more conventional than she is. So is her mother. "One day fifteen years ago," she said, ' when I was a freshman at Vassar, I called up to say, 'Mom! I'm not a nonconformist after all! It's just that before this I didn't want to conform with what was going on in St. Louis!' But my mother had the midwestern, upper-class kind of thinking, so she didn't understand the message."

"What message?"

"That *women don't feel any more that we're what's left over after the men*. We don't just weep over books in the middle of the night any more; we do something about it. We find each other. When that professor questioned whether there was enough about women to fill a three-month course, I got so angry we put out a list of women in history, and people would write in to say, 'Please send a copy to my sister in Iowa; she feels so alone.' Well, a lot of people's sisters in Iowa and other places aren't feeling so lonely any more."

"Have you had much to do with chronicling the gay movement?"

"As a fierce civil libertarian, that's one of the things I've been vilified for. A lot of women have decided to become gay, you know, since they got into the movement. There's a woman at San Francisco State who's been trying to pull all that together. If you want to read a good piece about lesbianism, look for an article in *Women: A Journal of Liberation* by Christine Mimichild."

"Mimichild? Seems to me I've run across other names like that—Susanchild, Bettydaughter."

"Probably. Mimichild means 'daughter of Mimi'. I guess she didn't want a man's name, either."

"If I felt that strongly about it," I mused, "I'd be Jane Eleanorchild." Laura nodded.

"You don't, though, do you?" she asked.

"No," I said. "But I'm glad you do." I toasted her with buttermilk.

Were it not for the special way the fog rolls in, Mavis Hoffman's street could as easily be Ann Arbor or Cambridge as Berkeley. It is unmistakably a street of graduate students, lined with Volkswagens, Volvos, bicycles, and old shingled houses divided into more separate units than their builders had intended.

Inside Mavis's house, too, the style is graduate student. There are gaily repainted Salvation Army chairs, a hooked rug, candles, plants. In the bookshelf are Malraux's *Anti-Memoirs,*

R. D. Laing, the Psalms and *Babar and Celeste*. The Babar is for Susie. Susie is Mavis's daughter, deliberately conceived out of wedlock.

"I wasn't very involved with Susie's father," Mavis told me. "I didn't even tell him he was the father until after she was born. He asked me if it was his, when I found out I was pregnant, and I said no, but my psychoanalyst told me I ought to tell him the truth, so later I did."

"Do you still see Susie's father?"

"He's visited us a few times, but the visits were more of a problem than anything else. The problem wasn't financial, because he's on welfare and there was no question ever of his supporting the child. He did give us money when he could. He's not a bad guy; it's just that I didn't ever want to marry him."

"Did you ever want to marry anyone before him?"

"At Penn I was involved with and engaged to a French guy. We lived with and cared for each other, but I didn't feel committed enough for a lifetime with him, even though he did want a child by me. I wanted one, but not by him. That's really why I moved out here: I thought it would be far enough from Philadelphia so that if I did decide to act on my desire to have a child, I could do it covertly, without hassling my family or being hassled by them."

"Your family knows now?"

"Oh, sure, I took Susie home to Hatboro, to show her and my parents to each other, and I didn't make any bones about wearing a ring. My parents are German immigrants, and they were shocked at first, but not for too long. Now they're supportive about it."

"How about your friends? Were they supportive?"

"When I was pregnant some of my friends advised me to have an abortion and thought I was crazy not to. But others understood, others were great about it. I had Susie in the hospital, under Medi-Cal, which was atypical, because home deliveries out here are the common thing.

"The worst part wasn't pregnancy but a period of isolation after she was born, after the novelty wore off and I was suddenly a mother, to a certain degree immobilized, with these heavy responsibilities. Sometimes, when I was alone with her, I was afraid. In the first three or four months of her life, I slowly exchanged my sets of friends.

"I guess I was a little hurt not being invited to parties or to go off on weekends. People don't seem to realize that it is possible, despite the hassle, to go camping with an infant. And I took her to classes with me, and damn anyone who didn't like it. There were a few people who objected to having me nurse her in class, but I tried to enroll in small, sympathetic seminars.

"I had very few boyfriends the first year of her life, which didn't bother me too much. I missed the company of women more. There were certain things men don't understand. Men tend to be overawed by certain things, more easily embarrassed than women.

"When she was five months old I could put her in a child-care center, so I did. Those first four or five months were difficult, but you forget about that sort of difficulty."

"Like labor pains?"

"Yes, sort of. Do you have children yourself?"

"No, but I guess like most single women I've often thought of doing what you have."

"It was always much stronger than the need for a man, this wish to have a child. It started, I guess, when I was in the Peace Corps in Peru. I sort of semiadopted a child down there. I was working in a hospital there and this baby was born, the product of an incestual union, and someone handed him to me and said, 'Here, you're a rich American, *you* take him.' If I hadn't, they'd have let him die."

"What happened?"

"I called him Juanito and raised him with the peasant family I lived with. The woman of that family was very poor, but she and I were sort of dual mothers to him. One night she just sort of migrated with him. I tried to track her down, to send money, but I never did reach her. Maybe she was afraid I'd take him away. I guess it's just as well: she could spend more time with him than I could."

"How old would he be now?"

196

"Well, he was born in June '65, so that would make him seven—God, that's incredible."

"Did you go straight from Peru back to Philadelphia?"

"No, I came home and did civil rights work in Mississippi, and there too I saw a lot of single mothers handling things just fine. I felt a desire for a child so strongly, so much more strongly than a desire for marriage, and the desire just got stronger all the time, especially when I worked in orphanages, spending all those hours taking care of other people's kids."

"How old were you when you finally had your own?"

"Fairly old, I was almost twenty-six. I'm almost twenty-nine now. And now I'm going to have another one."

"You *are?*"

"Oh, yes, didn't I tell you? I'm married. I never thought I would be, and I didn't think I'd even find a man at all for five years, because most men don't like little kids; little kids don't become people until they're three or four anyway. But I was lucky. I found Seth. When Susie was a year old, Seth started taking care of her at the child-care center. Six months later, we started living together."

"Does Seth still work at the child-care center?"

"He does now. He's going to go back to graduate school in linguistics, but not until after I finish my Ph.D. I've got three more years to go."

"What's it in, your doctorate?"

"Cultural anthropology—partly medical and women's studies, partly Latin American peasantry, partly research about counterculture styles of birth."

"Are you involved with the movement?"

"I'm very much concerned with the issues of the movement," said Mavis, "but I'm not directly involved, because the impression I get from movement heavies is pretty negative."

"I think I know what you mean," I said.

"Hey Mommy!" called a voice from the backyard. "Come look at the worm!"

"I will," Mavis answered, "in a minute."

"*Not* in a minute! Now!"

Mavis went.

"I would be livid," Marcus said, "if any woman had or aborted a child of mine without telling me. Doesn't a man have a right to know, too? Isn't it a matter of some interest to him?"

"I didn't say it wasn't," I said.

It was Joan and Jim's anniversary, and they had asked us to join them at their favorite restaurant in all San Francisco, the place where they had become engaged. In motif and cuisine it was rustic Japanese. Marcus winced to note that everyone sat on the floor.

"Could we possibly get chairs?" he asked.

"I don't think they even have chairs here," Jim said. We sat on mats near a window overlooking a garden. Night had not yet fallen.

"Isn't that a wonderful garden?" Joan asked.

"Such clever use of space," I said, eyeing Marcus.

"Do you think the waiter could bring me a flashlight?" he asked. "I can't seem to make out the menu."

"May I have a fork, please?" he later asked.

"I should think anyone who ate half his New York meals in Chinese places would have learned to use chopsticks," I barely managed not to say.

Most tourists come to the Bay Area to look at redwoods, drink Irish Coffee at the Buena Vista, ride cable cars, and shop at Gump's. Not me. Not this trip, anyway. What I seemed to do, most of the time, was talk to single mothers. I have not found, in San Francisco or elsewhere, anyone more articulate on this subject than Shirley Boccaccio, mother of three, wife of nobody.

"Society says it's okay, although pathetic, if a woman gets pregnant by accident," Shirley said, "but not if she calculatingly chooses a certain man to be a father. Women aren't supposed to be self-directing and autonomous, they're just supposed to let things happen to them. But I should think a man would be delighted to be chosen the way I chose my children's father. God, what an ego trip it must be! On the one hand upholding the patriarchal ideal, and on the other, fundamentally, what ultimate flattery, to be seduced by a wicked woman!

"The man I picked out is a lot older than I am. He was a bit taken aback to learn that I chose him for the express purpose of having a child by him. Maybe if he'd been in his prime, he wouldn't have gone along with my plan."

"It was a conscious plan?"

"Absolutely. Women don't often have such a sense of plunging into something adventurous. I knew no security, I knew I was taking a chance, but I was determined to make it work. I think that's why it *did* work. Not taking chances makes life narrow and uninteresting, but when you *do* take risks, the possibilities just expand. One radical step opens up all sorts of other doors—politically, sexually, economically."

Shirley lived on the sunny, spacious second floor of an apartment building in the Haight-Ashbury section of San Francisco. Her three children were gone that afternoon, visiting their father, so we drank coffee and talked in what for her was unaccustomed quiet. She showed me a deliberately nonsexist book she had written, *Penelope and the Mussels,* and plans for another, *Penelope Goes to the Farmer's Market.* She also showed me two controversial posters she had done, using the nom de plume Virtue Hathaway. The posters were captioned, respectively, FUCK HOUSEWORK and FUCK OFFICEWORK.

"Funny thing about those posters," she said. "My family at home in Chicago rejected me more because I'd used the word 'fuck' than because I broke the law. When I was evicted for having an illegitimate child, when I didn't have enough food or money, when I needed to suffer, that wasn't so bad, they could be sympathetic. What in their eyes was unforgivable was when those posters started to *sell*—when I started to succeed, when my letters home got more cheerful." They can't forgive me for not being a middle class housewife. They think of the movement as a bunch of 'sex-obsessed failures,' and the idea of single motherhood appals them."

Shirley makes three or four speeches a year and hopes when her youngest child is in school to get a full-time job, but when

I talked to her she was earning so little that she was on welfare.

"If there were just enough money, if women could have a clear choice between staying home to raise their children or finding good quality child care while they went out to work, then raising kids on welfare wouldn't be bad at all. There are so many agencies, and people are so eager to help. There's an eighty-three-year-old woman down the street here who never married—she likes to feed my kids and give them piano lessons."

"I wish I could meet your kids."

"I wish you could too. I'll tell you one thing: they're not going to be like *we* were. They're going to be a lot freer, not nearly as hostile and aggressive as the traditionally reared child. They'll have a lot fewer sexual hangups and ego identification hangups. They'll have a very strong sense of their own value, because there's no question that they were wanted."

The more middle-class a delivery, she said, the more important was the convenience of the obstetrician, and the less the mother mattered. Her own three children had been born under increasingly less middle-class circumstances. "With the first one I was drugged and had a Caesarean, the second was a little more free, and the third was down all the way. I liked the third birth best, because I knew where I was at. I fought them against having a Caesarean and being sterilized—no way. There is a sentiment, you know, that the mother of the third child born out of wedlock should be declared 'morally depraved'. I think that's outrageous, but when I was in the middle class I didn't have the courage to speak out against that sort of thing."

"You're definitely not in the middle class any more?"

"Do I look it?"

"You could pass."

"I don't want to. I really believe society should take part in taking care of children and that priority should be given to a woman's needs. If a woman chooses to have children, all possible help should be given to her. It's terrible that women are made to feel degraded by having children outside the patriarchal system. The words 'bastard' and 'illegitimate' are outmoded these days. I'd like to write a book called *Bastard Is Beautiful*. I don't think any child should be carried who isn't welcome. But then relating to children as people is a new concept, for those of us who were brought up to see ourselves as authoritarian oppressors of children."

"Have you ever been married?" I asked Shirley.

"Yes, a long time ago, to a lawyer. We moved out here from Chicago together because we both liked the idea of the mountains and the sea. But at age twenty-six I realized that marriage wasn't where it was at, so I painted and bummed around, went to Mexico for six months, came back, and realized I wanted a child, but not marriage: the idea of marrying again was just appalling. All of this points up the failure of marriage, how marriage oppresses women and children, how the whole male authoritarian political thing makes the mother and the child both scapegoats. All this is very threatening to the status quo too."

"So you just decided to go ahead and do it?"

"Yes. I was thirty then—that was seven years ago—and suddenly it struck me that if I was that motivated to become a mother, I'd better get on with it, because what difference, ten years hence, would my marital status make?"

"You don't live with the kids' father now?"

"No, now I have a more fundamental relationship with another man. Now that I've satisfied my desire for children, I do have a man, for the first time, and I'm really glad. When people can be liberated from sex roles, the relation between the sexes is so much better."

"You're not lonely, then."

"Not now, but I have been. Loneliness was much more devastating before I had the children. Now when they're not here I miss them, but I'm too tired to be lonely. At times when there are no men in my life, I go bike riding and visit the neighbors. I don't like to compromise to escape loneliness— you won't ever catch me saying to some man, 'I'll scrub your floors, I'll do anything, if you'll only relieve me of my loneliness.' "

"Do you think you'll ever change your mind about marriage?"

"It would be easier now to get married than it was in the middle sixties, because now at least it's socially acceptable to have a marriage based on equality."

"Do you think you'd like to have more kids?"

"Probably not, though maybe someday. What nobody told me was what a terrible drain pregnancy is on energy. Nature really does something, hormonally. I felt I was *occupied,* literally—that I didn't belong to myself, couldn't do anything creative. We just lived in sloth. I dropped out from everything, because I had to. All I did was take long naps, go for walks, and stop smoking, because I couldn't bear the idea of smoking. I didn't care how I looked, either, so I got fat, I got gross—all the way up to 170 pounds.

"We really went through some bad times, but I realized the most important thing was not to allow myself the luxury of flipping out mentally. I absolutely couldn't afford that. So as long as we had enough food and a reasonable roof (and by the way there's a lot of discrimination against women in housing), everything extraneous had to go by the wayside."

"If you were in charge," I asked Shirley "how would you change things?"

"I'd have a noncompetitive society," she said, "where every individual would be welcome for his or her talents and resources I don't think anybody should be hungry or without a roof, because technology gives us so much potential. I think women should learn a hell of a lot more about the technology of dams, sewage, that kind of thing.

"We really have to totally re-orient ourselves to understand the system politically and economically. Women have got to get out of this middle-class neighborhood-center housewife recycling trip—that stuff is just a drop in the bucket—and learn what's going on with sewage, find out what we're doing to oceans. The ecology movement is just a way to use women and lay another useless trip on them."

I was ready for a simple, actual trip in a car. The John Muir Redwood Forest so awed both Marcus and me that we spoke in whispers the whole time we walked through it. We both smiled when two German-looking men wearing hats and overcoats, who appeared to be in their sixties, took solemn snapshots of each other standing at the bottom of a tree. But Marcus didn't understand about the lady at the table next to ours in the coffee shop. The lady in the coffee shop had this truly colossal sculptured gray hairdo, and I could not restrain myself from asking her how she maintained it.

"Oh," she said, "I have it washed every Tuesday and combed every Thursday, and I sleep on a satin pillow." She and her husband, she added, had come to California from Alabama, for the accouchement of her daughter, downstate.

"We were down there waitin' on my grandbaby for three weeks," she said.

"*Why,*" asked Marcus later, "did you want to talk to her at all?"

15

None, They Say, Have I

Marcus was spending the day with some friends in Palo Alto, and my two interviews in northern Marin County were finished much earlier than I had expected. I stopped in a phone booth to call Polly Andrews, who had just moved into a new house in Sausalito. I didn't think she would be home. Polly and I are forever leaving messages with each other's answering services, saying, "Never mind, tell her I'll call again next time I'm in town." We both travel often, sometimes on little notice. What has kept us friends is not the nature of our work; I know as little about city planning as she does about journalism. It is not that we look alike; she is four inches shorter and her coloring is Mediterranean and intense. What we share is the quality of our energy. We both care more about what we do for a living than it was fashionable, until recently, for women to admit caring, and we both have avoided, for any number of reasons, getting married. Since we always find plenty to talk about, I was happily startled when Polly answered her phone herself and told me to come on over right away.

"What do you mean you don't believe the complementary

neurosis theory?" I was asking her an hour later. "Come off it, Polly. I've told you to watch that jargon stuff if you're going to stay in California." She had quit her job in a city planning office and opened a consulting firm of her own, operating out of her home. By the look of this secluded house, fragrant with eucalyptus and evergreen, rimmed with a patio, business was good. We sat outside in bathing suits. (I had learned never to go anywhere without my bathing suit.)

"Speaking of jargon," Polly said as she disappeared into the house, "I've got to read you something I eavesdropped at a restaurant in Tiburon. There was this really incredible woman." She came back out to read from a notebook. "How's this: 'I'm just getting into the whole new area of intuition and loneliness and ethics and defensiveness and love, and I have such *ambivalence* about it. I don't know *how* it will turn out, but it feels like the right place to be.' "

"Way to listen, Poll. You do have a good ear. Terrific, lean syntax, that, comparable to Ronald Ziegler's when he's confused."

"So," said Polly as she poured me more ginseng tea, "don't pounce on me about jargon."

"I won't, if you'll explain complementary neurosis theory."

"It's what it sounds like: the idea that a woman like me—and for that matter you too, Ms. Jane—should keep attracting men who want to be *de*pendent—nice guys, God only knows, but they put us more and more in the mommy position."

"There are a lot better ways of being a mommy," I agreed. "Hey, what's happened to Enid? Is she still out here?" Several years earlier, in New York, Polly and Enid Lunt and I had worked together on a crash project in so urgent an atmosphere that we quickly became close friends. Our temperaments were markedly different. Polly moved through episodes of work and love at so fast a pace I could barely keep track of her. Enid was cautious and deliberate; she reminded me of a slow-motion movie. My tempo was somewhere there in the middle. When Enid fell in love with Kurt, our married boss, Polly and I had helped her to agonize over Kurt's offer to divorce his wife and marry her. Ultimately and with great pain, Enid had said no.

She could not see herself as a homewrecker, even though the home in question was no model of harmony. A while later his company transferred Kurt to Brazil, and Enid had moved West.

"She's gone back East to live with her family."

"Her family? She didn't even like her family."

"She couldn't stand to stay here, though, because Kurt was transferred back here."

"He *was?* Here?"

"When she found that out, she spent about two weeks working up nerve to phone him. She decided she'd been wrong to turn him down. Since they broke up all she had were these two very gloomy, disappointing affairs. So she finally phoned the office here."

"And?"

"They told her to call him at Mount Zion hospital. He'd had a stroke."

"Dear God. Poor Kurt. A bad one?"

"No, a slight one as it turned out, but still. When Enid got his room there, his wife answered and said she'd give Kurt her message."

"What a body blow. What stellar times we live in. I guess that was more than Enid could take."

"It was."

"Hey, Polly," I said, "is there anything to eat around here?"

"Sorry," she said, "I figured you'd had lunch. Sure, I just unfroze some turkey soup I made the last time I was home, three weeks ago."

"You always were a famous soup maker," I remembered.

"It gives me a sense of home, which really matters a lot since I'm gone so much," she said. "Come on, we'll heat some up."

"Look at these *skylights!*" I said as we headed toward her kitchen. "This place is really remarkable."

"It should be, if you know what I mean," she said, using one of our standard old phrases. "But what's money for, etcetera etcetera? Hey, have a look at my sunken bathtub."

"All but decadent," I marveled. "It looks like something Phil thought of." Phil was an architect friend of Polly's, whom

I had met the last time I was in California. "What's become of him? Is he still on the scene?"

"That's over, too. It was hard for me to end it, because he had this hypnotic power over me. I took stuff from him I wouldn't have stood for from any other man on earth. But what finally did it was that he kept wanting me to go off with him on these swinging weekends. Us and two strangers he'd find through some special interest magazine ad, all piled up together. Discreet little adventures, don't you know. A bit too adventurous, even for my taste."

"You don't need me to tell you you're well rid of him."

"I know, but sometimes I still miss him."

"Surely you've got others?"

"Several, but mostly they're the kind who don't even ask to come in for a drink at the end of an evening, who look at their watches a lot and say, 'Must dash, early breakfast appointment tomorrow.' Where, will you please tell me, are all those importunate beasts of yesteryear, the ones we had to fight off?"

"I guess they're past their primes."

"Swell, just when we finally reach ours."

"Theoretically women our age are supposed to take up with teenagers—initiate them, as it were."

"I tried that number. This twenty-year-old in my office kept telling me he'd been having fantasies about me, so one day I saw to it that his fantasies came true. It was all very nice, if only we'd had anything to say to each other. It does seem to be true that younger men are more with it, sexually, because older men seem to spend all their energy competing and getting ahead. *Most* older men, that is."

"What about Sam? He's still back with Margaret?"

"Well, more or less."

"What do you mean, more or less? *You* don't still see him, do you?"

"Once in a while."

"Paula Winifred Andrews, you, of all people, are blushing. How often? Three times a week? Will he be here any minute?"

"More like twice a week. Sometimes once."

"Does Margaret know?"

"I guess she suspects, but she herself has taken up with that divorced archaeologist. Sam knows about that. Everybody's civilized. They all get along."

"*A trois?*"

"Please. *A deux.* What kind of circles do you think I move in?"

"Oh, Polly, doesn't it get confusing?"

"It can, but the so-called eligible ones seem to be so screwed up. I can't take all that wondering: is this one of those marvelous old-fashioned courtships? Should I be glad it's moving so slowly? Or do I scare him away? Or does he secretly not like any women?"

"Do you still see guys like *that?*"

"Sure, because they have redeeming social value: they take me places I want to go. Some of them make me laugh."

"How do you manage the logistics?"

"It can get complicated. Once in awhile there's a Beaumarchais scene I could do without, when I practically have to tell one to hide in the closet because the next one's ringing the doorbell. I must say that sort of thing doesn't seem as amusing as it used to."

"Did it ever, really?"

"Maybe I just thought it did. Sometimes I think maybe I'd better cut out all this shall we say diversity and have a baby. Look at Olga over there; *she* has babies." Olga was Polly's calico cat.

"Oh, let's have a look at them," I said. Polly led me to the box where the kittens snuggled together. "I'm not a great cat-lover, but they are cute, aren't they?"

"I'm thinking of naming them Chastity, Fidelity, Promiscuity—the central concepts of our time."

"You've never been *randomly* promiscuous though, have you?"

"Just that once, in Rome," said Polly. "I told you. I'd just arrived, and the conference I went there for didn't start until the next day and I was missing Sam terribly—I'd never missed anyone so desperately and specifically before or, for that matter, since; it was uncanny. So I did actually not only pick up, but go to bed, with a total stranger. Maybe it's something every woman should do once in her life."

"Like those Greeks, or whoever they were, who offered themselves one day a year to whoever came along at the marketplace?"

"Something like that. But I wouldn't make an annual practice of it. Once was enough."

"What about that maître d' in Guadeloupe?"

"Your memory, my friend, is uncanny."

"It isn't always, there are lots of things I forgot. I never remember the difference between a condominium and a cooperative."

"Well, that was a long time ago. And it wasn't a random pickup; I'd seen him around for several days before I, so to speak, succumbed. And after all, one had never known a black man. One did wonder about those clichés. And, having finished a crash course at Berlitz, one did want to practice one's French."

"You know something, Polly? I wish I were half as sure of myself as you are."

"Why shouldn't you be? Why should aggressive women feel they have to apologize? I think aggression is a positive force as long as you know how to use it."

"Like fire."

"Exactly."

"But shouldn't aggression have more focus? Wouldn't you like to settle on one man, regardless of whether you were married to him or not?"

"I've got nothing against it, but the really ideal arrangement would be to see a guy on weekends who had his own house and his own trip.

"Does it bother you," I asked Polly, "if a man earns less money than you do?"

"Funny you should ask. I just clipped out an article about that. It's getting slightly less odd for wives to out-earn their husbands. The percentage is up nearly two points since 1960."

"Who but you would work a fact like that into a conversation? But that's not really much, and those are *married* people."

"I wonder how they do it? The idea of a joint banking account alone would take a lot of getting used to."

"Joint *anything* would," I said, "much as I love the idea of commingling, fusing, uniting."

"Romantic nonsense," said Polly.

"Have we gone too far to ever be romantic?"

"I wish not, but I'm afraid we have. Still, I wouldn't want to be a man for anything. Would you?"

"No. Their problems seem worse by far. I saw a great graffito on a billboard in the IRT: 'This ad exploits men.'"

"Men *are* exploited. We have to help them along. I spend a lot of time cueing guys as to what's expected of them under the new system. Like if a guy opens a door for me, I'll say, 'Tell your mother she really raised you well, but there are *some* women who would find that offensive.'"

"I wouldn't think of saying that," I said. "Talk about condescending."

"That's what Sam says."

"I'll bet Sam would be crushed if you ever stopped bring available."

"I guess he would. I guess he *will,* rather."

"You mean you're going to . . ."

"I mean there are mornings when I wake up at four or so and look at my fine strong chiseled face in the mirror and see a whole new network of incipient wrinkles and wonder what, if anything, it all adds up to, other than a good consulting firm."

"That's something you should be proud of. Besides, who ever said it all added up?"

"Who ever promised us a rose garden, right?"

"Just so. Well, maybe the answer *is* having babies."

"If we haven't waited too long," said Polly. She and I were of an age. "What if I haven't even needed all the contraceptive stuff I've used all these years?"

"Look at the fog come down that hillside," I said. "It's like a huge, fat snake. I wish Marcus could see it."

"Too bad you couldn't bring him along."

"I'd better head back to join him for dinner. I guess we haven't been getting along all that well. No, I don't guess, I know. I know damn well."

"Travel," said Polly, "is a real test."

16

I Wanted Just What I Got

"Why, Officer," I said as I dutifully pulled over to the side of the road, "I had no idea I was going over the speed limit. I guess we were so busy trying to find a motel to stay in that I just wasn't noticing."

"Let's see your driver's license, lady." For the next twenty minutes, it seemed, the patrolman laboriously copied the data from that document onto a ticket, which led to a twenty-five-dollar fine. The moral of this vignette is that you don't mess around while driving through Eureka, California. That cop did us a favor, though. He said if we wanted to press on a bit more we might find an okay place to sleep up ahead in the fishing village of Trinidad.

Coastal California, north of San Francisco, is the part of that state where I am most at peace. Its terrain and particularly its trees fill me with awe, but I don't feel obliged, as I do farther south, to issue constant manic testimonials of praise. I suppose this region must have its chauvinists, but they are an admirably low-key lot, with sense enough not to keep shaking visitors by their shoulders and asking, "Well?"

Even in the dark I could tell I was going to like Trinidad. It was a small town on a harbor, probably like the stage setting for some West Coast version of *Carousel,* only it wouldn't be real nice clambakes of which the people would sing, but real good crab feeds and real good smoked salmon, too.

The Ocean Grove Lodge seemed a promisingly unfranchised, individual place to stay. The manager showed us to a cabin around which there seemed to be redwoods, and when we said we were hungry he said that even though the café part of the place was about to close up, he would let us go on in. Our vegetable beef soup and apple pie, all flawlessly homemade, were served by a stalwart tall waitress named Doris Van Velkinburgh.

"If I didn't work," Doris told us as we ate, "I'd get fat as a pig and weigh 200, but as it is I keep down to 170." She allowed that in addition to being a waitress in this café, she was also, like her husband and her father before her, a fisherman. She did not say fisherperson.

From the bar right next to the café we could hear somebody announcing he had just arrived in "a titty-pink new car—now ain't that a pretty son of a bitch?" Doris wiped off the counter and said she believed she would go on into the bar and have a beer, to unwind a bit.

"Hey, Marcus," I whispered. "She might be my lady shepherd."

"Your what?"

"Remember, I told you I've been hoping to find some terrific western woman who does a man's work? That was why I was thinking of going on to Utah or Idaho after this?"

"You mean Doris is a shepherd? Fish are sheep?"

"Something like that."

"You'd like to go in there and talk to her."

"And you'd like not to, I know. Would you mind if I did?"

"Do what you have to do," he said. He retired to Cabin Nine and read a few pages of *The Bell Jar.* I asked Doris if she would mind if I joined her, just to visit a little. Mind? Doris?

"Oh, yeah," she said as we sat on adjoining stools in the bar, "you go out there fishing and I'll tell you something, you forget your troubles, especially when it gets a little nippy. Our boat don't have railings, and I tell you, you've got to have nimble feet. Sure, I wear rubber stuff and outdoor gear. Last winter we lost a big boat, three hours after I'd been in it. If I'd still been in it, I could have saved it. That boat was worth $22,000, and you can't get no insurance out of Trinidad, because it's an open harbor.

"Fishing's good out of Trinidad. Sometimes schoolteachers come up here in the summer to fish, and they earn as much as they earned all winter teaching. We fish for crab and salmon. Crabs are the hardest and most temperamental; they might bite fine here but not at all one fathom away." Not having a note-book with me, I was writing down what Doris said on the backs of cardboard bills the bartender kept giving me, bills that said "THANK YOU! Your Patronage Is Appreciated."

"Darn right I get paid the same as men," Doris said. "I get the same percentage of the day's haul as they do: fifteen percent for crab, twenty percent for salmon. I'm called a puller. I un-load the pots and do rebaiting. There's two sizes of pots: big heavy eighty-five-pound ones for the deep sea and lighter ones for in close. There's three sizes of fish: small, medium, and splitters. Splitters usually weigh twelve pounds or over, and you don't find too many of those. When you do, you get a bonus.

"On the big boats the men pee off the side and treat you like a man. They say if you want to work like a man, you'd better expect us to treat you like one, so when they cuss like the devil I just cuss back. My favorite expression is 'bull-shitty'. I can't say that here in the restaurant, because the boss would say, 'Now, Doris, be nice,' but on the dock it's different. At the dock, if I said, 'Will you please move?' they'd look at me like I was crazy. The thing they understand is, 'Get your ass over here.' I'm like one of the boys; you don't find them fooling with me. If they did, I'd knock them on the *kozitzke,* which is a Greek expression for ass.

"I have to wash my hair every day with oil shampoo, because it gets all fishy, scaly, and crabby. I don't care much for fancy clothes, but once when I had a pilot's license and ran a yacht out of San Pedro, a man gave me a $120 tip and I spent it on a dress.

"Oh, I've had some times. Once I was down to a drunken party in San Pedro and woke up the next day in Mexico. Had to fly home. I've been all over almost all the U.S., drove to Alaska once, been to Honolulu several times, and been fishing all the way up and down the coast from the Bering Sea down to Chile. I was seventeen when my dad took me to the Bering Sea. They've got some Indians up there—they're not called Eskimos—but mostly mixed breeds. Up there we fished for salmon. It was fun, but a lot of work, and when we got in storms my dad would treat me like a boy.

"Chile was dirty. I didn't learn Spanish. My husband and kids know it, though. I know some French. I know what *s'il vous plaît* means. Down there we fished for shark liver and got eighty, ninety cents a pound for it, because they used it for medicine and perfume, but the next year synthetics came along, and the price went down to seven or eight cents." The bartender looked wonderingly at all my notes. "If I knew you were going to write down that much," he said, "I'd have given you some big sheets of paper." Don't worry, I told him.

"We lived in Oakland when I was a kid," said Doris. "My father was a pilot out of the San Francisco harbor. My younger sister didn't care much for the water but I always did. During the war I lied about my age to run a water taxi across from San Francisco to Oakland. We go to San Francisco now, two, three times a year to take in a show, hit a couple of clubs, go shopping. Up here you don't get the good clothes, the buys.

"Where I used to live in Oakland is all black now, not that I'm against black, don't get me wrong. If any came up here we'd be nice to them, but none do. See, Trinidad's the oldest incorporated city in California, and it's kinda cliquery here. There's just 650 or 700 people, and you're not family unless you've been here ten years. That's why I try to be extra nice to new people. Most people move here because it's a good place to bring up kids.

215

"We get a lot of artists in the summer. One did a picture of our boat, just to be nice, and we got it hanging in the front room. We get a few movie stars too. They like to come up here because they don't get bugged. Not too much goes on here. Weekends there's dances here in the lodge and at the town hall, but in wintertime the place closes up at seven o'clock, tighter'n a drum. We've got a Catholic church—I'm Catholic—and a Protestant, and a beauty parlor, a grocery store, a gas station, and a grammar school up to the eighth grade. Then there's Mom's fishhouse. It's called Katy's Smoke House. She's been at it twenty-six, twenty-seven years, selling crab and smoked and fresh salmon. You might want to go talk to her too, if you're here in the morning."

I was, and I did, while Marcus prowled delightedly around a beach where there were astonishing small driftwood formations, a bit farther up the coast. They entranced him, just as striped rocks on Maine island beaches had. So did the sample I brought him of Katy's smoked wares. Katy didn't have much time to talk, but she told me how for eight years she had cooked all the crab for the famous Trinidad Chamber of Commerce crab feed, held every year around May twenty-first. "I did it," she said, "up to when it was 10,000 pounds and didn't charge them because I was a member of the Chamber of Commerce myself, but now it's up to 14,000 pounds. I married for the first time at the age of fourteen. I guess you'd say I was a child bride, but I knew more than some of these do now at twenty-four or thirty. I've been lucky to have the kind of husband who'd understand me, otherwise my marriage wouldn't have lasted two minutes. I don't need no man to tell me how to run my life.

"Let's see now, where's that ConTac paper—see? I just bought it, to put over the card table. Those plaques? You mean the ones with the starfish on them? You might say they're more or less a sentimental souvenir. I got them from my lady friend, the best friend I ever had in my life, barring any. She's been gone twelve years now."

"I met my husband in Southern California," Doris went on, "when we were fishing for albacore. We got married in Las Vegas, when I was twenty-two, against my father's wishes. My dad didn't want me to marry a fisherman, or if I did he wanted him to be at least a captain. My husband was a game warden for seven years, but the state don't pay that much. Now he's gone back to fishing. He gets up at five. Do I have any free time? Sure, between two and five A.M. Our younger boy goes out there too. He does water-taxiing in a sixteen-foot skiff with an outboard. The fishermen blow their horns when they want him, and tip him.

"I've worked here in this cafe for four-and-a-half years. I'm used to working. I've just always worked, and when I'm not working here I work at my mom's. I've got two in college now and three next year, and you know what they cost. My oldest is twenty, she's stationed with the navy in Washington State, doing security bomb disbursements. She loves it, and she don't even tell me where the bombs are. Another girl's at Humboldt College. She wants to be an ombudsman. The boy who's seventeen, he'll graduate this June.

"He got tipsy on sloe gin fizz once, and threw up in the wastebasket. It was pink. I asked him if he wanted another drink, and he said forget it. He has two Hondas and three trucks, all broken down, but he fixes them up. Whenever we ask what he wants for a present, he says something like sockets, calipers, tools. The girl who's fifteen, she don't think about nothing but boys.

"They're a whole bunch too free with their sex, kids of that age, or maybe it's just that that's what we hear. My Sue, she's eighteen, she's a good girl, she told me she had intercourse with a boy. Shoot, I guess I did it at eighteen too, but I wouldn't have dared to tell my mother. I always tell them, if you get into trouble, tell Mama first. I told my girl, if you're going to do it, we'll get you some pills, because I want you to finish college and I want to make sure you'll stay clean. If you ever suspect you're not, we'll go to see the family doctor. He's a swell man, he knows us like books and it would never go past his lips.

"Shoot, they teach sex education here in the sixth grade, and I think it's real good that they do. They showed a VD movie at a PTA meeting I went to. Pretty raw stuff; it made me cringe. Drugs worries me quite a bit, too. It'd just about kill me if our kids got on them. If that happened, the first thing I'd do would be find me a mental clinic and drag their fannies down there.

"I've been in the PTA for years but I don't have much time to help except to send them pies. I used to have the girls' drill team in high school. We took fifth place in the whole West. We went to Sacramento and Oregon and all over. We'd do stars, blocks, oblique rights and lefts, circles, and unwind. We'd practice two nights a week. The girls wanted to do it, so I figured, shoot, it'd keep them out of trouble. Oh, I was rough, though. Like I told them, no goofing. Any girl who misses over two practices without a medical reason, you're out.

"I went to college myself, two years in Skagit Valley, Washington, where my dad was fishing at the time. I studied sociology, of all things. Ain't that something? No, I didn't want to stay longer. I wanted just what I got: to get married and raise my family.

"The worst thing that ever happened to us was one Christmas Eve morning when our house burned down. We've got just one volunteer fire engine but it came, and I'll tell you what a small community will do for you: they brought us clothes and furniture and everything. Lisa was in the hospital for eleven months. She's been grafted twelve times. Ninety percent of her body was burned. She can't have no kids, because there's so much scar tissue her tummy won't stretch. For a while she thought she wanted to be a nun, but now she's had an operation so she can't get pregnant.

"It's pretty gossipy around here. Linda came home crying one time and said her girlfriend said, 'Your mama's always in that bar.' I said, 'You can tell them your mama works in the *café,* and if they want to come in and see my check stubs they can.'

"There's lots of poverty up here in the winter. Our two industries, woods and fishing, are both bad in the winter. I took a lady friend who was down on her luck to Eureka to get food stamps, and there were big, strapping, healthy, hulking men there getting food stanps too, and I couldn't help but wonder why they didn't wash windows or mow lawns. The ones who feel down on the world aren't doing anything about it, they just protest and cry and bitch. Those filthy hippies with their beards, what are they doing to help? They're trashy, that's what they are. My husband says he'd like to take them down to the ocean and dump them in.

"I like organ music and the music of my own time: calypso, Glenn Miller, Tommy Dorsey. In the winter I like to go skiing, not here, where we just get a sprinkle, but nineteen miles away. We don't have to go far to go hunting for deer, either. We smoke it and make venison jerky. Movies? I haven't been to one in four, five years. Seems to me they don't make good ones any more. I used to love John Wayne. I'd tease my husband and say, 'John Wayne can put his shoes under my bed any time.' "

With that, since my wrist was cramped from note-taking, I thought it might be time to take my own shoes off in Cabin Nine. Before I left, the bartender, to whom I had mentioned that I liked wine, insisted, "Here, you try some of this, it's Gallo cream sherry, and don't it taste good?" Another big seller, he said, was tomato beer: beer with fresh tomato juice. Would I like to try it?

"Another time," I said.

I really wouldn't mind going back there again.

17

A Citizen of the Realm

I could be wrong about travel being a metaphor for life, but I figure that if we cannot survive a single day on the road without squabbling and seething, then Marcus and I wouldn't be able to at home, either, and we'd better stop kidding ourselves. It isn't that he drove the car off the highway into a ditch along the Oregon coast; that was a minor error any novice driver might have made. It caused no harm except to his psyche. I knew, though I tried to deny it even to myself, that this mishap would probably stop him from ever resuming his effort to get a license. I also knew that I had been foolish to place such an emphasis on his becoming a motorist: in doing so I had been revealing nothing so much as my own shallow insecurity. Mea maxima culpa.

What matters is that our moments of tenderness and humor have been far too infrequent to outweigh the acrimony. When we get to Eugene, Oregon, where I am to talk to the writer Ken Kesey, it has become clear to Marcus and me both that our travels together are over. Both our teeth, or rather all our teeth, have been gritted most of the majestic way up the coastline.

Someone gave Marcus *The Electric Kool-Aid Acid Test,* Tom Wolfe's book about Ken Kesey, and he never got around to reading it. He is not much interested in such matters as the drug generation and the future, if any, of communal living. Nor am I nearly as interested as I might be in the gallery scene along Madison Avenue or in movies—it is true that I have an offensive habit of falling asleep even in the best of movies—or in baseball. He's a wonderful person and I'm a wonderful person, but at close range we have a grim effect on one another.

Still, although there have been times during our trip when I have physically longed for this moment of parting, it does not delight or even much relieve me to take Marcus to the Eugene airport. He has worked his way into some of the innermore labyrinths of my head, from which I could not banish his influence even if I wanted to. I don't want to. I shall always be flustered, just a bit, at the sound of his voice. In spite of everything he has understood me, and I him, in a way neither of us can easily duplicate. Maybe, after we have been apart for a while, we can experiment and find a good middle distance from which to check in with each other from time to time and cheer each other on. Not yet, though, nor should we expect any more than that. We cannot go through all this again. He is rare and fine, and someone of calmer temperament, beset by fewer, or at least other, demons, will if she is lucky discover and deserve him, as I do not. He is flying now to New York, by way of Portland, and after a few days he will proceed to London. London, with its Turners and its parks, gives him something I cannot.

Faye, you might have thought, would be the obvious one for me to talk to. Faye the beatific, Faye the Ur mother, Faye the keel who had kept the craft afloat through the sixteen years of her often stormy marriage to Ken Kesey, Faye who had not even minded when another woman bore a child Kesey had sired, "because," Kesey put it, "all that sort of happened under other auspices, and we all get along real good."

Faye, heedless of auspices, sewed and made applesauce bread

and fed Rumiyako, the pet macaw, and imperturbally minis-
tered to the needs of her husband, their three children, and all
other sentient beings in sight. She had slightly tilted, Finnish-
looking blue eyes, and the calm air of a madonna. It was said
of Faye that once, warned of the possible imminence of earthquakes, she responded by going out to prune the fruit trees. I
recognized her worth. I thought to myself, now there's a
woman we might all well model ourselves after, but somehow
even though she and I were of an age I could not seem to strike
up an unstilted conversation with her. I felt shy. Maybe we
both did. I doubt very much that she meant to, but she, and in
fact the whole lot of them at Kesey's place, made me feel just a
bit like a comparison shopping, super-straight Junior Leaguer
from someplace like Grosse Pointe. Maybe it's just that after
five weeks on the road I was tired.

Kesey and Faye and their kids live in a huge barn outside
Pleasant Hill, which in turn is outside the state university
town of Eugene. That same barn used to be a commune, before
Kesey had ejected the several dozen other residents. "What it
boiled down to," he said, "was we realized we can't all live in
the same kitchen. We're too human; we bicker and brood and
gossip." But a lot of those same people have settled close by.
Their lives still revolve around Kesey's. He is still, as he puts
it, the honcho.

Rumor had it, in June of 1972, that Kesey was nearly finished working on a third book, his first in nearly ten years, to
be called *Garage Sale*. Quite an unorthodox book, it was supposed to be, incorporating a screenplay called *Over The Border,* which would tell of the months Kesey had spent in Mexico
as a fugitive from justice when he was wanted for possession of
drugs. Those same adventures had inspired Tom Wolfe's book,
which had done as much to make Kesey famous as had Kesey's
own novels, *One Flew over the Cuckoo's Nest* and *Sometimes a
Great Notion*. Wolfe told of all this and of Kesey's ebullient
followers, called the Merry Pranksters, who shared his feeling
of evangelism about LSD and speed.

With so many of the Merry Prankster alumni living nearby,
all the ingredients of a topical magazine piece seemed on hand.
Whither, such a piece could ask, the drug generation? Is acid

really obsolete? If communes don't work, why don't they? Is
there any truth in all the talk about permanent brain damage?
What made Kesey change his mind, after he told Wolfe he
planned to write no more "because I'd rather be a lightning
rod than a seismograph?" How come he was suddenly into, as
some might put it, seismography?

But since *Garage Sale* was farther from completion than anybody wanted it to be, my interest shifted. I paid more attention
to the morning ritual of throwing coins for the *I Ching,* and to
the place of women in the counterculture. I didn't use the
word 'counterculture' much. I used it, in fact, only once, on a
hot afternoon when a dozen or so of us were sunbathing next
to Kesey's yard by a pond which we shared with ducks, geese,
and trout.

"We don't talk that way," Gretchen Babbs told me evenly
and pleasantly, after I had used the word. Gretchen had clean
dark blonde hair and wore a long Indian print skirt. She always had at least one child on her lap. "Counterculture" she
said, "isn't in our vocabulary. We're not into bagging people
here."

"How would you describe yourself?" I asked.

"I consider myself a citizen of the realm," she said. That was
what made me decide to focus on Gretchen, who seemed cir-
cumspect and kind. There was something accessible about her
gaze. I hoped she would tell me more of how it felt to be a citizen of that particular part of the realm.

Technically her name is not Gretchen Babbs. Not being
technically married, she is legally still Paula Sundsten, the
name she was given in Hood River, Oregon, in 1943. But having lived with Kesey's close partner Ken Babbs since 1964, and
borne him four children, Gretchen does not "feel I have to go
through somebody else's ritual to prove I'm married." * She
has been known as Gretchen—more properly Gretchen

---

* I am impelled to note the names of the Babbs children. They are called
Purina Casa (nicknamed "Mouse"), S.Q.Y.X. (pronounced "Squeaks"), O.B.
(short for nothing), and Eli. S.Q.Y.X. is acronymic for Simon Quincey Yancey
Xeus. Xeus in turn is acronymic for Xavier Emergy Ulysses Sqyx.

Euphoria Marie is the name of the daughter of Paul and Laura Foster, who
are also a part of this axis.

Fetchin—only since the momentous transcontinental bus trip of which Wolfe writes in his book on Kesey.

During that trip she met Babbs. "Babbs was still married then, so it was two years before we were together permanently, but he and another guy and I shot a movie and put it together in Santa Cruz. Babbs' wife lived around there too. She and I became good friends. I'd take care of her kids when she went to classes. In Santa Cruz we started doing the acid tests. After she met another guy and got remarried, Babbs and I got started with our own family. O.B. and Eli, he likes to say, are the only natives here. The rest of us are just colonists."

They have since been evicted and bought land of their own, but when I met the Babbs family in late June, 1972, they rented a sprawling, friendly farmhouse for $70 a month. Chickens ran around the backyard, which had giant trees and a beanfield adjoining. Babbs drove me there one evening on his way home from the office in the loft above Kesey's barn. Babbs always wore coveralls to that office with an ID badge, as if he worked in some mammoth aerospace corporation with real security problems. Three other people, counting Kesey, worked with him at the headquarters of the Intrepid Travelers Information Service, to produce, among other publications, a magazine called *Spit in the Ocean*. These ventures were not at the time visibly profitable, and so the Babbs family subsisted on a $125 monthly check Babbs' mother in Ohio sent them from his late father's insurance. For $8 they could then buy $180 worth of food stamps, and it pleased them that "you can use the stamps to buy anything you like, including marinated artichokes."

"I'm the oldest of four kids, "Gretchen told me as I helped her hang her wash on the line, envying her the fragrance the clothes would have. "My mother, she's divorced now, is a librarian. I think our mothers' generation had a harder time than our grandmothers did, or than we do. With the Depression and all, our mothers weren't so sure who they were or what they were supposed to be. Advertising just raised their expectations of what they were supposed to want, which made them all the more confused.

"My having a garden here really inspired my mother to do one of her own. That's just what she needs, something to deal with every day. She just planted the first garden she's had since the time I was ten or twelve. She gave up then on that sort of stuff, because a whole Oregon thing went down in that period. You'd raise one crop, like apples, and get everything else at the grocery. The farm thing went from survival crop to cash crop when the first supermarket came along, seventeen miles away. It was supposed to represent progress and advancement and prosperity.

"My mother wanted me to be a college graduate and have a professional job. I lasted one term in business administration. Then I tried art, which proved too unstable, and art education, which I liked all right because it dealt with people. I was expected to get married in a lovely ceremony at age twenty-two, but I think my mother must have figured out by my sophomore year in college that it wouldn't quite work out that way.

"Even in high school, when kids that age were just beginning to be radicalized, I did some political stuff as well as the typical rebellious stuff and was scolded for having a negative attitude. They told me if I didn't cool it in two weeks, I wouldn't graduate. I did graduate. At the University of Oregon I was the first freshman ever to live off campus. I started the whole movement and battle about that, and it was a good thing I did. Living in dorms and dealing only with a certain age group can fuck you up. It doesn't teach you anything about how to deal with real life situations.

"Although everyone told us not to, a girlfriend and I went to New York the summer between sophomore and junior year. Everyone mentioned crimes and rapes and muggings, but we were very determined; we went anyway. Miraculously, we got jobs as waitresses at Jack Dempsey's restaurant and had a fantastic summer. The next year I decided to go back. That year I'd met Kesey, who'd been hanging around the campus, and I thought he seemed to have pretty straight vision. He had this bus he was driving East, so I went along for the ride." So did Babbs.

"Eli," said Gretchen, "is the only one of our children to have been conceived and born in the same bed. I highly recommend having kids at home with your old man right there. I was the first one in our county health nurse's experience to do it that way. When Kesey's farm was a commune, the nurse came over and brought a civil defense movie to show us on emergency childbirth. All of us, including the kids, sat around with tea and cookies to watch it. It was great. The only other stuff there is on the subject, or was then, just said, 'Be sure to pack your toothbrush and don't forget to wear a brightly colored negligee.'

"Having a kid, somebody said, should be like training for the Olympics. If you think of it that way, you'll come out ahead, because you not only save a lot of money, but your body's in much better shape. It would be a bummer to have a baby without a responsible man around, though.

"Dope interferes with motherhood. Women seem to do less dope than men do, partly because dope breaks down your resistance, and women need strength to deal with more interruptions, like runny noses. If you don't pay attention to your kids, they'll really be screwed up. So the way it works out, men have a much better chance of finishing what they start than women do. To do dope with kids around is a waste anyway; the two things don't mix.

"When I get high I like to get *really* high, in nature. And I've taken so much dope over the years that now I can get loaded without it, just off nature and good air. One thing dope really did for me, though: it made me more aware of the universe than I had been since I was a child. I had an inkling of it then, but I lost it through the public school system, where they don't even touch on it. But being high, in lots of ways, gave me the courage of my convictions.

My own hallucinogenic experiences, confined to *cannabis sativa,* have been few, and, in every sense, laughable. The first time my friends Julian and Lloyd and I ever smoked grass was on a screened back porch of a house on Cape Cod, several summers ago. I still have notes I made of that evening:

"Feeling of strange truncating, then elongating distances between other people—as if dimensions of room were expanding and contracting. Considerable effort to stop looking, say, at the candle and start focusing on the Ping-Pong table or Julian or Lloyd. Uncontrollable laughter—wave of giggling and hysteria. Ever-changing medley of visual hallucinations which come, however, only when eyes are closed. Very clinical between our bursts of laughing. Kept trying to tell each other precisely in what manner this feeling differed from being drunk. Agreed it was much more pleasant. Lloyd said nothing had happened to him, even after I and then Julian announced, 'Something seems to be happening,' but he too said he felt very dizzy and strange. Then we all kept telling each other what we 'had,' like 'do you have that washcloth?' 'I didn't, but now I've got it.'

"Wheel (turnable) around edge of aces of clubs, spades, diamonds, hearts, and little pearl shirt buttons in the middle. I said 'Blue yarn.' Funny ambiguity about conscious control: involuntarily and instantly you see what others say they see. I laughed almost hysterically, and announced, theatrically, that 'Laughing is better than crying.' Triangles. New optical law: invent own principles. Julian said he saw triangles. Lloyd said he saw a triangle with a peon on a burro, riding through it in silhouette. I said 'It's the pyramids,' remembering aloud how I once had gone around a pyramid on a rented camel. Lloyd saw flames coming out of the top of the pyramid, like symbolic Byzantine flames, and saw me not on the camel but walking on foot around the pyramid, holding up an umbrella. I saw JoAnn Kleinman as a department store mannequin, laughing. Lloyd had plumbing designs, pipes and faucets. I had very sharp colors, a lot of blue and white and brown.

"Lloyd said, 'An important general sensation is that I cannot focus on anything unpleasant.' He tried to, but got four boxes with triangles on the end and a brightly colored bent neon tube. The brightness of the colors gave him great pleasure. One of his boxes opened and out came a lot of rats, but they merged into a solid mass of brownish-black velvety stuff. Things would change into other things.

"Julian had an Andy Warhol split-screen movie, with images of many faces. Lloyd tried to get *The Iliad* in mind, but only could get abstract designs of men's white shoes with brown tips at the toes and heels. He had an assembly line of men's hats, which changed from cowboy Stetsons to Boy Scout hats to Panamas. A machine came down and stamped on brims.

"He then got a conveyor belt with very pretty colored green beans in kaleidoscopic pattern, not a still life, always moving. I had a multi-lane highway with a brick bridge and Spanish arches over every lane. The highest arch, over the median divider, turned into an open fretwork flamboyant Gothic arch. Then I had a huge, immense Fresca bottle like the sardine man at the Maine state line. Lloyd saw a whole fan of pound packages of bacon, held up like a hand of cards. He also had a fan of flags from golf courses. I said, 'There's so much geometry here, so many rectangles.'

"We got to talking about the names of dogs, among them Prince and Princess. We reasoned that if male dogs were known as Bruce, then females ought to be called Brucess. This seemed the funniest thing any of us had ever heard of. Julian commented that he was looking at the soles of my sneakers, and I said, 'What's your primary impression of them?' and he said simply 'Big!,' which also seemed hilarious.

"I then saw a Planter's Peanut man, Mr. Peanut, and then he was multiplied into a whole chorus line of dancing Mr. Peanuts. We all began to feel a gradual dizzy heavy feeling, and if we got up to walk across the room the trip seemed to take hours."

"Dope," Gretchen went on, "has done a lot to change women. It's turned them on more to *being* women. It brings out their spirit. The vibrations I get from Women's Liberation make me shy away from it completely. They're blowing it. All the women I've met who are into it seem very unhappy. They're searching so hard that they're turning off the very thing they're really searching for, which is a good relationship with a man. By trying to force him into a certain position, and dealing with him as 'a man' instead of as a human being, they blow it."

I wondered what Marcus was doing right then. Maybe he was still in New York, where it was three hours later. Maybe he was already heading toward London, crossing the Atlantic, going farther and farther away.

"Dope's changed my feelings about religion, too," said Gretchen. "It's really helped with religion. We say grace every night here, because we think it's a good idea to give up your ego once a day to somebody else. My religion now is a daily, secular thing, rather than being a matter of Sundays. I've always believed in having it be a daily thing but I could never initiate it, because as a kid I was living with my parents. As a kid I was really into the Presbyterian religion. I helped out with Sunday School and Bible School, and when my best friend later on tried two or three times to commit suicide, I stuck with her until I convinced her not to. She's doing real good now; she's become a Mormon.

"I think about religion a lot and study it. You have to do *something* during the long cold winters up here. I'd like to go to Egypt and the Holy Land—spiritual, mystical places—when the kids are older, and I'd like to read the books in the Bible that aren't around, that kind of thing. Babbs always reads the full Urantia book rundown on Easter week—that's a book of reports on this planet by spiritual beings from other planets who have visited earth at certain periods and gone back. One year on good Friday we had a Passover ceremony. Bobby, this friend of ours who was raised as a Jew, led us. It was neat.

"We've talked about renting a hall on Sundays and singing

hymns and whooping it up. I hope we do it, because I like to play the piano, and I think we should keep that stuff going. Hymns and spirituals are good for the kids. We do other rituals too: jack-o-lanterns, Thanksgiving, Easter egg coloring.

"What would I do if I didn't have kids? Well, I wouldn't just be hanging out. I'd definitely have something going, go back to working in movies, maybe. There's a lot of things I'd like to do, when the kids don't need so much attention. Babbs says he has to laugh at birth control, at man's arrogant attempt to take over for what God does, because he says, to him, kids are like blessings. Well, they are, but I think I'd like to take a break from blessings for a while."

Another Oregon afternoon, while Kesey rode a tractor around the field in front of his house, Kathi Wagner and I sat on the ground in the sun and talked of how her thinking had been changing. Kathi, who then was twenty-four, was one of the four people who worked in Kesey's office, and she lived in a little cottage on the Kesey property. She apologized elaborately for asking me not to smoke in the office, and wanted to know where I had been and where I was going. Unflaggingly cheerful, Kathi was.

Kathi had gone along a few months earlier on a trip Kesey and Babbs had made to college campuses around the country, urging students to vote and assessing the temper of the nation. Kesey had told me about that trip too. "We'd stop in these truck stations to eat," he said, "and at each table you would see a little *bund*. Kathi has these terrific tits, see, and you could hear those guys at those tables pointing at her and saying 'Haw! Haw!' That's how they get their identity energy, I guess. She happened to be a woman, but they could just as well have found a Jew, a nigger, a Polack to make humor about. It's amazing, how thick our nation is into this."

The trip had made Kathi more aware than she ever had been of the women's movement. "I never paid much attention to it before," she said, "but ever since I saw Robin Morgan at a symposium during that trip, my thinking has changed. Where it's at for me right now, for instance, is not to have a man. The whole sex thing plays much too important a part, you know. You don't realize how important until you get away from it. Right now I'm thinking maybe I never will get married, or ever have children.

"I did have an abortion once. My child, if I'd had it, would be four years old now. Whenever I see a kid that age I can't help but think that's how mine would look. Sometimes, the way kids look at me, I just can't look at them back. I guess that's the price you pay. A lot of my friends have had illegitimate children, not out of choice but because they had to, because their parents wouldn't have thought of suggesting an abortion. Still, nearly all my friends are into the marriage thing. The only one who isn't lives in Hawaii, and she and I write letters back and forth all the time, just as if we were together.

"I was brought up by conventional, I guess you'd say upper-middle-class, parents in California. I get along with them a lot better than I did before I left home, two years ago. Right after high school I worked as a secretary, because I wasn't into the idea of getting married then. I had a year of college, then for four more years I was a secretary. It was dull, much different from working here. Then I worked in a Lake Tahoe bookstore, which was the first time I ever really read anything in my life. The farther away I've moved from the city, the better I've felt. I really like working here a lot. Things are really okay.

"I've got two older brothers, both divorced, one of them twice. One evening when Kesey and Babbs and I were in New York, during that trip, I made plans to see that brother for the first time in three years. Ken asked me, 'Are you *sure* you wouldn't rather spend the evening with us instead?' I said, 'That's silly. You'd want to see Chuck, wouldn't you, if you hadn't seen him in three years?' And Ken said, 'But I'd never *let* three years go by without seeing him.' He was right to warn me. That evening didn't work.

"Lately I've been thinking more about religion. Driving around the country, my old Lutheran upbringing comes back to me. Once I happened to be singing a hymn when we nearly

ran into this huge truck with hay bales all over it. I was driving. I said something about how maybe that hymn kept us
from crashing. Babbs looked at me and said, 'Keep on
singing.' "

At this point the phone rang inside the barn, and whoever
answered it called to Kathi. "It's for *me?*" she said. "Hey, good
deal!"

One afternoon Kesey drove me into Eugene to visit his
mother. She had invited him and his brother Chuck and their
families for Sunday dinner. "I used to hate my mom's place
when she first moved in," Kesey said on the way, "but I don't
mind it so much now, because the trees are growing up, and
she's even thinking of painting it some color other than pink."

Mrs. Kesey had never read Wolfe's book about her son. "I
guess if I had I could have let it bother me," she said, "so I just
didn't." She looked like everybody's mother, and reminded me
of a lot of my aunts. Her house was pink, all right, but it was
immaculate and cheerful. Her husband, she told me, had died
at age fifty-six of an incurable disease of the central nervous system, "which was ironic because he had been on a complete
health-building jag all his life.

"He was always in some sort of body-building situation, to
make up for having had an office job. He didn't smoke and he
scarcely drank. Gramps, though, my father-in-law, he's eighty,
and he dances three nights a week. There's never any problem
of what to get *him* for a present, because he always asks for
Black Velvet.

"When my husband was alive, I never took a job or even
thought of it. He was of the old school. If I'd left home when
the kids were little, there'd have been a divorce. He was in
business, you see, and he expected me to be on call at home. If
he phoned to say, 'I'll be home in half an hour with four
guests,' then I knew I'd better be ready, and I always was, too.

"Since he died, though, I've been working. I sell dresses in a
department store, and I like it. Ken wasn't so sure I should,
but Chuck, my younger son, liked the idea. I got bored playing

cards, drinking coffee with the girls, doing volunteer work, bowling, golfing, all that crap. You have to change your own pattern, because nobody else is going to feel sorry for you if you feel sorry for yourself."

Mrs. Kesey got up just then and went into her kitchen to fetch the coffeepot.

"Want another cup of mud?" she asked.

18

Achieve, Achieve

Thick tan humid smog shrouds the whole Eastern seaboard the day I land at JFK Airport. Burnt sienna might be just the color for it. My cab driver curses the clotted traffic. His radio says the air is unacceptable. It is, but somehow I don't care, because pretty soon I can unpack. Unpacking, after so long on the road, is an almost erotic pleasure.

The next evening I am invited to a party at, of all places, the Statue of Liberty. What better setting, I think as the ferry lands, for the start of a new, unfettered phase of my life? It is a United Nations party, with dancing, after supper, at the base below the statue's feet. A South Vietnamese asks me to dance, and so does a Portuguese. Not very unfettered.

A man I once met in Ohio phones the next day, to say he will be in town the following week and why don't I be thinking of a place for us to eat? "I always say," he chipperly adds, and indeed I have heard him say it before, "that the three ingredients of a successful evening are good food, good wine, and good company." I tell him I don't think I can make it.

"What happened with Marcus?" my friend Alice calls to ask.

She and her husband Dean are spending the whole summer at their farm upstate.

"He's gone to Europe," I tell her. "It didn't work out."

"Oh dear. How're you feeling?"

"Numb, really. Numb and of course guilty—as you know I have a *vocation* for guilt—because I'm two months behind in my work. I've got to do a lot of work, and I've also got to unwind."

"If you really mean it about unwinding," she says, "come on up here this weekend. It's been awfully quiet this summer; there won't be a thing going on. The only excitement we can offer is homemade ice cream: we just got a freezer for our anniversary."

"What about your famous corn on the cob?" I ask.

"You'll have to come back around Labor Day for that."

"I can't wait that long. I'll be there Friday."

Alice, as it turns out, was wrong about the quiet weekend. We are all asked to an impromptu pot luck supper by the couple up the hill, to celebrate the wife's big book advance. The neighbors not only ask five or six other families but they have a houseguest. The houseguest's name is Charles Lawrence Nicholson, and he and I are asked to take charge of making the ice cream. Our product, peach with rum in it, is inspired. It vanishes fast. Afterward we all play Red Rover, Red Rover. Fireflies appear.

The next day Charles Lawrence Nicholson, not known as Charlie or Chuck, gives me a ride back to the city. Two years my senior, he is a divorced geneticist at Rockefeller University, the father of three daughters, and as classic a specimen of an Ivy Leaguer as ever my mother could have envisioned. Seven inches taller than I am, with abundant blond hair just starting to grow gray, he is a breakfast-eating, Brooks Brothers type with steel rims. One thing leads to another. He and I seem to be ready for each other, at least momentarily. Entertaining the possibility that we may in fact have been born for each other, I make a private vow: this time I won't be aloof or coy or evasive. Maybe that's what went wrong with Marcus. I like this man, I like him a lot, and I'm not going to pretend I don't.

When the new edition of the Manhattan telephone directory appears, four inches thick, I think: ah, a book with his name in it. Only it isn't, not yet, because Charles has just moved from the Yale Club to a studio apartment of his own in Yorkville. I go with him to Gimbel's East to buy a rug. The thought of him obsesses me. Like a child, I count the days until I'll see him next: the day after the day after tomorrow. How wise song lyrics are, I think. Doesn't need analyzin' 'cause it's not so surprisin'. Blow thou wind southerly. I am reminded of him wherever I look. Even the King of Clubs on a deck of cards— something about the curve of the brow. Charles's eyes, it strikes me, are pools of green from whose edge I might dive. I do dive, and then float.

One bond we discover early on is that Charles and I are both compulsive achievers. In this respect we differ from Marcus, from Charles's former wife, who resented all the time he spent at his laboratory, and in fact from nine-tenths of humanity. "Listen to this," Charles reads me from a paper: " 'Only ten percent of the population is achievement-motivated, and women in that category are likely to experience intense conflicts, especially in regard to a possible loss of femininity.' Are *you* experiencing such an intense conflict, my dear?"

"Not with you around I'm not," I told him, "but I can't pretend I don't know what you're talking about. Maybe we ought to start an Achievers' Anonymous Society. Everyone get together once a week to exchange confessions. Hello, my name is Jane and I'm a compulsive achiever."

"If you felt an achievement coming on," Charles added, "there'd be this buddy network, so you'd have a name and number you could call any time, on a twenty-four-hour basis. 'Take it easy,' I'd say if you called me. 'One dull, drab day at a time.' "

"But don't you ever secretly wonder whether it might not be nice to be just a *little* more contemplative?" I asked him, no longer kidding. "Maybe we're too much caught up in accomplishing—too much defined by bylines and discoveries at the lab?"

"Not really," said Charles. "I honestly love what I do at the lab. I love the idea that I have a good chance to be named the next full professor. I love being good at what I do. And come on, Howard, you know you love it, too."

"You know something I don't love?" I asked him. "Being called Howard."

"Fair enough," he said. From then on that evening our communication was nonverbal.

"I'm supposed to go up to New Hampshire next week," I told him the next morning over strawberries. "I wish I didn't have to."

"Why?"

"I'd rather hang around here and see more of you." With a guarded, reticent past like mine this was quite an admission, I thought.

"That's sweet," he said, "but next week I'm really clobbered. I'm going to have to be late at the lab just about every night. I don't even know if I'll get to see the girls." His daughters lived with their mother in Manhasset.

"Then maybe it's as good a time as any for me to be gone?"

"I suppose it is," said Charles as he poured himself more coffee. "What have you got to do up there, anyway?"

"Well, New England's a part of the country I haven't really been to in years. I figure at some point I ought to go up there and just drive around, talk to different women for this project I've got."

"Quaint *Yankee* magazine anecdotes?"

"Please. That's the sort of thing I've been trying to get away from."

"Are you just going to drive around by yourself?"

"I thought I'd told you. This friend of mine, Peggy, is taking her vacation next week, and that's why I ought to go then, because she's agreed to go with me. She feels like just messing around somewhere, too."

"Is she the one you said was to you as Bebe Rebozo is to what's-his-name?"

"We've been each *other*'s Bebe Rebozos," I corrected him. "Rebozohood is, or should be, a two-way street." Rebozohood, Charles and I had earlier agreed, was a rare, distilled form of friendship beyond pretense.

"I used to have friends like that in the navy," he said, "and one or two in school, but not many since. I guess it's less common for men than for women."

"Of course you were married for so long."

"That *is* a factor. Friends are more important when you're single. I was just barely twenty when we did it—good God, half my present age."

"A child groom."

"I did it to stop having dates."

"An excellent thing to stop having." (Should I tell him in so many words how ready I am to stop having them?)

"What's Peggy like?" Charles abruptly asked. (Maybe I've gone too far already.)

"Game, sympathetic, curious. Comes on strong. Being with her is like eating a lot of very tart McIntosh apples. Men sometimes find her overpowering. Sometimes you wish there were a volume control dial, so you could tune her down."

"Better that than a mumbler."

"Do you hate mumblers too? I can't stand them. Mumbling seems to me an inverted form of arrogance. Anyway, Peggy is also capable of total silence. So, as long as I can't go up there with you, her company will do nicely. And she likes New England."

"Any sensible person would," said Charles. "Have you spent a lot of time up there?"

"Not recently, but over the years, yes, a lot." And almost always, I thought, with pleasure. Maybe it takes a Midwesterner to revere and savor New England. Images flash to mind. A yellow cottage on the Pamet River in Truro. Acrophobia along the Knife Edge Trail on Mount Katahdin. Ritual three A.M. stops at L. L. Bean; by God if they say they're open twenty-four hours a day, we'll make them prove it. Dislodging mussels from rocks in ponds. Rocks the size of rooms above timber line at Mount Washington. A fight with Lloyd on Mount Desert because he wouldn't take me to a Blueberry Festival. Sleeping bags, backpacks, binoculars. Learning with delight at Salem that a man named Nathaniel Bowditch had been America's first actuary.

"I do wish we could go up there together," I told Charles

when this reverie of mine was over. He had been reading the paper.

"Maybe we will, sometime," he said. "Maybe later this summer I'll drive around up there with the girls. It sort of clears the head."

"So do you," I heard myself saying, "and that's not all you do."

"Enough, woman," he said. He gave me a playful slap. "Begone. Or rather *I'd* better be gone. If I stay here you'll get me started, and I've got work to do."

"Of course you have," I said. "Achieve, achieve."

"What is it you women say? 'Right on'?"

"Some women do," I said.

19

The Cat Lady

A week had been the idea. A week's cheerful, loosely structured scavenger hunt, on Peggy's part for tranquillity and on mine for some regional ideas about women. It didn't really matter where we went, we had concurred, because wasn't all of New England agreeable?

Ordinarily it was, but we had not reckoned on finding such brutal humidity. Who would have? Wherever we went, the air before us was like a wall of water. I have always taken the weather quite personally, regarding it as either a benediction or a reproach, and there was no mistaking this for benediction weather.

"Hey," said Peggy. "Listen to that frog." From the far end of a spinach-colored pond by which we had parked our car there came a *thwonk* of amazing timbre, and then another.

"He must have the deepest voice of any frog in all New Hampshire," I said.

"How do you know it's a he?"

"Touché." We tossed pebbles into the pond and watched the resulting ripples, hoping to dislodge and see the contralto frog, but she was nobody's fool. She stayed in the water. Shortly afterward, we joined her there.

"I'm glad *I* didn't come up here to work," said Peggy.

"I envy you," I told her. "I'd cancel that interview appointment tomorrow, if I could."

"Not *that* interview," she said. "Anyone with 126 cats has to be worth meeting."

"I guess behind my back they probably call me the Cat Lady around here," Linda Witherill said the next day. She and her neighbor Jean Rice and I were sitting around on her screened front porch, drinking bourbon and waiting for lunch.

"I guess maybe they do," I had to agree. It was hard to imagine what more apt nickname the other 1,400 residents of Chester, New Hampshire, might have hit upon for Linda. The exact count varies, but the number of felines she had in residence that day was indeed 126. "Half registered," she said, "and half strays."

If Linda left Chester, the title of Cat Lady would surely pass to Jean Rice, who keeps twenty-one in her apartment above the town laundromat. Cats and propinquity have made the two women close friends. Otherwise, they might not be. Jean is by trade an Avon lady, a door-to-door saleswoman of cosmetics, and Linda, until she decided to change over to animals, was by trade an archaeologist.

Neither of them, contrary to my expectation, looked catlike. Linda, in short, curly blonde hair, harlequin glasses, nail polish, and levis, could have been the proprietor of an antique store. Jean, whose splendid violet eyes and clear skin were nearly as noticeable as the fact that she must have weighed well above what actuarial tables advised, could have been a pastry chef. Never assume.

There is, I reflected, a subspecies of humanity called Collectors, in whom there stirs some dark urge not to rest, if ever, until they have acquired far more than one of an object they fancy. I don't know why collectors collect; I guess it might have something to do with power. I can't prove that this species flourishes especially well in New England or among women, either, although I suspect it may. All I know is that Linda and Jean both belong without question in this, if the expression may be excused, category.

Linda also had thirteen horses on the premises, three teen-aged human assistants, four dogs, and I'm not sure how many rare and valuable stamps. But creatures capable of purring, it was clear, were the focus of her most abiding passion. As Creamy and Tigger and Sooty II and Le Chat Noir Bonfire and Briar Brae Merlin and Dizzy and 120 others stretched and pounced around us, or slunk across the lunch table, or dozed in special cages upstairs, I only wished that my niece Sarah could be with me. Sarah, whose Buber was once judged to have the Most Interesting Markings in Macon County, Illinois, would have been in ecstasy.

Sarah would have said things like, "Come to Mommy, fluffy little snookums—a vernacular I had supposed, sight unseen, Linda might lapse into from time to time. Or I had thought she might come across something like the Englishwoman an American friend of mine once met on a train from Rome through Florence. My friend boarded in Rome and was not allowed to get off in Florence, her favorite city in all the world, so she went to stand on the platform between cars in the hope of catching at least a glimpse of the city. The flustered Englishwoman climbed aboard and mumbled something about what a relief it was to be leaving that terrible place.

"But how can you *say* that?" my friend interposed. "Florence is one of the most wonderful cities on earth."

"My dear," said the English woman, "you should *see* the way they treat their cats."

Such excesses of sentiment were not Linda's style. Extraordinary as was her ménage, she discussed it as matter-of-factly as other people might talk of tax-free municipal bonds. Nor was Jean one for getting carried away in lyrical rhapsodies about kittycats. In the course of a long and loquacious afternoon, neither woman said anything effusive.

"Cats," said Linda, "are more abused than other animals are, I wish they had the status dogs do, and I often wish they could talk. They're much more intelligent than other animals. I'd like to know what they think. And they're convenient. You can pick them up under your arm and take them from one room to another.

"They're also a lot more dependent than they're reputed to be. They're all very different, especially in a household like this. With as much competition for attention as each one has, they simply have to be distinctive. Not that we wouldn't feed them or pay attention, but the other cats would make it hard for them. We have to put the namby-pamby, shy ones in cages, but not very many of them *are* shy. This situation brings out their personalities.

"Mostly, I suppose, I just like the looks of them. Especially the shorthairs."

I had sought Linda out at the suggestion of another New Englander, a friend at *Life* who was once described as "that girl who wears rugs and walks like a tree," back in the years before we all wore rugs or called ourselves women. My colleague, who had been Linda's roommate at Radcliffe, comes of legendary stock herself. Her mother, Linda remembered, used to hang dog leashes from a Ming vase on the mantelpiece and once served six consecutive meals featuring eggplant. When I called my old *Life* friend, to check this with her, she said, "That's nothing—didn't you know about the time my mother served a marvelous poultry dressing to some European count and countess who begged her for the recipe? She wouldn't give it to them, because she'd made it out of dog food." Another similar New England woman, I once heard, was said to have paid a butcher's bill by wallpapering his house. "And," my informant marveled, "he didn't even *want* to have his house papered!" Long live such ingenuity.

Linda graduated from Radcliffe in 1953 and then lived abroad for six years. Enthusiastically single, she supports her fourteen-acre establishment, officially named Le Chat Noir Stable, with the help of a private income. Her friend Jean had no wish to go beyond junior college. "I never have been much of a bookworm," Jean says. "Maybe I'm missing something by not reading, but I doubt it." She is devotedly married to the operations manager of a truck terminal outside Boston, a ninety-mile daily commute from Chester. "Jean's husband Dave *does* like reading," Linda told me. "In fact he'd really like to teach, but he found he couldn't only teach and make a living wage."

Neither Linda nor Jean regrets being childless. "I enjoy other people's children," says Linda, "*if* they're well-behaved."

"I like being taken care of myself," says Jean, "but I wouldn't want to have the responsibility of looking after other human beings." It also suits them both fine to live in so snugly small a New England community, "even though so many do keep moving up from Boston to avoid the state income tax." Chester is in fact a pretty place, reassuringly rectilinear as most New England towns are. (The clapboard of houses there somehow seems more than horizontal, and the trees more than vertical.) People there tend to rely on the *Manchester Union-Leader* and to vote Republican, although Jean said that George Wallace of late had developed a considerable following.

"But we're not used to minority groups of any sort around here," Jean added. "Once we had a cat we called Bernstein, because he was this very fresh, bratty, Jewish cat, and I told that to some people we were visiting in Maine, without even knowing they were Jewish! Oh dear! Talk about bloopers!" Linda and Jean are both Episcopalians—Jean in an indifferent spirit and Linda, though she rarely goes to church, much more seriously.

"My tendencies are high church if not indeed Anglo-Catholic," she said. "I think Catholicism has a discipline which is very good for people, especially people who aren't ecclesiastically educated. But the church also allows intelligent people to stretch their thoughts. I feel that ritual is a very important part of any church. My own interest is in ritual via historic repetition through a long period of time. Knowing that the Mass has been said over so many centuries gives me a feeling of continuity with the past."

Linda's house, where she has lived since 1960, is the oldest existing frame structure in Chester, "and I'm absolutely *sick* that all the old fireplaces and beams have been removed." What endears the town to her as much as its architecture are its people and customs: the Ladies Aid fairs with pot holders for sale, church bazaars, election-day bake sales, annual town meetings, functions of the Grange and PTA. Not—"Oh, my *goodness* no"—consciousness-raising sessions. "Maybe there are some Women's Lib meetings in Manchester or Nashua, but Women's Lib doesn't matter to women around here. Many of these old town families are matriarchies to begin with, anyway."

"There are a lot of six-feet-three guys around here who are ruled by their mothers," agreed Jean. "I don't see why every couple doesn't just make their own pattern, the way Dave and I do. He changes the cat boxes, because I don't like to, and I feed the cats, because he doesn't like the smell of their food. I can't recall any of my friends ever even mentioning Women's Lib."

"Oh, they're *aware* of it," said Linda, "but it isn't talked about. In my case, I've been cashing in on it. If people want to think of me as a 'poor, defenseless woman,' I don't stop them."

"Linda can put on the dummies pretty good," said Jean, "and I can, too. I can be as competitive as anyone, but I try to suppress my competitiveness, because otherwise I might hurt people."

In Chester, as in many towns its size throughout the United States, much of the social calendar centers on parties organized by saleswomen of such nationally franchised products as Tupperware. Tupperware, a plastic substance of which kitchen storage containers of all sizes and shapes are made, cannot be obtained except at such parties. Once a friend of mine in Washington, D.C., absently contemplating rival plastic dishes at a dime store, was sidled up to by a Tupperware agent who said, in effect, "Pssst—wanna know how to get the real thing? Wanna know where there's going to be a genuine Tupperware party?" Out of curiosity my friend went to the party, where she was obliged to play the sort of parlor games her eight-year-old daughter might have enjoyed. Out of guilt, she ordered a lot of Tupperware.

"I have more Tupperware than Carter has pills," said Jean. "Not a week goes by that I'm not invited to one of these parties. Oh, we have Tupperware parties and parties for Beeline Dresses and Dutchmaid Clothes and Stanley Products and Sarah Coventry Jewelry, all with games you play to get door prizes. There was a lot of cheerleading and that sort of thing at the Avon annual sales get-together, up at the Highway Motor Inn in Concord. As far as seeing the line, I might go again, but not for the fun and games. But I should talk; I'm going to be having a party myself for Philippine Wood Products, just because I really like the stuff."

Abortion is not a topic likely to come up at these or any other Chester parties. "That's one of the things you just don't talk about around here," said Jean, "because people are afraid they'll be struck dead for destroying a life. If young ladies get pregnant they're whisked off and banished until it's over with. Country people are afraid of that sort of thing. Country people feel different about nearly everything. Sometimes I feel quite complimented when my friend Tina'll say to me, 'They don't think the same way we do.' Meaning 'they' the city people and 'we' the country ones.

"What I like most about living here is being able to go to a store and always bump into somebody I know. I like to gab, though you've got to be careful *how* you gab. If you don't keep your business to yourself, everybody else will know it. On the other hand, you shouldn't seem mysterious, either. What I do, in order not to seem mysterious, is run off at the mouth with small talk—weather, the price of things, whose house is for sale, what happened at the fire.

"My Avon customers—I don't like to sell here, by the way, because generally it's not a good idea to do business with friends—they all like to talk about their neighbors, even while they're browsing through the catalogues. It's amazing, the personal things they'll tell me. The more insecure people are, the more they'll talk about this sort of thing. But I never feel that gabbing around to your friends about personal problems will make them any better. In fact, it makes them worse."

Linda is not one to wear her heart on her sleeve, either. "Friends have told me I seem a very disciplined person," she says, "and I guess I am. Many times I might go to bed feeling angry with someone, but I'll wake up in the morning wondering, 'What was *that* all about?' The way I was brought up, we were taught that you don't let down the side. Tears may be therapeutic, tears may come to your eyes when you have to have the old dog put down or something, but to bawl and throw yourself across the bed doesn't accomplish anything. I think it's more constructive to carry tears in your heart than to make everybody else miserable. I don't think I ever shed one tear over Barbara Stone, for instance, yet I think of her in everything I do."

Barbara Stone and her husband, Gardner, were Linda's partners at Le Chat Noir. Linda was an undergraduate when she first met Mr. Stone. He then managed a stable near the Radcliffe campus. Later, when she bought a horse of her own, she boarded it with him, and came to be a close friend of his and his wife's. After Linda decided that the expatriate life was not for her after all, she returned from England and accepted the childless Stones' invitation to join them in running what then was primarily a horse business. Cats, at first, were just a sideline.

Barbara Stone must have been in every sense a monumental figure. "Her Wrangler dungarees were size sixty-four," said Jean, "and her shirts took three yards of cloth. Now my husband is quite chubby, but he and I could *both* fit into one of her shirts. For all her weight, though, she bopped right along when she moved. She was a Christian Scientist, so she wouldn't have a doctor, and when she died it was like out of *The Loved One*. We didn't have much choice about which coffin."

"She had a very beloved cat named Star," said Linda, "and she got him into good show condition, but he had a urinary problem and he died the day after Barbara did. Her husband said we ought to bury the two of them together. The undertaker said we could only put the cat in the coffin if he was embalmed. We stuck the embalmed cat down at her feet—fortunately, having been sick, she'd lost a lot of weight, so there was room. Barbara's mother wouldn't have wanted to see that cat in there with her. Barbara, though, would have thought it was fabulous. She had one of those infectious giggles. The church was packed, and we cleaned the house to a fare-thee-well.

"When my mother sees my house she just wrings her hands. She's a bit fussy about her housekeeping. She goes to the point of ironing bras and the tops of stockings and slips, even though they're nylon. But she and I get along very well. My father and I do too. They both realize that I'm bullheaded enough so that if she says 'No,' I'll automatically say 'Yes.'

"I had an enchanting childhood, even though I was only allowed to have a couple of cats, because my father's absolutely terrified of cats and birds. He has a really bad case of fright. I've always liked animals. I was brought up by a German nurse named Anna, whom I adored and still do. I still gravitate to her when I go home to see them. They still live where I was brought up, in central upstate New York. Anna would give me a good clout if I said anything untoward, and so I shaped up fairly swiftly. My parents seldom saw me unless I was clean and well-dressed, usually when I was presented to them for ten minutes before dinner. Maybe that's why my mother and I never had the contempt for each other that sometimes develops between mothers and daughters."

Linda's biological mother was not the bra-ironer of whom she speaks. Like many of her 126 cats, Linda was adopted. "All I know about my real parents," she says, "is that I was illegitimate and that my mother was Irish but not Catholic. Do I wonder more about her? Not much. I just think how fortunate I was that she had such great good sense, because I've had many more advantages this way than I could have had otherwise. I think that if I'd got married myself, I might have tended to adopt children, rather than having my own."

Linda unmistakably is single by choice, not default. Once there was a suitor who "had delusions of being Albert Schweitzer," once there was an Arab legion officer, and once or twice others sought her hand. "But I'm immensely relieved that I didn't just grab whoever came along, the way a lot of young people do, just because they feel they're supposed to. Besides, anyone who married me would have to marry this whole establishment, which would be asking a lot."

It would indeed. The fragrance of all those cats, immaculate though they are kept, is not to everyone's taste, and the shop-talk, though exotic compared with most, might strike many as unintelligible. Five hundred pounds of kitty litter and twelve cases of Calo a week. No milk; milk gives cats diarrhea. No declawing. No selling of kittens until they are three months old and have had permanent distemper shots. Heat can last for thirty-five days. Claws must be clipped, because males are often attacked, for their pains, after breeding, and "to keep happy the males have got to have the girls; they need a female every two or three weeks."

Veterinarian bills come to $100 a month. Once, when eighty cats were sick at the same time, the vet administered 1,700 shots and 3,000 pills. The biggest litter Linda ever saw born was thirteen, the oldest cat on the premises is eighteen, the most expensive cat she ever bought cost $250. Thirty-eight cats are kept in cages, seventy live upstairs, and each has its own specific, sociometrically analyzed territory. Many cats have never met others under Linda's roof; God forbid they ever should. "Your Abbys," says Linda, "are a completely different cup of tea from your Siamese and your Burmese. I'm a short-hair girl myself, but when Mrs. Stone died I inherited her thirty Persians, and that's how it all got started."

Linda once had six horses on the premises under the age of four, which was too many—"You could only work with one with any consistency." Now she only boards horses and doesn't rent them out. She wishes she had more time to ride. "Kids think it's fine fun to gallop over the horizon, and it is, but they don't realize how much maintenance it takes." Nor is the breeding of horses any simple matter. "People consider that if they give you a $150 or $200 stud fee you must be raking in the shekels, but the mare could kick the stud or knock down the barn, and good vets are hard to find these days. A lot of them are going into the small animal business. The greatest joy is having a foal born and stand up healthy, because half the mares who are bred don't conceive, and half the ones who conceive don't have live foals. It's a very iffy business.

"Four people have to be on hand to breed horses correctly. If things go wrong it can be a real fandango. Once we had two studs here that were a riot. One would have bred with a Volkswagen if it had got in his way, and the other, even if we'd led to a mare in dead heat, he'd start looking at a bird or eating grass."

By this time the three of us *homo sapiens* had moved to the swimming pool back behind Linda's stable. Two or three others joined us as we splashed to keep cool and kept on talking.

"Oh, there's always something happening around here," said Linda. "Not long ago the female college president who lives here got married for the first time, at age fifty, to a widower of seventy. She had three bridesmaids, of whom I was one, and we all ended up in completely different pastel colors. It looked like a spring wedding, although in fact it was December, and the bride was so happy she wept all the way down the aisle.

"There's not very often a dull moment. The other Sunday I counted, and I served thirty-five different cups of coffee to thirty-five different people. I was glad to see them come but glad to see them go, too, because I do enjoy solitude once in a while, along with all the celebrations. It suits me that I should have been born on Halloween, because orange is my favorite color and this place is named for a black cat. I adore Christmas too. I'd like to see it come four times a year, and celebrate it even more stringently than Thanksgiving and Easter."

"You should have been here last Christmas," Jean told me. "Linda came down the road wearing a raccoon coat to mid-calf length, an orange mohair scarf tied around her neck, kids' galoshes with buckles, and a brown umbrella. She carried the umbrella, she told us, to keep the snow off her glasses."

"I do love to see the snow fly," Linda said. "I don't ski or skate, I just like to see it. That's one reason why I wouldn't live anywhere else, except under duress. Three or four days in New York now and then are fine, and a luxury trip to England on the *QE II* would always be nice, and now and then I like to go see my brother and his family in Santa Monica. He says he feels as if he had as many children as I have cats. But this is where I belong.

"There was a time when I thought of becoming a British subject. While I lived there, studying first Anglo Saxon churches and later Romano-British archaeology, I developed an accent nobody could crack. My best friends there were the librarian of the Victoria and Albert Museum and his wife and daughter. We all became quite close. The man and his wife were quite a bit older than I am, as many of my friends have been. Age doesn't matter a darn to me."

Quite by chance Linda got sidetracked into Palestinian archaelogy. Once, when someone had to drop out at the last minute from a dig in Jericho, her professor Sir Mortimer Wheeler asked Linda to go along instead. There followed field trips in Jordan and Iraq. Eventually she decided to come home. "As my friends moved off and drifted away, I began to realize how strong one's ties and roots really were. Although the British women I knew were damned independent, the average British housewives were more downtrodden than Americans, and the average British men more likely to philander."

Now, in the center of her microcosm in Chester, Linda is at something like peace with herself. "Maybe I'm complacent," she says, "but I like the way I live."

"Every now and then," said Jean as she clambered out of the pool, "some bird will ask me, 'How can you lead such an irrelevant life?' "

"Maybe it *is* irrelevant," Linda said. "Maybe I'm very insular. I use newspapers more for the dogs' bed at night than for reading, although I do look to see whether King Hussein's been assassinated. There isn't time to read as much as I'd like to. These days I'm lucky if I get five minutes without the

phone ringing or somebody coming by. I regret to say I'm rele-
gated to the area of a good mystery story. I prefer stories like
Agatha Christie's, in which everyone is well-bred, to those
about the Mafia and syndicates and that sort of thing.

"I like Renaissance and Baroque music and I like movies
too, although I haven't seen one since *101 Dalmatians*. It
doesn't really take much to make me happy. I'm not a cause
person, but I do try to lead a decent life. I try to do my bit for
civic duty. Two months a year I'm in charge of the fire phone,
which means you can't even go to the bathroom if you're alone
in the house, because you have to answer by the second ring.

"Clothes don't matter much to me. I recently threw away a
skirt I took with me to boarding school. A couple of years ago I
spent $150 on a matching shantung coat and dress, but all I
mostly wear around here is jeans and sneakers, and when my
mother gave me a fur coat I was absolutely stunned. My idea of
luxury would be to eat lobster, or buy a piece of jewelry—I've
been taking silversmithing lately—or get a new stamp for my
collection.

"Do I get up early? Not really. At about 6:30. And you
should see the delegation outside my room if I get up ten minutes late. There are five cages in my room and one cat who
sleeps with me, named Scooterpie. Scooterpie is my bedroom
cat. Out of her whole litter she's the one I'd have chosen last,
but she wanted me. There's a lot to be said for being wanted."

20

Honor Your Corner Partner

"How are the Jensens?" I asked Peggy. "I'm sorry I didn't get to see them."

"They were sorry too, but they had to get going." Sally and Lars Jensen were old friends of ours, especially of Peggy's. Just before my arrival they and their five children had left for a month's camping in the Gaspé Peninsula and urged us to stay in their huge farmhouse as long as we liked. The house was vacant except for Lucy, a twenty-three-year-old biologist whom the Jensens had hired to stay and look after the horses and dogs. Lucy, who was trying to decide whether or not she wanted to go to medical school, had a single dark brown pigtail and an imperturbable manner. She looked as if no crisis could undo her.

"How long ago did the Jensens get married?" she asked Peggy and me as the three of us sat having breakfast.

"Must have been ten years ago," I said.

"That was some wedding, wasn't it?" asked Peggy.

"Sure was," I said. "Now *there's* a union I'll bet no man will ever put asunder." Dozens, maybe hundreds, of us had been in-

vited from all over the Eastern seaboard for the whole weekend. It had been like a New England version of a house party
at Tara; I kept waiting for the Tarleton twins to come and ask
me to eat barbecue with them. Elaborate charts showed us all
where we were to sleep, and we would help each other get but-
toned into our dresses, chanting ". . . beggarman, thief, doctor,
lawyer, *merchant!*"

"Ugh, I hate retailing."

"Well, maybe he'll be in import-export."

"We can hope." On the eve of the wedding, there was a
square dance in Sally's uncle's barn, with old time fiddlers and
callers. Everybody did the Virginia Reel, even Lars's elderly
parents and my friend Lloyd. He wasn't ordinarily much of a
one for dancing, but he had swung the opposite lady and prom-
enaded home with the best of them.

A woodwind quintet had played at the wedding, and afterward Mrs. Jensen, a Latvian immigrant who worked as a cook
in the Bronx, went up to her son's new in-laws and said,
"Thank you for everything, but thank you most of all for your
beautiful daughter."

"You caught the bouquet, didn't you, Peggy?" I asked.

"They still threw *bouquets* in those days?" asked Lucy as she
put honey in her tea.

"I caught a lot of them in my time," said Peggy. "I'm sure
everybody figured I'd have paired off with somebody or other
long before this."

"Me too," I said.

"Are you sure you *want* to get married?" Lucy asked us.

"I don't know of any better ideas," said Peggy. "Devotion
and commitment—that's a pretty hard combination to beat."

"I'm not so sure *I* want to," said Lucy. "Three years ago I'd
have jumped at the chance, but now I'm not so sure at all. I've
been living with Zach for a year now—we went together two
years before that—and it's been a real eye-opener. I'm not so
sure I wouldn't prefer to have him live about a block away so
that we could see each other when we really both felt like it,
when we *wanted* to share space and time."

"Is Zach gone a lot?"

"He's been an intern this year, so he's been gone about ninety percent of the time. What I do is I sit there and wait for him. I don't *like* waiting. I'm not good at it."

"Where's Zach now?"

"He's gone home, to see his family. He hasn't been back there for six years."

"Back where?"

"Nigeria."

"Wow."

"The funny thing is, he's the one who urged *me* to get into feminism in the first place. He's the one who told me about this eight-week course called Women and Their Bodies. Out of idle curiosity, I went. What an experience. I didn't stop bubbling for the whole eight weeks."

"Why?" asked Peggy. "Hadn't you ever talked about your insides before?"

"Oh sure, some, at college, but never without tee-heeing and giggling, on a level not too far removed from an embarrassed eighth grader having her period who thinks the whole *world* wonders why she isn't in the swimming pool."

"You spent eight weeks just talking about Fallopian tubes and such?"

"Not just that. The great impact of the course was the idea that women really are just as important as men and should be respected as professionals. Since I took the course, Zach and I have had some heavy, involved discussions as to whether it's more important for him to become a big international doctor than it is for me to become whatever I might become."

"You've been with him three years? That's a long time."

"Maybe too long," said Lucy. "But I do miss him. We'll see. This fall I'm going to live in a house with other people, instead of just alone with him. That way I'll get more support when he's gone, and be with him when his eyes aren't closed, when he's in the mood."

"I envy Lucy her options," Peggy said that evening, "don't you?"

"I envy that whole generation," I said.

"So do I," said Rachel Winters. "I don't like to think of

what I did with my twenties. But maybe if I'd spent them some other way, I wouldn't have met Mike." Rachel had befriended in me in eighth grade, in my most unlovely thirteenth year, which entitled her to be my friend for life. She and her husband Mike had a vacation house in a town not far from where the Jensens lived. I called to tell her that Peggy and I were just knocking around New England for a week and that maybe we'd see her.

"Come over *immediately*," she said. "Mike won't be up from Boston till the weekend. I could use some grownup company."

All of us were programmed to be agreeable, but in Rachel's case the message had gone straight to the heart, unedited and loud. If there's anything vexing about her it is that her sweetness can border on the cloying, can make one long at times for the taste of horseradish. But during this visit, after she put her children to bed, an odd thing happened. She and Peggy and I sat there at her kitchen table in a New Hampshire farmhouse on top of a hill and swore. Convulsed with laughter, we used all the foul language we had ever heard or read or imagined, each trying to outdo the others. If a prize had been given for variety, Rachel would have won it.

"What a catharsis," said Rachel, wiping her eyes.

"I guess we're really doing this," said Peggy, "because we're mad."

"Mad at being born too soon?" I asked.

"Too soon to get to know the opposite sex as human beings. As Thou's, you might say, rather than It's."

"Right on, sister."

"Sister schmister. Ram it."

"But really, wouldn't you rather be twenty-three now, if you could, than in—when was it—1958?"

"I really would."

Orpha Smith was twenty-three in 1935, the year I was born. Peggy and I spent an afternoon talking to Orpha, in her kitchen near the Canadian border of Vermont, two days later. Orpha, known locally as the Maple Sugar Lady, was another specimen of that staunch breed of country women, liberally scattered around the United States, who might never give lip service to the feminist movement—might even, if pressed, speak against it—but who exemplify it whether they mean to or not. Peggy and I had never heard of Orpha when we headed north the day after our ribald evening at Rachel's.

"It'll *have* to be cooler up there in the mountains," Peggy said. "Let's just go north. North means good. North means cool. If in doubt, we'll go either north or left."

"But I've sort of got used to the comforts of the Jensens' house," I said.

"We can come back there later," said Peggy. "Besides, I want to spend at least one night camping out, don't you?"

"Yes," I said, "because if we don't, I'll have schlepped this tent up here in vain." I had used the tent only once before.

"It's a good thing you *drove* up here," said Peggy. "You always bring a lot more stuff than you need."

"Maybe when I grow up I'll learn to travel light."

"It's not as though you'd never been anywhere."

"You're right. Less is more and all that. I preach it, but I haven't learned to practice it. Did I ever tell you my parable about the Benjamin Britten record?"

"What parable?"

"Once Dr. Dyer and I were talking about French horns . . ."

"At a dollar a minute you were talking about French horns?"

"In context," I said, "the topic had relevance. Anyway, he mentioned this terrific record, Britten's 'Serenade for Tenor, Horn and Strings,' and I went to Sam Goody's to buy it that very day, and came home to play it."

"And?"

"And I found out I'd already had that same record for years, *without ever playing it.* Lloyd had given it to me."

"It *is* time for you to slow down and take stock."

Later that day, as we passed a post office just over the Vermont border, Peggy suddenly recalled that some friends of friends of hers had moved to a commune nearby.

"Remember I told you about Phoebe and Alex Kramer, those friends of the Solowitzes?"

"The Solowitzes are the ones you liked in the Peace Corps?"

"Right. Well, the Kramers are these friends of theirs who dropped out of tasteful Roslyn, Long Island, and started this commune up here. I'll bet they'd be glad if we dropped by." We asked a gnarled gnome how to find the Kramers.

"Just take a left at that softwood tree over the hill there," said the gnome.

"I guess he means as opposed to Christmas trees," said Peggy. My father, the planter of redbuds and spruces, would not have been pleased with our ignorance. Still, we found the Kramers.

"Far out!" they said. "So you're the famous Peggy. Come on in and stay for dinner."

"Oh, we couldn't . . ." Peggy began.

"You don't have to go through that number," Phoebe Kramer told me. "We know you're staying, and you know you're staying, and it's terrific. We don't see people from New York every day, or every month, even."

"Do you care?" I asked. "Is there anything urban you really miss?"

"I think wistfully of the *Times* now and then," said Alex. "But we can get it if we really want to, and we're into a lot of other stuff. Want to see our garden?" Sure we wanted to. The seven adults and six children who lived in the Kramer household, who all wore overalls, shared an enormous vegetable garden with another communal ménage a couple of miles down the road. As we admired the garden, Gavin, one of the Kramer housemates, led us surreptitiously behind a toolshed to a secret patch of land where grew a thriving patch of *cannabis sativa,* which we rolled into joints as we waited for dinner.

"So far we've been lucky," said Gavin. "Nobody's been busted anywhere around here. We get along great with the cops and the community and everybody."

"Hey, the Democratic convention is on this week," Alex remembered. "Want to go see if the television works in the other house, and watch Miami tonight?"

"Maybe," I said. I was curious about Miami, but the grass was already getting to me. Soon after supper, I could tell from past experience, I might drift off to a sleep too sound for even the most bellicose Democrats to interrupt.

"We'd better get going after dinner," I said, "and find some-place to sleep."

"Didn't you say you had a tent?" asked Phoebe. "You could just pitch it back there, behind the house."

"That might be great," said Peggy. "A wilderness experience at last. Hey, this stuff is *good,*" she said of the grass. "I've never really liked the taste of it before."

"You're not inhaling enough," said Alex. "Watch how I suck in air."

"Okay, I'll go get the tent," I said, "but I have an embarrass-ing confession to make. I don't know how to put it up. The only other time I used it, some other people assembled it."

"Jane," said Peggy, "is famous for her concept of spatial rela-tions."

"That and motor skills," I said.

"You shouldn't play dumb that way," Alex said. "You're the victim of sexist stereotype conditioning. If you *had* to put the tent up yourself, you could."

"At gunpoint, maybe," I said, "but as it happens I really *am* slow when it comes to such things."

"Alex is one of those male feminists who's always trying to raise everyone's consciousness," said Phoebe. "Never mind: *I'll* put the tent up." Before I knew it, she and Peggy had coaxed the amorphous mound of canvas from its sausage-casing bag and figured out how to prop it up on aluminum rods. While they did this, Alex was casting a horoscope for Nina, one of the commune's unattached women.

"Moon and Venus both in Cancer!" he exclaimed. "Far out. A lot of us here have heavy Cancer, which means we're pretty domestically oriented."

"I'd hate to think how their place would look if they had *non-*Homey astrological charts," said Peggy as we drove back to town to get some wine for dinner. "I guess I'm a bourgeois hy-giene freak, but the way their kitchen floor looks makes me nervous."

"Dinner's going to be good, though," I said. "Did you smell the bread Phoebe is making?"

Dinner in fact was fine, and Peggy and I were stoned enough

not to mind washing all the dishes in tepid, greasy water, by the light of one candle.

"You guys don't *have* to do that," someone told us. "We just leave them if nobody feels like cleaning up." Afterward we sat under the stars, swatted mosquitoes, admired the moonlight, and forgot all about the Democrats in Miami. The next morning there were blueberry pancakes.

"The only thing I really minded," I said as Peggy and I drove north and left after breakfast, "was that many people in that small a space. I kept wondering what in God's name they do when it rains."

"They must have to be exceptionally honest," she said, "and exceptionally kind."

"It was kind of them to tell us about the Maple Sugar Lady."

"Are we near her town?"

"Near enough to phone her, I guess."

"What makes you think she'll just be dying to talk to a total stranger?"

"Maybe she won't be, but a lot of women are."

Orpha Smith was. Before we knew it we were sitting in her kitchen, where she was taking a break from making maple candy, in the shape of maple leaves and little maple women and men, and little tinfoil boxes of maple fudge, and maple syrup, and betwitching stuff called maple butter. The furniture and floors in her house were, of course, maple. She must have waxed and polished it all a lot, because it smelled immaculate. It looked cheerful, with African violets here and there, but it felt a bit lonely.

"We built this house twenty-five years ago," Orpha told us with what could have been a catch in her voice, "and it's never been as empty as it is now. Now that the kids are gone, we don't have such big Thanksgivings and Christmases as we used to. Maybe this year they'll come home—who knows? This place used to be like a hotel. Some mornings we'd wake up and find the beds all full."

Orpha had thick, wiry silver hair and tilted harlequin glasses. When we first met, her voice sounded high and tight, as if she hadn't been using it as much as she might have liked to.

She wore a plaid housedress, which, like most of her clothes, she had made herself, and tennis shoes without socks. "I usually just go around in dungarees," she said, "though I had quite a lot of fun this past spring: I went out and bought me a new dress. The most I've ever spent on a dress is forty dollars."

Her husband, Hue, she told us, was off in Maine, working on a family construction project. "He comes home with the crows in the spring to help with the sugaring," she said, "but the other nine months of the year, he's gone."

"Don't you and he miss each other?"

"I guess, but I don't want to go to Maine. I'd rather stay here and keep the business going, and he *doesn't* want to stay here—so there you are. But we've been married thirty-nine years, which is more than what happens with some of your big hoo-rah church weddings. Some of them sure don't amount to much.

"I can't say I thoroughly approve of divorce, though. Nobody's ever happy with anybody all the time, and these days too many of 'em just seem to quit without giving it a fair try."

"Is Hue fun?"

"Oh, he can be, when he wants to be, but he usually says 'No' automatically, before he even knows what I'm going to ask him. He and his brothers just live to work."

"You're not exactly a sluggard yourself."

"I guess I'm not. I've been baking sugar cakes ever since I came back here from New Hampshire, four years after I was out of high school." She spoke of New Hampshire as if it were as remote as the Aleutian Islands.

"What were you doing there?"

"Oh, domestic work. I went there originally because I was all het up to save money to go to the YWCA School of Cooking, but then my mother got sick, so I came home. I never did go. I married Hue instead. It seemed like the thing to do; we'd both been brought up here on this same hill."

But motherhood and work, more than marriage, were what had defined Orpha. "I guess what I'm probably proudest of," she said, "are the kids and the grandchildren. Our three kids are all doing okay. If I hadn't had my own, I think I'd have adopted some. It makes me mad to see my sister living over there on the home farm just the way it was when we were kids, in her own shell, just there with her husband and cows and horses and dogs. Without children, what's she got to live for?"

"Will any of your kids take over the sugaring business?"

"It doesn't look that way, but when they're married their life is their own. Seems too bad: we've tapped every maple tree around this part of the country. I've been making syrup all my life, ever since I could go in the woods. It's a good quick income for your small farmer.

"We're retailers; we don't sell to the big coopers anymore. Your General Foods buys a lot of syrup, and a lot of it goes into your blended syrups. Tobacco companies buy some, too. And private customers."

"Do you have much competition?" asked Peggy, whose appetite for any sort of shoptalk is remarkable.

"Your competition's not like it used to be. You've got your big sugar companies in Newport and St. Johnsbury, but they're more like factories. We're more trying to get rid of our product than to sell to the big companies, because we don't have good display space."

"Are there a lot of tricks in this trade?"

"Sometimes I go to these things in southern Vermont called Maple-Ramas, where sugar makers get together to snoop around and trade secrets and learn about barometric pressure and jazz like that. I used to think those meetings were silly, but you know, you can meet some very nice people."

"Does this work keep you pretty busy?"

"As busy as we need to be. If we hired more help, there'd be more paperwork, and we'd need more government control. There's a satisfaction in just knowing you've done something as well as you can. It may not be perfect, but it's the best I can do. There's some sugar cakes over there on top of the stove that didn't come out right, because we cooked the syrup too hard. But we found out what we did wrong, so now we know. We're always experimenting."

"It must be nice to work outdoors so much."

"It is. I wouldn't want any part of living in a city. I lived in a city of 10,000 once, and I could hardly wait to get back to the grass. The grass and snow. Snow usually starts up here around November, and sometimes it gets to thirty below. Then in the spring we go tap. You tap as low down on the tree as you can. Some of these trees up there probably been tapped for seventy years. We had fifty-four barrels this year, thirty gallons a barrel. We get around one gallon of syrup to every thirty-five or forty gallons of sap."

That ratio probably applies to my work, too. Odd, the business of work. Orpha extracts sap from trees, Tildy sews together scraps of cloth to make quilts, Doris hauls fish out of the sea, Linda gives shelter to 126 cats, and what do I do? I take words and string them together into sentences and paragraphs and articles and books. Is that not a passing strange way to make a living? Because it is a living: in turn for stringing words together, I am given money, and with the money I pay my phone bill and go to places like Barney Greengrass the Sturgeon King, at Eighty-sixth and Amsterdam, where $1.39 buys a quart of borscht with sour cream so good it can all but bring tears to the eyes, like Orpha's maple butter.

Actual sturgeon, of which Greengrass has proclaimed himself the monarch, is a bit steep at fourteen dollars a pound, but if it were really important to me I could buy some of that too. Relative prosperity has made me a finicky snob. In ice cream my choice is Häagen-Dazs, not the new "health" flavors, carob and honey, but the old, honored coffee and boysenberry. I am also fond of the seafood mix sold at Citarella's, at Seventy-fifth and Broadway, for $1.95 a pound, and in cheeses I am eclectically partial both to Brie and Caerphilly. My neighborhood liquor store, it pleased me to discover, carries inexpensive gallons of good Spanish burgundy and Chablis.

One does get set in one's ways. When I am writing, I have to have either clear skies outside or else a fresh black typewriter ribbon. I can do without one or the other, but not both. I am done in by the combination of a frazzled gray ribbon and a temperature inversion obscuring the view of New Jersey. (The state of New Jersey has some lyrical vistas, but the one from my window is not among them.) I am pathologically impatient in traffic jams and would as a rule far rather shiver than sweat, believing as I do that it is more pleasurable to warm up than it is to cool off. I like very much the cheek-tingling sensation of coming into a warm room from the cold or touching the cold cheeks of a visitor from outside, if I haven't been out myself.

I like to say hello to total strangers during walks in parks, although one Sunday morning when I thus greeted a woman on Central Park South, her considered reply was "Pigshit!" There is a stillness and clarity of vision that comes over me sometimes which I consider holy and which I would give a great deal to know how to sustain and invite at will. I like hard mattresses and open windows, 100-watt light bulbs, strong coffee, and Vita-baths.

"Sure I think women are different now," Orpha was saying. "Definitely they are, because no families can live on one income anymore. When I was a kid women stayed home and took care of the family and minded their own business, but all that's changed. I'm not sure it's changed for the better. With your higher educational level, life's going on at a faster pace. Sometimes I wonder where we're racing to, what we're in such a hurry for.

"For two-thirds of the people," said Orpha as passion arose in her voice, "your days of personal pride and accomplishment are over and gone. In my time we either worked for what we had, or else we didn't have it, and that's all there was to it. But the girl down the road here, she just picks up with anything that comes along. She hasn't got the responsibility to hold a job and that, if you ask me, is stupidity."

"She doesn't work at all?"

"*No* she doesn't work, and I hate to work *my* fool head off to pay for someone else's fun. These bunch of leeches have no idea of honest living. Life's always been handed to them on a silver platter. They've never done an honest day's work in their lives. Welfare, to me, is the whole thing that's wrong. I don't mean if they're sick and old—if they are, then sure they deserve welfare, but a lot of them aren't."

"Do you think women like that should be able to get abortions?"

"If people don't want babies, why don't they just get spayed, like dogs and cats, and have it over with? Some people running around these days seem to have about as much sense as dogs or cats. Maybe less."

"You must like some of your neighbors here, though."

"Oh, some I do, certainly, though I don't belong to as many clubs and organizations as I used to. Lately the Methodist church is about it. I got involved with the senior citizens, but haven't been down there for a few months. Play cards there is about all I do. You've got your Eastern Star, your Rebekah, your Grange, but there's no use belonging to those if it's just to have your name on the roster."

If there is a kitchen somewhere in rural or small-town America in which there does not hang a framed motto expressing some sentiment of its owner, I haven't been there yet. In Orpha's kitchen the sign says TO A FRIEND'S HOUSE THE ROAD IS NEVER LONG, and the friend in question would appear to be her neighbor Lila, who lives just down the road.

"Lila's the one I call up when I want somebody to visit with," said Orpha. Lila, who came over while Peggy and I were there, would appear to be Orpha's Bebe Rebozo. "Oh, we've had some good times, driving around," said Orpha. "I think I'd hate to lose my driving license more than anything I've got.

"I'd just hate to lose that feeling of independence. I've traveled some, I've been to Vancouver twice to visit some of Hue's folks, and as far south as North Carolina, but I'd like to do it a lot more. What I'd do if I had money, I'd put it in the gas tank and just head out, in any old direction. I'd like to go see Alaska sometime; I've heard they have twenty-two hours of sunlight and that the fruits there get to be just huge."

"Why *don't* you go there sometime?"

"All that keeps me here is lack of money. If somebody came

along and said let's go somewhere, anywhere, it wouldn't take me long to pack my bag. And I'd take Lila along. Lila and I, we just like to poke along the back roads."

So do Peggy and I. Right then, in fact, we said we had better get going, because we hoped to go to a square dance that night at the centennial celebration in the town where Rachel Winters lived.

"Square dances, those used to be fun," said Orpha. "When we were kids growin' up, there was your country dances, your neighbors, you all got together. Things then weren't such a commercial mess; we were satisfied with less and got more enjoyment out of what we had."

"Which were you closer to, your mother or your father?"

"To my father, he was a wonderful guy. Oh, Mom was good too, but he was the one who showed us the enjoyment there was in the simple things of life. We'd have something we called a Kitchen Tunk; somebody'd clean out the kitchen, and if they had an organ they'd chord on it, or a banjo, and always a fiddle. 'Twas fun. Once in a while they dance and that around here, but mostly everybody sits and watches TV."

Suddenly it seemed urgent to get to that square dance. If we left Orpha's right then, we could make it and arrive in time to hear the fiddles and honor our corner partners.

"Wouldn't you girls like to have just a little spin around the mounting before you go?" asked Orpha. Well, since she put it that way, of course we would like to. We all got in the Volkswagen and had a spin, driving past the house where Orpha's barren sister lived, going to see the mill where the sap was piped in by plastic tubes, and at one point crossing the line so that we were technically in Canada. I liked Orpha and am sorry we didn't stay there longer to talk to her more. We were not too late for the square dance, but it was disappointing: they had it in a parking lot, and the music was recorded.

The next day, back at the Jensens', there was a message for me to call my sister. "Urgent," the message said.

"You'll never guess," Ann correctly predicted, "what Bob-bob is going to do." Bob-bob is what her children call their grandfather.

"What's he going to do?"

"Are you sitting down?"

"Yes."

"Bob-bob is going to get *married!*"

"*Madre de Dios,*" I said not very audibly.

"Hello?"

"I'm here; I'm just a tiny bit surprised. Have you met the lady? Is she the one he said was nice, from Philadelphia?"

"I have, and she is. That should have been a clue enough, shouldn't it, his even mentioning he'd met a lady. You know what she said to me?"

"What'd she say?"

"She said, 'Your father isn't a very good Frisbee player, is he?' "

"Did you say, 'No, and I'm not really good, yet, at doing root canals'?"

"Who ever thinks of one-liners at appropriate times?"

"Nobody ever does. Oh, my goodness. Imagine it. Well, good for him. Why wouldn't he? Good for her, too. How did he meet her?"

"She was in Springfield visiting her widowed sister, and someone had a dinner party, and I guess they figured there were too many women and they needed an extra man, and let's see—I know! What about Bob Howard?"

"What's she like?"

"Svelte and stunning. Salt-and-pepper hair cut short. Six children, all married, and twenty-two grandchildren. Cheerful, bright, and straightforward. She admitted she was nervous when he brought her over to meet us, and that was refreshing. She was wearing pants. She was nice with the kids. They liked her. I think we will too. It'll just take some getting used to, is all."

"How long have they known each other?"

"Since March, I think. She went back to Philadelphia in

267

April, but came back to see her sister again—*so* important for them to keep in touch, don't you know—in June. The June visit still isn't over." This was the middle of July.

"When are they going to do it?"

"As soon as they can. I guess it depends on when you can come out."

"I guess I'd better call him."

"You mean them."

"Okay, them."

21

Tears of Joy

"I *hope* those are tears of joy," our new stepmother, Beth, said soon after the Presbyterian minister had pronounced her and my father wife and man. Ann and I had both wept audibly during the intimate garden ceremony.

"Don't *do* that to your face!" Ann had whispered.

"Well, you're doing it, too," I told her. "You started it."

"*I* don't twist *my* face up that way."

Our Aunt Martha, down from Minnesota for the occasion with Uncle Henry, put an arm around each of us and said, "There, there." In a way, our tears were joyful. Why should we not be glad that this slim, energetic widow had given up all her boards and committees in Philadelphia to make a new life in central Illinois? Why should we not rejoice in our father's release from stoical homemade Granola and long-playing opera records turned up loud, mostly to have some sound in the house? Did we want his involuntary bachelorhood to last any longer than it had to? Of course not. Had we not said we hoped he would find some nice woman? Of course we had. But did we think he really would? Of course we didn't. Here the two of them were, though, looking and acting entranced.

Our faces might not have shown it, but we did welcome Beth even as she said "I *certainly* do!" to the minister's rhetorical questions (among them, at her request, a promise to "obey" her new husband). We welcomed her even as she exclaimed "Wow!" when the service was over. I guess we were not crying for any immediate, rational reason, but because this occasion, more than any other, seemed to mark the real end of our protracted childhoods.

Beth's kin and friends outnumbered us for the weekend festivities, which began with a picnic outside our house on the eve of the wedding. The next day, at a prenuptial lunch, we sat on a lawn with some of our new step-siblings to draw a family tree so we could see whom they had married and borne. Two of Beth's daughters had come with their husbands, from Washington, D.C., and Palo Alto, and one of her sons flew in from Seattle. Considering our ages it wouldn't have mattered if they and we had cordially disliked each other, because it was hardly as if we were going to all live under the same roof, but, as a bonus, we all got on fine. We had been to a lot of the same places and knew the same songs. We were almost late to the wedding, because just before it began we had all swum out to a raft in the middle of Lake Springfield and passed a bottle of wine around to toast the bride and groom. Much later that night we had another swim, and then a songfest around the kitchen table. Uncle Henry came down in his pajamas and joined us. We sang show tunes, hymns, Gilbert & Sullivan, and World War II songs. To the everlasting glory of the infantry/Shines the name, shines the name of Rodger Young. We all traded addresses and promised to send prints of the 35-millimeter film we had been shooting. Like most Howard occasions, it was a thoroughly documented affair.

I was tempted to stay on at Ann's house in Decatur after the wedding, and in the interests of that sacred commodity dailiness, I should have. I should have stayed to savor such simple pleasures as hearing crickets at night and walking down quiet streets observing that yellow lights in country windows looked warmer than the bluish lights of cities. I should have stayed to stare out windows at trees whose leaves looked individually rinsed and to play with that grand old gentleman, Perry the dachshund, and to hear John practice on Auntie Grace's piano.

"Why don't you ever come out here when you can hang *around* a while, Tolly?" my bearded brother-in-law asked, using one of the old nicknames Ann once gave me. (She constantly rechristens everyone around her.) "What're you rushing back to New York to see?" Not Charles Lawrence Nicholson; he had gone for a month's vacation with his daughters. In fact I was not rushing back to New York at all, but to Washington. I had an article to do on Eleanor McGovern. For an exciting short while I had been supposed to go with her to Vienna, where she would have looked at some child-care centers, but then came the news about Senator Eagleton. Scratch Vienna. Instead I would have a free trip to Pittsburgh, with stops in Philadelphia and Baltimore.

First there would be another trip: a two-day whirlwind, with two planeloads of journalists, starting in Washington. Our stops would be Manchester, N.H. (a shoe factory), Hartford, Conn. (Aetna Insurance and Governor Ribicoff), Providence, R.I. (to mend fences), Mineola, Long Island (to see other newsmen), and back to the Time & Life Building (to be interrogated by Hedley Donovan and his colleagues). I did something bad on that trip. During one of the motorcades in, I believe, Manchester, I got into the same car with Mrs. McGovern *without clearing it in advance with Mary Hoyt.* Mary, who was Eleanor McGovern's press secretary, had to be very careful about things like that. After all, I was not the only one who was constantly imploring her and scheming to have a ten-minute segment of Mrs. McGovern's time, just in case she should say something relaxed or offhand. Winzola McLendon and Wauhillau La Hay and Myra MacPherson and a good many others shared this goal with me that summer. We were caricature newshens. I felt sorry for the object of all this conniving, even as I resented her tininess. I could see why the more matronly wife of another senator once said, "Let's drown her in the punchbowl," I would have liked to make her acquaintance in some other season of her life, perhaps at a time when she could go to a ladies' room without a Secret Service woman.

"What am I going to *wear* for all that campaigning?" I asked Ann, who in emergencies often serves as my fashion consultant. The things I had in my suitcase, she ruled, would not do. Too casual. Just before I caught a plane to Washington, she rushed me off to the Pret-à-Porter dress shop in Decatur, where we found a couple of dresses in which I could masquerade as a grownup career lady.

Halloween is my stepmother Beth's birthday. I rather envy her that. I went back in 1972 to help celebrate and to congratulate my father on the publication of his history of the state and to see John (as a gaucho) and Sarah (as Little Bo-Peep) in their costumes. The next afternoon I put my feet under Beth's kitchen table and we had a talk. She told me how skittish she had felt, when she returned East just after meeting my father for the first time. Would he remember her? Would she ever hear from him? Once, miraculously, there came from him a postcard signed "Yours." She had been enraptured. "Yours," if you think about it, which she did, is a rather promising exit line. Once Beth decided to phone my father, from Philadelphia, and dialed the ten digits five different times, hanging up after each dialing, before she could summon the nerve to wait for his voice. I found all this quite human and familiar. It was nice to know that other grownups had such feelings. Moreover, hers was a story with a happy ending.

We talked about having children. "When I was a child," she recalled, "I disliked the world of adults so much I never wanted to grow up myself. For me, having children was a way to continue being a child myself and make sure I'd have friends who were children."

"Not such a bad idea," I said.

"Coming here," Beth said, "has been a kind of inner homecoming for me. Your father is the best thing that's ever happened to me. I think he's the reason I was born. When I married him, I truly felt it was something that would make an enormous difference—enough to give up the very good things I had in terms of geography and relationships.

"I found it a wonderment not only that I *could* do it—come and make a new life here, I mean—but was strongly impelled to do it. Your father is not at all like my own, or my late husband, but I feel that he's on his own base, and it's a sound base. He isn't static. Don't you think he'll like having his study moved to the old sunroom?"

"It is a lot sunnier down there," I said.

"And we'll have shutters on the windows, and we've taken the big table out of the dining room. That's not the way we're going to be living. We'll use individual TV tables if there are more than just the two of us, except for really formal occasions, of which I hope there won't be many. And we're going to move the gazebo from the back over to the side, and put another bathroom in upstairs—oh, it's going to be *chaotic* around here until we get it all done, but it'll be worth it, I think.

"There are so many things we want to do, places we want to go, but I'm just so happy staying right here that I don't feel any urgency about it. When your father quits working at the State House [upon his retirement three years earlier he had of course begun another job the very next day] he has such a world of things he'd like to write about, study about. The other morning he woke up at two-thirty and, not intentionally of course, woke me.

"I said, 'It's two-thirty, dear, don't you think maybe you could sleep a *little* longer?' He smiled sweetly and said, 'How do you think I'm going to learn about mutations if I sleep?' I thought: mutations? Okay, if he wants to read about mutations at two-thirty in the morning, then fine.

"The fact that I can be with someone as different as he is is the greatest growing experience I could have at this age. He wouldn't have been foolish enough to marry me, either, if he planned to stay stuck in one place. And I've found him a really good listener too. If there's one thing I know for sure, it's that marrying him was a really healthy decision."

"Good," I said.

"On a moonlit night I can stand by the window upstairs and

get this tremendous kick out of just looking at the sky, just knowing I'm alive at this point in time."

I told Beth she appeared to be one of the most positive women of any age I had ever encountered. "Oh, I've made mistakes in my life," she said, "but they're over with. I can't keep harking back to all that. How can I be sixty-three and make the same mistakes? The needle has to move on to another groove in the record."

To many new grooves, I thought. I also thought of something I had recently underlined in Margaret Mead's autobiography: "Watching a parent grow is one of the most reassuring experiences anyone can have, a privilege that comes only to those whose parents live beyond their children's early adulthood." She was right.

22

Potentially Frivolous

"Hey, Jane Howard Girl Writer," said Stanley Caldwell as we left the Palace Bar in Prescott, Arizona, "you know what?"

"What, Stanley?" We crossed the street and walked through the courthouse square.

"I'm enormously pleased that you came out here. You're an okay broad."

"You know better than to use that word these days, Stanley," I said by rote, "but thanks. Is it such a surprise that I'm okay?"

"I used to think of you more as a pen pal."

"Even when you were with me?"

"Even then."

"Was that my fault or yours?"

"Neither, maybe." said Stanley. "Or maybe both."

"Could be," I said. "Nobody's perfect." I had liked Stanley ever since we first met five or six years ago. He has a good deal of style. Of his several modes I like best the one in evidence the night we went to the Palace Bar, when he wore a Stetson and cowboy boots which shot his height on up past the six-feet-six mark. (It sometimes amuses waiters and other strangers to address him as "Mr. Tiny." He has a crewcut, which no wave of ideological fashion will tempt him to let grow out, and a lavish black handlebar mustache, which comes and goes according to his moods. He and I had come to be old family friends, in a manner of speaking, even though both our families consist of one person. We both are given to frequent travel, and we have visited each other's houses. The first thing I noticed when I went to his, in Albuquerque, was the signs he had written in Magic Marker on his refrigerator door:

THE ILLUSIONS WHICH EXALT US ARE DEARER THAN
A THOUSAND SOBER TRUTHS.

CHEKHOV

and

NOT TO DISCRIMINATE IN EVERY MOMENT SOME PASSIONATE ATTITUDE IN THOSE ABOUT US IS, ON THIS SHORT DAY OF FROST AND SUN, TO SLEEP BEFORE EVENING.

PATER

Once in New York Stanley took me to a Tennessee Williams play. The tickets had been very expensive, but we both hated the play. I was impressed when Stanley suggested that we leave at intermission: that's what I call class. He was glad to get back to Albuquerque, just as I am perversely glad to get back to New York when I have been away. One thing that has drawn us toward each other is the fact that we are both comfortable with, or at least fascinated by, juxtapositions of style and event. He told me of two consecutive fund-raising evenings he had been to. The first, at which Cesar Chavez was to appear, was in aid of migrant farm workers. The second benefit, starring a sociology professor, was for Princeton.

"Chavez was supposed to be there at seven, but by eight he still wasn't, nor by nine or nine-thirty, and all the while the man in charge of the rally improvised most cleverly. Group after group of Mexican families would get up there on the stage and sing and dance, and they weren't even any good at it, which made it especially touching. By the time Chavez finally arrived you had the feeling you were in the presence of a saint. They passed the hat, literally, and they passed tin buckets; they passed every receptacle they could find." The Princeton affair had been tasteful and punctual.

Stanley is, among other things, a rancher. He had come to Prescott to order some Hereford heifers. I was there because I had happened to be home when he phoned me in New York, a few days earlier. Sometimes we call each other up, just to talk about how things are going with us, or aren't. This time he called to say he would be flying soon to Prescott from Albuquerque, in his own plane. I told him that I would be out West soon myself: the following week I had to be in Colorado to do research for an article.

"Hey, Jane Howard," he said. He nearly always calls me that, as if it were a double Southern name like Mary Ann. "You know what you ought to do?"

"What?"

"Get yourself out to Prescott on your way to Colorado. It would be overshooting the mark a bit, but you've done less logical things than that, haven't you?"

"You know I have."

"So come along. Meet me in Prescott. Have a look at the country out there. You'll like it."

"I already do like it. I drove through Prescott last summer, and wished there'd been time to stay longer. I remember a wonderful town square, with benches where old men sit and a coffee shop with a terribly nice waitress and an old-time saloon I didn't think there were any of any more."

"See it all again. I'll fly you back to Albuquerque, and then you can catch a flight up to Denver."

"You know what, Stanley? You couldn't have asked me at a better time. You're on."

Charles Lawrence Nicholson had returned from a month's vacation with his daughters, and whatever it was that had been there between us had evaporated. It was yet another, after all, in a long series of those bells that now and then rings. I saw him once or twice, and he treated me with elaborate, chilling courtesy. Courtesy like that can be more cruel than rage. I could not bring myself to ask whether he had reconciled with his wife, or found somebody new, or just decided that more closeness with me was not among the things he wished to achieve. I should have asked him, and meant to, and tried to, and wrote a lot of drafts of hypothetical letters to him, which mercifully I did not send. But even when he phoned me, even when I actually saw him, I did not ask him.

"How many more of these interludes can a person *stand?*" I asked Dr. Dyer. "Wouldn't you think I'd learn some lesson from all these episodes?"

"Maybe you can," he said.

"How?"

"By talking it over with the others involved. But that's not something I, or anyone, can make you do."

"It's so much easier to pretend everything's okay."

"But everything isn't okay."

"Are partings *ever* painless?"

"Never," he said. Poor Dr. Dyer. Listening to me must make him feel like someone condemned to review daytime television soap operas. Well, at least I had learned something with Charles Lawrence Nicholson. At least I had dared to take his arm when we walked down the street, without worrying whether he would think I was too pushy and possessive. Maybe I had been too possessive, in my zeal not to seem too aloof, but better to lose than never play. Marcus, with whom aloofness had been my style, had come home from Europe with a new, and presumably forthright; friend. Maybe the next time I cared about someone, whenever that might be, I could be assertive to just the right degree. For me there are few things more difficult.

Long ago *Life* sent me for a weekend to the Concord Hotel in the Catskills. I was supposed to write captions for a photographer assigned to do an elaborate double-truck picture of a mass cha-cha-cha lesson. The photographer and his wife and his

278

assistant and I would report thrice daily to the hotel's extravagant main dining room. Each time we went in, a grinning female sentry would ask us, "Got any singles in your party? I meet 'em, greet 'em, and match 'em."

I had no wish to revisit the Concord, but I thought a trip to meet Stanley might be just right. Not that any match would be forthcoming between him and me, I knew, because he had already experimented with the state of matrimony, three times, and found it wanting. A loyal, long-distance friendship was all he had in mind. But a weekend with him would at least be diverting, and diversion was the very thing I needed. I felt like a pathetic man who a good many New Year's Days ago had sat on a stool in a bar in Greenwich Village, next to my friend Lloyd. Plainly this man envied Lloyd and me our jocular rapport.

"Wanna know something about me?" he asked us.

"Sure," we said, realizing we had no choice.

"I'm potentially frivolous," the man said.

That's how I felt when I flew to Phoenix and then rented a car to meet Stanley in Prescott. Not frivolous, but potentially so. Stanley saw to it that I had a manifestly frivolous weekend. More than that, from him, I knew better than to ask. The town square and the coffeeshop and the saloon were not disappointing, and one afternoon I sat in a pickup truck in a pasture while Stanley and some cowhands checked over the whiteface heifers he planned to buy.

The next day we flew in Stanley's tiny plane back to Albuquerque, gasping at the marvelous pastels of the Painted Desert below us. It looked like melting ice cream. At one point I saw what I was pretty sure was an Unidentified Flying Object, a strange white curved form, but I didn't mention it to Stanley until it was too late, and when I did he was, to say the least, skeptical.

In the two days with him that followed, I felt looked after but not fawned over. I drove off by myself in his jeep and looked at Navajo artifacts in Old Town. It didn't much matter that as soon as I got to Denver, as far as Stanley was concerned, I would be on my own. We were no more than friends, but no less, either.

"So long, Stanley," I said when he took me to the Albuquerque airport, "and thanks a lot. I'll be seeing you."

"You bet you will, Jane Howard Girl Writer," he said. "We keep in touch."

We do at that.

23

A Tunnel's No Place for a Woman

The two hundred people who live year-round in Georgetown, Colorado, tend not to know their exact street addresses. They walk to the post office to get their mail. Sixty miles west of Denver, just off Interstate 70, Georgetown is a renovated nineteenth-century mining center whose chief civic aim now is to attract tourists, especially those who ski. In all directions rise humbling Rockies, covered with evergeens and quaking aspen which in the fall turn a stabbing yellow. The houses of Georgetown, painted in fanciful colors, have steeply gabled roofs. On the main street are a couple of fancy restaurants, meant to evoke the good old days, a grocery where you can get excellent take-out sandwiches for picnics, shops with wide selections of fossils and geodes, and stores like Thelma's Son-in-Law, featuring candles and pot holders.

The air is fresh and sweet and fragrant around Georgetown, but thin. Real thin, as they say, until you've been there for a while. In the Pretzel Kaffeehaus there hangs a sign that says WATCH YOUR STEP: 8,513.76 FEET ABOVE SEA LEVEL. Leonard McCombe, newly arrived with his cameras from sea level, said he felt funny from lack of oxygen. So did I, even after my stop in Albuquerque. Our breakfast conversation shifted between two topics: the altitude and Janet Bonnema.

Our rendezvous in Georgetown was to do a story for *Life* (my last, as it turned out) on Janet, a thirty-four-year-old engineering technician who was suing her employers, the Colorado Department of Highways. She was suing them for $100,000, because they forbade her and all other women to work inside or even set foot inside the Straight Creek Tunnel, an awesome engineering project under construction fifteen miles away and another 3,000 feet up. It would be bad luck, they said, for women to go in.

Janet and her class action lawsuit were a tidy metaphor for the widespread struggle of women to find work in places where men did not welcome them. Living as she did in a genuine small mining town in the West, Janet called to mind Our Gal Sunday and other legendary folk heroes. Like the cowboys Gary Cooper used to play, she was by nature a loner. Like Baby Doe Tabor, she was stubbornly single-minded. Like Silver Heels, who had a heart of gold and nursed dying miners through a smallpox epidemic, she wasn't afraid to take risks. Nor, like Molly Brown who survived the disaster of the *Titanic,* was she easily sinkable.

Besides, Janet's goal was so nice and unambiguous. All we had to do was drive up past timberline to the Loveland Pass, near the Continental Divide, to see it: the mighty, four-lane Straight Creek Tunnel, which may come to mean to tunnel enthusiasts what King Tut's Tomb means to fanciers of Egyptology. Designed to carve for 8,900 feet through the Rockies, the largest high-altitude tunnel ever built, it had presented all manner of tricky engineering problems in the five years of its construction. Seven hundred men had worked on it. It would cost something like $90 million. I could not join Leonard on his guided tour, but I was given a lot of facts while I waited. It was, as one of the bosses said, "one *big* hole in the ground."

Janet worked in one of several trailers parked a few hundred yards from the eastern mouth of the tunnel. She worked ably, too; nobody denied that. "She's got a real good sense of the third dimension," her supervisor told me. "I've had her do a lot of special drafting." Her job, in the Rock Mechanics Section, was, as she put it, "knowing what they do in the tunnel, so I can make graphic presentations. I would be a lot more useful if I could get this knowledge firsthand, the way all the other technicians do." Her male counterparts had been issued hard hats and wet boots, so that they could enter the tunnel at will. Janet stayed behind and did paperwork and wished she could go in too. As her $100,000 lawsuit said, she was being denied "irreplaceable experience at a unique and highly important engineering project." It would have looked pretty good, in short, on the old resumé. But as things stood, Janet said, "I'm not advancing; I'm treading water."

Personally, tunnels make me feel claustrophobic, so at first I was actually relieved not to enter Straight Creek. But the more I heard about the superstition against females, I almost felt like sneaking in. This superstition, apparently the legacy of Welsh miners called "Cousin Jacks" who came to work in Colorado in the 1850s, held that there was no telling what dangers might ensue if a woman went into a tunnel or mine.

"Some years ago I took my wife into a tunnel," one of Janet's bosses said, "and the next day we had a man get killed. So you never really know."

"You never do," said another official. "A tunnel's no place for a woman anyway. You know how men are. They might relieve themselves right where they're standing and not wait to get to a toilet. You wouldn't want a woman hearing the kind of language we use down there, either. Besides, women couldn't take it physically. They don't have the stamina."

"That what *he* thinks," Leonard said later as we, in our sedate rent-a-car, followed Janet back to Georgetown on her Honda CL-350. "Look at her, tall in the saddle." Nearly five feet ten, Janet was tall anywhere. Zooming along in her day-glo orange flight suit she was an imposing figure indeed.

"When I wake up in the morning," she had told us, "I like to ask myself not 'What shall I wear today?' but 'Who shall I *be* today?'" She had already been a lot of things—a cab driver, a pilot, a teacher, a global hitch-hiker, the captain of Colordao

University's ski team, and the dutiful daughter of people who taught her to believe, as she still did, in the Republican party and in a life hereafter. The one thing Janet never dreamed she might become, but had, was a symbol of the women's movement. The style of her commitment to this cause was all her own. Unlike many feminists who are clannish and doctrinaire in their solidarity, Janet had never been to a consciousness-raising session in her life, much less allied herself with any sect or group. Rallies did not tempt her. She preferred to stay home crocheting hotpads, fixing her motorcycle, or playing with her cat.

"Here kitty, here love, come *on,* sweetheart," she would call at the end of a day's work. You never could tell about Janet. She made you reflect on the principle of Yin and Yang. Sometimes she would wear her waist-length hair in a single business-like pigtail, but on other mornings she troubled to arrange it in an elaborate eighteenth-century cascade of ringlets. At lunch you'd see her batting her eyelashes at a table full of elderly miners, and that afternoon, on a climbing expedition, she would be scrambling out of sight over a nearly vertical cliff.

She lived in the east half of a two-story turquoise frame duplex on Rose Street. In the other half lived her landlady, Olive Barnes. Janet went to watch television at Olive's sometimes, especially when she was on it herself. Olive worried about Janet. She wasn't sure it was wise for her to walk along the highway picking up beer cans. Janet did this not to beautify the landscape but so she could crush the cans beneath her boot and sell them for scrap aluminum. She was saving to go to Africa.

Janet's tiny living room also served as a garage for her Honda, which she kept under a giant paper parasol. She had brought the parasol home from the Orient, after three and a half years of hitch-hiking around the world. On the living room wall hung a signed color portrait of a beribboned Air Force general who had become her special friend in Saigon, and next to it a framed studio portrait of Janet herself. Across the room were framed twin pictures of her parents.

In the kitchen hung a poster of the Taj Mahal, in the bathroom a towel inscribed DEAR DIARY, I'M IN LOVE

AGAIN, and on Janet herself, at times, a tee-shirt that said
VIRGINIA IS FOR LOVERS. Upstairs was a chess set she had
carved herself, and in the icebox was split pea soup made from
scratch, as was her daily oatmeal. Here and there were books:
James Michener, Irving Wallace, Graham Greene ("He has
such a wonderful way of saying 'It stinks.' "), *The Last of the
Mohicans,* a Bible. No, two Bibles. "Just now I'm reading the
Book of Kings," Janet said. "It's like James Michener all over
again."

Plainly Janet stepped to music she alone could hear, an improbable medley of selections from the Christian Reformed
Church Hymnal and such tunes as might be overhead in a ski
lodge or a party for military men in Vietnam. "It was such *fun*
when I first got there, before the war slowed down and they
started inventing new rules and enforcing old ones. I could
have gone to ten different parties every weekend."

If people found Janet a puzzlement, as many did, then that
was their problem, not hers. Once, by writing to a male friend
on stationery decorated with roses, she showed him an aspect of
her psyche he had not seen. "When he wrote back he told me I
wasn't just schizophrenic but *polyphrenic,*" said Janet, "which
I guess meant a personality not split just in two ways but many
ways. Well, maybe he's right."

"Of course I'm in favor of equal pay," say people who are
tired of talking and even hearing about the goals of the wom-
en's movement, "but isn't everybody? Hasn't that been pretty
well taken care of?" In point of fact it has not. The average female college graduate earns $7,930 per year, only a little more
than the average male graduate of eighth grade, who earns
$7,140. The average male college graduate's salary is $13,320.
Of the forty-three percent of American women who have jobs,
making up thirty-eight percent of the total labor force, a min-
uscule seven percent earn five-figure salaries or hold managerial
positions. The wage differential, in startling fact, was worse in
1972 than it had been seventeen years earlier. In 1955, women
earned not quite sixty-four percent of what men did. In 1972,

the figure had dropped by four and a half percent. Women felt lucky and even proud to have jobs at all. "Oh, that gal's so bright; she goes to business" was sufficient praise for many.

"The worst thing about women," I heard the sociologist Dr. Jessie Bernard say, "is the low opinion they have of themselves." If pay was low and advancement slow, a good many women would rationalize, "Oh, well, it must be just me—I'm not really working as hard as I might anyway, and besides men have families to support." Moreover, among people who had been brought up, as Janet Bonnema put it, to be "conservative and blendy," it wasn't considered ladylike or nice to make trouble.

Niceness of that ilk, by 1972, had become about as unfashionable as short-sleeved cashmere sweaters. In legally challenging the old husbands' tale that kept her out of the tunnel, Janet allied herself with a whole new class of suddenly litigious women, of whom most had undramatic white collar jobs and few had any previous experience with barricades of any sort.

"From your sister I might have expected something like this," said the mother of one plaintiff in a $100,000 class action suit against Liberty Mutual Insurance in Pittsburgh, "but *you?* I thought you were our *quiet* daughter!" That particular quiet daughter was filing suit because, among other reasons, her male counterparts earned $2,500 a year more than she did, had access to company cars and expense accounts, and could leave the office to investigate claims while women stayed behind and used the phone.

In considerable numbers other wronged women gave up the habit of being nice. A clerk was suing Continental Can because they had not even considered her for promotion to buyer on the grounds that she was bowlegged. In many banks women were suing because they had not even been told of training programs routinely open to men or because they were never sent overseas. "The rest of the world," one bank personnel man tried to explain, "just isn't ready for our American gals, God bless 'em." On campuses, the level of rage at unjust treatment of faculty women was rising almost hourly. It was as if the spectre of Rosie the Riveter, that apocryphal wartime heroine, had come back, in a vengeful mood. "Women only make it," I heard someone say, "when the world is falling apart." Rosie had been sent back to her kitchen, when the brave boys returned from the war to reclaim their jobs. But now she was angry, and new laws had made her anger legitimate.

It used to be that employers could get by paying lip service to the principle and the laws of equality. There was no particular incentive for men at the top to let women in. "Nothing really gets done," said Todd Jagerson, one of an emerging new species of consultants to companies perplexed by new discrimination rulings, "until somebody breathes down their necks— until the cost of responding to the law becomes less than the cost of ignoring it."

That is what has happened. Ignoring the laws has become costly indeed. Companies which do business with the federal government, of which there are some 250,000, are now obliged not only to quit discriminating on grounds of sex but to file affirmative action programs for the hiring and the advancement of women. These programs must redress both present and past effects of discrimination. Until March of 1972, there was no federal statutory law that applied to state agencies like the one Janet worked for. About ninety-five percent of all employers had in fact been exempt, because the minimum number of employes—now lowered to fifteen—had been twenty-five. Religious and academic organizations had been exempt too, but were no more. Equal pay, it was ruled, was due not only for the same work as men did but for comparable work, and to executive, administrative, and professional employes, as well as to outside sales personnel.

"The trouble with suing state agencies," said Janet's lawyer Sandra Rothenberg, "is that it's overpowering politically. They usually stall for a long time and say they're negotiating, but who can tell whether they really are? Janet's suit, though, potentially could be embarrassing. It could stop the whole tunnel."

The biggest legal advance was the new ability granted the

Equal Employment Opportunities Commission to take errant employers to court, in class action suits like the one in which Janet, on behalf of a "class" including all women, sued to get into the tunnel. The cost of settling these charges, in or out of court, was coming to threaten employers. "Some of these suits could get into the hundreds of thousands, maybe millions of dollars," Jagerson said. "Some could wipe out three years of profits." By late 1972, women had filed something like 6,000 discrimination complaints. An exponential rise in this figure seemed possible, as employers were made to face such stringent demands as reinstatement of dismissed workers, forced promotions, punitive damages, and back pay. Back pay made employers especially nervous. Since 1965, more than $43 million had been awarded to 104,604 workers, nearly all of them female.

Janet was eager to show us around. We saw her office in the trailer, we watched her go climbing near Boulder, we took her to lunch at a Mexican roadside place. ("Excuse me," she said, "I think I'll wash my hands before I enjoy this guacamole.") Leonard kidded her about Arby's Roast Beef Sandwiches, which she fancied much more than he did. We went with her to the Denver public library, where she made Xerox copies of some briefs. The clerical work of filing a lawsuit, she told us, could take up a good bit of time. She told me there was a paper on engineering in that library of which she was a co-author, and sometimes she looked her name up in the card catalogue, just for fun. That evening she took us to a high-rise apartment building in Denver to meet her widowed mother, who had spent the afternoon on a birdwatching expedition.

Mrs. Bonnema, who had a doctorate in education, was more taken with birding and with a movement to reform spelling than with feminism. She did not embrace Janet when we came in; that apparently was not their style. But it was clear that she supported her daughter's struggle, and she thought her late husband would too, for all his conservatism. She told us he used to confide to her a private worry he had about his three daughters.

"They're all the first ones in their class," he would say, "but what good, since they're girls, will that do?"

When Janet applied to work at Straight Creek, in the fall of 1970, she had just come home from three and a half years abroad. At that time she had not even heard of Women's Liberation. All she knew of sisterhood was what she had seen at the Kappa Delta house at the state university, from which she had graduated ten years earlier as a history major. She had been persuaded not to study engineering, her first choice, on grounds that she would never find a job.

"Even in high school," she said, I always scored high in the Mechanical and Natural Science categories of aptitude tests, but the guidance counselors would always tell me there must have been a mistake; girls weren't interested in those things. So I got off on the wrong foot, and I've been trying to make up for it ever since."

She did manage to get work as an engineering aide for Boeing Aircraft in Seattle, and liked it, but quit. Less qualified men around her were being paid more and promoted faster; who needed that? (Another friend of mine recalls having been advised by her fatherly Boeing boss to look elsewhere "because you've gone as far here as a woman can go.")

After Seattle, Janet went to Vermont for a Peace Corps volunteer training program. Half the students in her class were chosen to go to Afghanistan, to give smallpox vaccinations. Janet was in the rejected half. "One person told me I was a prima donna, and another said I was too quiet and didn't mix enough. A psychologist worried about what I'd do instead. I hadn't the slightest doubt. That was the last summer of the *Queen Mary,* so I got a ticket and went abroad anyway." With two friends she set forth to hitch-hike, twice, around the world. In Saigon, where Janet ended up spending most of her time, she made friends with pilots and unofficially learned to fly a plane herself.

Broke by the fall of 1970, she returned to her native Denver to job-hunt. She hoped to find interesting work, related to engineering, near the ski slopes. Straight Creek sounded ideal. Applying for a job as an engineering technician, she scored eighty-seven on a written exam and was notified in a letter mis-addressed to "Mr. Jamet" P. Bonnema that an opening was available, at $492 per month. The work sounded relevant to what she had done before and reasonably interesting, but the salary was not what she had in mind. She called to see whether there had been some mistake. Imagine the surprise at the other end of the line when "Mr. Jamet" spoke.

"*You* don't want *that* job," said the voice at the other end.

"I think I do," replied Janet.

"Well, you can't have it," the voice said. "No women are allowed in the tunnel." But Janet, encouraged by her mother, protested. Two months later a special technician's job, limited to office work, was invented for her. She was awarded back pay for the time she had had to wait, but the money mollified her no more than did manful efforts to explain why she could not go underground. Chivalrous fretting about sanitary facilities and dirty language cut no ice with Janet. "Do you think there were all that many toilets for *anyone* in Vietnam? Do you think I don't know how men talk?"

"Economics was the basic issue, for all the talk about superstitions and sanitation," said Janet's lawyer Sandra. "The Civil Service Commission just wasn't in the habit of hiring women for jobs like that. Her case was the strongest of its kind in the state, and it was fun too." Economic insecurity is probably at the root of most such grievances, and the cause least discussed. Men politely evade talking about their historic tendency to replace themselves with women only in emergencies. In Victorian England, in fact, women and even children worked in mines, and the ancient saw that "woman's place is in the home" is said to have begun as a battle cry to get women, for their own sakes, out of the mines.

Like her fellow plaintiffs elsewhere, Janet gradually became aware of a complex of interwoven issues hostile to their cause. Much more to the point than the Welsh superstition, it seemed to Janet, was the fact that men simply like to get away from women. Lionel Tiger's book *Men in Groups* calls this phenomenon "male bonding." Bonding is what the four suburban dads were doing in James Dickey's novel *Deliverance*, when they set out to test themselves in the wilderness. Although aggrieved feminists have been known of late to do a good bit of bonding themselves, they don't forgive the tendency in men. "It's like a boyish effort to keep girls out of the locker room," one plaintiff said, "while the men snap wet towels at each other's bottoms."

Even less popular with women is the tendency of their male adversaries to suggest, as one executive did of a plaintiff, "All *she* needs is a man—if I'd known about *her* before all this started, I could have taken care of her myself, if you know what I mean." I knew what he meant. There were also those who thought that all Janet Bonnema needed was to locate that elusive fellow Mr. Right, but fortunately they had the sense not to say this to her face.

"There's a lot more to life than having a husband," Janet told Leonard and me one evening as she served us lasagna in her kitchen. "It might be nice to get married someday, sure— to have a regular audience when I fix a good dinner and someone to share things with. But what business is it of anybody's if I have a boyfriend? Maybe I do have one someplace, but I don't need 'the boyfriend', strong and silent, to lead me by the hand into the tunnel and bail me out when I get in trouble.

"A lot of my girlfriends find the social stigma of being single unbearable. Not me. I don't want to have children at this point, either. I'm too old to commit my life to a twenty-year program of any kind, which is what having a child would mean. I wouldn't want to do it as a lark or a fling, but only if I could guarantee the child what it would need. Rather than breed new children, I like the idea of taking care of existing ones. I do have a stepdaughter in South Africa, through the Christian Children's Fund, and if I go through a spell of feeling motherly, I can write her letters of advice.

"I have a lot of very good male friends too, who are very understanding through thick and thin year after year, but it all goes on year after year and nothing happens. I write to several of them, telling them all more or less the same thing. I'd have a hard time choosing between them now, because what one has, another lacks. And when none of them is around, if it's a question of going alone or not going someplace at all, I'll go alone. I'll land on my feet too."

True to form, Janet did land on her feet. In July of 1972, after a year-long investigation, the United States Department of Transportation ruled that to bar women from Straight Creek Tunnel was to practice sex discrimination. When her bosses chose not to heed this ruling, Janet filed the suit that came to a triumphant end on a snowy morning in November.

Suddenly there were no more affadavits, no more conniving to have Xerox copies made of briefs. Suddenly Janet was surrounded by television crews and inevitable banter about light at the end of the tunnel. She put on a hard hat and goggles and was ushered all the muddy way through to the other end of Straight Creek. Her case had been settled out of court for $6,750. From then on, the tunnel was open to women.

Observers noted that the tunnel did not cave in. Sixty-some workers threatened to quit, but in fact only one did. Janet felt philosophical. Her small step into Straight Creek, she hoped, might help speed that giant leap for womankind in which, before long, all females might find work wherever they liked. Meanwhile, Janet thought she would use some of her winnings to go to Africa. Later she might look for a job having to do with mass transit or the rebuilding of South East Asia. She also had another idea.

"I hear they aren't hiring women as highway patrolmen," she said. "Maybe I'll send my application over there."

24

Cream Can Curdle

As soon as I was old enough to have friends who had been through law school, I learned a practical lesson: lawyers are hardly ever home. Even at 11:45 P.M., even on a radiantly sunny Fourth of July, chances of finding an attorney right by the phone at his or her office range from good to excellent. But compared with Sylvia Roberts, my lawyer friends seem indolent laggards.

"All these lawsuits are such a fantastic waste of time and energy and money," Sylvia was lamenting as the waiter rolled our lunch into her New York hotel room. Meeting her in person made me feel like a birdwatcher spying her first pileated woodpecker, or a movie fan getting a glimpse of Ida Lupino, whom Sylvia somewhat resembles. Maybe Garbo would be more like it: Sylvia is not an easy woman to reach. In the several months I had been trying to keep tabs on the phenomenon of women taking to the courts, I had often phoned her office in Baton Rouge, Louisiana, with one question or another, and nearly always been referred to some other distant area code. She might be off almost anywhere, trying one sex discrimination case or another.

In five or ten years, the phrase "lady lawyer" will not sound nearly as novel as it does now. It sounds less novel, in fact, all the time. Two all-women law firms have recently set up shop in New York City. One plans to undertake nonprofit cases to challenge discrimination against women, supporting itself with a private practice. The other has a grant to start a program of test cases in matrimonial law and sex discrimination in mortgages, loans and other credit procedures. "These firms," a *New York Times* article said, "are going to have a collective instead of a competitive feeling, and show other women they can do such things themselves, without waiting to be invited by men."

Sylvia Roberts has a practice of her own, but her philosophy is kindred to that of these new collectives. She is president of the NOW Legal Defense and Education Fund, and it was she who tried and won the landmark case of Weeks *vs* Southern Bell, the first sex discrimination case to reach the federal appellate court. Lorena Weeks, the plaintiff, was awarded thirty thousand dollars in back pay, and became Southern Bell's first female switchperson. Her case set the precedent that women may apply for all jobs except those which employers can prove that "all or substantially all" women cannot perform. That made Sylvia happy. So did the case of Dr. Sharon Johnson, a University of Pittsburg biochemist—the first time a court ruled that a university seemed to be discriminating on grounds of sex.

As a leader in the emerging new species of experts in the laws of discrimination, Sylvia is resigned to the schedule of an underdog political candidate. "It would be so simple to prevent all this, though," she said. "If women could just be promoted right now to the jobs they deserve, it would be so much less traumatic for everybody concerned. Still, if it takes five hundred more class action suits, we'll do it. Women aren't after blood or a pound of flesh. They're not bitter. They're just hurt —terribly hurt. Don't let anyone say they're happy. Black people were thought to be happy too, with soul food and music, until the rejection was apparent to the rejects."

"Now they'll have to invent a *new* superstition," said Sandra Rothenberg when her client Janet Bonnema won her lawsuit to get inside Straight Creek. "Now they'll have to say it's *good* luck for women to go inside tunnels."

Sandra had in her twenty-nine years been, among other things, a traveling baby photographer, a teacher, the "token woman" at the University of Miami law school in Florida, a short-order cook at her father's hotel in the Catskills, and a psychiatrist's wife. When I met her she owned a total of one dress: half a winter one and half a summer one. A friend of hers, another woman lawyer, owned the other halves. "Fortunately," said Sandra, "we're the same size. It's our joint superman costume. Whenever either one of us has to go to court, we put on one of the dresses."

Sandra has since moved to Washington, D.C., to teach law, but we met in her cheerful three-room office in a rundown part of Denver. No diplomas hung in that office. Not that she didn't have them—she was graduated from Miami in 1968 and later got a master's in criminal law on a fellowship from Georgetown University in Washington. It's just that hanging diplomas on the wall isn't her style. Neither is working for a big firm, which she tried and found distasteful. "Practicing alone, the way I do now," she said, "is much more to my liking."

One evening several months before I met Sandra and Janet, I was dining in a San Francisco restaurant with Barbara Phillips and one of her clients. Her client was a plaintiff in the class action suit against the Bank of America. Our mood was conspiratorial. The three of us resolved, as we ordered our meals, that we would try to refer to the bank as "the company," lest we be overheard by hostile ears. That was a hard resolution to keep, since our conversation was spirited and spontaneous. What I found more interesting even than the suit against the Bank was Barbara's account of how her own thinking had evolved in the ten years she had been practicing law.

"I've changed a lot just recently," she said, "but basically I'm so conservative that even the green stationery we're using for the cake sale seems a bit bizarre to me."

"Cake sale?"

"For the Women's Defense Fund. Very few women, you know, can afford to pay the costs of their litigation. We need to raise money, and we thought this might be a good tactic. It's funny: none of us has ever been involved with a bake sale before."

"What a disarming idea," I said. "A bake sale is just what those gray-suited men on Montgomery Street need. It's quite a departure for you, you say?"

"I was programmed to be conventional," Barbara said. "I started out as a tax lawyer, after all: how conventional can you get? I worked very hard at first for one of the most prominent tax firms in San Francisco, earning much less money than the going rate for men. When I suggested that I needed more pay, even after they'd given me a raise, they said, 'But after all, we started you out above the secretaries, didn't we?'

"I'd worked hard there. They'd said I was one of the best associates they ever had. I was brought up, as we all were, to believe that cream rises to the top, and virtue is its own reward. But when I had the temerity to ask for a better office, they said, 'Look, apparently something hasn't been made clear to you. You're never going to be a partner in this firm, because you're a woman.' Not only that, but I was fired."

"You learned that cream can curdle, and virtue go unnoticed?" I asked. Barbara nodded.

"I found out for myself," she said, "how it feels to get to the gate with all my marbles in my hand and be told, 'Oh, sorry, you're in the wrong race.' I don't think anybody who hasn't experienced discrimination personally can know how totally demoralizing it is or how much stamina and determination it takes to fight one of these battles. You need to make a very deep commitment which can last for a period of years."

"These firings," Sylvia Roberts said over lunch in New York, "are the ultimate in rejection. After you've been told a certain number of times that you're not wanted, you begin to think, 'Well, maybe they're right, maybe there *is* something wrong with me!' What's so crazy is the waste, the voluntary throwing away of resources, the irrationality of all this. Take these women who get Ph.D's, for instance, they're supermotivated, because they've *had* to do a better job than their male counterparts.

"These are distinguished women, and the effect on them is just deadening. People say, 'But the discrimination isn't deliberate.' Even so, does that make it any better? And I'm not at all sure that it's completely unwitting. Good men and true, after all, are responsible for these decisions. Maybe these men aren't malevolent, but their habit of discrimination is ingrained so deeply that they don't even *know* how they demean women. So women will have to keep on begging for whatever crumbs they get thrown, until men start to understand that we won't accept such treatment, that we *do* rock boats, even if boat-rocking makes us seem uppity and aggressive."

"Is there more coffee?" I asked. Persuasive as it was, I was not used to such rhetoric at lunch.

"Yes," said Sylvia. "Sometime you ought to go see a client of mine named Margaret Cussler."

One sultry afternoon in Washington, D.C., I did. It was right after I had lunch with Ila Pennington, who was understandably much less guarded than her identical twin sister, Eleanor McGovern. I caught a cab to Margaret Cussler's house in College Park, Maryland, right after Ila gave me a thorough tour of the McGovern headquarters on K Street. The headquarters was not a very cheerful place.

Dr. Cussler's house shouldn't have been, either, considering, but somehow it was. A sixty-one-year-old associate professor of sociology at the University of Maryland, Dr. Cussler had been struggling for ten years to be promoted to full professor. In April, 1972, she had filed suit for $400,000, half compensatory and half punitive, on grounds, Sylvia had said, that "she had been hamstrung and had her career eroded during her peak productive years". The defendants were the University of Maryland, its board of regents, its president, its vice-president for academic affairs, its chancellor, and the present and acting heads of the sociology department.

Dr. Cussler kept refilling my glass with iced tea as I read a thick file of data on her complaint. She had been on the Maryland faculty, off and on, since 1947. From 1951 to 1954 she left, to work first for the United States Information Agency and then at Radcliffe. On her return to College Park, she was demoted to instructor from her previous rank of assistant professor, and stripped of all honors.

Her story was a Kafkaesque nightmare of red tape. Two committees had been appointed to study her case. The first ruled she should be promoted. She wasn't. The second said she deserved a raise and that a panel of outside experts should rule on the promotion question, but that the administration should have the last word as to who would be on the panel. Dr. Cussler declined to be judged by such a panel.

"They can't call me a Communist," she said, "because I'm a member of the DAR. Some of us Daughters still *are* Revolutionaries." Her credentials did not impress those who judged her. Reminded she had published five books, they told her she should have done articles. Told that she had been elected president of the District of Columbia Sociological Society by the largest majority ever, they did not respond. Nor did they say anything about ineffectiveness or incompetence on her part.

"What they did accuse me of," Dr. Cussler said, "was 'capricious grading'—I guess because I refused to change failing marks for two students I considered illiterate—and 'abusive language'. The worst language I can recall having used was 'slick operator' and 'scalawag'." Still, the *Diamondback,* the campus newspaper, later selected her "one of College Park's six best."

Margaret Cussller earned her doctorate in 1943 from Radcliffe. "For anyone who's graduated from a good university," she said, "it's hard to realize that there can be this kind of expediency and salaciousness in academic circles. It's quite disillusioning to find that there are so few thinking minds and so many people willing to put knives in others' backs if they can get away with it."

"It's not just me, either. Of ninety-four faculty members who got promoted here in June of 1972, eighty-six were men. I've slowly come to learn that what you don't ask for, you don't get."

To supplement her income, Dr. Cussler had earned extra money on seventeen outside grants and research contracts, nearly all with United States government agencies. "Many times these contracts were awarded to me personally rather than to the university, which except for its physics department is supposed to be less than first rate. There's too much spurious affluence here, and the place is much too big. It's getting to be a multiversity, trying to be the UCLA of the East."

"Why do you stay here?" I asked.

"Women have to take what they get," she replied. "The only consolation of all this, so far, is that what's happened fits into my field, which is social psychology, the study of social movements. It's not the kind of adventure I most enjoy, but it is fascinating to see this switch from abstraction into realism."

"What would you do," I asked her, "if you really won anything liked $400,000?"

"Form a research institute and study old age. Old people are the real concentration camp sufferers of Western civilization. I've just been reading Simone de Beauvoir on the subject, and she has a lot of prescriptions I'd like to follow. Nobody will give money for this cause, because it's so unpopular."

"But what if you were forced to spend the money on yourself?"

She had to think a while. "In that case, I guess I'd like a really nice sailboat. I'd sail around the Caribbean. I'd start a repair firm too, repairing appliances. I'd take the time to learn fine cabinetmaking. I'd like to work more with my hands. It gave me so much satisfaction to learn to put up my own aluminum gutter. I'd do what I do now, only more: garden, tennis, theater, reading."

Dr. Cussler had shared her house in the past, she told me, with foreign students. "One year my students were Korean and

Thai, and I didn't eat a single potato but I sure learned a lot of things to do with rice." She had done a documentary film on starvation and a book on nutrition. There had been other books, other films, any number of other pursuits. It occurred to me that if I were a student at Maryland, I would go out of my way to study with this woman.

Her middle name, I noticed reading through her curriculum vitae, was Thekla. Thekla? "She was a saint who followed St. Paul around," Dr. Cussler said. "She was the first female Christian martyr."

"Do you think naming you that was prophetic of your parents?"

"They were used to controversy too," she told me. Her father was a Dutch Reformed Church minister, who had been run out of his upstate New York town for making it known that town funds had been stolen. Her grandfather had been scorned by rumrunners and slaveholders. She went to get her mother's plush-covered autograph album, in which there was an original and personal quatrain inscribed by John Greenleaf Whittier:

> Thy father kept the good old plan,
> A good, a wise, and upright honest man.
> Hating pretense, he did with righteous will
> What others prayed for, while their hands were still.

"There's kind of a tradition in my family," Dr. Cussler said, "that no matter what it costs you, if it's a matter of principle, you follow it through."

And then, because I had a dinner date with one of my new stepsisters and her family, Dr. Cussler drove me back to the district border. I wished her well.

"A lot of women are afraid to sue," Sandra Rothenberg said when I visited her Denver apartment, "because jobs are scarce. Sometimes it's a matter of bullying companies. One woman client of mine hadn't had a raise in six years, so I wrote her boss a letter implying that this might be a discrimination case. Guess what? Quick like a bunny, she got a raise. I'm involved in suing the State Board of Education too. They discriminate blatantly. There's not one female superintendent of schools in this whole state. Some factories start women off at $1.60, and give men a minimum wage of $2.50."

"Have you been specializing in class action suits all along?"

"I was too busy to know much at all about sex discrimination until last year," Sandra said, "when I brought suit against the FBI for not hiring me as a special agent."

"Did you *want* to be a special agent?"

"Not really, but I wanted the training. I wanted to know what it would be like, and it made me mad that I couldn't find out. Since Hoover's death they've changed that policy and started hiring women, only you have to be five feet seven and weigh 140. It occurred to me to make an issue about that, because what woman voluntarily weighs 140?"

Sandra was brought up in Greenwich, Connecticut, where her father ran a stationery store until, in her thirteenth year, he moved his family to Florida. "I was the only Jew in my class," said Sandra, "except for Joel Feldman, whom I concluded at the age of seven I would have to marry. If you think women in Greenwich are any happier than women anywhere else, you ought to see how much they drink."

"I don't suppose they *are* any happier," I told her. "Once, come to think of it, I almost did an article on women alcoholics in Fairfield County."

"You wouldn't have had any trouble finding subjects for it," she told me.

"I didn't," I said. "It was a sad scene."

"There's so much sadness among women," Sandra said. "When I worked for the Federal Communications Commission in Washington I found it excruciatingly painful, because most of what I had to do was busywork, but sometimes I'd stay there late at night, and see these enormous, pathetic black cleaning-women, carrying around these fifty-pound pails.

"A lot of women clients come into my office and tell me they feel out of tune because they're not emulating Doris Day, or

301

whoever the model of their time was. A lot of them say that nothing's *happening* to them, that they have the feeling they're *missing* something."

"What sort of practice do you have? General?"

"No, there are a lot of things I wouldn't like to get into. Estates, tax problems, corporate stuff, complex wills. I don't do much landlord-tenant stuff, either, because it's depressing; it's a pathetic thing with no rewards at all. I like rewards. In Washington, so that my clients wouldn't look like bums in court, I'd ask them what size they were and go all over to borrow clothes for them. We had them looking like Harvard sophomores.

"Now I do criminal work, and I think and hope I do it very well. This is a dingbat trade, though. I get a lot of dingbats in my office. Some of them need my ex-husband more than they need me."

"The psychiatrist, you mean?"

"Right. That's how I came out here to Denver in the first place. We both wanted to. We got married in a classic ceremony; I wore a beautiful white dress. It was all just right, but one morning we woke up and realized, 'We're not happy, we're not making it,' and that was pretty much that. As a golf pro once said when someone asked him how it felt to be great, 'It's the getting there that counts.' Actually *being* married, I found, was a letdown.

"I was married to a hell of a nice guy, too, but I work as hard as I can, and I'm often not home until late, and that didn't make me any dutiful wife. Besides, law and psychiatry don't mix. A lot of psychiatrists are caught up in strict, Freudian, anatomy-is-destiny theories, and they're not equipped to deal with women. I'm beginning to feel that all psychiatrists try to get women to do is adjust to *their* concept of what we should be. They tend to dismiss all problems as unresolved Oedipus. A lot of women today just aren't into patterns like having children in order to fulfill themselves."

"Do you want to have children yourself?"

"I'd love to," said Sandra, "and I intend to, but I think they'll have to be illegitimate. Legitimacy, after all, is only a matter of property rights, and that's not too important. Not that I have anything against men. I like my father and brothers a lot, and I like my ex-husband too. But marriage? It just seems too confining. I can't imagine ever not being preoccupied with my work."

"Early in life I realized I'd have to work," Barbara Phillips said in the San Francisco restaurant, "or I'd live everyone else's life instead of my own. It's my temperament, my energy level, and that's all there is to it. My husband's a lawyer too, and we're both competitive, but I don't compete with him. I compete with myself. He and I have an amazing balance worked out between us.

"Before I got into discrimination cases I always had a lot of projects—I was president of the San Francisco Barristers Club, for one thing—but I was never a cause person. Now legal specialists in sex discrimination are a rare new breed of experts. There's a limit to how many of these plaintiffs a one-woman band can handle.

"I took on women's cases because they're not only interesting but socially worthwhile and constructive. Not all law work is. A few lawyers are socially destructive. Essentially, we lawyers are information brokers. There are those who call us the witch doctors of society. Our work gets more burdensome and complex all the time, the more complex society becomes.

"But with these women's cases, we're not trying to screw anybody. All we're asking is that the skills and talents and loyalty of employees be taken into account. Is that so much? When we win, everybody wins."

A few years ago, some women who worked for *Life* and other Time Inc. magazines got together and instituted a class action suit, charging that the company discriminated against females. I was invited to be one of the plaintiffs. I declined. Of late, I explained to my more litigious colleagues, I had been treated quite decently at *Life*. But hadn't I been exploited, they asked me, in my early years? Hadn't men been promoted much faster and farther than women in those years? Couldn't I see the in-justice? All that was true, but I had not been raised to be a rocker of boats.

I think now that if I had it to do over, I would have joined the plaintiffs.

25

Tooth and Nail

Thank you. We're down here in Washington, D.C., folks. I'm speaking to you, as I guess you can see, from the playoff room of the annual Thanksgiving Night Double Solitaire Classic in the Julian Alexander residence, and a fabulous classic it is again this year. The score so far in the tourney is five to three, and on the losing end—here he comes now—is Julian "Daddy" Alexander, dapperly dressed as always, imposing in his new mustache, but looking a little shaky as he takes his place on the blue chair by the bridge lamp, sitting down, adjusting the lighting. Coming in now to deafening applause is his redoubtable opponent and daughter Molly, nine years young, seated in the ochre wingchair. It looks as if Molly's really up for this game, eyeing her opponent with a glance of withering scorn Bobby Fischer himself would find unnerving. Just a minute; I think I can hear the bell. Molly's beginning to deal her hand, and what a hand it is with the ace of clubs in the number-one spot moving right on over to no man's land as she moves over the king of spades from the sixth row and there it is . . . a red nine to slap right under the black ten in the third! What a beginning! Molly's Daddy is trying to seem calm but he looks stymied; he's already begun to flip through his deck three at a time, and although it's a little early to be certain, it doesn't look as if he has much of a chance.

"Remember," said Julian, "it's only a game."

"That's not what you say when *you're* winning," replied Molly, as she turned up the three of clubs that cinched her victory. "Hey, Mommy," she called, "you want to play next time? Make it *Triple* Solly?"

"No thanks," Liz answered from the kitchen. She was in there doing something about a *ratatouille* for tomorrow. Liz is so efficient and organized that if I didn't like her so much, as they say, I would hate her. She has a strong chin and stubby, capable hands. You might think on meeting her at first that she was too composed to be interesting. You would be wrong.

"How's your career coming?" I ask her. "Still clawing your way to the top?"

"Tooth and nail," said Liz as she cubed the eggplant, "and in the ichthyology racket, as I hardly need to tell you, you never know whose knife you'll find in your back next. It makes the Seventh Avenue rag trade seem tame."

It is a fine thing, every few Thanksgivings, to go to Washington and be with the Alexanders. I did so in 1963, when we were all reeling from our first national assassination, stunned after a time to the point of absurdity. We would ask each other, "How do you rate the riderless horse [or Haile Selassie or young John's salute, or Senator Mansfield's speech about the ring] on your Grief-O-Meter?" We went together to Central Park the night of the first moon landing, and once we drove three hundred miles to have an ice cream cone. The Alexanders have seen me through many seasons and weathers. We listen to the same music, scorn the same politicians, read the same books, and love the same friends.

Although we have found few answers, we puzzle over the same questions. Should we adopt Vietnamese orphans? Why, if we like the country so much, do we keep on living in cities? Why wouldn't it work if we tried to start a commune? Wouldn't you resent not knowing you had a fatal disease? Why is it that very rich people eat Silvercup bread? Why is money the really dirty subject, the real taboo, the cause of more euphemisms than sex? Why do Molly's schoolmates gauge their birthdays by the amount of loot they get? Why can't we all simplify our lives and stop having to make so many arrangements? Why should Princess Anne be fourth in line for the British throne after even her little brothers? What time is it? Is there any more of that Cointreau? There isn't? What will morning be like if we finish off these two inches of Old Grand-Dad?

"Come back soon," Liz once wrote me after one such visit. "It's unlikely you're properly appreciated up there among the heathen." Few people anywhere appreciate me as they do. I can say no more than that when I am Worse they make me feel Better, and when I am Better they don't even act surprised.

"I'll have my thank-you note in your mailbox early in the week," I assure them as I leave.

"You do that," they say.

26

Didn't You Almost Drown While Interviewing Saul Bellow?

"And of course you love your job," a fond uncle of mine told me when he came to New York and took me out to dinner, not long after I had arrived there. He didn't ask me; he told me. At that point, in fact, I did not love it at all, since my task was to wear a smock and sort photographic negatives, then file them in translucent sleeves. Still, according to the ethic by which I had been raised, one unquestioningly loved one's work. Was it not what defined one? Certainly it was, until some more biological definition came along. Meanwhile, until that happened, one got oneself hired if possible by a large, generous daddyish corporation, of which there may never anywhere have been or be a more classic example than Time Inc.

I was on the payroll there for fifteen years, mostly with *Life*. (Early and briefly I worked for *Time,* but I didn't like it. A woman named Content Peckham intimidated me.) One more year, *Life*'s last, I was on a contract. The contract took up more time than I had thought it would, and in the fall of 1972 I often announced to people that I had decided I wouldn't take such a demanding one the next year, or that I might even let it drop altogether.

"That," said a friend who had bought me a pastrami sand-wich, "is a chronic decision. What else is new?"

If anyone had asked me, as a neophyte employe, to guess what I might be doing on December 8, 1972, the day *Life*'s death was announced, I would have envisioned being a faculty wife somewhere, with a Cub pack or maybe a Brownie troop, and a lovably disarrayed chignon. I would have guessed that before my marriage to this nice ironic Mr. Chips—"my mis-ter," I would jokingly call him—I would have studied or worked abroad for a couple of years, on one pretext or other. On crisp autumn afternoons, I would have said, my mister would haul leaves around our yard wearing a red and black checked wool shirt, with a funny hat of some sort shoved back on his head. I'd have guessed we might have a cheerfully shabby house with big rooms and a porch. (A friend of mine said she bought a house she hated, just because of its porch, and I could see her point.) We would have season tickets to lec-ture and concert series and I might have learned to say things like, "Of course we left before the Dvořák." I'd also have said we might have a bounding, amiable black Lab, though possibly a yellow one, that we would take most of our vacations in a Volkswagen camper, and make our own Christmas cards out of linoleum blocks. That's what we'd have been doing in early December: getting those cards done.

Instead, *Life* had become my arena, my stage, the channel for most of my energies. Its masthead was such a nice coherent hierarchy, and the bylines it gave were such a nice outward and visible sign of merit, like A's in English, sure to invite ap-proval. *Life*'s assignments, much if not all of the time, in-volved travel and invited us to stretch our minds. I spent a whole season, it seemed a year, studying the habits of *eciton burchelli*, a species of marauding army ants. I was obliged to be, or at least to seem, conversant with the argots of pianists, hairdressers, diplomats, soothsayers, poets, sculptors, evangel-ists, a professional atheist, politicians—maybe not all sorts and conditions of men, but a good many.

Life's rituals and traditions, moreover, gave my own life an order and a structure I would otherwise have been obliged to seek elsewhere, and the notion of "elsewhere" became less and less inviting as time went by. The office gave me a semblance of a family; a *mishpocha*. It made me feel connected and important. It is said of George Hunt, the managing editor in what so far as I am concerned was *Life*'s golden age, that when he learned of one reporter's plan to quit he called her into his office and said to her, in unfeigned puzzlement, "But Dolores! *Life* is the best!" He heartily believed that it was, and his faith was contagious, even among chronic cynics.

My employee number was 3274 and my office, toward the end, was 3022, next to Dick Meryman's and well within earshot of Dita Camacho's and Tommy Thompson's. I had to walk half a block to the ladies' room, but only a few short steps to the Xerox machine, that now most lamented of lost amenities. By some fluke I had two phone lines, and if someone else called while we were talking, I could put you on hold. One afternoon in early 1971 an affable writer named John Thorne stopped by my office, looking affably desperate. He had to find someone whose recent adventures in the line of duty might inspire copy for a slow week's Editor's Note. "Come on," he implored me, "are you *sure* you didn't almost drown while interviewing Saul Bellow?"

Alas for his purpose, I had not. There was a myth of glamour and danger about the place, all right, but near-drownings were the lot chiefly of war correspondents and superstar photographers, with whom I associated only peripherally. But my own timing was lucky. If I had turned up there five years earlier, I might have resigned myself to the anonymity that was then the norm and never have shed my cocoon—more an armor, really—of timidity. I might have become one of those good-natured, whiskey-voiced, unobtrusive corporate women, whose ego never got in anybody's way. I might, for example, have been persuaded to stay on answering letters to *Time,* which I did for a while in my trainee period. I was good with those letters, and it was hinted that I could have a future there.

But I turned up just at the time when kindly mentors began

to encourage some of us to try to write, or rather Write, and some of us did. The old joke that to be a writer for *Life* was like being a photographer for the *Reader's Digest* gradually stopped seeming funny. So I wrote, at first just a little. What I did, for quite a while, was to follow around persons who had written bestsellers or won elections or choreographed hit shows or otherwise distinguished themselves and take down what they said. The resulting quotes would appear in articles called Close-Ups, overseen by my friend Dave Scherman. Later, promoted to staff writer, I did longer stories and once or twice, to my chagrin, was billed as *"Life's* Jane Howard."

The hell you say, I thought, but the extent to which the magazine did encroach on our lives could worry both us who worked there and those on the outside, "real people" we sometimes called them, who cared for us. "You'd better get out of there," more than one friend advised me, "because you're in a rut, a nice, elegant rut." Right, I would answer. Sure. I'll do that. But even after I took a year's leave of absence to write a book, I came back, back to where it was warm and where projects were finite and where if you were so disposed you could make off with the odd roll of typewriter ribbon here and toilet paper there. (I always forgot to buy my own.) The out-of-town bureaus, always chicly located near Saks or the American Express, whichever might apply, were cordial places. Our colleagues there tended to be helpful and funny when we showed up, pulling bottles of Jack Daniels from their desk drawers for impromptu "pours," at which they would roll their eyes skyward as they confided what indignities "New York" made them suffer. Still, they and we all felt part of something imposing. Few of us were so explicit as the photographer who said, on the way to Churchill's funeral, that "this is like a back seat to history," but that was the general idea.

If we thought we were hot stuff, the outer world could either disabuse us at once of that notion or else unctuously concur. Sometimes we had to defend our connection with what was seen as the enemy pig imperialist homogenizer, but more often we were the objects of blatant and shameless fawning. A Mr. Heep was often on the other line, waiting to talk to us. (One of the pleasures of no longer working there is the appreciable drop in the number of calls from flacks—whom we did not often call Public Relations Representatives—who used the word "area" more often and in more contexts than you might think possible and who said things like, "I'll have that *on* your desk *in* the morning," or "I'll get back *to* you *on* that." It is nice now to be *at* a remove *from* that mentality.) Of course we had to get in there and fawn ourselves from time to time, convincing our story subjects or their lackeys that nothing could suit them better than coverage in *Life*. And although I don't like to remember it, there was such a thing as interoffice fawning, too. We were never fawned over, naturally, by people whom we esteemed. If they were nice to us, it only confirmed what we had known all along: that they had superior judgment.

A few among us had been rich kids, but most of us were raised by Depression-minded parents who had taught us to scrimp, a habit we gradually lost at *Life*. Not only were our paychecks quite handsome by general standards, but there were a number of other blandishments: taxis instead of subways, picking up the check at costly lunches ("to discuss possible future story" we would explain on expense accounts), and the assurance that if it were really a desperate emergency, we could go ahead and charter a plane. Such extravagance seeped its sinister way through the thin membrane that separated our professional and personal lives. I did not know how far I had come along this road myself until one day during a vacation in Maine when I stopped by at my hosts' bank to cash a check.

"I'm a houseguest," I explained to the teller, "of one of your parishioners—oh, sorry, I meant *depositors*." But the slip had slipped. Banks, down there in my subconscious, had got mixed up with churches. Better watch it.

To work at *Life* was to possess to dizzying degree what Marianne Moore said was the charm of New York City: accessibility to experience. "I'm programming myself for life," said that same photographer who went to Churchill's funeral, and although a lot of us wouldn't have admitted it, we felt that way too. The magazine was such a vast and diverse organism that every set of memories of working there is unique. My own include the time I chartered a seaplane with Bob Peterson, a photographer who early on had resolved to become a living legend in his own time. In the wilderness of British Columbia we descended, literally out of the blue, onto an armed camp of right-wing extremists from Indiana. There had been no way of letting them know we were coming or imagining what their scene would really be like. Our story never did run, because it turned out there were only two families of extremists, and they did not seem as menacing as we had imagined they might. But the trip was a glorious way to see Wakeman Sound and to learn something about abandoned lumber camps and paranoia. It was a good way to learn how not to cook a beautiful sirloin too. Our hosts fried the steak we brought until it was beige.

In Tangier one day (where else could I have got license to begin a sentence that way?) the photographer Terry Spencer was lecturing a hotel maid who scolded us for cluttering up our rooms with real flowers from the marketplace instead of plastic ones. "But, Madame," Terry told her in courtly French, "You too will grow old, and you too will die like these flowers, and you too must be appreciated while you are in bloom." Terry quoted a maxim he had learned on assignments with Hugh Moffett: "Wherever you are in the world, if you're looking for fun, go downhill." The story we had been sent to Morocco to do, on the expatriate authors Paul and Jane Bowles, never did run. Too bad. We both did a good job. But those things could happen, especially back in the days before economy waves. The Bowleses weren't as manifestly commercial as our next subjects, the travel author Temple Fielding and his wife, whom he usually called My Nancy, who lived in Mallorca. It wasn't bad being in Mallorca, either.

Parties were frequent and lavish in those days. After one, in New York, Sally O'Quin and Marc Crawford and I felt moved to go down onto the street and raise our voices in hymns in front of the Taft Hotel. Our esprit de corps was famous; the *mishpocha* extended and extended. Once, when I was in Paris where Jordan Bonfante was stationed, he and I got to talking for some reason about midwestern politics and decided we ought to send a cable to our unobtrusive New York colleague Dave Martin, who comes from the same state I do. We paid for it ourselves. It began: SERIOUSLY CONSIDERING MOUNTING GIGANTIC JUGGERNAUT ELECT YOU GOVERNOR ILLINOIS 1968. UNREQUIRE IMMEDIATE COMMITMENT BUT PLEASE GIVE URGENTEST DE-LIBERATION. WON'T REST UNTIL YOU IN STATE HOUSE. I guess I like that cablese word "unrequire" as much as anything.

On the grounds of the Royal Palace in Gangtok, Sikkim, Farrell Grehan was one day making telephoto portraits of the palace's momentarily unkempt mistress. "Your Highness!," he kept yelling to her (she had not yet granted permission for us to address her otherwise) "Your hair!." After that assignment Farrell and I were stranded, by no means for the first time, in the then unrenovated Dum-Dum Airport of Calcutta. Our plane out was cancelled or postponed or something, and we had to stay in Dum-Dum all right. Toward dawn, I was able to get a bit of prone rest on a narrow bookshelf from which a stack of *Kama Sutras* had only recently and for a short time been removed. Earlier, Farrell and I had chatted with another transient, a jocose Japanese gentleman who said, or so we thought, that he was by trade a "Phariseeist"—one, presumably, whose business was the study of Pharisees? That didn't sound quite right. Finally we puzzled it out: he had been south to see the fabled erotic sculptures of Khajuraho. It was *phalluses* he was interested in.

Once, on less than a day's notice, I was assigned to rush from Lansing, Michigan, where I had been working on a story about a child mathematical genius, to Jamaica in the West Indies, to ghost-write a piece by Wiley T. Buchanan, who had been chief of protocol in the Eisenhower Administration. It was Mr. Buchanan's opinion that the guest artists at White House functions of late had lacked a wholesome common touch. "Mind you," he said, "I've got nothing *against* Pablo Casals—after all, he's tops in his field."

There are any number of really tops people I probably

would never have encountered had it not been for *Life,* and tops places I would not have seen. I think that as a result of these undeniable perquisites some people, certain of my relatives, for example, thought of me as they would have thought of a totally irresponsible, carefree go-go dancer, unbound by anything but whim, at liberty at all times to jump from one exciting, cushy world nerve center to another. Need I say that this notion, if anyone in fact really did entertain it, was mistaken? In retrospect I resent very much the fact that in my early years there my only tested quality was endurance. The fourteen months or so which Charlotte Smith and Tira Faherty and I spent on the Clipdesk (a year after Charlotte and I had been hired, with maximum fanfare, and told how promising we were) felt like a decade. We consoled ourselves by keeping a file called "Ugly Brides," on the unliberated late-fifties theory that if they could find husbands we could, too. Our lives were engrossing otherwise, which was to say socially. We further trusted that one day Marian MacPhail would phone, in her constantly imitated baritone, to ask "Got a minute?" which would signal the fact that at long last, like Brownies flying up to Scouthood, we could become bona fide Reporters.

I resent that long wait, to be sure, and I resent the hackneyed notion that the average reader's mental age is twelve, and I resent the emphasis on brevity and alliteration, which subtly caused me, for one, to think of my own life in terms of snappy 800- or 2,500-word episodes, instead of as a more seamless whole. I could name a good many more things I also resent, but that would sound vindictive now that the big beached whale has expired. That would be to overlook the fact that every once in a while, after painful retreats with armloads of notes, I learned more about myself than I had about any celebrity subject of a Close-Up. I learned that if I put my mind to it, I could begin to transcend the limits set by textblocks and captions. *Life* not only gave me experiences, and friends, but it taught me my craft.

I didn't think I would cry on December 8, when we all trooped into the Ponti Auditorium to learn that the magazine really was going to fold, but I did. I cried even though I had heard the rumors, known the magazine was ailing, expected this news to come one day. But I no more thought it would come that particular morning or even that season than I had been prepared for the sudden death of my mother. It makes me uncomfortable to think how similarly these two passings hit me. Maybe it shouldn't. My mother, after all, was more or less in charge of the first seventeen years of my existence, and *Life* of the sixteen that began four years later.

Wakes for the magazine went on for a week or so, until even the most compulsive wits among us, who were many, had been wrung dry of gallows humor. After so many weepy hugs and farewell speeches and post-mortems, it finally became a relief to pack up our stuff, or start to anyway, and get busy Christmas shopping. Now that some months have passed, I have "adjusted," as you might say, more "bravely" than the bereaved sometimes do. I have spent most of the intervening days in the room where I sit at this moment, all alone to be sure, but not quite so piteously cut off from the mainstream of society as I had thought I might feel. My phone works. I still see, or hope to see, most of the people I cared about at *Life*. It gives me pleasure to write "Self-Employed" when I have to fill out forms. The only thing I really miss, as I said, is the Xerox.

Once in a while I find myself in midtown, looking up at the giant building in which for so many years I got most of the signals that mattered to me. I feel no more emotional than I do when I walk past a building where I used to live. I think, "Hmmm—what was *that* all about?"

27

Fragments of Comfort and Joy

Steady, girl, I told myself. Easy. Think of the space-time continuum. So what if there isn't so much as a sprig of holly in this whole house? Aren't the birds outside as vivid as ornaments and the flowers as gay as packages? Is not the tropical sun a deal more warming than a hearth in the north? Maybe you wouldn't be so crazy about rituals either, if you had been raised in the Roman Catholic church of Central America. And so what if the custom here does seem to be nonstop firecrackers, sounding like cannons and machine guns, instead of medieval carols? And anyway, when you wake up tomorrow it will be the twenty-sixth, and then all this won't matter any more.

It wasn't as if anyone had forced me to spend Christmas in El Salvador. I had come quite of my own choice because my friend Miguel, Miguel with the eyelashes, had invited me. Miguel is a designer who speaks five languages, plays chess, knows the constellations, draws masterly sketches of unsuspecting people on buses, and can make me laugh. When he lived in New York he referred to himself as a wetback. He had often asked me to visit his country. What better time than now, with no more paychecks in sight? Funiculi funicula, right?

Besides, this little lecture to myself went on, you're going to the beach today; won't that be fun? You know how you've always loved the shore. And look: Miguel is placing a cased revolver in among our picnic stuff. Just think, an armed picnic, baby's first, on Christmas Day! Not to shoot, Miguel explained, but to scare off drunks with machetes, in case we should encounter any. One never knew. That was true. The people in Managua, for example, had not known they would have a *terremoto* two days earlier.

Well, I had to admit, one never knew back where I came from, either. My friend Edith had not known that a bullet was going to zing, one recent night, right through her bedroom window on East Ninety-third Street and lodge in the door of her closet. She was, in fact, quite surprised, and she had to agree with the policemen who told her it was a lucky thing she had been recumbent at the time instead of, say, sitting up reading in the path of the bullet. Nor had another woman known, when she went to the ladies' room of a Wall Street office building, that a man with a knife would leap out at her from a booth to snatch her purse and slash her face. She too had been surprised. So: in Central America you had machetes and earthquakes; in Manhattan there was equal craziness; other places might be dull. *Entonces, vamos a la playa. Feliz navidad.*

The landscape became a seascape as we drove downward for half an hour past magnificent vistas and billboards advertising seven or eight rival brands of panty hose. Panty hose must be very big down here. Although plenty of Salvadoreños were celebrating Christmas by the Pacific, we did not encounter a single drunk with a machete. What we encountered instead, besides amiable boys who offered us fresh oysters, was what I, for one, least expected: a houseful of *norteamericanos* who seemed to be having an impromptu seminar on a topic close to my heart: the decline of families.

"Maybe ten years from now, when I'm in my late thirties, I'll be sick of all this moving around," said Diane from her hammock on Tony's porch, "but for now I just can't see staying put. After Argentina I think we'll try Africa, and then maybe the Middle East." By "we" Diane meant herself and her pig-tailed, ten-year-old daughter, Denise. Denise, whose ears were pierced, was fussing restively with a coloring book. Tony, their host, was an acquaintance of Miguel's we met on the beach, who asked us to stop by when we had had enough sun.

Diane and Denise had with them two sleeping bags, two hammocks, a backpack, a daypack for Denise, three airline flight bags, and two large suitcases, one filled with clothing and the other with toys. "You might think that's a lot," said Diane, "and it *is* a lot to carry, but remember: we have to think about the high Andes as well as the tropics, and we'll be gone for a year. We have to get to Argentina by March, because that's when the school years starts. Every now and then I like to have Denise spend a whole school year in one place. I think it's good for her.

"We're going to live in a ski resort. There are these two guys I met in Paris who live down there. They'll help us find a place to stay, and I'm sure they'll help me find a job too."

"Do they know when you're coming?"

"No, they don't know we're coming at all. But it'll be cool. Even if they aren't there. I won't have trouble finding work. I've worked as a bookkeeper, receptionist, chambermaid, waitress—I've done a lot of things. All I care about is being where there's skiing, where there are exciting panoramas you can get to without a motor.

"A resort town would be the only place I could stand to stop for a whole year. At least there's a steady flow of new people in a resort town, and they're not the kind of people who care whether you have a nice car or apartment. That's why I keep traveling; the people you meet on the road don't care about stuff like that."

"Do you ever wonder if you're running *from* or *toward?*" asked Tony.

"I don't feel into heavy questions," said Diane. She was wearing an embroidered Guatemalan blouse over her bikini. You would have guessed that she was from California by her luminous skin, flabless body, and open mind. Such minds are sometimes, though not in her case, so open as to seem unfurnished. Ah, the open symmetry of Californians. All that sun and orange juice, or something, has deprived them of (they might say freed them from) the quirks, both physical and otherwise, that mark (they might say mar) the rest of us.

Tony, who lived in Ventura, had that look about him too. By avocation Tony was a surfer, by profession a successful enough architect to have bought this two-room joke of a house, a quarter of a mile from the beach. The house had no kitchen, but there was a cheap restaurant across the way, and there was a vast long porch from which could hang any number of hammocks. A hammock and a surfboard were about all Tony needed when he came down to El Salvador. Something about this particular beach caused wave formations whose renown drew surfers from as far away as Australia, and now and then some of them ended up sleeping on hammocks at Tony's. One of these, named Neal, had yesterday run into Diane and Denise outside the bus station in San Salvador, looking as confused as they probably ever did, which wasn't very.

"We were supposed to get right onto another bus to Costa Rica," said Diane, "but because of the earthquake no buses were going south at all. Neal noticed us wondering what to do and we started rapping and he said Tony probably wouldn't mind if we crashed here for a few days, and Tony didn't. Hey, Tony? Thanks." She toasted him by lifting the coconut we had all been passing back and forth, to which had been added a local fluid called Tik-Tak. Watching lizards darting up and down tree trunks from my own hammock, I pretended the drink was eggnog.

"We left San Diego in October," said Diane, "and we planned to be a lot farther south than this by now, only we got hung up in Belize. The people in British Honduras were so *nice!* They weren't at all like the Mexicans; they actually talked to each other and they called each other, and us, 'Darlin'. One truckdriver gave us a ride to a town where there were no hotels, so we put up our hammocks in his house and made friends with his wife and six kids.

"And the Guatemalans—the Guatemalans were dynamite.

Up there in the mountains they look like elves. They're all around three feet tall, and each town has its own special costume, and they're very big on shaking hands and smiling. People here seem nice too. I could see staying on this beach for a long time, only I can't wait to get to Costa Rica, because in Costa Rica we'll have our first mail in two months. I'm sort of worried. For all I know, everybody could be dead."

Everybody, to Diane, meant her thrice-married mother, her alcoholic father, her suburban sister, her ex-husband, and assorted other relatives. "I don't speak to about ninety-percent of my family," she said, "or rather they don't speak to me, but I really do care about my mother. She's a good lady, and she's all for what I'm doing. We're pretty tight. She wouldn't leave my dad until I talked her into it, even though she said the last fifteen of her twenty-five years with him were hell. She's the self-sacrificing type, you know? It's funny, my mom's more like a daughter to me than Denise is. Lots of times I feel like Denise is my mother and I'm her daughter."

"I know what you mean," I said. "I often feel that my niece Sarah is in fact my aunt. Sarah's seven now, but her true spiritual age, my sister says, is and always has been forty-two. She's forever lecturing us to quit smoking."

"Hey, Mom," asked Denise, "how many packs of cigarettes have you smoked today?"

"Five," said Diane.

"No come on, really, how many?"

"Not even half, so far, but it'll be a full pack by night. Hey, Denise, why don't you go get a Sno-Kone at that restaurant across the way? Here's some money.

"She doesn't like my life-style," Diane said when her daughter had gone. "She misses cold milk and television, but she wasn't into staying with her father or my sister, either. Her father is remarried to a bitch, and my sister has two little boys who tease the daylights out of Denise, so I figure she's better off on the road with me. She's been around a lot, for a ten-year-old: she's lived in Seattle, L. A., the French Alps, Spain, Germany, Paris, back in the States a while, and now here; now this trip.

"Do I give her lessons along the way? Sort of, sometimes. She's quick to pick up languages, but she forgets them after we leave. Now and then I read to her. This guy at USC, I asked him before we left what I should bring along on the trip to read, and he not only recommended but gave us *The Wind in the Willows*. And the other day I read a Harold Robbins book. Magazines like *Newsweek,* though I never care about them at home, are like gold on the road. What I really miss more than reading, though, is music. I'd give a lot for a radio right now."

Had Denise not been conceived, Diane would never have married Mike, a salesman who referred to her as 'the wife' even when she was in the same room. "But he made one mistake," said Diane. "He bought a second car for me to use, a Volvo, and the minute I laid eyes on it I knew that this would be the way I'd escape, and one day it was. One day, before Denise could even walk, I packed us both up and drove off."

By the time Denise was three she and her mother were settled in the French Alps. Diane worked as a chambermaid and fell in love, "for the first and only time in my whole life," with a French skier. "It was really dumb of me to leave there and go to Spain, but I did." In Torremelinos and Marbella, "a really mellow town then," she worked for an artist who did flattering twenty-minute portraits of tourists. In Garmisch, Germany she put Denise in a Montessori school and worked as a governess. Army wives, grateful that although Diane had long hair she did not appear to be on her way to Turkey to score for hash, trusted her with their kids and were kind to Denise, who one year had three birthday cakes.

In Paris Diane found "a so-so job at a snobbish club for very rich American women who were totally out of touch with France. Their idea of a really big deal was to be invited to a luncheon by Eunice Shriver." Diane got free rent in exchange for baby-sitting for another American couple, and discovered a night club "where they had this really neat, fantastic South American music, which was what turned me on to coming down this way in the first place. That was where I met the guys we're going to look for. In that club they had every kind of instrument you can think of, including a harp. Have you ever heard a harp played with rhythm and life? You can't imagine what it sounds like. Before we leave here, I'd like to get a couple of cane flutes for Denise and me."

Diane's mother, whose second husband had been killed in a motorcycle crash, came over to France to job-hunt, but nobody wanted to hire a fifty-year-old American widow. Before long she took her daughter and granddaughter home to California, where Diane stayed put a couple of months before she hitchhiked, by air, to see an old flame who had moved to Philadelphia.

"Mail planes are a good way to go," said Diane, "if you've got guts. Those guys are all bush pilots; they're wired. They probably all take pills. They'll fly at night or anytime. It didn't work out with the Philadelphia guy, so I spent the summer of '71 at my sister's house, working as a cocktail waitress and just sort of freeloading.

"My sister's friends, I noticed, were all really nervous about their husbands. If they didn't get home before their husbands did, or if they hadn't waxed the floor or watered the lawn or whatever they'd promised they were going to have done by that night, they would be literally *scared,* to the point of real fear. It was like their daddy, instead of their husband, would punish them, by not letting them go to the prom next week or something."

Diane's mother, who is "always into Zen or astrology or something," went to a singles dance where she met a man who also had a Gemini daughter. On the strength of that coincidence they were married. "He's a nice guy," says Diane, "but you know where they live? In a mobile home moored in concrete. It's got bigger rooms than a lot of mobile homes, but still. His idea of a vacation is the Disneyland Hotel, which is around five miles away. He never wants to *go* anyplace."

My own father, unlike many American husbands, likes traveling just fine. He studies guide books in advance, gets out of the car to examine historical markers, and always knows what railroad goes over an underpass. He and my mother went to Europe twice, on charter flights, and they were forever driving around the States. The last Christmas of her life they went to California. Ann and I urged them to, promising we would have our annual reunion later. When they finally agreed, we felt as Kenya must have on the day of Uhuru: free but nervous. But then Christmas always made us nervous. It obliged us to declare who we were and to whom we belonged, questions I never felt ready to answer. At other times of the year we worked and played and got and spent more or less as normal grownups do, but Christmas meant a mix of regression and guilt I thought peculiar to our age and place and time until I asked a psychoanalyst if anyone else felt the same way. "They *all* do," he said.

The Christmas of Uhuru, Ann and David and their children went to the Caribbean. I joined them later, after devoting the twenty-fifth to a lame-duck reconciliation with a man about whom my feelings had long been mixed. He and I went to the farmhouse of some friends in the Berkshires. The farmhouse was idyllic, and the friends were stouthearted and true, but I cannot recommend lame-duck Christmases. This one was confusingly bittersweet, to say the least. Late that afternoon I bade the man in question another in a series of farewells, dropped him off with other friends in Dutchess County, and drove back to New York to give a dinner party. Some party. None of the guests knew each other, or wanted to. They included a poet from the beatnik days, a rosy-cheeked secretary, a Jewish mountaineer and his wife, and a dogged attorney-at-law. We all make jokes about the 100 Neediest Cases.

Santa and I, before then, had always returned to Illinois, for a pagan amalgam of tributes more to him than to Jesus. We would go either to Springfield or Decatur, my parents' or my sister's. He would arrive by his traditional means, I via Ozark, the All-Jet, Go-Getter Airline. For him there would be cookies and milk, for the reindeer carrots, and for me a few rounds of the perennially challenging "Guess Which Ornament I'm Thinking Of?" That

blue one up near the top? No. That candy canish one toward the bottom? Mmmp-mmm. The Mexican angel?
Yeah! Way to guess! Okay, your turn. Gol, Mom, this is a
dumb game. Play it anyway, it's a tradition.

Sometimes in the Springfield years we made it to the
First Presbyterian midnight service to hear Dr. Graebel
sing "Stille Nacht" as his immigrant mother had taught
him to, and sometimes we didn't. When we didn't we
would hear such reassuring phrases on the phonograph, or
voice them ourselves. Mark my footsteps, good my page,
tread thou in them boldly. Wrapped in swaddling clothes.
Natum videte. The luster of midday. Tiny tots, Ann
would always add, with their hair all ablaze.

What a jumble of memories. Some of the memories are
sweet. The primal smell of the greens, for one, and the
chance that in some day's mail there might come a half-
inch stack of cards with a handwritten message on each,
and my favorite rite of all, the wrapping of presents. Buying them makes one feel a caricature consumer, and opening them for those above the age of nine is often an anti-
climax, but all the fuss about paper and Scotch tape and
tags, and the way they all look under the tree, makes me
feel actually merry, the way you're supposed to.

My mother would permit only the most terminally
crumpled tissue paper to be sacrificed in the fireplace.
Everything else she would fold and perhaps iron for next
year. She was a rewrapper and proud of it, just as she was a
petty thief of soap and stationery from hotel rooms. A
number of the gift enclosure tags were kept from year to
year, too. One of these said, "To the woman whom I selected to become the mother of my children."

Nobody was ever too old, or too canine or too feline, to
hang up a stocking, nor could anyone ever lollygag abed
after daybreak. Down we would file in our bathrobes, to
say, "You *should,* if you know what I mean," when others
said they liked our Serious presents. Serious presents,
which cost in the two-figure range, were supplemented
with cheerful unserious stuff, edible and otherwise, and all
manner of nontoxic notions and knicknacks. One year my

mother gave me a Baggie, tied with a red ribbon, of stones she had collected the previous summer in Michigan, and polished by hand.

After we had opened the "gifts" we had "received" we would "display" them for a while, each taking over a chair surface for the purpose and then, with carols on the phonograph, go eat sausage and eggs and coffeecake. Later would come dutiful phone calls, if the circuits were free, to or from distant loved ones ("Here, come on, *you* talk to her.") and thank-you notes. One record year we had all our acknowledgments posted by the twenty-sixth. Sometimes we would rate all the cards, on a one-to-ten scale.

There were always some random fragments of comfort and joy, especially if it had snowed, but rarely when expected or of much duration. One year a thoughtful friend in New York had given me four mildly hallucinogenic cigarettes—wasn't that a nice gesture? Late that December twenty-sixth, when everyone else had gone to bed, Ann and I smoked two and laughed a lot as we played, I believe, *Rigoletto*. I don't know to this day what happened to the other two joints. Search the house though we did the next morning, refluffing the cushions behind us, we never could locate them. The mistress of the house was most oddly nonchalant as her two daughters ransacked the premises—up, down, under, behind, around—in search of some unnamed lost object. Odd indeed. Normally it was we who would yawn and say, "Oh, never mind, it'll turn up," no matter what was missing, and she whose heart would leap at the thrill of the hunt for its own sake, regardless of the prize. Could it possibly be that she herself had found that which we sought and flushed it down the drain (afraid to confront us), lest banner headlines read NAB HOWARD GIRLS IN DOPE RAID?

Different parts of the world offer different comforts. Down here there wasn't a phonograph, but up home nobody in my immediate ken had much in the way of servants. Miguel had a

326

live-in cook, and even at Tony's beach shack there was a defer-
ential caretaker called Segundo, who said things like *A sus or-*
denes and *Para servirle*. Segundo had just carved a hole in another coconut, and Neal, the surfer who had met Diane at the
bus station, had forsaken his hammock to go find some more
Tik-Tak. Earlier Neal had been talking in hearty praise of
President Nixon and the space program, sentiments Diane
was not used to hearing.

"Neal's an odd one," she said. "He looks like a hippie, but
you know what he told me? He told me he's saving money to
get married, as soon as he finds the right girl. It's funny, but in
the last seven years, since women have been into not marrying,
men have been *dying* to find wives. Being married simplifies
their lives so much. If they have wives, see, it means they don't
have to go to the laundromat."

"I guess the old game of snaring Mr. Right *is* pretty obsolete,
isn't it?" I said. "Especially if laundry has all that much to do
with it."

"Well, a contract of property is part of it, too," said Tom.
"Marriage is essentially a matter of finding someone you can
stand who can stand you too. Don't knock it; it's a lot. Only
dreamers like both my wives think there's more to it than
that."

"If there's no more to it than that, forget it," said Diane. "It
would be different if I wanted another child, or if I had faith
that any marriage would last, but who needs divorce and the
hassle of *suing* somebody? I could only see it if I fell in love,
and I don't think I know what love is any more. I've met so
many guys I like, I can't imagine settling for just one."

"We're spoiled," I said.

"You are," said Tony, "and you're too impatient. You split
from your marriage as soon as it wasn't groovy, right Diane?
That's the trouble with a lot of women. Marriages take around
five years to mellow. This friend of my wife's, she got screwed
up and drove off in her husband's car with a sleeping bag, so
she could see the sunrise. She left her kids behind and now all
she wants to do is screw everyone in sight, probably because
she never had any fun before she got married."

"Things are more balanced in Europe," said Diane. "American men, especially divorced American men, are the worst: they don't know what it's all about. That's one reason I'm glad to be leaving; other places where they marry later I'll be more likely to find single men my own age. In Europe, generally speaking, men know how to make women feel special. Frenchmen in particular. Having doors opened and being admired on the street is great, as far as I'm concerned."

"So you're not liberated?" asked Tony.

"What's liberated?" said Diane. "Sure I am, in a lot of ways. I like women more than I used to. I used to avoid them and say, 'Give me a man any time.' There are lots of things I'd rather talk about with women than with men. There's a lot that men miss. Hey, Miguel, you've lived all around the world: what do you think about women in the States?"

"Generalizing is dangerous," he said, "but North American women do seem obsessed with money, with having their incomes increase annually and regularly."

"I was having dinner with a friend in New York a while ago," I said, "and you know why he said he wanted to take a year off and travel around the world? He said, 'I just wonder what folks in other places *do* with all that energy, when they don't spend it *buying* stuff.'"

"Another thing," said Miguel, "is that a lot of North American women want to change their men."

"Why do the men put up with it?"

"Because they saw their mothers do it to their fathers; they don't know any other way."

"When I was a kid I used to love my uncles," said Diane, "because I was a tomboy and they were the good guys. They were all hunter-fisherman-cowboy types, and they could all hardly wait to get away from their wives, I guess because their wives really screwed up their egos. We'd have these family reunions at Lake Tahoe, and my mom and aunts would all sleep late, and I'd get up early when the men did. You know something? Those uncles would make breakfast for themselves, but not for me, because I was a girl. Boy, *they* sure must have hated women."

"Hey, Tony," I said, "doesn't your wife mind that you're gone for Christmas?"

"I guess so," he said, "but she's going to Europe in the spring, so it all evens out. I'll get her something in Guatemala on the way home."

"But how come you married her, if you don't even want to be with her on Christmas?"

"You're really Miss Yule Log, aren't you? Christmas doesn't have to be that big a deal. I married her because I couldn't get rid of her. She hung around my house all the time and her parents were after me too. So was my own mother. You know what my mother said when I asked her to give me one good reason why I should get married again? She said, 'Christ, who're you going to *yell* at, if you don't have a wife? You don't want to be all alone when you're pissed *off*, do you?' And maybe that's as good a reason as any."

"Hey, Mom," said Denise, who had come back from climbing some trees and rocks by the beach, "how long did you say we're going to stay here?"

"*You* know," said her mother, "until the buses start running south. It might be soon."

"Anybody want to play Hangman with me?" asked Denise.

"It's getting too dark," said her mother. "We'll play it tomorrow, in the daylight."

"Do you ever miss having roots?" I asked Diane.

"Not much," she said. "Everyplace I happen to go to there's something worth seeing. I don't figure that any experience is wasted. It's all the planet earth; it's all got vegetation."

Suddenly I thought of one reason why Mark Van Doren had been a part of my triumvirate of heroes. There is a sentence in his *Autobiography* which strikes me now as much as it did when I first read it: "I tend to approve of any place I am in, simply because I am there." Or, as I once heard a Yoga teacher tell his class, "Wherever you are is where you should be." Oh, to believe that more often. Diane had something of that spirit in her, for which I envied her. She also made me think of Tom Tuttle, with whom I had recently had lunch in New York. Tom Tuttle, a prosperous Detroit businessman, told me he was worried about his twenty-seven-year-old daughter, Sigrid. Sigrid aspired to be a sculptor, but she survived mainly on food stamps and what she could earn as a part-time gardener, which was not at all the future her father had envisioned for her.

"The trouble with her," her father had said, "is that she doesn't even know she wants to get married."

"How do *you* know she wants to?" I had the impudence to ask.

"Well, of course she wants to," he said. "Every girl wants to. How else can she support herself? How else can she find any sort of lasting security?"

As I lay in that hammock, my head felt like a television set with all the channels on at once. What would happen to Sigrid Tuttle? Could she and her father ever understand each other? Would Diane find cane flutes for herself and Denise? Would the guys she had met in Paris be there when they got to Argentina? Would the skiing panoramas match her hopes? Would the music? Would Denise be better equipped to face the twenty-first century than little girls whose Brownie troopmates would grow up to be their bridesmaids? What of Diane's mother, stuck in the immobile trailer with a man who never wanted to travel? Were families truly obsolete? Was Christmas?

Usually hammocks make me feel so blissfully weightless that I never willingly get up from them, but gravity suddenly seemed an inviting idea. Miguel rose from his hammock too, and we walked together down the dirt path to the shore, to watch the tide come in and the sun go down. The sun disappeared resplendently, not directly out at sea but a bit to our right, because we were not facing due west. We stood there in stillness and watched it for quite a while.

"Tomorrow *will* be the twenty-sixth, won't it?" I finally asked Miguel.

"Indeed," he said. In the dark I could barely see his smile.

28

Oh Taut Stretched Beam

Maybe I was being punished for the sin of pride. I had felt smug, during my time in San Salvador, not to succumb to so banal a complaint as diarrhea. This was the sort of thing that happened to ordinary gringos, I had figured, not to me.

Besides, should I not be immune at this point to all misfortune? Had not an astrologer told me that on January 6, coincidentally the Feast of Epiphany on the church calendar, I would commence a sparkling new phase of my life? My planets, she had foretold, would so arrange themselves that "the three-year period of stagnation and despair you've been having" would dramatically end: just wait and see. Wow, I thought. My own personal epiphany. Maybe I'll have a vision.

What I was having instead, as Pan Am Flight 903 headed toward Miami via Guatemala, was acute gastric distress. This was only January 3; the planets were not to be hurried. They, or the gods of the Mayans I had left behind and the Presbyterians I was about to join, had conspired to chastise me for my hubris. Or maybe it was that the previous night, my last in San Salvador, I had urged Miguel to take me to some darling little ethnic, regional place to eat. He had. It was all delicious too. But now my intestines felt like the epicenter of an earthquake.

The trouble with such maladies, as with common colds, is that they are so utterly preoccupying. I had expected to read and muse and maybe write a bit en route north, but all I could do was squirm in my seat, between hasty lurches to the lavatory, and feel sorry for myself.

The Miami airport that day was bedlam. Quite a few other people seemed also to be in transit. The air was scented with jet fuel and the loudspeaker kept summoning passengers to something called the White Courtesy Telephone. Redcaps were not to be found. In addition to three serious pieces of checked-through luggage I had another three "carry-on" items —a leather L. L. Bean bag full of reading material, a "portable" typewriter, and a plastic tote containing the duty-free Grand Marnier I had thriftily picked up during the Guatemala stopover.

My name was paged as I waited in a long queue for Customs officials to appraise the contents of my baggage. A message from my brother-in-law, who knew when I was to arrive in Miami, suggested that I join his family at St. John in the Virgin Islands, where they had decided to stay on for an extra five days.

Now generally I pride myself on spontaneity, as well as on freedom from upset stomachs, but the prospect of this change of plans brought about a grand mal seizure of indecision. I recognized the symptoms; it had happened before, and nearly always in airports. (It is possible to have such attacks elsewhere, but airports, proclaiming as they do such an infinity of options, are ideal for the purpose.) Once, at the airport in Cincinnati, it was a tossup between LaGuardia or Springfield, Illinois. A couple of years earlier, in Athens, my dilemma had been whether or not to stop off in Cairo on the way to Zurich. I have been known on such occasions not just to weep softly, like a lightweight neurotic in a Joan Didion novel, but to sob, right there in public.

"Evil," as Martin Buber once wrote, "is lack of direction." I think he was right. He was also correct to add that one must relinquish "undirected plenitude in favor of the one taut string, the one stretched beam of direction." Fine, but which taut string? A Caribbean beach where I might snorkel over coral reefs with my niece and nephew? I had been specifically missing John and Sarah, the way one misses beloved grownups, and the temptation to see them made me ache. But, since thousands of other people apparently had tickets to the Virgin Islands, I could only go as a Standby.

A Standby is a person who waits with feigned serenity at an airport gate without a reservation to the place he wants to go, hoping ticketed passengers won't show up so that he can get aboard at the last minute, after all. It isn't so bad to be a Standby if you don't have diarrhea and aren't carrying much, but such was not my state. Nor would it be a matter of just one trip. First I would have to stand by for a flight to San Juan, then to St. Thomas, and then a long taxi ride and a ferryboat. It would cost a lot of money, stir up a good bit of anxiety, and the chances of losing some or all of my luggage were excellent.

It would also mean postponing my trip to Denton, South Carolina, and maybe missing the Magnolia Ladies. This was the very day I had told Virginia Bingham I would probably show up in Denton, her birthplace, where she was spending a month's holiday. She knew all about my project to talk to different American women. When I told her about the Cat Lady and the Quilt Lady and the Maple Sugar Lady, she had said I would be remiss to overlook the Magnolia Ladies of Denton (the "t" in which, incidentally, is almost silent, as if the town's name were Dennon).

One would not know, to talk to Virginia, that she has not lived in South Carolina for decades. "The minute some people hear my accent," she said, "they ask me things like 'Why don't those people at that Louisiana college go back to Africa?' It can get tiresome, I tell *you*."

As she described the Magnolia Ladies in an eight-page letter, they sounded like a classic microcosm. They tend, Ginny wrote, to look fifteen years younger than they are and to spend most of their lives in or near the places they were born. Gifted cooks, they serve things like peach leather and syllabub and

green pepper jelly at luncheons and bridge parties, and sometimes at 10 A.M. Coca-Cola parties too. Many of them are regal
in their gentility and skilled at denying the existence of anything unpleasant. For some reason, those among them who had
the most wretched childhoods seemed to grow up happiest, and
vice versa. Some were "vapid kittens," others "vindictive tar-
tars," but still others, Ginny stoutly maintained, were delightful.

It puzzled her, she went on, that "people my age [she was
born in 1922] are forever dying early, years before their time.
My mother has more friends alive than I do. I wonder if her
generation doesn't live longer because they were given rules to
follow, rules that held up. Things were laid out for them in
certain clear patterns. They knew what they were supposed to
do, and they did it, with no doubts or questions."

All this sounded meaty enough to warrant a five-year visit by
the likes of Faulkner or Flannery O'Connor. How could I,
passing through for a few days with my notebooks, hope to do
it justice? All I knew for sure was that I wouldn't go unless
Ginny herself was there to interpret. Seeing her would justify
the trip anyway. (Come to think of it, she looks fifteen years
younger than she is, too. She has short brown hair and a sculp-
tured-looking face and a deceptively antebellum laugh.) One
must not lose touch with tenured members of the Committee
to Keep One Sane. Ginny is on that committee because of the
way she listens. She should give lessons in how to listen. She remembers things you told her in passing three years ago and re-
lates them to the present, like a shrink. She will let you know
with surgical finesse if she thinks you aren't making much
sense. If she thinks you are, you will feel in her presence like
that most fugitive of phantoms, the best imaginable real you,
seldom seen by tourists.

But.

But John and Sarah make me feel that way too. With them I
feel positively delightful, exactly the opposite of the way I felt
in the Miami airport. I particularly like to be with them, for
some reason, by such bodies of water as the Caribbean. Should

334

I just put off the South Carolina trip by a few days and go to join them? To solve the problem, I did what I always do. I made a long-distance phone call—my first, for a wonder, in ten days.

"Well," said Ginny when she heard my dilemma, "I always think you ought to do what you *want* to do."

"Oh, come on. Anyone could tell me that. It's no help. Can't you see that I don't *know* what I want to do?"

"Then come here."

Ginny can't walk. She has not walked since 1941, when she was eighteen. She could before that. Before that she was a state champion women's-doubles tennis player, a cheerleader, and a drum majorette who liked to dance. But she was thrown out of a convertible car on the way home for spring vacation in her sophomore year.

"The wheels of the car were still spinning when I landed flat on my back in a cornfield. The car must have turned over several times. I looked at my feet, which I couldn't move, and thought how odd that my shoes had been knocked off. When I tried to raise myself up on my arms a great long shooting pain went through my back, as if someone had stabbed me with a sword. After that there was no pain at all."

No wonder. Her spine was broken; from the waist down she was totally paralyzed. In vain did her friends wish, in yearbook autographs, "a real speedy recovery to a really swell girl." During World War II, when Denton's young men went off to fight, their wives and fiancées came almost daily to Ginny's house to knit and play bridge and visit.

It was during that period that Ginny's mother quit smoking. Her quitting smoking is a family legend. "I didn't even *want* to smoke, but somebody said if I tried Kools it would help my hay fever, so I did," says Mrs. Bingham. "I just hated it. It was right after the accident, and I was workin' all the time. When I was workin' I was too busy to smoke, and when I was relaxin' I was too tired, so quittin' was the easiest thing I ever did." Every night in those years it took Mrs. Bingham two or three hours to get her daughter ready for bed.

Althea Newell Bingham was a Yeomanette during World War I in the U.S. Navy. She believes that God is like the Jungfrau, to which she made a pilgrimage during a European trip, while Ginny stayed in Tuscany to practice her Italian. "I waited for three days to see that mountain, and the clouds completely covered it until the last morning. I think that's the way God is; we can't always see Him, but we must never doubt that He's there." She would no more skip saying grace before a meal than she would ever say anything more harsh than *"Darn* it!" or cast a vote for Richard M. Nixon. "I can't *stand* that man," she says. She and her cook Roberta Small and Ginny had to draw the blinds and lock the doors lest anyone observe them cheering as they watched McGovern at the 1972 Democrat convention. Such sentiments, in Denton, were not fashionable.

But Miss Althea, as some of her friends call her, is forgiven her politics. Her house is, in fact, a focal point for the female gentry of Denton. While I was there the doorbell rang quite a lot.

"Why, Cousin Rowena! Why, Mrs. Marsh! Did you ever! Imagine your droppin' by! I declare, I was just saying to Jinki and Bowman and Loretta that it's time *we* came to see *you!*"

"Law, darlin', I meant to get over here sooner, but with all the company we've had . . ."

"Oh, I know, it's been like that here too. Now: let me go get some of that Tunnel of Love cake. It's so nice with the coffee, don't you know."

Legs are crossed at the ankle. Coffee is served. A wastebasket some retarded child made of tasseled styrofoam egg crates is admired. Hugs may or may not have been exchanged, but generally people touch each other a lot, hold hands, administer little backrubs. It is sweet. So are nicknames. Cousin Rowena Taylor, for example, is known to some as Sweetheart. Down the street lives Little Nanny ("in reduced circumstances," Miss Althea explains). Little Nanny, a retired schoolteacher, is so called not because of her height, which is five feet eight, nor her age, which is upwards of seventy, but to distinguish her from Big Nanny, who used to be Miss Althea's wet nurse. "We're all just unbelievably intertwined here," said Miss Althea. Big Nanny had been so beloved a part of the family that on her deathbed Miss Althea took her daughter and two sons, then children, to see her. The old nurse was so happy to see her visitors that she forgot herself and hugged them.

After the war, Ginny went to New York for a two-year rehabilitation program, learning among other things how to hoist herself from her wheelchair onto the driver's seat of a hand-controlled car. Entranced with the city, she found a job as a typist for *Life*. After twenty years she was an assistant editor, and later was transferred to the bureau in Beverly Hills.

There are persons whom Los Angeles intoxicates with its magic, its tolerance of diversity, its very freeways, but Virginia Newell Bingham did not turn out to be one of them. The only thing she did much fancy about that city was Synanon, the therapeutic community for former drug addicts. A pharmacist's daughter and sister—"I'd always been curious about drugs, from watching so many secret addicts come into the store for their daily paregoric,"—she was pleased to learn that Synanon welcomed unaddicted "squares" like herself as well as ex-users. All were free to join "tribes" and take part in weekly "games," a form of encounter group in which everybody hurls honesty at everyone else.

"At Synanon they used to ask me why I didn't just wheel myself on over to the VA Hospital, where they had a big paraplegic ward, to find myself a soulmate. 'What are you waiting for?' they'd ask me. They all thought I was too mousy. But can you see it, all that clanging and banging of wheelchairs? Can you imagine the *logistics* of it?"

Several perfectly nice ambulatory men had sought to marry Ginny, wheelchair and all. Twice she was tempted, but neither alliance worked out. "With the others I never felt the spark of the irresistible attraction that makes it easy to give up independence and freedom. Anyway, it seems to me that most women

337

get married for security and status. I never wanted to do it just for the sake of being married. If I had, my life would have been a lot more solid and stable, but I resisted security. I may be sorry tomorrow, but there it is.

"Besides, if you've lived by yourself for a while, you wonder how married couples, no matter how much they love each other, can stand all that constant, twenty-four-hour-a-day proximity. Still, paradoxically, I find it harder and harder to live alone. You might think it would get easier as time goes on, but it doesn't."

"Continuity is what I crave when I have attacks of loneliness," I told her. "The idea of seeing someone without having to fix my hair first, without it being a special occasion. I guess that's one reason some people have kids, so they won't be lonely."

"Do you want them?" she asked me.

"Well, I think I do."

"Why? Power and vanity?"

"That could be part of it. What could be more flattering than a tiny little adorable version of me, with none of my faults of course, to instruct and amuse? But that's idealistic, isn't it, and they do seem to take up a fair amount of time, don't they? Did you ever wish you had children?"

"Oh, I thought about it. Paraplegics can be mothers; it's been done, you know. But I figured it's hard enough for kids whose mothers *aren't* in wheelchairs to grow up. As I say, talk about logistics."

Even her Synanon tribe could not keep Ginny from moving for good to Tucson, which during an earlier visit smote her on sight, just as New York had. My cousins Kathy and Steve became her close friends before I did. She analyzed their handwriting and got interested in their cactuses and children. Now it's as if we were all cousins.

Ginny puts a lot more stock in graphology than in horoscopes, and truth to tell so do I, but she was excited for me when I told her what the astrologer had said about Epiphany. "Good night! I feel *responsible* to think that you're going to begin a whole new cycle right here in Clinton! Maybe it was something to do with the Magnolia Ladies. Let's see, which ones should we arrange for you to talk to?

"But what am I thinkin' of? First we've got to get you well." Oh, yes, of course, poor pitiful me with my tropical indisposition. The way Ginny and her nearly blind mother fussed over me, you would have thought that they had never themselves suffered anything more serious than a hangnail. (Mrs. Bingham, as the result of glaucoma, can see through certain special very thick glasses, sometimes, at a certain angle, sort of, well enough to read a giant-print edition of the Psalms and the large type weekly *New York Times*.) Their solicitude was so embarrassing, and the pink medicine Ginny's pharmacist brother Ronnie brought over so effective, that I began to take notice of my surroundings.

Freight trains still toot through Denton, over tracks that separate Us from Them. I did not actually hear anyone whistling "Dixie," or humming "Beautiful Dreamer," but the town could provide quite a suitable background for a filmed operetta set to the music of Stephen Collins Foster. It is an hour away from any airport, and thus from the vexations that plague more accessible places. Oh, there had been some interracial unpleasantness at the high school, I heard, and someone had been arrested for homegrown marijuana. Murder, embezzlement, and kidnapping were not altogether unheard of, but gentleness prevailed, or appeared to. One afternoon, as I strolled alone in the Presbyterian cemetery, the carillon was playing "Blest Be the Tie That Binds."

A good many of Denton's 10,000 inhabitants work in the two cotton mills. Cotton fields surround the town. It is too far north for hanging Spanish moss, but magnolias abound, and everybody said I should come back in spring to see the azaleas. Camellias were blooming even though it was January; when I first arrived it was warm enough to walk without a coat across Newell Street to the imposing house of Ronnie, the pharmacist. I did just that, in fact, because his wife Patty Ann had a perfectly lovely sit-down luncheon, more or less in my honor, for seven ladies who declared themselves thrilled to meet Jinki's friend from New York.

Jinki is Ginny's name when she is home. To her five nieces, one of whom is her namesake, she is in fact known as Big Jinki. She is closest to Kitty, the eldest niece, whose high school classmates voted her the senior girl with the Best Personality. Now a law student at the state university, Kitty says Big Jinki has influenced her plenty.

Once, when Kitty came to visit in New York, Ginny asked why her niece was so edgy. It turned out Kitty's father had cautioned her: "Jinki might take you to some play or someplace where you'll hear the kind of language you're not used to, and if that happens you just excuse yourself and go quietly to the ladies' room, hear?"

"Can you imagine?" says Ginny, *"Me,* the straightest person you ever heard of, coming across as some corruptin' Auntie Mame?" The next night she took Kitty to a Frank Sinatra concert in Forest Hills, "mainly because *I* wanted to go myself." At one point, when the euphoric singer exclaimed "Hot damn!," aunt nudged niece and said, "Well, Kitty, you want to go find the ladies' room?"

A few years later, around the time when she was writing a college paper in support of the Vietnam war, Kitty went to visit Ginny in Los Angeles. "I can't believe I ever really thought this," says Kitty, "but I did: I said to Jinki, 'Those hippies who don't like the war can just find somewhere else to go.' Jinki just looked at me and said, 'Why should *they* move?' I told her to go to hell. Grandma was there too, and the next morning she had to *make* me say goodbye to Jinki on her way to work."

Kitty's views have changed. In a congressman's Washington office, where she worked for two years, "I was the token liberal." When a law school classmate asked if she were serious about becoming an attorney, she exploded, "You jerk! I'm more serious, than *you* are!" She hopes to do legal aid, specializing in criminal law, and is more concerned with the plight of blacks than with that of women.

Ginny, since her return to Tucson from Los Angeles, has become a student too. There are 500,000 women over the age of thirty on college campuses in America, and she is one of them. Roberta, her mother's cook, is not quite accurate in addressing her as "Lily of the Field," on the grounds that she toils not, neither does she spin. By the fall of 1972, she had become a junior at the University of Arizona.

"To get in the swing of things," she wrote me, "I'm making it a point to attend as many protest rallies as possible and to sign a lot of petitions. The U of A is not exactly your Berkeley campus—they're a pretty phlegmatic bunch—but they did manage to scrape up a protest the other day against raising tuition to finance an eleven-million-dollar addition to the football stadium, which nobody ever goes to.

"I attended that, of course, and it was pretty good. They ceremoniously burned a jock strap. I don't have any blue jeans, because I really can't get into them, but am looking around for some denim skirts. My hair would look lousy long too, but maybe I can sign extra petitions to make up for wearing it short."

She returned to college for the same reason Kitty says she enrolled in law school: "Because I got tired of not usin' my brain. The first year it was enchanting to put new stuff in, but now it's just plain hard. All the studyin' is so hard I haven't had time to help much with the women lawyers' movement. First I was disillusioned, because I did go to one of their meetings where they talked for a whole hour about where to put the Tampax machine, but I got to feelin' guilty, so I volunteered to help with the convention comin' up this spring, when women law students from all over will be comin' to our campus.

"They asked if I'd plan a cocktail party for the convention, and I said sure: I've been plannin' parties all my life and thought nothing could be simpler. They said I'd have to line up a band for the party, and I thought, 'Easy, there're plenty of musicians at the law fraternity house.' Then they said it would have to be an all-*girl* band—can you imagine, for a four-hour

341

cocktail party? *That* part's not going to be easy. I may have to end up with the five Bingham sisters in puffed sleeves doin' a piano recital."

"Maybe *I* could help you," offered Ginny. "If I worked at it I might still be able to remember 'The Frolic of the Lambs.' "

How, I asked Kitty, did people react to the idea of her as a woman lawyer? "Men seem to trust women more," she said, "on the grounds that women aren't smart enough to be as sneaky as men. But I think that's all wrong. I had to go talk to one lady to get her to sign an easement, and even though I tried to show her how it was for her own good, she didn't want to sign it and wouldn't. Okay then, I asked her, could I come back later and talk to her husband? She said he wouldn't see me. I asked her why not. 'Because,' she said, 'I won't *let* him.' "

In Charleston, South Carolina there is an organization called the Saint Cecelia Society which since the middle 1700's has annually sponsored balls of such exclusivity that their fame has spread throughout the state, if not the whole South. "You are born into this society," Ginny wrote me. "You do not get into it any other way. I actually visited one of THEIR homes a couple of times, during dance weekends when I stayed with a college friend of Mother's who was IN IT. She was an adorable eccentric who lived in a ramshackle house but on the RIGHT STREET." This society has no equivalent in Denton. In Denton there were no coming-out parties at all until 1966, when Patty Ann Bingham, wife of Ronnie the pharmacist, inspired a campaign to establish such a tradition.

"Girls these days are in danger of not knowin' how lovely it can *be* to be a young girl," Patty Ann told me as we sat sipping 1918 Chianti at Loretta Whitcomb's dinner party. Rowena Carr had brought the smoked Rock Cornish game hen, having smoked it herself, and even though it was sleeting outside, of all things, we all felt quite cozy by Loretta's baronial hearth. Patty Ann looked absolutely stunning, but then I never saw her when she didn't. No mother of five in all Laurens County could have a smaller waist, I'm sure, nor a complexion more

like that of Vivien Leigh playing Scarlett O'Hara. Nor can I remember a more pronounced Southern accent, either: I don't
think anyone else made "yes" a two-syllable word. "Patty Ann's
a better Southerner than I am," Ginny had said, but the fact
is that Patty Ann was born in County Limerick and raised in
Yonkers, New York.

"This Women's Lib business just seems silly to me," she said.
"They can have it; it's a waste of time. These feminists, or
whatever you call the ones in the movement, they're only hurt-
ing themselves. I just don't understand all this talk of 'Who
Am I?'

"If only women would try to do things in a *feminine* way,
without causin' such an uproar, don't you think they could just
do so much more good? Doin' good, it seems to me, is basically
a feminine quality. Not that men can't be good too. Take Ronnie. Ronnie is just perfect. You should have seen the way he
chased a bat out of our bedroom.

"For our twenty-fifth anniversary he took me for a long
weekend at the Pierre in New York. I'd have been happy just
to buy hot dogs from vendors and go walkin' in the park, but
he insisted on doin' everything right. But I tell *you,* he
dragged in and skipped out, and I skipped in and dragged
out."

I saw less of Rita, Ginny's other sister-in-law. Rita is married
to Gus, who is a dentist. She calls Gus "D.P.," short for Darling
Precious. They have no children, but they do have a swimming
pool in their backyard, and two bars. One of the bars is in the
back seat of the Lincoln in which they were kind enough to
fetch me when I finally arrived, as a Standby of course, at the
Greenville-Spartanburg airport. The other bar is in their basement, and it is remarkable. Strings of Christmas lights arranged
like constellations twinkle, all year around, on the ceiling. Similar lights glitter onto the tops of pilsener glasses and brandy
snifters and other specialty crystalware arranged on shelves
under Gus's definitive collection of different beer cans.

The walls are covered with cocktail napkins imprinted with
humorous slogans and with signs that say such things as VD IS
NOTHING TO CLAP ABOUT, and REMEMBER THE

GOLDEN RULE: HE WHO HAS THE GOLD MAKES THE RULES. On the far wall is an ultraviolet, shine-in-the-dark representation of the Chicago River as it looks from Wacker Drive, with the Wrigley Building and the Tribune Tower in the background. Staring at this vista through a long evening of rather too much Wild Turkey, I was put in mind of my own adolescent fantasies of romantic evenings in cocktail lounges, hushed but for tinkly piano music.

Ginny did all in her power to make my Day of Epiphany a meaningful one. She drove me across town to visit the house of Harriet Cooper, the matriarchal sister of Mrs. Bingham's cook Roberta. As we arrived Harriet's husband Ben asked how Miss Jinki had been feeling.

"Oh," she replied, "a few humidity aches." I misunderstood and thought she said "humility," and small wonder. For her to describe her condition as "a few aches" was a polite Southern lie. Paraplegics are prey to a great many ailments of arms, shoulders, and insides, which grow more pronounced with the passage of years. "Before there was such a thing as sulfa," Ginny once told me, "there weren't even any paraplegics, because if you broke your back at all, you'd automatically die of kidney and bladder infection. We of Paraplegicdom, Class of '41, are the oldest surviving relics of spinal cord severance that I know, that is in length of service. World War II of course produced a big batch, as did the various other little wars the country has indulged in since."

"So you've had the opportunity to be a pioneer," I said. "That must be a real comfort to you."

"Oh," she said with total irony, "it is."

"How can you stand it?" I asked her.

"My essential nature has always been optimistic," she said. "When I was in the fifth grade I still believed in Santa Claus, and my mother actually had to take me aside for a private talk on the subject. If she hadn't, I'd have believed until I was in college. Oh, I'd heard rumors, of course, but I just dismissed them. Mother gave me a little speech that actually began, so help me, '*No*, Virginia . . .' "

"Were you crushed?"

344

"You know something? It's only now, now that I'm fifty, that I'm beginning to believe Mother was right."

Harriet showed us pictures of her only son, who had been killed in World War II. She introduced me to his six impish grandchildren. Thinking of John and Sarah, I played with these children and made faces at them. When we first went in the house Harriet asked, 'Won't you rest your scarf?' I rested it for quite a lot longer than I had meant to, because Roberta took me for a long and lovely walk at twilight, just when the trees were beginning to stand out in silhouette. Ginny had gone home, and I was easily persuaded to stay for pork backbone and rice.

I asked Roberta and Harriet what they would like to do, if they could choose any fate in the world. They both thought for a while and replied that they would like to be missionaries. Later that evening, back on Newell Street when we were all snug in our bathrobes, I asked Ginny and her mother the same question. Ginny allowed that she wouldn't have minded being Cleopatra, or maybe Elizabeth II.

"Oh, Jinki," said her mother, "they were *awful* women!"

"Maybe, at that, I'd rather have been Aspasia," Ginny said. "Aspasia was Pericles' courtesan, and she had plenty to say about what went on in fifth-century Athens. How about you, Mother? Who would you be?"

"If I had another life to live I think I'd want to be the wife of an English professor," said Mrs. Bingham. "Wouldn't that be nice, dealing with language and literature at the same time you were helping and being close to the young people?" Ginny agreed, and I confessed that this was an old fantasy of mine too.

"How about being a professor *yourself?*" I asked Mrs. Bingham. "Wouldn't you like to do that, if you could?"

"Oh, *no,*" she smiled. "Being one's wife would be close enough for me." Unobtrusiveness, I reflected as I went to bed, is really programmed into American women, at least into those whose circumstances were not, to begin with, reduced. Two friends of mine both have a habit of laughing very expressively and responsively, whenever anyone around them makes a joke, but they laugh silently. They make no noise. To laugh along with them, making full use of one's vocal cords, is to feel raucuous indeed. Both these friends, as it happens are alumnae of a New York City girls' school whose former headmistress, a Miss Stringfellow, is said to have admonished them to "make yourselves conspicuous by being inconspicuous." Maybe Miss Stringfellow came from the South.

Periodically Althea Bingham would announce to her sons that since her vision was not improving, and since she did not wish to be a burden on them or on anyone, she would soon be moving to a perfectly pleasant senior citizens' home for Presbyterians in the southern part of the state.

"Fine, Mammy," Ronnie and Gus would both reply, "but isn't it a mighty long walk? *We're* sure not going to drive you down there."

Something astonishing happened that night. It snowed. Waking, I marveled like a kindergartener to see ice covering the camellias and magnolias and everything else. Highways leading to both airports were, of course, impassible. An invasion by Cambodians could scarcely have unsettled the populace more. Piedmont Airlines phoned to say that my flight out had been cancelled and so, later, did Delta and Eastern. At first I was vexed about being late for my next appointment up the road, but then something caused me to uncoil. Maybe it was an overdue epiphany. "The rare moment," Joseph Wood Krutch wrote somewhere, "is not the moment when there is something worth looking at, but the moment when we are capable of seeing."

I went outside for a walk, under heavy clouds that looked pregnant with more snow. Marcus always used to say that gray was his favorite color, and I always used to sneer, but these clouds were a gray even I could like. I wandered over to the library of the town's small college, knowing that I would no longer be mistaken for an undergraduate, not caring, leafing through magazines. I picked up burrs which had fallen from trees I assumed were exotically Southern, until I later discovered their exact facsimiles along the path at Riverside Park in

New York. The ice on the treetops was magical. Twilight fell quickly, and as I trudged up one street I came upon a trio of boys about my nephew's age, careening around on a sled they had fashioned from a metal Greyhound Bus sign, bent to curve like a sleigh.

"Would *you* like to have a ride?" they asked. I could have kissed them. How miraculous for them to sense that within my respectable, grownup frame there lurked the soul of a ten-year-old who at that moment craved nothing more in the world than to ride on a sled. For a lovely while, on that hilly street, I did.

I was glad not to add more airport tags, just yet, to my suitcases, having already been to JFK, GUA, ELS, MIA, ATL, and GSP. Another day had stilled my soul, and so would another late night sipping bourbon with Ginny at her mother's table, under the framed motto that declared MY HOUSE IS CLEAN ENOUGH TO BE HEALTHY AND DIRTY ENOUGH TO BE HAPPY. Another Southern lie, that sign. The house wasn't dirty at all. Although I have never shared the reverence many feel for *The Little Prince,* I preferred the banner that hung in the hallway outside Ginny's room, exactly like the one she made for Kathy in Arizona. One of her nieces had made this one for her by hand, from the text of Antoine de Saint Exupéry, and on it I read, again, IT IS THE TIME YOU HAVE WASTED ON YOUR ROSE THAT MAKES YOUR ROSE SO IMPORTANT.

29

You've Got to be Buried by Oliver

She-crab soup, more succulent presumably than he-crab, is the perfect thing to have for lunch if you happen to be stuck between planes in Charleston, South Carolina, just after the South's first big blizzard in fifteen years. She-crab soup is fortifying, and at such a time a transient needs all the fortification she can get. Airport runways tend to be icy, and schedules are subject to capricious change.

I was more than an hour late arriving at the airport in Norfolk, Virginia, called NOR on baggage tags. It was my fourth airport of the day, the others having been COL, CHA, and NPN. NPN, Newport News, had been a last-minute surprise. But never mind all that: there waiting for me, God love them, were Mr. and Mrs. H. M. P. Tunstall, all bundled up in unaccustomed extra scarves and full of the solicitude for which their region is famous. Apart from a few phone calls I was a total stranger to them, but they welcomed me as effusively as if I were a foreign student newly arrived on a nonstop flight from Pakistan which, come to think of it, is more or less how I felt. Not only had they driven over perilous roads to fetch me to their house for dinner, but they wouldn't hear of my spending the night in a motel.

"Unless," Caroline Heath Tunstall said, "you *mind* sleeping on the narrow, hard little sofa-bed in our library." I minded not at all. I wouldn't have turned down a straw pallet on the floor of their garage. An hour in an airport is as draining as a day anywhere else, and a four-airport day ought not to end in the impersonal anonymity of some TraveLodge or Chez Raton Motor Inn, however posh. I was in no mood to be handed a plastoid key to some Room 218 (I always seem to stay in Room 218), even if it did have a toilet sanitized for my protection, a Moorish bedspread with tigerskin curtains, a cunning little coffee machine, and a plaque on the wall with coy Fragonard cupids and the legend SERENITAS. Once I had stayed in just such a room, but not tonight. Tonight my idea of *serenitas* was not to dial 2 for Room Service but to sit with a leisurely drink, and then perhaps another, in front of the Tunstalls' fireplace, to which my host kept adding more logs.

A common friend in New York had suggested that I might find Cro Tunstall, as she is known, to be one of the champion talkers of the entire South. Our friend had met Cro while he was stationed in Norfolk during World War II. When I mentioned my wish to discover the true essence of Southern womanhood, or some such modest goal, Cro's name leapt to his mind. "She's got as deep a sense of roots and her own identity as anyone I can think of," he said. "That's what impressed me about her in the first place. If you ever get around to it, you might want to look her up, and give her my love." That's one thing I'm good at, running around giving people other people's love, and so, to the surprise of all concerned, I did.

Cro, her old friend had added, was the first person who ever made him want to—no, feel he had to—read Proust, "It was in self-defense," he remembered. "She and her sister would gossip about Madame de Guermante's party as if it had happened next door, last week. Someone else told me that when her sister was dying Cro sat there in the hospital reading Trollope to her. They were real autodidacts, both of them."

"Harriet was truly beautiful," Cro said of that sister. "See

349

this picture?" I saw; it was true. "Of the five of us, she and I were the closest two, and I was desolate of course when she died. The only consolation was that she didn't have to grow old and lose that beauty. It's not much, but it's something, to think of it that way." Cro herself was more arresting than beautiful, with prominent brown eyes and a chignon which kept coming undone. (I found this endearing because my own rare attempts to affect a soigné chignon had been disastrous.) I had not often met women as energetic as Cro, or couples as content with each other as she and Hugo, as she sometimes called her husband, seemed to be. They had been married during the Depression.

"Hugo never finished college until later, when he was forty," Cro told me. "When he fell in love with me he couldn't see any percentage in having a diploma, so he went into real estate. We got married on a $100 a month and had a child on $125. Hugh hated and despised the real estate business. His father was the kind of man who had a golden gift. He could look at a brothel and see a hotel, or look at a hotel and see a brothel, but Hugh didn't share that. He got the hell out of real estate and worked for a while at the plant of a heap-rich uncle up in Bristol, Virginia, until he and several other people got axed. Then he got the idea of being an accountant, so we went on up to Charlottesville for a year to study, and then we came home here to Masters Corner at last."

Their cheerful small house in the Masters Corner section of Norfolk is, in fact, only eight blocks from the one in which Cro had been born sixty-one years before. "Essentially a lot of the people we know best have been here for most of their lives," she said. "They aren't the people we're necessarily most in sympathy with, but there's something to be said, isn't there, for all that shared history? If you meet someone new who turns out to be a chump, you dismiss him and don't pursue the acquaintance, but if an old friend's a chump, he is forgiven. There's someone who lives near here who you might think was a prize bitch and an idiot, but we'll still always be friends, because we always have been."

It was not usual, I gathered, for young ladies of Masters Corner, members of certified First Families of Virginia, to grow up and teach Black Literature to college students. That isn't all Cro teaches at Old Dominion University, where she was one of the first students ever to get a master's degree and where she is now an assistant professor. She also teaches freshman and sophomore English, and Latin when there is enough demand for it. But she is especially animated when she talks of Black Literature.

"This black renaissance," she said, "is really something. There are so damned many extremely gifted young blacks writing now that it's like Periclean Athens. I've got all my friends alerted to send me anything they find on the subject, and they all do, so I'm reading constantly to keep up. The course has been made required, and there are usually two or three quite shockable lower middle-class students in it, but that doesn't bother me. I can usually win them over by showing them injustices.

"I've always *gulped* books. I read every waking hour like a boa constrictor. I pay a price for it, though. The price is I can't listen to music any more. When Hugo and Alec [their thirty-five-year-old son and only child] are in the other room listening attentively to a record, they don't talk, they don't read. They truly listen. Then Hugh might come in and ask me, 'What would you like to hear now?' and I'll say, 'Oh, play the Brahms Violin Concerto,' and he'll smile and say 'But we just *played* it.' I think it's been ten or fifteen years since I really heard music.

"Would you like to change into something more comfortable?" Cro herself had changed into a long wool skirt with an orange top, but my own pretty long wool skirt, along with other costumes suitable for the tropics, was in a suitcase checked at the airport. As a sign of comfort and trust I kicked off my shoes, while Cro and Hugh took turns being busy in the kitchen. Nuts. Drinks. More drinks. Steak. Potatoes. Salad. Wine. Ice cream. Apologies for a hastily assembled menu but snow, you know. Oh, I know.

Just past the airport I had noticed a sign that said AZALEA GARDENS. This, the Tunstalls told me, used to be one of their favorite places to walk. It still is, in fact, but they feel personally deprived by someone's decisions to take over several acres of the park and add them to the airport grounds. The Tunstalls are devoted to places like azalea gardens. "Wherever we travel," Cro said, "the first place I always want to have a look at is the zoo. Zoos are wonderful, because you tend not to see so many other tourists. At Chapultepec Park in Mexico all we saw were children and nurses. This summer we're going to London for a month, and I can't wait to see Whipsnade; they're supposed to have hippos browsing over acres and acres of English countryside. I understand the Regent's Park Zoo is nice, too."

"It is," I said.

"There's been a diminution of our involvement in civic affairs as the years have gone by," Cro said. "We've dropped the chamber quartet, and before Hugh retired—he's semi-retired, actually, from working as a CPA—he worked hellish hours and we also dropped the little theater. Ther's no denying that live music has a lot to offer, but it's a hell of a strain to go out on a school night. Oh, it's *possible* to give an evening quiz and then make it to the concert, but only just.

"Hugh was on the symphony board for a while. Oh, we dressed for that, it was black tie, and we had to go to these God-awful crummy parties. Parties down here aren't to everyone's taste, there's sort of a rule that you never let people talk more than three minutes together, so as to keep things moving. To be candid, it's sometimes rather tacky ladies who get involved with the symphony sort of thing. Is tacky a word in your vocabulary? It is? It's a good word, isn't it? It says so much.

"I've just read Thomas Pynchon's *The Crying of Lot 49,* and it has the most marvelous beginning: 'Oedipa came home from a Tupperware party whose hostess had put perhaps too much kirsch in the fondue.' I didn't think so much of *V,* in fact I couldn't really get through it, but that first line made me think maybe I'd better give Pynchon another chance.

"Class angles just fascinate me, don't they you? If you'd lived in the South, you'd know the special way in which people ask 'who is she?' Why, you might answer, she's Jane Smith; but you'd be missing the point. 'Who *is* she?' means whose wife, whose daughter, whose descendant, where her grandparents lived, all sorts of other things."

I had heard similar tales from my friend Carol, who a long and improbable time ago had been part of a team of traveling liquor salesmen whose territory included the South. "When we'd go into a bar or tavern or package store down there to do our number, they'd look at me and say, 'Hmm, "Einhorn," what kind of a name is that? What's your background?' I'd say 'Austrian and Russian.' They'd say, 'No, I mean your *background*,' and I'd say, 'Oh, well I'm Jewish, if that's what you mean.'

"Ah, when I think of the magic of it—two whole weeks in a place like Shreveport. One became so convinced of the condition of the men of this country. They just had the hots constantly, even for women in the employ of a hugh national corporation. I mean they assumed we'd been sent around just as playmates. Certainly it was fuel for Women's Lib, now that I think of it. A man and I would go into one of those places and I wouldn't say anything, I'd just stand there looking bored or pathetic while the man made his pitch, then I'd say, 'Well, please buy three bottles anyway,' and the owner would say 'I guess they must have paid a lot of money to send you here.' Originally we were supposed to give talks on the women's viewpoint, like tell them that vodka was a woman's drink because it didn't taste or smell."

"One thing you have to know, if you live in Norfolk," said Cro, "is that you've got to be buried by Oliver. If you're buried by anyone other than Oliver, you're disgraced, or your survivors are. Oliver buries you and that's all there is to it. When my sister's husband died she had him buried by one of his friends, who owned another firm, and she had to explain and apologize for weeks.

"Most of the people I've known all my life are untouched by Women's Liberation. They don't think in those terms. They all have their stories about how they worked hard, were brilliant, had it made, but ran into opposition because they were women, but *Ms.* and all that sort of thing leave them absolutely cold. If they ever ran into Steinem and all that masturbation talk, they'd have none of it. Language, that's what really shocks them most. Generally speaking, anyone over fifty is simply not going to whip out those four-letter words. In their forties they will, a few, and from there down to age seven, they will any time."

The power of four-letter words is something I would someday like to understand much better than I do now. In 1969, researching an article on the mood then prevalent in Springfield, Illinois, I asked a neighbor of my parents what he thought people there were truly worried about— the war? pollution? inflation? He and his wife had just been kind enough to give me a ride down a channel of the lake in their pontoon, christened the *Booze 'n' Cruise*. He reflected for several minutes on my question and finally said, "Four-letter words, in conversation and in print. I just don't see why people have to talk that way, when there are so many other *delightful* words to use."

My mother herself was profoundly offended that seven or eight such words appeared in dialogue I quoted in my earlier book. Ultimately she absolved me from guilt and came to laugh and help make *hors d'oeuvres* at a party celebrating that book's publication, but for a couple of weeks the silence, from her to me, was eloquent. It was as if she could not bear the knowledge that I, her own issue, had been to places where people talked that way. Her Auntie Grace commiserated by post: "I cannot approve of all [Jane's, my] selection of words, and think she could and should have spared your and Bob's embarrassment. All your nice friends, I am sure, feel the same way. Guess some of us are still old-fashioned."

"Students in my classes," Cro went on, "think I'll be more shocked than I am when they use such language. One of them said, 'As far as I'm concerned that book was bullshit—Oh, excuse me, Mrs. Tunstall.' What really shocks me more than that is that some of them don't even know who Martin Luther King was.

"Of the thirty-four kids in one of my classes, seven are Jesus freaks, so I've got to be careful how I grade their themes. They're involved in all kinds of projects: ACTION, helping the retarded, helping Indians. One of them wrote a paper equating atheism with immorality, and another is involved with a new minor sect called Christadelphia that advertises in the papers. She kept inviting me to dinner and I kept regretting, saying, 'No, sorry, I can't make it that night.' What I should have said, of course, was, 'No, I make it a point never to dine with my pupils,' but since I didn't say that, eventually I had to go. Her father, who was from Sicily of all places, asked me, 'Do you read the Bible, Mrs. Tunstall?' I said, 'Oh certainly, I've read it often, of course I have, there's wonderful stuff in there.' But that didn't do. He asked me, 'Do you read it *constantly,* Mrs. Tunstall?' Of course not, do I read Thackeray constantly?"

I told Cro that in the South Carolina town where I had waked up that morning, the Presbyterians appeared to have the most prosperous and established church. "They're not the top of the heap around here," Cro said. "They're allowed, of course, but Episcopalians are *it*. It was the shame of my mama's life and still is [her mother died at age 95 shortly after my visit to Norfolk] that she had an aunt who got converted and became a Baptist. My mother knows perfectly well that this happened, but she can't bring herself to recognize it. One of the pleasures of senility is that as you grow old, you can successfully deny such things.

"When my sister Harriet moved to the little town of Urbana, Virginia, all the neighbors brought her over a dozen rolls or a cake or something and asked her what church she belonged to. She didn't belong to any damned church at all, but from habit she said Episcopalian. Well, from then on the others were cordial to her, but only the Episcopalians, it was clear, were expected to keep in touch with her socially.

"Daddy had four of us daughters and presumed we'd all marry. It never occurred to me to find a way to make a living for the rest of my life. It seems to me that's the big difference. Any girl now automatically thinks of how she'll earn a living. All I wanted to do—I guess I was resigned to wanting to do— was learn a lot of languages and read a lot.

"Our father was a lawyer, and although he knew it was wicked he was a compulsive book-buyer. We had these bills every month from the publisher, and my mother would have to sneak antiques out to the market to get some extra money. She never knew now much he earned. Neither did Hugh's mother. When I was little, I can remember poor Mother saying, 'Oh, the poor girls, they need thus and such.' Money, I sometimes think, is a much more personal subject than sex. Asking how much money Daddy makes is, in many families, as unheard of a question as any you can imagine. I've had friends who've said, 'I don't know what Jim makes and I don't *want* to know; he pays all the bills and gives me an allowance.' That's not the way Hugo and I've done it. We've had a joint checking account, and before I worked, I paid the bills and we discussed it all."

Cro is an alumna of Sweet Briar. "I wanted to go to Vassar," she said, "but we didn't have the railroad fare. The only reason I went at all was because my sister did, and she only went because her friends went. I finished in '31, and the main aim we all talked about then was to get married or to go to New York and get a job at Macy's, because it was fun in New York, it was swinging. Daddy'd never have let me gone there, though. Fat chance. When I got out of college I made my debut, and that took up a year. Then I decided I'd like to be a teacher, but I had no education courses. I wanted to study law, but my father didn't like the idea of women lawyers. He wanted women to read, sure, but not go out into the world.

"My older sister had a job in a bookshop, and Daddy was very doubtful about that, because *men* might come in and buy books. She and Daddy would argue at dinner over the hideous problem of how she should address a certain Nigro—I use that word deliberately—who lived in Norfolk and sometimes came into the store to buy books. What was she to call him? Surely not Tom, but just as surely not Mr. Diggs. I was a radical then already. I'd think, 'Jesus, why *can't* you call him Mr. Diggs?' But it was resolved that she should address him simply as 'you.'

"I finally got a job as a school librarian. I'd never heard of the Dewey Decimal System, so I made up my own. It wasn't much, but it was mine. The man who got me the job was the first Jew on the Norfolk school board. He said us minorities (meaning Jews and Episcopalians) have got to stick together.

"The sad thing about girls nowadays, I think, is that the bulk of them set their sights so low: nursing, dental hygiene. You'd be amazed how many of them say, 'I want to be a dental hygienist because I'll meet new and interesting people.' I always wonder how interesting anyone can be with cotton in his mouth?

"Every now and then I get a class of whom sixteen—count them, sixteen—will *all* be nurses. They all say, 'I want to be a nurse and when I get married I'll quit and then later I can go back and help my husband.' They have no background in reading, but they can tell you that the drapes of their house will be Provençal and that they'll have two cars and two TVs and that their children's names will be Steven and Brenda. It's real pitiful; they're nice little girls with real wit, some of them. I guess it's purely economic. I guess they're the first ones in their families to make it.

"Of course the real hope for the whole women's thing, don't you think, is when women's jobs start to attract men."

"That's begun to happen, I think," I told her. "Haven't you read about men becoming stewardesses—stewards, rather? And I believe there are a lot more male nurses around these days."

"Good," said Cro. "And also you're beginning to get a guy now who really *wants* to teach fifth grade. It used to be that men could only teach physical education. You'd find that the average administrator of a small town public shool system had been a coach or a PE teacher.

"I have my freshmen write papers on What They Want To

Be, and I ask them, 'Whatever it is, what's it going to cost you? Have a pot belly when you're forty?' My son has one at thirty-five; he's a systems analyst in the very rareified upper reaches. I took a course at ODU to see what the theory of it was. One of the great things about being on the faculty is that you can take advantage of all the courses. I wanted to take logic—one of my great temptations had been to learn about syllogisms and tautologies—and I finally did, and it was beautiful, it was gorgeous.

"As I said, I try to call my students' attention to what they're giving up when they make their choices. Whatever it is, they're giving up a hell of a lot. You know that Frost poem 'The Road Not Taken?' I call their attention to that."

Cro did not say, nor in my amiable cognac buzz did I think to ask her, what sacrifices her own life had entailed, other than not really listening to music. Whatever they were, they had not visibly diminished her.

"From '35 to '38," she told me, "Hugh and I were very hung up on radical politics. We were Mr. and Mrs. Spanish Civil War. For our generation that was it. Czechoslavakia was sad; Hitler was expected, but the Spanish Civil War was what did it for us. It really got us all. Then in '38 we had Alec, and I put in three years nursing. I wrote a detective story but quit after I got two rejections. Alec drew pictures on the back of it. I wrote some book reviews, for the *New York Herald-Tribune* and for the local papers, and I wrote a short story that took third place in a local contest for which I'd been a judge before. Mortifying, that third place.

"When Alec was in kindergarten I got a job teaching, and that's what I've wanted to do ever since. That and keep learning. When I retire I'll go down there to the university and take geology and the whole works. There was a circus clown up at Charlottesville who took all the courses they had there. He wanted to take them all, and he did. Who knows, maybe I'll end up taking Pre-Stressed Concrete 101.

" 'Did you take?' is a very American, middle-class expression, isn't it? Mostly of course it refers to music. I think all children should learn to read music, the same way they should know basic arithmetic and how to sew, drive, take a car apart, and fix the plumbing or the television. It's awfully nice to sit around of an evening picking out music the same way you'd try a new Shakespeare sonnet, saying, 'Oh look, here's a good one; let's try this!'

"Oh look at the time! It's nearly midnight, and I've an eight o'clock class." My wrist was tired, and so was the rest of me, so I did not object, except to wonder what would happen to the dishes.

"Never mind," said Cro. "We'll get to them in the morning."

My "narrow, hard little sofa-bed" had been comfortable indeed but, being in the habit of rising early, I did so the next morning and thought I might get at the dishes. But Cro was up and, having had breakfast, urged me to do the same.

"The snow's really beautiful, isn't it?" I said.

"No," she replied, "it's a bastard." At about 7:30, earlier than she usually left for class, Hugh drove her off. Bundled against the freak cold she looked like a nine-year-old on her way to fourth grade.

"I'd better take a book along," she said. "The maddening thing is I might get there twenty minutes early after all, in spite of the icy roads. Must go, give me a kiss. If you sit in this room here while you have your coffee, you can watch the sun come up over the house next door and see the birds at the feeding station. The dishes? Oh, Hugh's done them."

When I grow up, I thought as I watched the bluejays fighting over suet, I could do a lot worse than to live this way.

30

Carrot Juice

It's cold out. I like that. It's clear too. The outline of the
George Washington Bridge is vivid, and if there isn't ice on the
river, there soon will be. I am wearing a nightie designed to resemble or suggest two motifs: a cowboy's gay bandana and mattress ticking. It's me, don't you know: funky, homey, unpretentious, cheerful, and yet warm. It has a tear in it too. Once
somebody said that if I were a car I would be a Volkswagen
with a dent in the fender. Little did he then guess that someday I would own just such a vehicle. I own it now, in fact, but
I haven't even seen it in I can't think how long. Not only have
I not been for drives in the country of late, I've scarcely left
this neighborhood. I have a lot to do, and since the best place
to do it seems to be my own apartment, there are Oblomovian
days when I don't even go outside.

I draw more and more into myself, shedding several layers of
the gregariousness I had thought was at my core. Expeditions
to such places as the stationery store seem momentous. I have
my choice of two stationers: Levy's, near Eighty-fourth Street,
and Houston, at Seventy-third. Both give me shameful plea-

sure. I take to loitering around them, furtive as a pederast in a schoolyard. What if someone sees me? Hmm, a new line of ring-binders at Levy's, not just primary colors but such departures from tradition as HoJo coral and turquoise. Those I don't care for, but there's quite a nice three-hole forest green. Can you show me something please in gummed reinforcements? Will there be anything else? No thank you, I already have a three-hole punch. (I would no sooner be without my three-hole punch than without light bulbs.) Just looking. All right, if you see something you want to try on, I'm Miss Estelle.

I get to know Dot at the checkout counter at the Shopping Cart, which seems a more agreeable place by and large than either Daitch's or Food City. I have switched to the neighborhood branch of my bank, and no longer go much at all to midtown, where I bought the nightie I have on which is not, by the way, one of your suggestive numbers, reaching at it does from my collarbone down to the floor and provided as it is with long and somewhat puffed sleeves. I am also wearing a silver ring about half an inch in width which fits my right ring finger but is a bit too large for the left, perhaps because everything on my right side, being by definition less gauche, gets used more and is therefore better developed—even the nearly vestigial ring finger.

When I wish for any reason to appear married, I switch this ring to the left hand, because it could pass for the wedding band of some emancipated, dare I say young, woman who had left most of the traditions and conventions of the 1950s behind her but who still had some regard for the past. I am also, for added warmth, wearing a white cable-knit cardigan and on my feet, instead of the more usual slippers or scuffies, a pair of nearly knee-length mottled oatmeal-color gray socks. I would rather dress warmly in the cold than turn the radiator on high, because when it is on high the plants get sick, and they are thriving none too well anyway in this season.

Sometimes the radio is on and sometimes it isn't. It comforts me to know that they are all there, Ralph Lowenstein and Piano Personalities and Fleetwood and the WNCN Anniversary Concert and all the rest of them. This morning I heard a

Brandenburg Concerto as soon as I woke up. That's what I call a way to begin a day. Maybe I should switch oftener to WBLS, the Total Black Experience in Sound. Maybe I should have more black friends, come to think of it, but can such a state of affairs be willed? Can any friendship? I suspect not. I have had some off and on, but since the assassination of Malcolm X, they have seemed less available, and I hesitate to call them up for fear of seeming patronizing. It's all confusing and annoying. I do phone one such old friend, but she doesn't call me back. I go to see another, a perhaps atypically assimilated one, and she tells me she fell off her wedgies and that she has become interested in the race track. Another tells me she is pregnant but her man has left, "and let me tell you, girl, having a baby without that dude around isn't so easy." She asks me to lunch and I tell her I'll come. I will, too, but not just now.

These days I don't have lunch with anybody. Lunch dates break up the day too much; they interrupt whatever flow of thought has been generated in the morning. Rather than have lunch, I prefer to take a long ruminative bath and stare at the tile wall but not, of course, without the long-corded telephone readily at hand. I am not prepared to give up the phone, not just yet. I understand there are people who never make long-distance calls or even run up extra message units, but then there are also people whose hair is never out of place, and I wouldn't want to know them socially, either. Orwellian though it may be, I depend shamelessly on my long-corded connection. So do a number of my friends, one of whom calls to report that he has recently experienced "a few fugitive moments of repose and self-esteem." Hang in there, I tell him, it sounds like you're on the right track.

I watch, and doubtless am watched by, the neighbors directly across the way. If their building is like a dollhouse to me, why should mine not be so to them? At a certain interlude around dusk all our facing Venetian blinds are discreetly drawn. Someone's maid, meanwhile, steps out onto a balcony and shakes out a blanket. Feathers fly. Pigeons fly too. As John Updike has observed, they are beautiful for all their banality. I watch them, motionless. As soon as I stir even a little, they are off. I return to my typewriter, which I use a good deal these days. How many pages, I long to ask someone, do you get to a roll of ribbon?

I make lists of words to look up: demiurge, meliphic, aniate, hierophant, antinomianism. It pays to increase your word power. Thirty days to a more powerful. Cudgel. Now there's a nice word. Use it sometime. Cudgel my brain. Just settle my brain for a long winter's nap. No nap this, though. I don't sleep much. Maybe a sign of advancing age. I'm awake an hour at least before the heartening thud of the *Times* on the doorstep. I love to read my paper in the morning, tearing out clippings as I drink coffee and separate, with attention otherwise not like me, each segment of grapefruit from its membrane. Some days I read the Lost and Found notices. Poodle, ans. to "Coco." Pearl bracelet, vic. 37th & Mad. Reward. The *Saga-fjord* sails this morning from West Houston Street. Showers likely through Thursday. Not responsible for debts incurred by my wife.

On a less cold gray day I walk up Broadway in pink slacks with an orange turtleneck. A woman with an elaborate head-dress and the translucent complexion of a newly-saved vegetarian approaches me.

"You know that's Russian?" she says.

"Excuse me?"

"Russians mix orange with pink," she tells me. "When I first became an Episcopalian, I used to know this little girl who chose to wear orange with pink quite often, and her mother would say, 'Oh, she's such a little Russian.'"

"I'd thought of the combination more as Mexican," I tell the woman.

"That's true," she says. "Puerto Ricans *do* tend to mix their reds."

"Well, nice talking to you," I tell her, and head on north.

I stop to buy some vermouth in a tiny narrow liquor store where an enormous Great Dane named Orpheus is trapped in a corridor, to frighten off miscreants. A large Airedale outside attracts Orpheus' interest. There is a fuss. Since Orpheus has been here, the clerk advises me, there have been no holdups. Small wonder. But, I ask, what about exercise? Does he ever get a run in the park?

"On weekends," the clerk says. "Besides, they're trained to stay in places like this."

"Oh," I say, unconvinced. I head west for a walk along the riverside promenade, past the boat basin. I have come to feel possessive about the cherry trees, in a positively Chekhovian fashion. A whole orchard of them would be super, but these must sustain me, and they do. I am a glutton for nature as for certain foods. I had deluded myself into supposing I was only a social ice-cream eater, but who was I trying to kid? No more than an alcoholic can forget an old bottle of cooking sherry, can it slip my mind that I am under the same roof with some Häagen-Dazs. There are occasions when a whole pint of the Rum Raisin will disappear at one sitting, with nobody else in sight. Such occasions tend to be followed by Green Pepper Emphasis weeks. Yin and Yang. One trusts it will all somehow balance out.

"Small or large?" asks the waitress in a health food store I wander into.

"Large." What the hell; live a little. "How much?"

"Two."

"Two *dollars*? For a glass of *carrot juice*?"

"It's a whole pint," the waitress says, avoiding my eyes. (Health food personnel never have seemed like the sort I'd like to have over.) Oh all right, you win. I do like me wee jar now and again.

The elevator is not broken, but just because I feel like it I walk the five flights to my front door. Talk about self-esteem. It won't be long before the sun goes down behind New Jersey. A barge makes its way up the river. On somebody's windowsill, across the way, a tomato ripens.

The last time I stayed put in one place this long it was because my leg was in a cast and I had no choice. Imagine, being grounded three months without the excuse of a fracture.

This must be dailiness. A person could get used to it.

31

Rapid Pips and Bongo Drums

It furthers one, the *I Ching* sometimes tells us, to cross the great water. Not having been on British soil in six years, I arrange to leave early, before an assignment in Ireland, so as to spend some time on my own in London. I have become so preoccupied with my own countrywomen that a change of scene seems in order, and that most gently civilized of capitals ought to give just the right perspective. My only worry is who I'll eat dinner with when I get there, because most of the Londoners I used to know have moved away. Dinner alone, abroad, can be strangely despondent, but I trust in providence and call BOAC.

Besides, I have to get away from this lugubrious apartment. It wasn't lugubrious to begin with, but of late it has come to resemble a shrine. There might as well be faithful peasants, crazed with devotion, crawling from room to room on their knees. Everywhere is the smell of burnt wax. The smell is there because I have taken to the nonstop, day and night burning of candles. Two people I care about have been critically ill, and since I have no credit with any deity, burning candles is the only thing I can think of to do to help. The candles are a sort of protest gesture, a pagan's prayer.

"Well, I guess it beats cursing the darkness," my friend Carol sighs on the phone, "but what *kind* of candles?"

"Those twenty-four-hour Jewish ones from the supermarket."

"But those are *memorial* candles. You're supposed to burn them on the anniversary of a death."

"You think I can't read? It says so, in English as well as Hebrew, on the labels. But I soak those labels off and replace them with special ones of my own."

"What do your labels say?"

"It varies. 'Hang in there' was one sentiment."

"Too flippant."

"Another was *Salud y amor y pesetas y tiempo para gustarlos.*"

"That's better. Cosmopolitan, and yet apt. Especially *tiempo.* You keep them burning all the time?"

"Sometimes I start a new one before the old one goes out. Some of them last a lot longer than twenty-four hours. I've had them go, oh, as much as thirty-seven. I write the times on the labels: '11:10 A.M. Sat.–2:40 P.M. Mon.' "

"How many candles do you buy at a time?"

"Oh, eight or so."

"Jesus, the checkout girl must think your entire family perished in a flash flood. What do you do when you go out?"

"Leave them burning. I mean an eternal flame is an eternal flame; you can't cheat. As long as you leave them on a plate it's safe. But I do have a bit of a turn whenever I hear a fire engine. And they do burn up a lot of oxygen. If I had a canary, it would have long since died."

"Then you'd have to burn a candle for *it*. You do feel, do you, that all this helps?"

"Let me put it this way: my first caseload is much improved. I actually heard his voice on the phone."

"*First?* How many have you got?"

"I may have several, as word spreads of my powers."

For the descendant of several unbroken lines of stolid Protestants, none of them at all high church, I have an unusual tolerance for the occult. The way I look at it is, you never know. Although I prefer *Kyries* to *Oms,* I'm an eclectic pushover for the mantras and chants of all creeds, and there hangs on my wall a diploma proclaiming me to be a Psi Op (psychic operator), issued after a four-day crash course at the New York branch of the Mind Control Institute of Laredo, Texas. I was a loyal customer of the Astroflash booth at Grand Central Station, where computerized horoscopes of uncanny accuracy could be bought, until Astroflash's own planets apparently went haywire and the booth was shut down. Once when I lost my wallet I took the advice of my butcher, a man of German descent who lives in Queens and had recently become a Buddhist. He told me that if I kept repeating *Nam myo ho renge kyo* over and over to myself, the wallet would be returned. I did, and it was. As I say, you never know. Hence the candles. My friend Sally said she would keep them burning while I was abroad.

I never usually talk to strangers on planes, but Celia Bates, my seatmate on the flight to London, was an exception. We both got up to sit in another section when the movie went on, agreeing that there is something fundamentally wrong about seeing any movie on any plane, and thus began what could become a friendship. It cheers me, as I age, to think that I can have friends fifteen years my junior or, as appeared to be the case with Celia, my senior. It also cheers me to think that somebody I have at this moment never heard of, or only just met, may in a year's time have become important. (Once I told Marcus this, and he said "I find that frightening.")

Celia's red hair was just beginning to go gray. She had one of those expressive Eleanor Roosevelt faces, a face designed not to stop men in their tracks but to register such of the world's sorrows as it encountered, which in her case had apparently been many, and also to laugh. "Two frightful clichés apply to me," she said as we sipped bloody marys. "I'm 'of a certain age' and 'in reduced circumstances.'" A short marriage, long ago, had been childless, and she had never felt close to her own family in Wilmington, Delaware. She had just returned there "for the last time ever, I hope" for the funeral of her father. For ten years now she had been living on a small inheritance in London, working for a musical publisher only in the mornings so as to have afternoons free for whatever might come up. Once in a while, she said, she thought of looking for more involving work, "but who'd want to hire me at my age? They're all looking for buxom young vixens."

She did not wish ever again to live in the States, because among other reasons, she said in a whisper, "if I did I might get to look like *her*," a woman across the aisle with dyed, backcombed, and sprayed blonde hair and a raucous whiskey baritone voice. Her like, Celia assured me, would not be found among Englishwomen.

The next afternoon a message in my box at Brown's Hotel said to call Celia. The simple act of phoning made me feel even more euphoric than I had in a morning of blatant materialism on, or rather in, Regent Street. "Have you ever noticed the instructions inside phone booths here?" I asked Celia. " '. . . wait for continuous purring, dial number or code and number, when you hear rapid pips, press in a coin.' "

"Continuous purring and rapid pips. You see why I don't want to move back to the States?"

"We don't purr as continuously as we might," I had to admit.

"I'm surprised *you've* never lived overseas," Celia later said as we climbed to the upper deck of a bus to Trafalgar Square.

"I was always afraid to leave New York, because I didn't have a nucleus of friends anyplace else. There was this grim image of myself Starting Over on alien turf, away from my loved ones. Shortsighted, maybe, but there you are."

"One Starts Over, as you put it, wherever one is, all the time."

"So certain people say in my country. Today is the first day of the rest of your life."

"Doctrinaire, but true. I like your new Aquascutum."

"So do I, thanks. The one thing I minded in a morning of shopping was being addressed constantly as Madame. 'Yes, Madame,' 'No, Madame,' 'Right this way, Madame.' "

"What do you expect them to call you? Honey?"

"Little girl, maybe. Miss, I guess. Madame sounds geriatric."

We agreed that the National Portrait Gallery was depressingly filled with compulsive achievers and that museum postcard shops could be as enticing, though this was not a feeling to be proud of, as the original paintings themselves. "Once," I told Celia, "a friend of mine in New York had a rendezvous at the Frick, and the man she was meeting asked *where* in the Frick, and she said, 'The postcards—the *Fauve* postcards.'"

Celia invited me to a concert with her and some friends that evening, but for a wonder I had already been asked to dinner in Chelsea.

"So much for my tragic fantasies of existential loneliness in London," I said. "People here are so *nice*."

"Sometimes too nice," said Celia. "Sometimes I try in vain to provoke them to be more critical. Who was it, Dame Sybil Thorndike I think, said of someone 'Oh, I know he's a bastard, darling, but he does tie the most marvelous packages.' They're quite unlike us, the British. We say (A) Isn't she a cruel bitch, but (B) She means well. All they'll admit is that she means well. It can be boring."

Americans should only be so boring, I thought as I set out for a walk the next morning. If we were more boring we might have more tolerable public places. St. James Park, now, why it made our parks seem rubble heaps. Who could deny that that's what our parks were? I had promised a friend that I would go jogging in St. James Park, as a gesture of international sportsmanship, but a jog didn't seem the right pace. The waterfowl in the long lake there deserved the careful attention of a stroll, if not a full stop. But band music in the distance quickened my walk to an involuntary march. I didn't know what I was marching toward until I got to Buckingham Palace and witnessed that majestic ritual, the Changing of the Guard.

"Just think," said a man with a Konica to his wife, who had a Pentax, "they do this *every* morning!" I wished I had someone to nudge in the ribs. One does not nudge a strange rib in front of Buckingham Palace.

At the quick lunch counter at Fortnum & Mason's the waitress brought seven different utensils connected with my order of tea for one. Sipping the tea as I ate an open-faced prawn sandwich, I took one of the postcards I had just bought at the Tate Gallery to send a birthday message to my friend Liz, back home. "*So* like Nedick's," I began. Damn. Suddenly I missed her and Julian and wished they would walk right in and sit down on the next two stools.

"Maybe someday," I said when I called to tell Celia goodbye, "I'll make more of a habit of doing things worth doing with people worth doing them with, if you follow me."

"Your syntax is staggering," she said, "but I do follow you."

"I wish you could follow me more often," I said. "That's part of what I mean. What if we hadn't met on the plane? Seeing a bit of London with you has meant so much more than seeing it alone would have."

"But seeing it alone is better than not seeing it at all?"

"I'm not even as sure of that as I used to be."

"Here's something for you to write on your next list: 'Arrange life so that next time great experience comes along, great companion is available.'"

"You make it sound so simple. Well, anyway I can enjoy myself here among the ampersands—Fortnum & Mason, Marks & Spencer . . ."

"What'd you buy?"

"Cookies in a can called Easter Cakes, which I hope will make some unknown American household a happier place on Easter Morning, and some oranges . . ."

"Why oranges? Why carry food around if you're in transit?"

"To keep things on a homier, more human scale. I'll take the oranges with me to Belfast and pretend they're just ordinary groceries."

"Oh, yes, Belfast. Those random bombs. I'll worry."

"Don't. I'll send you a postcard."

The random bombs did not interrupt the research I had been sent to Ireland to do, but they did preclude any recreation other than eating and drinking. I wasn't eager to step onto a scale when I got home.

"It was as if some cruel dietitian had conspired to keep me on an all beer and butter diet, to fatten me up," I announced on my return. "Fish and chips, wheaten bread, Jameson's, Old Bushmill—hey, I've got some Old Bushmill right here! Want some?" They did not; they were happy with Almadén, the dozen or so people in my living room. Sally, who had stayed to mind the candles, had invited the others in honor of the legendary Jacobses of Tucson, who for a change were my houseguests instead of my being theirs. The Jacobses had come to celebrate the eightieth birthday of Grandma Moo, as Steve's mother, Josette Frank, is known to the nine persons whose names are on her favorite bracelet. Never in her life has Josette been called Mrs. Jacobs, not even when she registered in the maternity ward. For fifty of her eighty years she has worked with the Child Study Association. The Children's Book Committee, which she manages, reads and evaluates 3,000 books a year.

"A lot of them," she said, "make you weep for the trees cut down to print them."

Kathy, the wonder woman and earth mother, stayed on in New York for a few days after Steve returned to Arizona. She had brought along her serious L. L. Bean hiking boots. Scorning public transportation, she set forth in her boots to revisit the city and shop for food, hiking to Yorkville to get a certain kind of paprika and to her favorite old butcher's in the Village to take a rare cut of veal back to Tucson.

"You don't mean to tell me *she's* older than *you* are?" asked my cleaning woman, always the soul of tact. "She sure don't look it." Oh well, once Kathy had been asked for identification in her own liquor store at home.

The cherry trees in Riverside Park had not quite erupted into bloom when I came back, but the ones in Central Park, just a few blocks away, were at their peak. I went to pay homage, but doing so was difficult. New York's less fortunate citizens, those who had not the option of rides to the country, much less to England, were brazenly stripping whole boughs off the trees and making off with azaleas and daffodils as well.

My response to these misdemeanors lacked force. "I can see how busy you are," I more or less said, "but it would be nice if you wouldn't take any more of those branches." If this were England, I began to think . . . no. Mustn't become one of those anglophile bores.

From several directions came the throbbing mantras of bongo drums. Maybe it was barbaric to denude the trees, but those who did the denuding came from places where blossoms were free and where there was music like this, no easier to ignore than the brasses outside Buckingham Palace. I joined a large crowd around one trio of drummers on a park bench near the Tavern on the Green. Others in the crowd began to dance. I stood tapping my feet and longing for the nerve to wave my arms around as well, in abandoned tribute, alone if need be, to spring in Central Park. But this was not Esalen, so what I did instead was find a phone booth and call a friend who lived nearby. No continuous purring, no rapid pips, but he came to join me and we jogged across the Sheep Meadow to watch the drummers, agreeing that they sounded better from a distance. We did not dance. My friend had to go. He had an appointment. I had to go too. I had to get some rest. When you fly home from east to west, your jet lag bill comes due.

32

Chicanos Don't Say Olé

When I was a child in Winnetka, Illinois, I used to wish we had a car. Until we finally did get one, when I was in high school, we'd have to borrow other people's or make do without. It was embarrassing. Everyone else had a car. Some families even had two. Once in a while I would imply that we had one too, only it was away somewhere, maybe being fixed, maybe off at camp. I also used to wish my cardigans were cashmere instead of lamb's wool and that we had a shower as well as a tub and that I had a closet of my own so I wouldn't have to share the one in Ann's room.

Nelba Chavez grew up in Pascua Village east of Miracle Mile in Tucson, where families of ten commonly live in two-room houses. She was born there in 1941, six years after I was, and her childhood was about as filled with conveniences as that of Abraham Lincoln. Nelba took two baths a week. Her house had kerosene lamps and dirt floors and a wood stove. Nelba's grandmother, who raised her, took in ironing, doing large bundles of ironing for twenty-five cents each, and the only way she had to heat the irons was on the stove. Flour to make tortillas came in sacks from which her grandmother made Nelba's underwear.

"Wasn't it scratchy?" I asked.

"No," said Nelba. "She'd boil the sacks with a bar of lye soap for several days, until they got soft."

Nelba was raised by her grandmother because her mother (one of fifteen children of whom seven survived infancy) was an alcoholic. She married an alcoholic too. Nelba's parents lived right across the unpaved street, so she saw and heard them fight. They fought most of the time. Nelba had many relatives. Some of them were in and out of jail.

When Nelba first went to school it amazed her to learn that not all children had parents who drank and that there were people who had hair the color of a yellow Crayola. At school she was hit if she spoke Spanish on the playground and tied with a jump rope and put in the closet if she spoke it in the classroom. Nelba decided, she still is not sure why, that she would be different from the people around her. She did not, for example, join her friends who all had crosses tattooed on their hands when they were seven. She took part in gang fights only when she had to, for survival's sake. By the time she got to fifth grade, she had a teacher she liked. As a junior in high school, she decided she would apply for a scholarship at the state university. Her guidance counselor laughed at the very thought. How could Nelba, whose annual family income it said right here was $1,600, expect to afford college even if she did win a scholarship?

"Besides," the guidance counselor added, "people of *your* kind *never* make it."

Nelba did, though. When we met, she was dividing her energy in three directions. She taught at Pima Community College, she led groups of pre-delinquent children, and she was a psychiatric social worker at La Frontera, which treats the highest percentage of Mexican-Americans of any mental health clinic in Arizona. When I met her, Nelba was one of two Spanish-speaking masters of social work in the state. The other was her friend Grace Burruel. They both got their advanced degrees in 1971, from UCLA, and they were both nationally regarded as experts, which seemed to them both funny and sad.

This expertise made them special, but what made them truly freakish by the standards of their culture was their marital status. Nelba was thirty-two and Grace twenty-eight, and both were uncommonly attractive, but they did not have husbands.

"My mother went into a severe depression when I went to graduate school," Grace said the evening I met her and Nelba in her office at La Frontera. "The more educated I am, the less men want to have to do with me. I've been ostracized by my brothers and brothers-in-law, because I'm threatening to them. My family nag me constantly because they know of no definition of happiness outside marriage."

Grace was wearing a pink jumper-style pantsuit and pearl earrings. Her features and stature were more delicate than Nelba's. Nelba made me think of the heroine of some comic book: Barbarella, maybe, or Wonder Woman. She had coarse, shoulder-length black hair, a full mouth, and volatile eyes. Like Grace she was quick to laugh, but in repose Nelba's face had about it a look of anger. I guess mine would too if I had to deal with people like the woman Nelba encountered in the Safeway checkout line.

"I asked this woman if she would please let a friend of mine who'd gone to get something she forgot back in the line. The woman said, 'You goddamn SOB greaser, I'll be damned if I'll move an inch for you—I'm going to hit you with this bottle.' I said, 'Go right ahead; it'll be the last thing you ever do.' I contained myself, but it took every ounce of energy I had. In another supermarket, in West Los Angeles, the checkout lady saw my full cart and asked, 'Why didn't you separate your items for Food Stamps?' Since I look Mexican, it didn't occur to her that I could afford to buy any other way."

I had to wait until their workday was over to meet Nelba and Grace, because they were booked all day long with nonstop therapy sessions, some with individuals and some with couples and families. "We deal with Mexicans and Chicanos of all age levels," they said, "and every conceivable problem."

"Let's get this straight," I said. "Who's a Chicano and who isn't?"

"Any Mexican-American who feels like one is a Chicano,"

Grace said. "Chicanismo—awareness of the roots of Mexican-American culture and concern about injustice—is a state of mind. But to some 'Chicano' is a dirty, derogatory word. Elderly people think it's too radical and militant. You'd no more call an old person a Chicano to his face than you'd address him as *tu* instead of *usted*. People who've just arrived from Mexico don't consider themselves Chicanos, either."

"It used to be hard to get help from the community when I was working my ass off over in the village where I grew up," said Nelba, "until suddenly the word 'Chicano' became fashionable. Do-gooders would all of a sudden rush over to help, and I'd feel like saying, 'Where the hell were you when we needed you? These are the same people they've always been, no matter what you call them.' "

Grace, having spent most of her childhood in Mexico, did not speak English when she arrived in Tucson and enrolled in high school. "They gave me an IQ test and I came out a moron," she said. "My counselor suggested I might be a beautician, and she meant it as a compliment.

"You know why the statistics show that Mexican-Americans don't have many mental health problems? Because ours is one of the few clinics where Mexican-American needs are met in the whole Southwest. We are, you will find, quite well represented in penal institutions, alcoholism, drug abuse. Oh, is it really seven-thirty? I'm going to have to go. The group will be waiting."

"Stay a bit," said Nelba. "They'll keep waiting. They wouldn't miss it."

"Who's in the group?" I asked.

"Mostly Mexican-American women concerned about emancipation," said Grace. "We have a lot of groups devoted to that subject. Sometimes we get women as old as forty-five who still live at home with their parents and still feel guilty about wanting to get out.

"One Mexican father came in here, very serious, and said he needed our advice. He said, 'I need a court order to stop my older son from interfering with my role as a father.' I asked how the son was interfering. The father said, 'He's been saying his nineteen-year-old sister ought to be allowed to go out and have dates.' I asked if he'd like to send his daughter to one of our groups. He asked, 'Are the groups all women?' I said yes. He said, 'Can her mother and brother come along as chaperones?'

"Sometimes men come in here and want to get us," said Nelba. "They threaten to kill their wives, kill us, put a bomb in the place. The idea of emancipated women totally undermines their authority. It's very traumatic what happens to a man when his wife sees herself as emancipated. My reaction to the women's movement is you Anglos don't know how lucky you are. If you only knew *our* problems!"

"I was beginning to think there was no such thing as an old maid anymore," I said.

"Are you kidding? One lady came in here, forty-two years old, she nearly had a psychotic break, with fainting spells, extreme depression. She'd been very active in her job, but suddenly her whole defense system fell apart. I called her up and said, 'Look, you're going to work at eight o'clock tomorrow morning and no buts.' She liked her work and got involved again, but her mother started rejecting her. It wouldn't do any good if I went to talk to the mother—I'm only a female social worker—but I got the male doctor, a Jewish doctor from Hartford, Connecticut, to go to that home and tell the mother to start encouraging her daughter to work, that if she didn't work she'd get sick. The whole concept of male authority was what did it."

"Do you have male patients?"

"Some. It's easier to engage Anglo males in therapy than Mexicans. There's such emphasis on *machismo* that when Mexican men come in here they've mostly been referred by MDs, and they all have psychosomatic complaints—backaches, legaches, stomachaches. Women can come in with *los nervios,* nerves, because being women it's okay for them to be a little crazy.

"Some of the diagnoses we get are ridiculous. One woman was referred here by another clinic with a diagnosis of paranoid schizophrenia, because she said her husband's ex-wife put a hex on her. Hell, she wasn't any more paranoid schizophrenic than I am. That hex business is a very common thing in our culture."

"A lot of what we try to do," said Nelba, "is have women come out and *do* something with their lives. Unless Mexican women emancipate, we're lost. In our culture the double standard is far worse. Latin men can do anything they like, but women are sheltered, protected, chaperoned, and raised from birth to be slaves to men."

"But what about your extended families?" I asked. "Isn't there supposed to be something special about having all those *copadres* and *tios* and *sobrinas* and *primas* and *cuñadas?* Doesn't it give you a warmth and security we could use some of to have them around?" That was the impression I had got from talking to Mexican-American women my last trip to Tucson, the previous June.

"My own family," said Grace, "is so close it's suffocating." She and Nelba had been to a conference in Washington, D.C., where, much to their wonderment, Anglo psychiatrists had presented different proposals for the rediscovery of roots of extended families. To them this made about as much sense as bringing back polio.

"You Anglos," said Nelba, shaking her head. "You don't know how lucky you are. Hell, we've been living in extended families for years. Some of what you say about closeness and security is true, of course, but those ties can be *too* close. What you're trying to bring back is what we're trying to get away from."

To me it had seemed miraculous to spend Easter, whose potential for nostalgia is about half that of Christmas (which is to say still a lot), with the other daughter of the late Eleanor Howard and her husband and their children. Buffeted around the globe as they and I are by choice and chance, it seemed a splendid coincidence that their plans and mine and the Easter Bunny's should bring us all to Arizona. I said as much.

"Oh, Janie," my jaded niece Sarah said, "there's no such *thing* as the Easter Bunny."

"That's what you think," I said. "What do you call *him?*" I pointed to the surreal papier-mâché figure of a turquoise rabbit hanging like a lynching victim from the bough of a cottonwood tree. This particular bunny was, by persuasion, a piñata. His destiny was to hang from that tree and be whacked at with a stick by a series of thirty or so blindfolded children, starting with the very smallest, until somebody aimed hard enough so that a cache of jellybeans, artfully hidden in the bunny's torso, would shower down onto the squealing young celebrants.

"You can't say this scene isn't ethnic," Ann observed as we sat getting too much sun, having eaten too much food and drunk too much wine. She had bought the piñata bunny in California somewhere. For her and David and the kids, this was the end of a two-week trip which began with a convention in Los Angeles and continued to Disneyland, the San Diego Zoo, and the Grand Canyon, with liberal doses along the way of fellowship with relatives. Of these the last was David's mother, known as Gragra, who had been persuaded to come along from Phoenix for this multi-generation, super-ethnic Easter in the desert. Our hosts, of course, were the Jacobses.

Sensory overload, as it is called in some circles, had been a problem throughout our tribal day. We all got up soon after the kids did, at daybreak, to look for candy and eggs. Everyone got at least one personalized egg. Mine, dyed an imaginative shade of mauve, said "Greetings From Arizona, Janie Bird" in John's newly learned cursive script. Breakfast, at a poolside table with a sweetpea centerpiece, was like something out of *Sunset* magazine. Strawberries with sour cream, homemade hot cross buns, served with Irish butter sculptured into the shape of a chick. Oh, we are clever with our hostess presents. The previous night Steve and Dave finally figured how to open the clams and oysters brought packed in New York dry ice: on the vise in Steve's workshop.

Handel's "Messiah," which Kathy always likes to play on Easter, was turned on loud enough to be heard above the vacuum cleaner. At midday the eleven of us joined a caravan of five or six other full Land Rovers for a picnic in a canyon and the ethnic piñata ceremony. Later we came home to swim and split into special interest sub-groups. Maybe it was that some of us had been in too many time zones lately, but nerves grew frayed. Rich though the day had been, misunderstandings arose. But I thought . . . How could you have expected . . . When was I supposed to . . . I'll just have a tray in my room.

Oh, be nice, everybody.

A few nights later, slowing down as I drove along First Street in South Tucson, I squinted to see whether I had come to the right place.

"Is that you, Jane?" called Irma Villa from a patio between two houses.

"How'd you know?"

"Your hair." Even in the dark, a head of straight tan hair stood out in this part of town. Irma's own hair, black with a bit of gray here and there, hung in a ponytail to her waist. She had a pre-Columbian profile and intense brown eyes. She was as tall as I am and probably outweighed me even when she wasn't four months pregnant, as she then was. She wore a lot of silver and turquoise jewelry and won my trust as soon as I saw that she carried a big, floppy patchwork suede purse. I am just a bit suspicious, at first, of women who organize everything tidily into tiny handbags.

I was supposed to have dinner that night with Irma and her husband Joe, for whom her nickname is "Viejo" (old one), but that plan had to be canceled because Joe, a carpenter, had an accident. A power saw cut off the tip of one of his fingers, exposing the bone. When Joe came back from the emergency ward, all his relatives had come to offer solace. All Irma's had come too, which wasn't a logistical feat as most of them live right next door or right across the street. If ever there was a casebook example of an extended family, and a matriarchal one at that, I had found it. Irma's well-named mother, Reina

Basurto, who lived next door, clearly reigned over her brood, which consisted of Irma and Joe and their nine-year-old son Joey and Irma's sister Pat, across the street, and her family. Reina and her husband Reynaldo also had in residence five foster children. Over the years they have had fifty, in addition to three of their own.

Reina was a matriarch, all right, a role to which Irma was clearly heiress apparent, but these households also paid homage to the principle of *machismo*. Irma waited for Joe to walk around the car to open the door for her; she would not think of doing otherwise. "It's a sign," she said, "of the respect between us." Irma waited for Joe to come home before she went shopping for supper, in case there was something special he might crave to eat. Irma didn't *tell* Joe she was going out of town on business, she asked his permission.

Irma was, most remarkably, on the national board of Planned Parenthood, a cause not generally held in high repute among Latin Roman Catholics. "I believe in my religion," she said, "but I don't want to be a hypocrite, I went to confession and confessed I practiced birth control, because I don't feel I should have the luxury of more children than we can afford to educate." Most women her age, which was thirty-two, had five children. A cousin three years her senior was already a grandmother.

Irma also had what could be called a career. She was a manpower specialist for the community branch of the Office of Economic Opportunity. Her mission was to break down barriers and find jobs and a sense of involvement for minority people. Her dread was that wholesale budget cuts by the federal administration would shut down the grass-roots programs she had spent seven years helping to develop. She was prominent enough to have enemies. One man in the community, she said, "is anti-Irma Villa, period. He'd go all the way to Hell just to heckle me at a meeting."

For several hours, that soft night in South Tucson, these two matriarchs and I sat on the bricked patio between their homes and talked. Irma told of the time she was sent to the store, as a little girl, and got the order confused: she asked for a dozen beans and a pound of eggs instead of the reverse, and the dead-pan grocer obliged. We talked of Reina's fifty foster children, most of whom came to her as adolescents. "Everyone loves a baby," she said, "anyone can mold a baby, but teenagers, set in their minds already, they're more of a challenge. They need more patience and more love, and they give more satisfaction. Two years is the least I can work with a child and see a little change."

Irma talked of politics. What made her mad was "administrators who try to get rid of the grass roots so they can save their own jobs. Excuse me, but it's a whole bunch of bullshit. And we can't keep electing wonderful old men with no fight in them, who automatically second all the motions. We need younger people who'll stand up for what they believe."

"Most people around here are domestics," said Reina. "A lot of them work for government programs, but when the programs fold up, the people will be in a bad way. I feel sorry for these people. They need to better their standards of living. Standards of living is what makes people happy, not education. I feel that the more education people have, the more unhappy they are."

"I didn't start thinking of myself as a Chicano until the last couple of years," said Irma. "Before that I was just a Mexican-American person, not aware of any special identity. I'd be considered militant now, compared to the way I was eight years ago."

"It's the union people who are really fighting for a real cause," said Reynaldo Basurto, who did not call himself a Chicano. "My son would be classifed as real low class if his father wasn't a union member."

We talked of *machismo*. "To me," said Reina, "*machismo* is pride. Children should be proud of their fathers, no matter how much money there is or isn't. I've had foster children whose fathers gave them nothing but expensive toys. That's not *machismo*."

"In fifty percent of the homes," said Reina, "the man thinks he's the smart one and the woman should have to go along with what he says, but I don't believe that. I believe that if I'm right I'm right, and if I'm wrong I'll admit it. A weak wife will pull a man down. A strong man with some dreams in the world will need a strong wife."

"I don't think *I'd* want a tamer woman," Reynaldo Basurto admitted.

"Two people like me," said Reina, "we'd burn up the world."

Sure she remembered who I was, Julia Soto said on the phone. That was a nice surprise. She and I had talked for two hours ten months earlier, and I was afraid the meeting had made much more of an impression on me than it had on her. I had said very little, spending most of my time taking notes. "I'm very nosy and very honest," Julia had said. "I'm an advocate and an activist. I get my ears pinned back now and then, but when I see issues not being taken care of, I get very vocal. I sit on a lot of boards and negotiate with a lot of important people, and I tell them right away 'Look, if I can manipulate you, I will.' "

I drove with Julia to pick up her four-year-old daughter, the youngest of her seven children, at an experimental pre-kindergarten for parent and child education. Twenty children were in that classroom. "Most of the mothers are not very vocal," Julia said, "because they represent generations of not rocking the boat." She dropped her daughter off at her grandmother's, and then we talked more.

Health is Julia's foremost interest, probably because five people in her own immediate family had died of tuberculosis. She has an arrested case of it herself. "There used to be tent cities set up for people with TB when I was a child," she said, "and orphanages and WPA camps. The people who ran those places gave us sputum tests and a lot of cod liver oil and good advice, but their attitudes were shitty as hell."

Julia's own attitudes toward injustice were once rather mild. "I used to just plan school parades, make cupcakes, march for the March of Dimes, work in rummage sales. Once when I was fifty pounds lighter I did La Raspa—the Mexican hat dance—

at a PTA party." But then certain things started making Julia mad. One of these was the huge dropout rate of Mexican-American students from high school. She learned that a poor command of English was grounds for classifying students as retarded or shunting them automatically into vocational instead of academic programs. When Julia organized parents of these "retarded" students into a walkout, the papers called her "an irresponsible liar." A year later, her charges were proven valid.

"I began to get hooked," she said. "Activism got to be to me as water is to a dying man." Having dropped out of school at age eleven, she took a general equivalency test and got a high school diploma. Having worked as a maid, cook, and aircraft inspector, she took an OEO leadership training course, learning how local resources were funded and how little money was being spent on the aged. "It made me furious to see how federal funds ignored the elderly," she said. *"Doghouses* on the east side are better than the living quarters of old people on the west."

Observing that politics mattered, she got elected district committeewoman and started a legislative club. "I urged people to register to vote, and not just so they'd get Christmas baskets. A lot of people never thought of things that way before. My husband and I took around a little voting machine, which is confusing as hell, and set it up in supermarkets and shopping centers so people could see how it worked." She protested if she saw a young Mexican mother ignored at a Well Baby Clinic, or an old Indian man treated rudely in an unemployment line.

Meanwhile, she raised her family of seven. "We never questioned having a baby a year," she says. "I wouldn't want to do it otherwise. But things are different now. In my father's *epoca* they'd never talk of sex in front of children, but I do to my kids. I tell my daughters, 'What if you marry someone and he turns out to be a lion?' We talk of premarital relations, sex problems, drugs, everything. Even my seven-year-old asked me about sperm; he said he'd heard that 'from your dicky you get sperm and that's what makes babies.' I said, 'Well, that's true, *mi jito.'* My daughter asked if she needed a bra, and when I said no she said, 'Well then, can I get bikini panties?'

"My older daughter, who wants to be a correction officer, asked her father if she could live in the dorm at school. He said no. He says the law emancipates them at eighteen, but they're never emancipated from him as the parent until they say good-bye.

"My husband is proud of what I'm doing, but he says, 'Remember you're a lady, so you don't need to rant and rave and use four-letter words.'"

"I wish I could meet your husband," I told Julia. He worked, she said, as an inspector for the Arizona Corporation Commission, inspecting trucks for safety and health violations and cargoes. He was often away on duty at a border town. That day, however, he was in his office in Tucson, so we went to meet him. He was tall and magnificent in his uniform and not much given to small talk. I got the idea he took me for yet another sociologist from some federal agency, come to write yet another in a long series of boondoggle reports on the status of minorities.

Hoping to dispel him of this notion, I said "I just wanted to meet you."

"It's been my pleasure," he said, ending the interview five minutes after it began.

Even though Nelba was offered a scholarship to the University of Arizona, she turned it down to prove she could work her own way through. She did, supporting her grandmother as well, finding jobs in a carwash, an office, and a factory. Five years later she graduated and applied for a job as a probation officer in Juvenile Court. The judge in charge said he didn't want to hire her, because he had seen some of her relatives in court too often.

"If that's why you're denying me the job," Nelba told the judge, "then you're a farce and your court is a farce." She got the job and spent most of the rest of her time doing extra-curricular work with children who lived where she had grown up, in Pascua Village. One thing she did was organize a softball tournament. "I didn't know a thing about softball, in fact I *hated* it, but it was a way to work those kids so hard they wouldn't have any time to be delinquents."

Promoted, she decided she needed a master's and got a grant from the National Institute of Mental Health to study at UCLA. Her grandmother cried the day she left and begged her not to go. "I had to kneel down in front of her while she gave me the Last Blessing, a special prayer which meant, 'God guide you and take care of you wherever you're at.' What my grandmother really wanted was to see me married."

Nelba has been engaged three times. "I don't think I'll ever find a liberated Mexican male," she said. "A Latin male would have to be a superman before I'd marry him. Latin men are the worst of all. The best husbands are Anglos, some Mexican-American women say, and the best wives are Mexicans. If a fourth-generation Mexican-American marries a first-generation Mexican man, then she's in trouble."

"I had a German boyfriend in college," said Grace, "and my family ostracized us both at family gatherings, but if I brought him around now they'd think, 'Well, he's better than nothing.' Later, in graduate school, I met a Mexican male who was emancipated intellectually, but not emotionally. He felt very threatened by me, so that didn't work out either.

"Marriage was very tempting to me when I was eighteen," said Grace, "but I'm grateful I didn't do it. If I had, I would have had five kids by now and be stuck. I wouldn't have got where I am. Not that I *know* where I am—if I had the money I'd rather be analyzed than take a trip, to find out where—but I do at least know that I'm getting somewhere."

Grace went off to lead her group of women concerned with emancipation, and Nelba and I decided to go to La Fuentes, a fancy Mexican restaurant on the Miracle Mile, to talk some more. We were shown to a table as close as we could ever dream of being to the mariachi band. The musicians didn't stay put, though. Glittering in their sequins, they wandered around the restaurant's several rooms, playing whatever songs people asked for. It was understood that everyone would have a favorite song to request. I felt unnerved; the only song I could think of was 'South of the Border,' a shameful choice for a Muzak-hater like myself. A veil of white by candlelight indeed. But I asked for it anyway, and the musicians obliged with gusto. When they were through, some tourists at the next table shouted "Olé!"

"Chicanos don't say *Olé!*, do they?" I asked Nelba.

"No," she said, smiling. "Just you guys."

33

Vodka Gimlet to Go

I'm too tired to stay awake any longer. Even though it's only eleven o'clock here, it's midnight in Tucson, where I've just flown from, and tomorrow in Europe, where I was last week. Besides, I'm still taking pills called V-Cillin-K for the flu I caught last week. Everyone understands. This is a kind hospice. I am shown to a room with a king-size bed. The patterned sheets remind me of tomato soup, egg yolk and raspberry sherbet. There is a Disneyland poster on the wall and a blown-up plastic giraffe and a collage of mementoes of a trip to Ireland and a copy of that parchment labeled "Desiderata," which I have seen often of late, beginning, "Go placidly, amid the noise and haste, and remember what peace there may be in silence." I try to remember. Tomorrow, if the fog lifts, I can look out at the Pacific. I am in California again, La Jolla this time, in the bedroom of a nineteen-year-old named Robin.

"Oh, poor Robin, I'm putting you out."

"No, that's fine," she says. "It means *I* get to sleep on one of the waterbeds."

It is a measure of my fatigue and general churlishness that

my first, barely suppressed reaction to this news is annoyance: why didn't they assign *me* to the waterbed? Don't they know I've always wanted to sleep on one? But how, my voice of reason retorts, could they possibly know that? "They," this time, are my hosts Audrey and Bill McGaw. I have come to talk to Audrey because Bill has told me "she *really* knows what it is to be an American woman."

I suppose there is not an adult female between Samoa and the Bay of Fundy who could not lay some claim to expertise on this subject, but something in Bill's voice has lured me. He met me at the San Diego airport in his hearse, the famous glittering black hearse he bought last summer in London, the very one which once belonged to the Beatles and which appeared in "A Hard Day's Night." What panache; I am grateful enough if anyone meets me in a battered pick-up truck. Driving home, we practiced waving regally at those who stare at us. Many do.

When Bill bought the hearse the previous summer it had taken four days of his total attention. That made Audrey mad. "He got *obsessed,*" she said. "It smelled of such selfishness. While the kids and I waited for him to do all that paperwork, we had to change all our plans. I was tempted to just take the kids and leave, instead of hanging around. I don't like losing control of my life, being at the whim of somebody else. In those three or four days I didn't feel loved by him. We had it out, though."

"We always do," said Bill. "We fight big and love big. We don't let anything slide anymore. Neither of us will settle for anything less than a really good relationship. We both know what it's like to have a bad thing, because we had bad things before." Between them the McGaws have six children. Robin and three boys now live in La Jolla. A son of Audrey's is in Hawaii, and a daughter of Bill's lives most of the year with her remarried mother in the East.

I first met the McGaws five years earlier, when they were leading an encounter group. They had co-led seventy or eighty such groups, mostly for married couples and families and many under the auspices of the Center for the Studies of the Person. The Center, in La Jolla, was established by a group including the psychologist Dr. Carl Rogers. I had last seen Audrey in Pittsburgh four months earlier, when she and Dr. Rogers both helped lead a filmed encounter group of nine Irishmen imported for the occasion from Belfast. Bill had produced the film. I had gone with him and a colleague to Belfast in early April, when they showed the movie to its stars.

I thought that after having led so many groups for troubled marriages, Audrey might have some sage things to say about how women were changing. The next morning she was eloquent on the subject. "The big difference I notice," she said, "is that women are realizing now that they're responsible for themselves, instead of feeling like society's victims. We're getting to see that we shouldn't blame our troubles on men, God, the president, or our mothers, but on ourselves. It's ridiculous to say you can't change yourself, because you can. You don't have to be a loser.

"The new thing is looking inside yourself, instead of out at society, to find out how you got to where you are."

"I've always thought it was pointless for people over the age of twenty-five to blame their parents for anything," I said. "Just as you're supposed to be responsible for the way your face looks after forty—God forbid—I think you're responsible for your life after twenty-five. I just made that up, but don't you think it makes sense?"

"I think it does," said Audrey. "But a lot of women like to stay in the past. As long as they stay in the past, instead of right now, they're very secure, because they can always avoid responsibility, always say, 'What can you expect, with a mother like I had?' "

"Why," I asked her, "do you think women come to encounter groups?"

"Mostly from a gnawing hunger for some sort of recognition. In the groups we've done I'd bet that eighty percent of the women bring their men along, instead of vice versa. Men are bewildered when they get there, they say, 'Well, of *course* I love her; I wouldn't *live* with her if I didn't,' but they don't understand. They think it's just a matter of sex. Women don't mean just that. They mean being touched, as opposed to being fucked. What women have to learn, and it's scary, is that if they want to accept freedom, an enormous responsibility comes with it. It's safer to avoid the responsibility and choose enslavement.

"And a lot of people are screwed up by images. Bill and I used to have big scenes because he didn't like gardening and woodwork. I might have got some joy out of the yard if I'd worked in it myself, but I didn't because it was *his* job. Some women often say, 'How do you expect me to make love when I've been up till two in the morning doing your job?' Withholding of sex is often a punishment for not living up to images.

"Women often don't realize how powerful they are in the house. All the time I hear, 'I love him more than he loves me, because look: he has his job, that's his first love; and he has the house, the kids, the dog, and finally me. I keep slim, cook, dress well, have my hair done, and all he does is take.' Women don't see that men too can feel hurt, and hungry for affection and rewards."

"Do you think women run the show most of the time?"

"They do, in a peculiar way—not hypocritically or even consciously, but because they don't accept responsibility for the position they're in, from resentment."

Outside on the lawn, in the light drizzle, I saw a long lumpy Day-Glo orange sleeping bag, which appeared to contain a human form. Every once in a while the human form would shift.

"Who's *that?*" I asked.

"That's Par," Bill said. Parlan is one of Bill's sons.

"Oh, so it was *his* waterbed Robin slept in."

"Nobody minds."

Two years earlier, Audrey had been so full of resentment herself that she wrote Bill a letter. He wasn't off on a trip, although he frequently is. He was right there in the house with her, but somehow she felt like writing down what was on her mind instead of saying it aloud. "There've been four or five times in our marriage," she says, "when I haven't been able to find words. I brood about it for a while, whatever it is, then write everything down and give it to Bill when I'm quiet."

The letter she wrote him then said, among many other things, that "I'm dull & uninteresting most of the time. I'm unkempt & dishonest. Nothing I do is lasting. . . . I'm not comfortable with myself. I'm getting older & gray & wrinkled & I smoke & eat too much & I don't do anything worthwhile for anyone or myself. I complain & cry & scream & smart & avoid & hide. I feel sorry for myself. I feel taken for granted, overworked, misunderstood, underappreciated, ugly, wronged, helpless, lost, ashamed, pitiful. I feel disgust for myself. . . . I find I am easily irritated by you, the kids, our friends, the yard, the house, the laundry, the kitchen, the refrigerator, doghair, dogshit, trash & dirt & dust & mess & clutter & lunch & dinner & endless dishes & ashtrays & chairs out of place & telephones & crumbs & cats & meals & food & marketing & cars & bills & bathroom mirrors & the patio & the windows & the walls & making the bed & picking up clothes & being fat & not having clothes look right & cooking & marketing & spots & etc etc etc."

Could this be the Audrey I saw before me? This stately, radiant, expressive, in fact beautiful, if not emaciated woman? Apparently it had been, but then she and Bill went with another couple for a weekend camping trip which turned into a critical nonstop marathon. "We didn't mean for it to be that," Audrey said. "We'd been fighting for a couple of days after that letter but we figured since we'd planned the camping trip a long time we'd postpone the fight until we came back. But our friends were so sensitive they probably figured 'What's going on here?' and *made* us talk about it.

"We'd done the same thing for them once, on a trip to Puerto Vallarta. In fact we met them when they were in a group of ours. We fought it out for that entire weekend, hour after hour, stopping only to fix meals. It really got heavy on Sunday morning, but in the end it was very neat."

"The marvelous thing," said Bill, "is that Audrey has the courage to communicate this stuff."

"And," said Audrey, "that Bill cares enough to listen, no matter how threatening it is."

"How did things change afterward?" I asked.

"Well," said Audrey, "before that letter, I used to take pleasure in housework. My house shone better than anybody's. There was no dust, no clutter, because I had no other way of proving my value. My children were well-behaved, whatever that means."

"What about the groups you led with Bill?" I asked. "Didn't that give you value?"

"Not enough," she said. "Besides, by then I'd tapered off from doing them."

"What else have you ever done for a living?" I asked her.

"Mostly I was a service operator for the telephone company. Also I worked in a pool hall, and in a P-X once. Nothing much. I didn't go to college. Of the seven children in my family, only one did."

"So you felt that housework was what defined you?"

"Sure. When Bill would say, 'Come on, drop what you're doing and meet me for a drink after work,' and I'd say, 'I can't, I have to do the floor,' and he'd say, 'Oh, the floor isn't important,' I'd explode: if the floor wasn't important, since the floor was my work, what did that make *me*?"

"And I got sick of saying, "Would you please feed the dogs for me?' Suddenly it hit me that they were everybody's dogs, not mine. Why should I say please and thank you to the bunch of very big people who live here? So I didn't.

"Another thing: before two years ago, if Bill was out of town I'd never go to a party by myself, I'd just lie or make up some excuse. Then I began to start going. The other day I went to one at Carl and Helen's, and it was one of those really neat, rare evenings, and as I was leaving I said to a friend of ours, really meaning it, that I was sorry not to have had a chance to talk to him.

"He said he was sorry too, because there was something he'd

393

been noticing and meaning to tell me. 'I suddenly realize,' he said with tears in his eyes, 'that you're the most mentally sane and emotionally healthy person I know.' I was floored, as you can imagine. What a gorgeous thing to hear.

" 'It's our *business* to help people be mentally sane and emotionally healthy,' he went on, 'but we rarely know it or be it by ourselves.' "

"You know what I told him? I told him I thought he was right, that I *was* sane and healthy. Two years ago I'd never have said that. I'd have said something flip like, 'Thanks, I'm glad I *seem* that way, but you don't know the half of it.' "

"That's surely what *I'd* say, if the occasion arose," I said.

"Most people would," said Audrey, "but I think maybe that's what mental health is about: never forgetting to take credit for what you've accomplished. Want some more coffee?" Sure I did. Just then Robin and her cousin Cindy came in from church. Robin, her mother later told me, "believes in God and Christ and a lot of things I've always been negative about, but that's fine, because the kids she hangs around with are really alive, neat, marvelous people."

"Well, Cindy," Audrey asked her pretty niece, "are you in love?" Cindy blushed. "What about the boy with the Mercedes?" Cindy blushed more. Robin, I later learned, had recently reconciled with her boyfriend after a dismaying split. "It bothered me," Audrey said, "that she should have been *grateful* to him for liking her. That meant she thought he was the king, just as I used to think Bill was. Bill never asked for that throne in the first place, but as long as it was there, as long as he got royal treatment like having his socks picked up, he didn't want to abidcate.

"I was on the way into making Robin into a matriarch, a hideous role which would have made her brothers resent and dislike her. It used to be that they never did dishes because the kitchen was her place. No more. Since then I've tried to make her see that the path she picks for herself needn't be any narrower than anybody else's, just because she's a female.

"She's starting to think a lot of things out now, things which in the depth of her pain she didn't acknowledge, because all she wanted was for the boy to come back. She says she's in a very different place with him, that if he starts treating her carelessly again, she won't take it."

"Good for her," I said. "Do you think these changes came from the women's movement?"

"I think it's more a natural evolvement," said Audrey. "Since we had our showdown a couple of years ago, we all care more about each other and listen more to each other. Before, the male-female thing kept the kids from being as close as they are now. We've had so many little changes. Like the boys cooking. Sandy makes the best *quesedillas* now, no matter how hard the rest of us may try, and James came up with the idea of melted cheese on top of hamburgers. Par even said he'd like to learn to cook. Bill, too. He used to just do steak and lobster, now he's into tempura."

Par had risen from his sleeping bag outside. As he went up the stairs to the street, he tapped on the outside wall three times.

"I love *you*," Audrey called in response. That, clearly, was what the family code of three taps meant: I love you.

Bill McGaw first laid eyes on Audrey in a bar after a Christmas party in the office where they both worked, eleven years earlier. "I pointed to her and told a fellow girlwatcher that someday she'd be my number one. 'Impossible,' the friend said, 'I happen to know, she's married.' 'Even so,' I said, 'Just wait.' "

In time, when Bill heard that Audrey was divorced, which he had been himself for a couple of years, he began his pursuit. His was not a faint heart. "He really had to beat down an awful lot of defenses in me," Audrey said. Learning that she was in the habit of driving to a certain beach where her children could let off steam while she watched the sunset, he drove there, parked his car next to hers, stayed in his, and talked to her.

"If you weren't so stubborn," he said, "You'd have let me bring you a drink."

"You couldn't have brought the only kind of drink I like."

"What's that?"

"Vodka gimlet."

"Excuse me," said Bill. He drove to a bar, ordered a double vodka gimlet, poured it into a glass he happened to have in his pocket, returned to the beach, and said, "*Now* can I sit in your car, if I keep way over to the other side?"

"Still," said Audrey, "I was wary. I didn't want to get into another relationship that didn't work. I wasn't any better for my first husband, an artist who did technical illustrations for a living, than he was for me. He never finished things because he didn't want to be judged, but I kept *urging* him to. In his case, if I'd been a devoted wife I'd have just let it go.

"I was twenty-one when I was married the first time, but I might as well have been twelve. I married him mostly to get away from my mother." Audrey's then widowed mother brought up seven of the twelve children she bore. Audrey was the second youngest. That family, as Audrey describes it, could have been imagined by Joyce Carol Oates.

"Mother wouldn't let me sit on her lap. Her first husband had died in the flu epidemic, and I had a sister who died before I was born, a blue baby who died at age seventeen of spinal meningitis. I think those two deaths made my mother decide never to get close to anyone again. Something happened to her long before I was born that locked her away from me. She'd say things like, 'If I had my life to live over I wouldn't have any children.' I'd tease her and say, 'Oh come on, I give you *some* joy, don't I? You'd have *me*, wouldn't you?' And she'd say, 'No, I wouldn't have any of you.'

"When we had dates she'd set her alarm for midnight and put the chain on the door if we weren't home. She'd say, 'You little slut, if you want to be with him, *be* with him.' In my case, she was totally wrong; I was as naive a child as there ever was, a virgin when I got married." Not long thereafter, Audrey and her first husband moved to San Diego and began having children. In 1961 that marriage ended, and on the day after Christmas in 1964 Audrey married Bill.

"It was the kids who got him to move in, bit by bit, shirt by shirt. They'd say, 'Gee, Bill, you spend so much time here, why don't you bring your favorite painting over so it'll be more homelike for you?' They loved finding him on the couch in the morning. After a while they said, 'Why do you sleep on the couch when Mom's got such a nice big bed?' At first I was concerned what the neighbors would think, but as long as the kids were happy, the neighbors didn't give us any static. But it bugged me when Bill's parents came to visit and he moved back to his own house. All *my* friends and family knew; I didn't see why his shouldn't. I guess he was just reluctant to talk about marriage. But then once, when he was off on a trip, I sat and looked at my reflection in the window and had a conversation with it."

"With your reflection?"

"Yes. A textbook case of taking a look at myself. I asked my reflection what it was I wanted. '*You* know,' the reflection said, 'you want children and a dog and a house and to love and be loved.' And I said, 'Jackass, that's what you've got right now! The reflection said, 'I'll be goddamned, it's true—if you have what you've always wanted what difference does it make if you're married?' I said, 'None—who says a piece of paper will make things any better?'

"Then when Bill came home I totally gave myself to him for the first time. All the pressure was gone. Two weeks later, *he* wanted to get married, because there was no reason *not* to have a binding piece of paper. A few days after that he bought a washing machine and dryer to replace the clunky old thing I had, and that meant he was really going to settle in."

Settle in he did, and with him, off and on, his three children, who got along astonishingly well with Audrey's. When any friction developed, there were always the Tuesday night meetings. "We'd eliminate potential disaster at those meetings," Bill said, "by talking about and sharing our real feelings, with I-messages instead of U-messages—the idea was not to say 'You're a bastard and a bully' but 'I feel like a worm when you treat me that way.'

"Tuesday nights we also had gourmet dinners," said Audrey. "Sometimes they were extremely gourmetish and distinctive. The kids took turns planning them. After a while it got so there were no conflicts of any size at the meetings." Now the

McGaws have a new idea: each child will design a ten-day vacation within a 1,200-mile air range for Bill and Audrey and him
or herself. Bill belongs to a flying club and has access to planes.
"We're all excited about the idea of being with one child for a
whole week in a setting away from home. They're getting
older, and we'll lose them soon enough."

It pleased Audrey, she wrote in her letter to Bill, that he had
"broken tradition and chosen not to work eight hours a day
five days a week to pay the bills. You may work much less than
that, in spurts, and often don't even earn enough to support
the family. Everyone, including me, thinks that's marvelous.
No one expects or wants you to change. I'm ready to buck tradition too, in choosing not to work seven days a week at slave
work in the house. I don't care who doesn't like it or who
doesn't approve. Except you, of course. I do need you."

"I'm not a first-class crusader," Bill said later. "I'm a third-or
fourth-class crusader. I'm selfish, hedonistic, need time to be
with my family. I don't respect myself, nor do they, if I sit on
my ass for six weeks, but it is important for me to spend much
more time with them than conventional fathers do. Of course if
I had a shitty wife I might feel different about it. What I'd like
to do is a smashing couples group film, make a lot of money at
the box office so I'd have no financial worries, then do other
things I wanted to do.

"Why the hell be married, why have a family, unless you create a place where you can go to recharge your batteries, main-
tain mental health? We all have a strong need to support each
other in the family. Out in the world we all play roles like 'student', 'friendly playmate', 'helpful neighbor', but if home isn't
the one place in the world where you can get a support system
for role relief, you're lost. I can come home and be feminine,
she masculine, kids can be mother or baby. Churches should do
this for us, but they don't."

"Maybe the nuclear family isn't in such bad shape after all,"
I said. "Oh it's going to take a hell of a beating," said Bill.
"But it's healthy to have it battered. Marriage has been going
on a hell of a long time and it's only now being challenged. It's

good to rip it open and see how goddamn ugly it's gotten to be, and try to change it."

"Hey," said Audrey, "I'd better go to the supermarket."

"Bring me a surprise?" asked Bill's son, Sandy.

"A surprise to chew," asked Audrey, "or a surprise to drink?"

"Chew."

"Okay."

"Can I go with you?" I asked. I love California supermarkets. As a photographer friend remarked when he and I went shopping with Adelle Davis in Palos Verdes, "This is *super!*" So was the one Audrey took me to. It even had an elevator, and it made the ones I go to on Broadway seem like miserable company stores in a coal town. Although I was flying away in the morning, I could not resist buying some baby artichokes.

After we shopped Audrey and I drove around La Jolla. We stopped and looked at the ocean. "I look at it more often now," she said. "For a while I just took it for granted. I wouldn't go for months on end. I enjoy cooking more now too. I've been here twenty-two years now, half my life. I grew up really right here on Wind & Sea beach, and it's like my mother. I've done a lot of crying, screaming, walking on this beach. I used to bring David down here every day. He'd say, 'Hello, ocean, here I am.' He's in Hawaii now. He had some minor brain damage and dyslexia, can't read well. Not retarded, but slow. He's wise, though. A friend of mine asked him how she should try to be a good mother, and he said, 'Be a *person* with your child as soon as you try to be anything else, that's when you fuck it all up.' He needs to be by water, he went to live in Hawaii where he could build his own house, grow vegetables. He wanted to find out if the land was friendly to him, if he could make it. Now he says, 'I am in a part of the world that cares for me, and when I go into the ocean it is my friend. I have enormous peace with this land and this world.'

" 'I think patience is what love is,' he said, 'because how could you love somebody without it?' "

"He doesn't sound retarded at all," I said.

"When he was about fifteen I, like a lot of mother hens, wanted David and Bill to love each other as if they were a father and son. I didn't realize that they already did, in a different but no less real way than my image of how it should be. With all the problems, failures, and doubts I was constantly explaining David to Bill and Bill to David, and they were hot on each other, and I kept interfering, until David finally said, 'Would you please butt out of my life and let me have something with my father that's *mine,* even if he hates me?'

"My mother came out here to visit from Detroit after I had all three kids, which was a thrill because she'd never been able to afford to go anywhere. She didn't like my house, kids, style of life. I was thirty-two then, and during her visit she said, 'You know, Audrey, I've never really loved you and don't now, and I don't think I can, because I don't understand you, but I respect you.'

"I heard a roaring in my ears. I realized she was trying to do something nice but I couldn't stand it, and went into the bathroom to vomit. I think that was the moment I started to grow up. I went into a slump for a while thinking if my own mother doesn't love me then why should anyone else? But then I realized I'm not the child I was. The past can't comfort me; there's nothing for me in the past.

"All our friends thought she was the neatest person in the world. She could give to them, but not to us. Nor would she take from us. She wouldn't let any of us do anything for her— get her coffee, rub her shoulder, help her in any way. When we went to clean out the house after she died, we found boxes labeled for each one of us, filled with all the gifts we'd ever sent her over five or ten years. All the Christmas, birthday, Mothers' Day presents—warm sweaters, all the things we thought she might like or need. It was as if she was reaching from her grave to say 'screw you.' "

"How has this affected you?"

"I guess mine is the only good marriage of the lot. I'm the only one who has a good thing going, which makes me feel both lucky and sad. Bill's dad, when he died it was just the opposite. He went hideously, of cancer, but Bill gave up his job and family and everything a month before the end and was there: that was where he had to be. He didn't want to be anywhere else in the entire world, so he went. He stayed there in that hospital room in Cleveland and he'd say, 'I'm here Daddy, I love you,' and hold his hand. Let your parents need you. Let your kids need you."

"Let people in general need you," I said.

"Right," said Audrey.

34

Is That Miss or Mrs.?

My friend George is not an ornithologist, but he has a Life List all the same. His is a list of things he wants to see and do before he dies. He would no more miss a chance to stand on that Southwestern spot where four state lines intersect than he would turn down an invitation to a royal wedding. He might be called what someone once called me, an Experience Freak. Now and then he telephones to suggest that we have an Experience together. Our most recent Experience, at the Radio City Music Hall, was a midnight concert called "Colossus of the Keyboard." Colossal it was, too. First E. Power Biggs, that most aptly named of modern artists, played his heart out at the mighty Wurlitzer. Then no fewer than ten pianos rose in grandeur, as from Iolanthe's dark exile, into our range of vision. The stage revolved not only up and down but all around, like the setting for a Busby Berkeley musical. The master of ceremonies, a gentleman from one of the major recording studios, told us how grateful he was to have this chance to bring "culture to the masses." We, the masses, hissed, as united in spirit as Knick fans at a playoff game. The two musical highlights of the program were the "William Tell Overture," in which all the pianos seemed somehow miraculously to be galloping around on the stage, and then "Stars and Stripes Forever," with I suppose you can guess what unrestrainedly patriotic lighting effects. It was truly an evening, or rather a morning, to remember, and I always shall, among other reasons because George observed, as I don't think he or most men would have a couple of years before, that it wasn't fair: all the ten pianists were men, and their page-turners all were female.

Feminism has come to tinge all my thoughts, particularly those which concern my late mother. My sister recalls an evening in Winnetka, when we were both probably in high school, when we sat at the dining room table with our mother (our father didn't get home until ten most nights), and Mother's eyes nearly brimmed over as she said, "People *used* to think I was fun."

I don't remember that particular supper hour myself, but those were not years in which my mother would often say, "We just *howled!*"—a favorite accolade from the Blithe Spirit whose strong suit, it will be recalled, had been mirth. Corinne Stocker, the last in a sixty-six-year series of the Blithe Spirit's best friends, said what her predecessors in their different ways said, too: "What I miss most about Eleanor is her humor. I can't expect to find humor like that again." The last time they ever talked on the phone, just before Corinne left on a week's vacation, my mother told her: "Hurry home, I miss you already."

Toward the end, apparently, the Blithe Spirit had regained blitheness and a sort of peaceful balance. I'm glad of that. "She was starting, "Ann said, "to get to the bottom of her trunk." All her things were in such extraordinary order, as if she sensed how soon Ann and I would be throwing out her lipsticks, going through her drawers. We found these little ballpoint memos tucked everywhere: "Diamond ring mother and dad gave me when I was a little girl in Montevideo. How I loved this ring."

I guess it undid her to be faced suddenly with two galumph-
ing daughters of her own, no longer darling little things, before
whom suddenly stretched the fearsome options of adulthood.
What, for instance, was she to make of me, her firstborn, a
non-sewing, non-tennis-playing recluse not much sought by
swains, whose social calendar bore so little resemblance to
those of the soda-guzzling, hot rod-riding keen teens of popular
lore? How could she tell me what I would need to grow up? It
was all she could do to give me my first box of Modess. Almost
never did we talk of the long-range implications of womanhood, or of anything controversial or ambiguous or abstract. If
Ann or I would say, "Come on, what's really so terrible about
socialized medicine?", Mother would call, "Bob! *You* handle
this one!" The more we acted like docile children, the more we
were praised. "She's a good kid," we noted, was a compliment
paid as approvingly to octogenarians as to our own classmates.
We must have deduced that the thing to do was to keep on
being kids, good ones if possible.

To be a kid constantly, though, became a strain. Occasional
relief was needed. Early on I figured out how to escape. I fell
into the habit of retreating to whatever handy place smelled
the most like Daddy's office. I went wherever I could find the
urgent, pungent scent of newsprint, the heady excitement of
fast-breaking news, free passes to conventions, free tickets to
concerts, the shrugging martyrdom of last-minute cancellations
of plans. "In Bob's business we just *never* know," was a frequent refrain, as proud as it was wistful. I never consciously
planned to be like Daddy, but offices that smelled of newsprint, from grade school on, were a good place to find congenial people whose talk was not evasive. Anyway, writing had
seemed a glamorous thing to do since the time I was around
seven, when I spilled ink all over the dining room rug. That
certainly was careless and naughty, and I well remember my
punishment: "You can't use a pen until Thanksgiving." The
pen, and later the typewriter, were symbols of privilege. Using
them made me feel less a child.

The Blithe Spirit was proud of my bylines and clippings.
She pasted them all in scrapbooks, and showed them to her

friends, and that was nice, but it didn't make her relax. Nothing seemed to, for long. Yet compared with some women of her generation, a sad and confused one by and large, the Blithe Spirit was a model of serene poise. I know of one mother who wept to see her daughter marry, because there would be no more intrigue over girlish romances. "Since I got my first valentine from a boy in third grade," that daughter said, "those intrigues were all that kept my mother going." My own mother at least had a few other things to think about. She did not conspire with us to lie to Daddy about how much we spent on a hat, and she would have been as alarmed as I was to hear the beaming mother of a friend of mine say, "And he *never* gave us *any* trouble," as if that were something to admit in public.

Once in a great while the Blithe Spirit would even let slip that perhaps Mrs. X was not quite as darling as Mrs. Y after all, and that there were unresolved questions of relativity and degree even under the protectively arching elms of Winnetka. Almost in spite of herself she passed on to me a preference for tributaries over mainstreams, a curiosity about the peripheries of things, a capacity for certain intuitive leaps.

Sisterhood, as introduced by the women's movement, did not fall on my parched soul like rain on a desert. Whatever solace it has brought to others—a good deal, apparently—it only makes me think back to my nearly manless childhood in Winnetka, when nobody's daddies were around very much and ours, owing to the demands made on him by Colonel Robert R. McCormick, was hardly there at all. Perhaps because we saw so little of men other than our classmates and some teachers, we were not told we had to simper and be fluffy when we grew up. I wasn't, anyway. My attention was called to Mrs. Van Der Vries, who was in the legislature, and Mrs. Hahn down the street, who was a sculptor, and Aunt Janet, who had a distinct flair for management. I cannot say that anyone ever programmed me not to "succeed" in "work," or to be afraid of success. It has been said of late, notably by President Matina L. Horner of Radcliffe College, that women avoid success because they fear its consequences. If this is true of me, it is so in a

roundabout way. I am reasonably comfortable with professional success, and take pleasure in what I have done. What
would frighten me, by its very novelty, would be success in affairs of the heart. Victory on that strange terrain would be for
me as heartening as for a mother of six to go back to school and
get a doctorate.

I think sometimes of the Aldine paper dolls. They weren't
paper, really, they were oilcloth, bright red oilcloth, cut out by
Eleanor and Bob in an endless chain of alternating boy and
girl figures, holding hands, glued to the walls of a room called
the Nursery in our apartment on Aldine Avenue in Chicago. It
was assumed that one day we, the occupants of the Nursery,
would grow up and find partners to dance with too, just as
symmetrically. Symmetry, perhaps as a consequence, means
more to me than it might. I have sense enough to go to parties
alone at times when I'm not involved with anyone, but doing
so makes me feel conspicious. What am I supposed to do, I
asked my sister, pick up one of those darling nineteen-year-old
French sailors with red pompoms on their caps like I saw at
the Central Park Zoo? (Why not? she asked. Why don't *you*
take up with the garbageman? I asked her.)

Shirley Chisholm said if she could choose anybody in the
world to take with her to a desert island, she would take herself. Maybe if I were a politician I would too, because in that
line of work people don't have many opportunities to encounter themselves. But creaking along as I do in reactionary old
Consciousness II circles, I would elect to go to a desert island,
or just about anywhere, with a mature specimen of the opposite sex. I guess that friend was right who told me once, "Of
course you shouldn't get married until you feel like it, but
hurry up and feel like it." I guess John Berryman was right,
too, when he said, "It's terrible to give half your life over to
someone else, but it's even worse not to. It's too bad that when
you get married they won't let you say 'I hope so' instead of 'I
will,' but it's still important to try. You've *got* to try." Okay,
I'll hurry up and try, as soon as I find someone who is so busy
doing what he does that he'll not mind my doing what I do,

with whom I need not play games, and who knows that I'm a
Ten on a One-to-Ten scale. Not everybody recognizes that fact
at a glance. Some people can't even tell, the dummies.

I would not like to live like the ladies who sat in Jack and
Millie's living room the sunny April afternoon of Jack's sixty-
fifth birthday party. Millie, she of the snakeboots, summoned
people from as far away as Illinois to come to Jack's birthday at
their farm in the mountains of Maryland, and many of us did.
Women all sat inside in the living room, visiting about their
children and grandchildren, saying how proud they were of
them, while the men were outside in the sun.

"Aren't you proud of *yourself,* too?" I could not help asking
a woman who had been talking of her grandson's stamp collection.

"That sounds like a Women's Lib question to me," she said.

Sometimes I go to Jack and Millie's with my friends in
Washington. We went this past year, the day after Thanksgiving. Julian had to work, but Molly and Liz and I went. We
hiked up a long series of ascending meadows, squeezing under
barbed wire fences when we had to, until we got far enough up
to look all around us and see the diffuse glow of red sunset all
over the stands of cedar and birch, everywhere wheat and lavender and gold, a day for Turgenev to describe, a late afternoon of no pollution, no smog, no haze even, with Molly there
in her duffel coat gathering dried milkweed pods and all of us
climbing, climbing. And in the distance came the cracks of
guns, because it was hunting season. Liz, who knows about
such things, who knows of many things, said the guns were
probably farther away than they sounded, but still the shots
were unsettling, marring the peace of the lavender day.

"Don't shoot us," I called, half in jest, as if the hunters could
hear.

"Don't shoot *anything!*" cried Molly in her duffel coat.

"Quiet," said Liz, "or they might get ideas."

They might have, too. The human race, as you may have noticed, is not entirely rational. It is *meshuga,* as some of my best
friends say, and its lunacies certainly affect women. "There's

something crazy about our society," I heard one woman say, "if half the women in it are going nuts because of child care and the other half because nobody needs them any more."

Gretchen Babbs, whom I phoned in Oregon several months after we met, said that during the long winter just past she had been doing a lot of thinking about spiritual matters, had been doing a lot of reading. A lecture by a Christian mystic had caused her to reflect on the uncanny New Testament prophecies about the end of the world. She said there are times when she wonders if maybe those Biblical prophecies aren't coming true, if maybe Agamemnon isn't almost here.

"Agamemnon? You mean Armageddon?"

"Right, Armageddon." It didn't seem all that absurd.

My friend Lenore is the daughter of Japanese immigrants to this country. She was born and raised in a tiny town in the state of Washington and has lived for many years in New York. One early summer evening we decided at the last minute to go try for tickets to a play on Washington Square, but a line snaked practically around the block, so we had to think of an alternate plan. As we stood there looking at the *New York Post* movie listings, a menacing person with a black eye lurched up to us and asked if we had any change. We said we had not.

"Let me give you some advice," he said. "Next time, you'd better have a couple of dollars on you, because the next time you might not get asked. I know, because I've got a .44 on me to back me up." Lenore and I went to the most reassuring place we could think of, the soda fountain at C. O. Bigelow's Pharmacy, and talked of her childhood near the Pacific Coast.

"During World War II, around when I was in fourth grade, things were tough if you were Japanese, and I figured out that the way to avoid trouble was not to have any eye contact with anyone. Once I went into the post office and made the mistake of looking a man in the eye, and he started a tirade about how he was going to slit my Jap throat. Me, a nine-year-old kid. He was crazy, right? But lately I'm starting to get that same feeling, like on subways and buses, the feeling that it's safer not to meet people's eyes. That old friendly openness of the sixties, when there was a lot of eye contact and sometimes you'd even smile at strangers, that's gone.

"There's one exception, though," Lenore said. "I've also been noticing lately that *women* are starting to look at each other, in a way we never used to, checking each other out as people. And that part is nice."

That part is nice. I like it too. I like not being so hesitant. I like not saying that-is-I-mean-to-say. My grandmother used to say that all the time. She'd qualify everything. She wouldn't just say, "It's raining." She would add, "That is I mean to say there's moisture on the ground." If she were alive now she probably would feel more sure of herself, because crazy though things are, most women these days do.

Some women object to getting mail addressed "Ms." I don't mind at all; I like it. I like being snippy to airlines personnel, too.

"Is that Miss or Mrs.?" they usually ask when I call to make a reservation.

"Are you Mister or Master?" I answered once, when the voice was male.

"It's Reverend," I said another time.

"Fine," said the voice. "Tell the Reverend he can pick up his tickets half an hour before flight time."

"But *I'm* the Reverend," I said.

"You *are?*" Well, I guess I could be. I guess I could aspire to be just about anything, and I don't doubt that I owe this profusion of options to legislation which surely would not exist without the feminist movement. For the energy which has transmuted yearnings into laws, I and all women must be grateful. We owe whatever support we can give to continuing efforts to remove archaic barriers. Many such barriers remain. Not all can be legislated away. Some will last until attitudes are softened. To soften such attitudes, we have to be persuasive. That's where some of us make mistakes. Nothing is less persuasive than a tirade from a rigidly orthodox heretic.

I'm a sympathizer, a femsymp if you will, but some feminists come on so abrasive they alarm even me. I can only lament the impression they must make on the undecided. Some of these zealots remind me of Pentecostal Christians who grab your elbow and stare you down and demand, "Do *you* know the Lord?", when everyone else in the church is keening and writhing and speaking in tongues. Since I'm there too, having heard the sermon and the altar call and the hymn, I am accountable: why am I too not seized with ecstasy? But Pentecostal fervor happens not to be my style, nor does evangelical feminism. There are ways and ways of being saved. I have heard the message, *sorores*. I agree. But I'd rather be in the woodwind section than the percussion, and I don't think you can afford to alienate the piccolos, or to forget that there are other contexts in which to view life. Is not your cause more important than that?

I think your cause—okay, our cause—is important. Do not, for all my reservations, misunderstand me. I think that if women felt they had access to more realistic power, were permitted to run corporations and become full professors (to name two of innumerable possible examples), that our homes would be less damagingly matriarchal. Yes, I think our homes are damagingly matriarchal. I think we run the show at home, to too great a degree, in part because we have sensed we cannot run it elsewhere. And something about the way we run the show at home scares men away. They have abdicated. They and we have drifted apart. To fill the vacuum their absence creates, most of us have become more vital and imaginative and resourceful than most of them. We are also funnier. When I dial the phone numbers of most households I am close to, by no means all but most, I catch myself hoping the woman will answer instead of the man, because I have more to say to most women than to most men, and I am more curious about what they will have to say to me. We understand each other better. Men, as one man I know neatly put it, are more wary and mooselike.

I do not applaud this state of affairs. It alarms me. Intuition and humor and alert peripheral vision are qualities I deeply esteem and would like to find everywhere. I don't want us to have any monopoly on them. But have we robbed men of these strengths? Does our being strong mean they must be weak? If I'm up must you be down? Can't we both be up together? If the only way I can make you feel strong is to feign coy frailty, then we're both in trouble, because in this one respect I have changed irreversibly: I can no longer pretend to be submissive and helpless. I can't dissemble any more. It's too strenuous, too demeaning. Besides, and note this well, in some ways I truly am weak, less gifted than you are whoever you may be, and while I am not proud of my shortcomings, I no more intend to conceal them than my strengths. Maybe we can all take a lesson from the Mexican-Americans of South Tucson. Maybe if matriarchy and *machismo* can coexist there, then the rest of us can seek such balance, too.

I think we need each other. Much as I love certain women, I am not signing up for any separatist Amazon commune, to get away from those men who are dolts and beasts. I should sorely miss those who are not. I think W. H. Auden was right to write, "You shall love your crooked neighbor with your crooked heart." I think men need us as much as we need them, and that it is urgent for us to figure out how to talk to each other, not always with words, until we have stopped scaring each other or boring each other or whatever it is we have done that has made things go so sour.

Wholesomeness is exotic to me. I pretended to like the era of strobe lights and deafening acid rock in discotheques, but a lot of that sixties frenzy really just made me nervous. More and more I am drawn toward stillness. So it is with the women's movement: its theorists interest me less than those Closet Feminists, as I have come to think of them, who wrest sap from the trees, fish from the seas, or fashion quilts from scraps of cloth. Yoked to their menfolk, to whom they are faithful and whom they survive, they flourish on a fraction of the options granted most of us. Without being ideological about it or even articulating it at all, these women embody the movement's best principles. They don't confuse strength with gender, nor do they use their sex as an excuse to avoid responsibility. There are still a lot of these American noblewomen around. Maybe before their breed dies out, which as society grows more complex and labor more abstract it surely and sadly will, the rest of us can learn something from them.

This is a watershed time in my own life. Motherless, I have nobody to paste my clippings into scrapbooks, so I shall achieve, or try to achieve, what I want to and because I want to. Maybe some of my achievements won't even involve the printed word. Jobless, I have no office to go to, no boss to tell me where to be next Thursday, and so I shall move at my own pace away from the conventions that structured my past. Perhaps in so doing I shall seem at the same time appallingly brassy to those I leave behind, and hopelessly timid to those on the farther shore. Tough.

I am not making any resolutions. Anyway, there are certain things about myself I like; I'm not in the market for a total metamorphosis. I don't plan to stop getting out of cars to pick wildflowers along highways (although I would prefer to pick them elsewhere). I shall continue to bring butter home from Ireland and artichokes home from La Jolla when the opportunity arises. I hope it arises somewhat less often; I should like to lead a life less episodic and picaresque. "Seamless" is a word that keeps occurring to me. I'm not such an Experience Freak any more; the Life List doesn't matter so much. I am not so indiscriminately receptive. Some things human *are* alien to me. I still grope, but the spectrum of my mistakes narrows. Most of my worries are over how to mix honesty with charity. The poles to avoid, for me, are glibness at one extreme and self-pity at the other.

What matters to me now is staying home long enough to eat the leftovers in my icebox before I go off on the next trip. I hope not to go anywhere for less than two weeks, to carry less luggage, to simplify. I hope not always to be phoning people in different time zones, recovering from jet lag, making Grade G decisions like should I stay here another night or go on there, and if so when is checkout time?

I hope when I do go away it will be either to learn something worth knowing, or else to be fussed over by people who don't need to be reminded that I am a Ten (they will be Tens too, of course), or both. I wish to hold and be held, laugh and be made to laugh, commune in every way I can, but solitude doesn't scare me. I can always stay home and alphabetize my phonograph records, learn languages, maybe figure out how to read music.

It might be nice to stop being a kid, too. My sister and I according to the actuarial tables, are at the midpoints of our lives. We are older than some Astronauts, older than some Watergate defendants. She is, after all, the mother of a person five feet two inches tall. I have, after all, been on the Johnny Carson show. We are both taxpayers, voters, concerned citizens. Just because our mother defined us as children doesn't mean we have to accept that definition. We can transcend it. We can try to be what we hope to be in spite of her, as well as because of her. We can also extend amnesty to her spirit. She deserves forgiveness no less than the war resisters do. So do we.

Her death, we thought, was surely, at last, the long-delayed end of our childhood. We were wrong about that, though, because our father's remarriage inspired an even more final feeling; we could all but hear that great door ceremoniously shutting. But the door must not have been locked, because I had the same terminal sensation still another time, on the occasion of the death of *Life* magazine. Such reflections force me to consider the possibility that maybe that door is not meant to be shut. Maybe we should leave it a bit ajar, and try to be good kids.

You know what I wish the three of us would do, if my mother came back? We would get into a car and drive off somewhere, drive up past the undecided pin oaks to the zone where the trees grow tall and straight, and we would stop and have a picnic with a bottle of rosé, because she didn't like dry wine. We would talk about how things really were, how we really felt, and what we really were afraid of. And while we were at it, we would laugh.